MW01087185

NATIONALISM AND ETHNOSYMBOLISM

HISTORY, CULTURE AND ETHNICITY IN THE FORMATION OF NATIONS

edited by Athena S. Leoussi
and Steven Grosby

EDINBURGH UNIVERSITY PRESS

For Professor Anthony D. Smith

© in this edition Edinburgh University Press, 2007
© in the individual contributions is retained by the authors

Edinburgh University Press Ltd
22 George Square, Edinburgh

Typeset in Garamond Pro by
Koinonia, Manchester, and
printed and bound in Great Britain by
Antony Rowe Ltd, Chippenham, Wilts

A CIP record for this book is available from the British Library

ISBN 978 0 7486 2112 5 (hardback)
ISBN 978 0 7486 2113 2 (paperback)

The right of the contributors to be identified as authors of
this work has been asserted in accordance with the Copyright,
Designs and Patents Act 1988.

CONTENTS

NOTES ON THE CONTRIBUTORS

Dr David Aberbach is Associate Professor in the Department of Jewish Studies, McGill University, Montreal, Canada. He is also Visiting Academic in the Government Department of the London School of Economics and Political Science, UK.

John A. Armstrong is Emeritus Professor of Political Science at the University of Wisconsin-Madison, USA.

Mark Bassin is Professor of Human Geography in the Department of Geography, University of Birmingham, Birmingham, UK, and Associate Editor of *Geopolitics*.

Dr Bruce Cauthen, who formerly taught International Relations at Emory University in Atlanta, USA, is the Regional Director of the Sigma Alpha Epsilon Foundation.

Dr Daniele Conversi teaches in the European Policy Research Centre, Department of Policy Studies, University of Lincoln, UK. E-mail address: conversi@easynet.co.uk.

Dr Peter Ferdinand is Director of the Centre for Studies in Democratisation in the Department of Politics and International Studies, University of Warwick. E-mail address: peter.ferdinand@warwick.ac.uk.

Allon Gal is Emeritus Professor at Ben-Gurion University, Israel, in the Department of The History of the Jewish People and in the Ben-Gurion Institute for the Research of Israel and Zionism. He is on the Academic Council of the Ben-Gurion Institute and of the American Jewish Historical Society, USA, on the Editorial Board of Bialik Publishing Institute, Jerusalem, and on the Editorial Advisory Boards of the *Journal of Modern Jewish Studies*, University of Oxford, *Studies in Contemporary Jewry*, The Hebrew University of Jerusalem, and *Nations and Nationalism*, the Association for the Study of Ethnicity and Nationalism, UK. Email address: algal@bgu.ac.il.

Dr Sebastian Garman is Senior Tutor in the School of Health Science and Social Care at Brunel University, UK. A long-standing member of the Association for the Study of Ethnicity and Nationalism and at one time the editor of its Bulletin he is a member of the International Advisory Board of the journal *Nations and Nationalism*. E-mail address: Sebastian.Garman@brunel.ac.uk.

Haim Gerber is Professor of Islamic History at the Hebrew University of Jerusalem, Israel. E-mail address: gerberh@mscc.huji.ac.il.

Steven Grosby is Professor of Religion at Clemson University, USA. E-mail address: stevengrosby@yahoo.com.

Dr Natividad Gutiérrez Chong teaches Ethnicity and Nationalism in the Instituto de Investigaciones Sociales at the Universidad Nacional Autonoma de Mexico, Mexico. E-mail address: nativid@servidor.unam.mx.

Dr John Hutchinson is a Reader in the Government Department of the London School of Economics and Political Science, University of London, UK. He is Deputy Editor of the journal *Nations and Nationalism*. E-mail address: j.hutchinson1@lse.ac.uk.

Dr Obi Igwara was, until her sudden death in 2002, Director of the Centre for Comparative International Development at the Department of Sociology and Anthropology of the University of Hull, UK. She was one of the founding editors of the journal *Nations and Nationalism*.

Dr Sudipta Kaviraj is Reader in Politics with reference to Asia in the Department of Politics and International Studies, School of Oriental and African Studies, University of London, UK. E-mail address: sk7@soas.ac.uk.

Dr Athena S. Leoussi teaches Nationalism and European Studies in the School of Sociology, Politics and International Relations, and is an Associate Member of the History Department, University of Reading, UK. She is a founder editor and currently an editor of the journal *Nations and Nationalism*. E-mail address: a.s.leoussi@reading.ac.uk.

David Martin is Emeritus Professor at the London School of Economics and Political Science, University of London, UK, and Visiting Professor in the Department of Theology and Religious Studies, Lancaster University, UK.

Dr Joanna B. Michlic is Assistant Professor in Holocaust and Genocide Studies at the Richard Stockton College of New Jersey, USA. She is a member of the international Advisory Council of the journal *Nations and Nationalism*. E-mail address: michlicj@stockton.edu.

Dr Polly Rizova is Assistant Professor of Sociology at Boston University, USA. E-mail address: prizova@bu.edu.

Jim Samson is Professor in the Department of Music, Royal Holloway College, University of London, UK. E-mail address: Jim.Samson@rhul.ac.uk.

Anthony D. Smith is Emeritus Professor of Nationalism and Ethnicity in the Department of Government, London School of Economics and Political Science, University of London, UK. He is a founder editor and currently Editor-in-Chief of the journal *Nations and Nationalism*, and President of the Association for the Study of Ethnicity and Nationalism (ASEN), at the London School of Economics and Political Science, UK.

J. E. Spence OBE is Visiting Professor in the Department of War Studies, King's College, University of London, UK. He is also Academic Advisor to the Royal College of Defence Studies, London, and Chair of the Advisory Council of the Association for the Study of Ethnicity and Nationalism (ASEN), at the London School of Economics and Political Science, UK.

John Stone is Professor of Sociology and Chairman of the Department of Sociology, Boston University, USA. E-mail address: jstone2@bu.edu.

David Welsh is Emeritus Professor in the Political Studies Department, University of Cape Town, South Africa.

INTRODUCTION

The problems of better understanding nationality have, since the 1970s, been considerably clarified. Much of that clarification has been a result of renewed attention given to the subject, even though expressed through numerous, sharply divergent analyses, for example in the works of Walker Connor, John A. Armstrong, Ernest Gellner, Benedict Anderson, Anthony D. Smith, Pierre L. van den Berghe, John Breuilly, Eric Hobsbawm, Liah Greenfeld, Dominique Schnapper and John Hutchinson. No one during this period has done more to clarify those problems than Anthony D. Smith, first by refining, through his 'ethno-symbolic' approach, the analysis of nationality in the context of enduring ethnicity (*The Ethnic Origins of Nations* 1986), territorial kinship ('Nation and Ethnoscape' 1997), and long-term cultural, political and symbolic development and coalescence of collectivities (*The Antiquity of Nations* 2004; *The Nation in History* 2000); and second, by examining the presuppositions of those divergent analyses (*Nationalism and Modernism* 1998). To be sure, the differences among these analyses suggest that problems remain. This should come as no surprise; for as Herder (1774) observed, and scholars like Friedrich Meinecke and Hans Kohn after him, nations are protean. What are some of the reasons that justify this observation, and what are its implications for understanding better the national question?

The variability and malleability of the characteristics of any particular nation over time and from one nation to another, conveyed by Herder's observation and attested to by many of the chapters of this volume, is one reason for those problems that remain in clarifying our understanding of nationality. These problems are unavoidable, as this variability and malleability are features common to all forms of human association because of the unavoidable presence of a developing multiplicity of meanings arising out of the heterogeneous pursuits of humanity. These different meanings coalesce into a complex, are recognised, and thereby shared by a number of individuals who by doing so constitute a bounded collectivity. We refer to such a bounded complex of unevenly shared, changing and heterogeneous meanings as 'culture'. These commonplace, sociological observations, in turn, indicate that no nation can ever be thoroughly uniform or stable as if it were made out of inanimate material and designed by engineers. The historical evidence clearly confirms the changing, shifting character of nations, both over time and from one nation to another. There can, thus, be no such thing as the 'classic' form of the nation. As a consequence, analytical problems arise in the determination of the categorial specificity of nationality. Scholars must not lose sight of the merit of Herder's observation; indeed, it must be incorporated as central to their understanding of nationality.

The very character of a shared, but changing, complex of meanings in the formation of the intersubjective world of the nation – the nation as a community of collective self-consciousness – poses methodological problems. This has, of course, long been recognised, for example in the debates at the end of the nineteenth century and continuing into the twentieth over the differences between the so-called *Geisteswissenschaften* and the *Naturwissenschaften* involving Droysen, Windelband, Dilthey, Rickert, Meyer, Weber, Simmel, Freyer, Cassirer, Knight, Parsons, Oakeshott and many others. Although rarely recognised as such, many of the differences between various analyses of nationality actually represent a continuation of these earlier, methodological debates. Thus, while Anthony D. Smith has done crucially important work in advancing our understanding of nationality through developing further the ethno-symbolic approach, mainly from a historical point of view, this approach can be further enriched by philosophical considerations.

All scholars of nationality obviously agree that the materials out of which nations are formed are living, human beings. Thus, to say that the nation is neither made out of inanimate material nor designed by engineers may be viewed by some to be little more than rhetorical excess in the service of erecting a straw man. Yet this is in fact the implication of overly deterministic, whether historical or sociobiological, accounts of nationality, where the existence of one form of the nation is presented as a necessary, uniform result of either the 'historical forces' of 'modernity' (as in the work of Gellner, Anderson and Hobsbawm) or our biological drives (as in the work of van den Berghe), and where the 'engineers' are elites manipulating or inventing traditions to further one interest, for example 'power' in the form of the state, the market, or the 'inclusive fitness' of kinship, depending upon the analyst. Such accounts minimise, if not altogether eliminate, what is crucial to the existence of the nation: its meaning to its members such that the nation is, as Smith has rightly put it, 'a community of history and destiny'. Moreover, these accounts avoid the merit of Herder's observation: the fact that any nation can be only *relatively* stable precisely because of this centrality of meaning to its existence. This manifest, historical fact of relative stability, or the potential for instability, is because the meaning around which the nation is constituted: (1) emerges over time, and is seen as doing so by its members, thereby presenting the philosophical problem of tradition and its reception, specifically the character of historical consciousness; (2) as such, is susceptible to change, given the myriad problems that arise in the course of life and that require response; (3) varies not only over time, but also from one individual to another and from one group (or region) to another; and (4) is, in fact, a complex of heterogeneous meanings (corresponding to different pursuits or interests, for example, economic, political and religious) which can be in varying degrees of tension with one another, which often are expressed as political differences (for example, over trade, immigration, church–state relations), and where at any particular point in time one of those meanings may be ascendant over the others (for example, at the outbreak of war). Such a complex of meanings can never be free from ambiguity; it is always contested. Thus, nations can only be (to resort to the title of a recent book on nationality that captures well these above observations) 'zones of conflict' (Hutchinson 2005).

These observations about the analytical problems that arise from the place of meaning in the constitution of human associations indicate that the nation, as with all 'cultural forms', is, to borrow a felicitous phrase of Cassirer (2000 [1942]: 51), an 'active form of expression', or as Smith has recognised, the characteristic features of nationality and their institutional expressions are 'processes'. It is precisely this character of being 'active' that scholars of nationality must take into account, even if by so doing analytical difficulties arise, for example tolerating ambiguities, above all, with the demarcation of the categories of one 'intersubjective world' from another such as ethnic community (or 'proto nation') from nation.

Both the centrality of meaning to the existence of a nation and the contingencies of its historical forms and continuation should force the analyst of the nation, as a cultural fact in space and time, to steer a course between deterministic 'naturalism' and ahistorical 'metaphysics'. Here is where there exists another source of the problems for understanding better nationality: the necessity for developing procedures to investigate cultural forms.

Clearly, for the social and historical sciences to be scientific, there must be a subordination of particular to universal. The most well known attempt to do this has been Max Weber's use of 'ideal types', the positing of which permits comparative analysis. Smith (2005: 98; 2004a: 18) has followed Weber by formulating a definition of the nation as a named and self-defined community whose members cultivate common myths, memories, symbols and values, possess and disseminate a distinctive public culture, reside in and identify with a historical homeland, and create and disseminate common laws and shared customs. This definition implies that the existence of a nation presupposes the relative stability (the recurrence over generations) of symbols whose referents are explicitly territorial of relatively extensive, but delimited scope. The analyst, however, must not allow this definition to lull him or her into a historiographical or sociological myopia, where an assumption renders moot investigation of evidence, because the analyst, of necessity, will be confronted with varying degrees of ambiguity in the active, processual expression of each of these characteristic components for reasons that have been previously alluded to.

The methodological problem is that the forms of participation in a changing tradition such that a shared meaning exists is different from what occurs in the subordination of a physical fact to a natural law or – let it be emphasised – to any number of socioeconomic developments, because key to the existence of the nation is that the subjects are aware that they are involved in actions of varying kinds that are viewed by them as common. As Cassirer (2000 [1942]: 75) observed, the wavering constancy of the shared awareness of such common actions is not one of the properties or laws of either physical objects or socio-economic developments, but rather of *significations*.

To be sure, any number of socio-economic developments may facilitate the likelihood of the stability and shared recognition of the symbols of a common culture. Obviously, modern means of communication and democratic citizenship would do so; but in and of themselves such developments are not sufficient to account for the existence of a nation. Indeed, these developments may undermine the nation by creating conditions for empire. Moreover, they may not even be prerequisites for the existence of spatially extensive solidarities. One should, for example, remember that the shared understanding of the self, created through the spread of the world religions of Buddhism, Christianity and Islam, took place in the absence of modern means of communication. Key for the existence of a nation is the development and relative constancy of unavoidably ambiguous significations of territorial kinship that make possible involvement in actions that are viewed as being common, that is, a collective self-consciousness. These two, crucial components deserve emphasis: (1) we are dealing with the existence and continuation of a shared awareness, of a self-designating collective consciousness; and (2) the justification of that collective self-consciousness as being distinctive, that is, delimited through focus on a temporally deep territory that implies the perception of generational succession.

It is precisely this central problem of a shared consciousness that achieves a relative constancy through the establishment of significations that is pivotal to the study of the nation. Smith (2005: 98) has rightly recognised this centrality in his formulation of the ethno-symbolic approach.

What are the main assumptions behind the selection of [the] particular processes and the ensuing ideal type of the nation? . . . The first is *the centrality of symbolic elements* [our emphasis] – myths, memories, traditions, values, rituals and symbols – in the formation and persistence of nations.

This recognition places the ethno-symbolic approach to the investigation of nationality within the *Geisteswissenschaften*, that is, within the study of symbolic vehicles of consciousness. To do so is, once again, most certainly not to engage in a kind of metaphysics, that is, to ignore historical contingencies, socio-economic developments, or the biological realities of humanity within the animal kingdom. It is, however, to recognise problems of human consciousness that are *sui generis* – problems that are not to be submerged under those contingencies, developments, and realities such that they are, in effect, ignored. To refuse this recognition is to reintroduce, paradoxically, either a naturalism or a metaphysics into the analysis of nationality by riding roughshod over the historical evidence of the development of, and problems posed by, symbols, even if that is not the intention of those social scientists who seeks to formulate an 'operational' or 'predictive' 'model'.

In the limited space available in this introduction, we will allude to only a few, additional problems specific to collective consciousness, its structure, and its symbolic representation, that indicate the necessity of different procedures of investigation. It is often assumed that in order for the *community* of the nation to exist, there must, *qua community,* be the condition and recognition of equality. This is the implication of how the categories of citizenship and 'modernity' are used by many analysts of the nation. It is thus concluded by such analysts that nations can only be modern. However, the assumption is incorrect.

All associations, beyond that of true friendship, of enduring, intense attachment are differentiated. All have 'representatives' who serve as symbols of attachment, embodying the purposes of the association. Such symbolic representation is a necessary property of consciousness, if the latter is to be more than fleeting. For example, a father may represent a family, a chief for a tribe, a bishop for a church, a king for a kingdom, and a democratically elected president or prime minister for the modern state. An inegalitarian family, tribe, kingdom or religious association may also be a *Gemeinschaft*, and certainly a territorially extensive one when customs, laws, language and religion are unifying factors that further distinguish that community from another. *Pars pro toto* is a phenomenon of collective consciousness, where the sense of belonging to, of membership in, the nation is facilitated through the symbol of the representative as an object of attachment, as a referent of consciousness. The place of symbolic representation in the formation and continuation of a national collective self-consciousness has certainly been recognised by scholars of nationality; but that recognition has usually been confined to monuments and works of art. The phenomenon of representation of the collectivity through a 'representative' individual as a structural property of collective consciousness has not received proper attention in the study of nationality.

Furthermore, the historical evidence of belonging to a territorial collectivity is too rich and varied to be conflated with only one form of political participation, specifically modern expressions of democratic citizenship. To insist on such a conflation is to ignore the historical and symbolic expressions or representations of the collectivity and its self-consciousness not only in the past, but also in the present. It is to ignore representation as a phenomenological property of consciousness.

Another problem is to ascertain just what is the meaning that is being designated, often ambiguously, by the symbol. For a nation to exist, there must be a symbolic representation of a territory such that, when acknowledged and thereby incorporated as part of the understanding of the self, a territorial relation, a territorial kinship, is posited over time. Smith has consistently insisted that the scope of the investigation into such a symbol and its acceptance, persistence, rejection and revival must be across different epochs of history over the long term (*la longue durée*). Philosophically, this insistence presupposes that symbols, once created out of the ebb and flow of life, 'take on a life of their own', that is, they can no longer be reduced to the circumstances of their creation. In this sense, the symbols are 'objective'; however, they are only relatively objective, for their continued existence as symbols requires recognition. This subjective component of the collective self-consciousness – the requirement of recognition (affirmation) of the objective symbol – may also result, given changing historical and socio-economic conditions, in a modification of the meaning borne by the symbol, thus, as Herder observed, the unavoidable malleability and variation of the symbolic complex of any nation. The ethno-symbolic approach in no way denies this influence of historical and socio-economic circumstances on the creation and continued recognition of symbols; but it avoids the mistake of reducing those symbols to those circumstances. It affirms symbols as cultural resources capable of shaping collective responses to changing socio-economic and political circumstances; but it does not collapse the meanings borne by those symbols into those circumstances.

Despite such variation, the category of the nation, if it is to have heuristic utility, indicates the ascendancy of the recognition of kinship, both biological and territorial, and its symbols within the national cultural complex. This is, in fact, the significance of Smith's proper attention to the ethnic component of the nation. Now, to raise the problem of the ethnic group is to raise the problem of myth.

What is the place of myth in the constitution of a nation? First, myths, such as that of being a 'chosen people' (Smith 2004b), provide the collectivity with justification for its distinctiveness. Second, and as the historical record shows, myths or existential ideals that are not capable of empirical verification clearly have a bearing on the orientation of action, in this instance, in the formation and continued existence of a nation. In recognising this historical fact, the ethno-symbolic approach continues the methodological tradition of Max Weber and Talcott Parsons (1954 [1938]), namely, that ideas borne by religion and myth are often factors influencing human conduct. Thus, while scholars of nationality should avoid a metaphysical analysis of the nation, to do so in no way means a refusal to acknowledge the significance of a metaphysical orientation in human action. Indeed, the implication of the ethno-symbolic approach is the recognition that a metaphysical component in human affairs is seemingly inexpungeable; that is, these nonempirical, justificatory ideas about collective existence appear necessary for the distinctiveness of any nation. Thus, and of great importance, the ethno-symbolic approach follows Jaspers (1958: 15) in the recognition that 'mythical thinking is not a thing of the past, but characterizes man in any epoch'.

These are a few of the important, methodological and philosophical implications of the ethnosymbolic approach to nationality which richly deserve greater attention and elaboration than has generally been recognised: (1) the relative objectivity, hence independence, of symbols; (2) the heterogeneous character of the symbolic complex – the centre – of a nation; (3) the phenomenon of representation; (4) the problem of distinctiveness; and, finally, (5) myth, both as a problem for the social sciences and as a fact of human consciousness. This volume focuses on precisely these issues, elaborating on their implications and problems. Of course, more work needs to be done. It is the hope of the editors of this volume that these essays will contribute not only to a better understanding of the ethno-symbolic approach, but also to undertaking further investigation into these historical, methodological and philosophical implications of the ethno-symbolic approach to the study of nations.

The book is broadly organised into thematic and 'area' sections, the latter cutting across different historical periods. The thematic sections consist of a section on theories of nation and nationalism, and a section on the role of the arts, and especially music and poetry, in expressing and constituting national identities. A separate section is devoted to antiquity: ancient Greece and Rome, and the ancient Middle East.

The book opens with the theoretical section, placing ethnosymbolism in the context of the large body of literature on nations and nationalism. Focusing on those theories which have directly collided or colluded with ethnosymbolism, Daniele Conversi outlines their salient features and points of contact with ethnosymbolism and provides an assessment of the latter's capacity, as an analytical tool, to describe and explain historical and contemporary national issues. John Stone and Polly Rizova supplement Conversi's theoretical considerations by tracing the revival of ethno-national and racial identifications, symbols and affiliations since the end of the Cold War and their transformations in the context of global interpenetration and hybridisation of societies and of new waves and types of international migration. Hutchinson completes this section with an ethnosymbolic analysis of warfare that shows the importance of war in nation-formation. He examines, first, the idea of the nation as a community of sacrifice; second, the importance of memory in the reproduction of nations; and third, changes in the nature of warfare and their potential to subvert national solidarities.

Music has been a subject much neglected by nationalism studies. Drawing on a variety of European examples, from both the centre of the European 'classical' tradition and its peripheries, the second thematic section shows, with essays by Jim Samson, David Martin and David Aberbach, first, how ethno-national affirmation might be achieved through music and poetry; and second, how the national idea, with its re-evaluation of folk, ethno-historic and mythical motifs, has given impetus to musical and poetic creativity, renewed established canons, or combined folk with modern, global idioms.

The section on antiquity shows, with essays by Steven Grosby and Sebastian Garman, first, the antiquity, persistence and potency of the idea of 'successor territory' in forming, maintaining and symbolising communities, as exemplified in ancient Israel; and second, the importance, in ancient Greece and Rome, of beliefs and symbols of common ethnicity as the basis of political community, regularly invoked in public games, festivals, funerary orations, statues and altars located in central sites of public life.

The area sections show the usefulness and relevance of the ethnosymbolic approach to illuminate conditions and processes of collective identification and coalescence in a variety of local and historical circumstances. Thanks to our specialist contributors, these sections include areas that have not received adequate attention in nationalism studies.

Eastern Europe and Russia are examined with an essay on perceptions and symbolisations of the Jews as a threatening 'other' in modern Poland from the 1880s to the present day (Joanna Michlic); an essay considering the ideological conflation of territory, landscape and ethnicity in the writings of Lev Nikolaevich Gumilev during the1960s and 1970s, a period of revived Russian nationalism (Mark Bassin); and an essay on the ethno-cultural symbols and re-orientations of the constitutions of the seven post-communist states which in 2004 joined the European Union (Athena S. Leoussi).

The Middle East is examined, first, with a general essay surveying the significance of Islamic faith for the emergence of nations and national symbolisations in the Middle East (John A. Armstrong); second, an essay which shows the tolerance of ethnic diversity within the Islamic *umma* enabling, over a *longue durée*, the development of a distinctive Turkish ethno-national and literate culture on which modern Turkish nationalism was to be based (Haim Gerber); and third, an essay on the religious continuity of Zionism and the modern state of Israel with the Jewish past (Allon Gal).

The Far East and India are examined with two essays: one essay on China and Taiwan, showing, first, that key elements of modern ethnic and national Chinese identity go back not just centuries but millennia, and second, the problems of establishing a distinctive Taiwanese identity without a prior ethnic identity to underpin it (Peter Ferdinand); and another on the development of a new language of emotion and sacredness regarding the nation in late-nineteenth-century Bengal, one that was based on the traditional language of piety and its associated iconography (Sudipta Kaviraj).

Africa is also examined with two essays: one on the national and religious components of political identity in Nigeria which, since the 1970s, have given rise to Islamic and Christian 'holy nationalisms' (Obi Igwara); and another on South Africa that offers, in a study of the rise and fall of Afrikaner nationalism, a rare case study of demobilisation of a once-powerful ethnic nationalism (David Welsh and J. E. Spence).

Finally, the Americas are examined with an essay on the profound identification, during the American Civil War, of Southern women with their native, Southern landscape thereby transforming it, to use Smith's term, into an ethnoscape, and an active participant in the Southern Secession (Bruce Cauthen); and an essay on contemporary Latin America that explores the importance, among indigenous and underprivileged groups, of the idea of ancestry, and of ethnic myths and symbols, as ways of self-understanding, and contexts for demanding recognition and political participation in the multicultural states of Latin America (Natividad Gutiérrez Chong).

The book closes with an essay by Anthony D. Smith that explores two antithetical visions of global society: 'cosmopolis' and 'ethnopolis', showing that even the most 'civic' and 'cosmopolitan' societies of both the past and the present have been infused by ethnic elements of native landscape, language, history, symbols and traditions.

In bringing this book to life we drew sustenance from a number of kind associates and friends, to whom we are deeply grateful. Above all, we are grateful to Edinburgh University Press, and especially Nicola Ramsey and Stuart Midgley, for giving us the opportunity to produce this book and for being the ideal publisher-patrons: generous with time, instantly and positively responsive to our requests, and with impressive understanding of the intellectual implications of the subject matter of this book.

We are grateful to the readers of our initial proposal to Edinburgh University Press. Their imaginative and positive engagement with our proposal improved substantially our original plans by suggesting wider and more varied vistas of investigation. We wish to thank Professors David Martin and Richard Boyd. Professor J. E. Spence's counsel opened up, yet again, great and new possibilities for us.

Of course, this book would not have been possible without our contributors. Their enthusiastic embracing of and commitment to this book are tributes to the work of Anthony D. Smith. His ethnosymbolic approach has attracted to its orbit many distinguished scholars of nations and nationalism who have either shared or been inspired by his intuitions and extensive research. The consequence has been the amplification and consolidation of what we might call an 'ethno-symbolic school' of nationalism.

Finally, we wish to remember in this introduction, Dr Obi Igwara. She was the genetrix of the idea of a monograph showing the manifold applications, wide appeal and crucial importance for a fuller and deeper understanding of nations and nationalism, of Anthony D. Smith's ethnosymbolic approach. Her sudden death, in 2002 in a car accident in Nigeria, stopped her from realising this important project. As her co-editor, I took it upon myself, with the help of Professor Steven Grosby as co-editor, to see that her vision was realised. Together, we also ensured that her own ethnosymbolic contribution to the study of nationalism is appreciated and recognised by including in this book an essay by her.

Athena S. Leoussi and Steven Grosby
February 2006

REFERENCES

Cassirer, Ernst (2000 [1942]), *The Logic of the Cultural Sciences*, New Haven: Yale University Press.

Herder, Johann Gottfried von (1774 [1877–1913]), *Auch eine Philosophie der Geschichte zur Bildung der Menscheit*, vol. 5, Herders Sämtliche Werke, ed. B. Suphan, Berlin: Weidmannsche.

Hutchinson, John (2005), *Nations as Zones of Conflict*, London: Sage.

Jaspers, Karl (1958), 'Myth and religion', in K. Jaspers and R. Bultmann, *Myth and Christianity*, New York: Noonday.

Parsons, Talcott (1954 [1938]), 'The role of ideas in social action', in *Essays in Sociological Theory*, Glencoe: Free Press.

Smith, Anthony D. (1986), *The Ethnic Origin of Nations*, Oxford: Blackwell.

Smith, Anthony D. (1998), *Nationalism and Modernism*, London: Routledge.

Smith, Anthony D. (1999), 'Nation and ethnoscape', in Anthony D. Smith, *Myths and Memories of the Nation*, Oxford: Oxford University Press, 149–59.

Smith, Anthony D. (2000), *The Nation in History*, Hanover: University Press of New England.

Smith, Anthony D. (2004a), *The Antiquity of Nations*, Cambridge: Polity Press.

Smith, Anthony D. (2004b), *Chosen Peoples: Sacred Sources of Nationality Identity*, Oxford: Oxford University Press.

Smith, Anthony D. (2005), 'The genealogy of nations', in A. Ichijo and G. Uzelac (eds), *When is the Nation?*, London: Routledge.

Part 1

THEORIES OF NATIONALISM AND
THE ETHNOSYMBOLIC APPROACH

Chapter 1

MAPPING THE FIELD:
THEORIES OF NATIONALISM AND
THE ETHNOSYMBOLIC APPROACH

Daniele Conversi

To be fully understood, the ethnosymbolic approach, developed by Anthony D. Smith, must be placed in the context of a larger body of literature on nations and nationalism. Two streams of thought are particularly important here: *instrumentalism* as opposed to *primordialism*, and *modernism* as opposed to *perennialism*. This chapter will explore those theories with which Smith has most often engaged, placing his own approach within a larger cross-disciplinary context. The scope of this volume compels me to be highly selective: I will only deal with those theories with which Smith has most persistently interacted. The reader will not find here much about other theories like rational choice, which still dominates US academia.[1] The chapter will conclude with an exploration of the limits of ethnosymbolism as a tool for interpreting current events and conflicts.

PRIMORDIALISM

Smith's initial polemics were directed at two contrasting vogues in scholarly research: primordialism and instrumentalism. Primordialists appeal to emotional and instinctive constraints as ultimate explanations for national mobilisation. They typically date the origin of nationhood back to remote epochs, treating them as emotional givens. Their approach is often associated with nationalist discourse, which occasionally reverberates in academia. For Steven Grosby (1995), 'primordial' refers to the 'significance of vitality which man attributes to, and is constitutive of, both nativity and structures of nativity', including lineage, family, and, most importantly, territory. Donald Horowitz (2004) postulates the existence of a broader scholarly category called '*the primordialists*', distinguished by their reluctance to analyse ethnonationalism as a relevant phenomenon in its own right. Classic nationalists proclaim the immutable nature of their symbolic universes. 'Nation-states' seem to have the power, tools (media) and legally enforceable apparatus (official education) to impose their primordialist vision as the only acceptable one.

But what happens when self-defining 'nation-states' fail to absorb recalcitrant minorities? In the heyday of the nation-state (till about the end of World War Two), this was a common goal. Dominant nations responded to the challenge of mobilised nationalities by stressing further their primordialist 'pedigree'. Far too often, ethnic cleansing and mass expulsions became the ultimate culmination of denial of difference. Thus, the state's determinist eschatology was constructed as a powerful obstacle vis-à-vis the feared transformation of rival '*ethnies*' into fully fledged 'nations'.[2] The very institutional continuity of existing states was often proffered as evidence of the primordiality of the nation they embody. As Smith notes, these visions were 'heavily influenced by an organic nationalism which posited the "rebirth" of nations after centuries of somnolence, amnesia and silent invisibility' (Smith 2004: 53).

No wonder primordialists have been an easy target for more positivist, calculative approaches, becoming 'the straw man of ethnic studies', indeed 'the most maligned for their naivete in supposing that ethnic affiliations are given rather than chosen, immutable rather than malleable, and inevitably productive of conflict' (Horowitz 2004: 72–3). By accentuating the explosive and unpredictable nature of ethnic bonds, primordialists seem to discourage further scholarly enquiry, particularly into the causes of, and possible solutions to, ethnic conflict.

An approach that encompasses both primordialism and instrumentalism is *sociobiology*. Smith describes this as a radical variety of primordialism. In fact, Pierre Van den Berghe, who began to use the term '*ethny*' as early as the 1970s, considers ethnic and racial sentiments as an extension of kinship ties (1981: 80). Sociobiological and 'kinship' perspectives bring forth the centrality of descent in defining ethnic groups. However, Van den Berghe's idea of *kin selection* can also be read as an extreme form of 'individual instrumentalism': if the overriding criterion is the reproduction of one's own genes, everything else becomes a tool to this end, the epiphenomenon of a larger biological drive for group survival. The idea of ethnic ties as 'kinship' ties is also embraced by Donald Horowitz (1985), who defines ethnic groups as '*super-families*'. Indeed, nationalism conveys the idea that members of the nation are somehow related by birth. No real biological relationship is needed, a mere unproven belief could turn nationalism into a *placebo*, a potion with no chemically active ingredients but miraculous effects.

INSTRUMENTALISM

Instrumentalism conceives ethnicity as a dependent variable, externally controlled according to its strategic utility for achieving more secular goods (formally in the name of the group, in fact solely to the elites' advantage). Instrumentalism is also often referred to as *constructivism* (Brown 2000), while 'the claim that ethnic group boundaries are not primordial, but socially constructed is now the dominant view' (Hechter and Okamoto 2001: 193).[3]

For radical instrumentalists, the category 'nation' does not correspond to any objective reality. They postulate a sharp fracture between political-economic elites and their followers, seeing the latter as passively manipulated by the former. For Eric Hobsbawm (1995), they are ambitious *'social engineers'* deliberately stirring up the atavist emotions of the masses. Elie Kedourie (1960) rather saw nationalism as a conspiracy devised by German Romantic intellectuals. In short, instrumentalists try to single out the 'manufacturers' of nations among those social groups that have most to gain from it.

Hobsbawm's term *'invention of tradition'* has acquired a nearly iconic meaning (Hobsbawm and Ranger 1983). Hobsbawm belongs to a Marxist tradition that Smith sees as over-confident in locating national manipulators with surgical precision (1998: 117–24). For this line of thought, it is rather irrelevant whether or not the repository of ethnic symbols from which elites attain power persists through the ages. They reject the claim that nations are fixed, pre-determined, natural entities, and identify nationalism as deriving from discursive and political practices. Unscrupulous leaders such as Adolf Hitler, Slobodan Milosevic and Saddam Hussein can engage in an unprincipled, deceitful, devious use of patriotism, deforming it into annexation, conquest, subjugation, imperialism, war and genocide. They manipulate public feelings for the only purpose of holding on to power. Of course, this does not mean that elites can instantly invent the symbolic material from which to draw on their mobilising power.

Smith does not deny that ethnicity, as an independent variable, can be abused and manipulated. But he stresses that it can scarcely be created. Therefore, elites can distort and dramatically alter existing myths. Yet, it is questionable whether, and how far, they can 'invent' them. In their pristine version, instrumentalists also failed to recognise that key activists in the mobilised groups may simply be interested in the maintenance of their cultural heritage, rather than gaining material goals. There may well be no cynical aspirations there, but a sincere desire to preserve something from the past, if not merely a positive self-image.

Nevertheless, ethnonational mobilisation often results from the conscious efforts of elites to obtain access to specific social, political and material resources. Such goals are better pursued in the name of 'alleged' common interests. Sociopolitical elites are particularly efficient in deploying the ethnosymbolic complex to the full: they often engage in top-down 'myth-making' – or at least they attempt to do so. But does this mean that they can invent myths *impromptu*? Not quite so.

MODERNISM

Speculations about the timing of nations ('when is a nation?') and the emergence of nationalism ('when did nationalism become an influential force and dominant ideology?') has led to two contrasting calendars: *modernists* date their formation to the rise of modernity, in whatever form the latter is defined; *perennialists* see them as enduring, inveterate, century-long, even millennial phenomena, certainly predating modernity.[4]

Modernism remains one of the few postulates overwhelmingly embraced by most scholars, in itself a rare achievement: even primordialists may see nationalism as the *modern* re-enactment of a pre-modern idea. Modernism has long been the dominant trend not only in nationalism studies, but also in related fields: for genocide scholars, ethnic cleansing tends to be a substantially modern phenomenon (Kuper 1981; Levene 2005; Mann 2005), whether or not one includes '*colonial*' (antipodal) genocides within an expanded definition of modernity (Palmer 1998).[5] Similarly, and more obviously, Fascism studies (Gentile 2000; Gregor 1979) and totalitarianism studies (Griffin 1991) share a fully fledged modernist view of history, arguing that both these phenomena cannot develop outside modernity. Most scholars of nationalism are also modernists and entirely associate the nation, not only nationalism, with modernity.[6]

Can anti-instrumentalist primordialism combine with modernism? Connor (1993; 2004a) adopts a critique of instrumentalism while pursuing a robust modernist agenda. The Connor–Smith debate is highly representative of this contrast: while Smith (2004) argues that it is possible to date an embryonic development of modern nations to ancestral times, Connor (2004b) retorts by defining such a task as purely speculative and rejects sweeping *longue durée* explanations.[7] If nationalism is a mass – not an elite – phenomenon, then it can only occur at a quite advanced stage of modernity. That is when the development of modern mass communication makes it possible for an ethnic core elite to spread national identification amongst larger and larger sectors of the population.

GELLNER'S THEORY OF INDUSTRIAL HOMOGENISATION

Since Gellner was perhaps the major modernist influence on Smith's work, it is appropriate to dedicate a separate section to his theory. A former disciple of Ernest Gellner (1925–95), Smith has questioned and challenged the latter's deterministic and modernist grand-vision. This has been a daunting task, not least because Gellner had, since the 1970s, been the revered doyen and most influential scholar in the field. Not only has Smith succeeded, he also fruitfully tackled a broader range of approaches, producing an alternative vision that vigorously challenged established wisdom.

Gellner (1983) associates modernity with the spread of industrialisation. The latter brought about an unprecedented, all-pervasive change that disrupted the traditional balance of society, creating new constellations of shared interests.[8] For Gellner, nationalism was the offspring of the marriage between state and modern culture, celebrated on the altar of modernity. With the passage from agricultural to industrial society, a 'high', scientific culture, carried by standardised, national languages, becomes an all-pervasive requisite. However, only the state has the power to inculcate the new standard on an uprooted labour force. A nation is hence defined as common membership in a shared 'high culture'. In turn, nationalism is defined as 'primarily a principle that holds that the political and national unit should be congruent' (Gellner 1983: 1).

In his typical lapidary and terse style, Ernest Gellner pushes the 'invention' of nations argument to its logical consequences: 'Nationalism is not the awakening of nations to self-consciousness: it invents nations where they do not exist' (Gellner 1964: 168). But he also argued that state-enforced homogenisation, metaphorically identified as the Empire of '*Megalomania*', provokes the reactions of those who have been either excluded, or opted out by their own choice in order to protect their own culture. These latter are bound to form their own national movements, in which a low culture is promoted and transformed into a High Culture. Their political project is the establishment of a new '*Ruritania*', the prototypical nationalist homeland (reminiscent of historical occurrences in Eastern Europe, including Gellner's native Czecho-Slovakia).[9] In the homogenising world of nation-states, societies find themselves at a radical crossroads: either organise themselves on the basis of the nation-state model or succumb (Gellner 1983).

Smith has accepted in part Gellner's focus on nationalism as replacing the social cohesion of pre-modern societies, but did not share his radical modernism, or his dogmatic stress on the relationship between industrialism and socio-cultural homogenisation. Contra Gellner, he has argued that industrialisation is not a prerequisite for nationalism, as there are instances of nationalist movements emerging well before the latter's advent. He mentions the cases of Finland, Serbia, Ireland, Mexico, Japan and many others, including post-revolutionary France and pre-Bismarckian Germany (Smith 1998: 36ff.). The critique is commonly accepted by most scholars. Gellner himself acknowledged the Greek 'exception'.[10] He also quoted the Kurdish experience, as a case where 'a modern nationalism might appear in a region in which tribal organisation survives' (Gellner 1964: 173), even though Kurdish nationalism was mostly born as a reaction against the imposition of the Turkish state's secular nationalism (Rugman and Hutchings 1996).[11] Moreover, Gellner's evolutionism (Smith 2004: 65) postulates a view of mankind advancing through a series of progressive evolutionary stages leading to socio-political paradigm shifts. This grand theory is too deterministic and associated with over-ambitious neo-positivist paradigms.

PERENNIALISM

To the perennialists, the nation is reassuringly granted for posterity, indeed destined to eternity. This double projection towards past and future represents nationalism's greatest force, but also its greatest weakness as a generalisable principle.

Smith (1999: 5–27; 2000: 34–41) has identified two varieties of perennialism: *continuous perennialism* focuses on the continuity of nations over the centuries, indeed millennia; *recurrent perennialism* focuses on the broader recurrence of the nation as a general phenomenon – particular nations 'may come and go, but the phenomenon itself is universal' (2000: 35). Again, it is the idea of ethnic chosenness, which can better explain persistence and articulate the stress on continuity.

For Adrian Hastings (1997), the very act of translating the Bible into the vernacular turned the reading public into a 'chosen people'. By allowing translation of Sacred Texts from Hebrew/Greek into the vernacular, Christianity encouraged the development of ethnicities and pre-modern nations. It also endowed the latter with a new sense of sacredness attached to their collective identities by supplying a ready-made sense of God-sent chosenness. Even in a secular world, the most powerful election myth remains a Biblical one: ensuing secularisation, the sacred object of devotion shifts from God to the 'chosen people' themselves in a self-idolising frenzy. Many authors have viewed nationalism as a religious surrogate: the spread of secularisation, and perhaps atheism itself, was accompanied by this sense of divine election, stressing the profane essence of neighbouring groups. Smith (1972) has identified here continuity with pre-modern ethnocentrism.

Islam, by contrast, 'deconstructs' nations, remaining one of the most powerful antidotes against nationalism (Hastings 1997: 200–2). The sacred centrality of Arabic as a God-given tongue makes the development of vernacular nationalisms unlikely. In the West, religious print literature and, in particular, vernacular Bibles play a key role in generating national feeling and cultures. Firmly rooted in Judeo-Christian values, nationalism then spread outside Christianity in the wake of colonialism. It is through the mirror of the Bible which nations are initially conceived: 'The Bible provided ... the original model of the nation. Without it and its Christian interpretation and implementation, it is arguable that nations and nationalism, as we know them, could never have existed ...' (Hastings 1997: 4). In particular, the role of territory is comparable to that of biblical Israel (see also Grosby 1995). The concept of a Holy Land has been passed on to all significant nationalist movements, either civically or ethnically based.

Hastings' work is a critique of mainstream 'modernism' and its claim that nations and nationalism are a product of the modern era, ignoring – among other fallacies – the early examples of English and Irish nationalisms. For most modernist historiography, nations did not exist before the French Revolution (and occasionally before the Polish Rising of 1794). Instead, Hastings argues that English national identity can be dated back at least to 1066 and that the main European nations had already emerged by the sixteenth century. 'England presents the prototype of both a nation and a nation-state in the fullest sense' (1997: 4). The English case in Europe is unique and as such it became a model 'which was then re-employed, remarkably little changed, in America and elsewhere' (1997: 5). But English nationhood preceded English nationalism, the latter manifesting itself visibly during the long fourteenth-century wars with France. 'Divine election' can also help explain the self-righteous character of British imperial patriotism or *'missionary nationalism'* (Kumar 2003). Despite the nation' s antiquity, a formal political philosophy of nationalism only appeared in the nineteenth century. It was universally canonised even later, after World War I, when President Woodrow Wilson turned it into the building block of the US-led post-Versailles new world order (1920).

One aspect that has been left unexplored is the association of chosenness with the state, rather than the nation, particularly noticeable in fascist and totalitarian regimes. Some of the excesses of such secular nationalisms are to be found in the idea of chosenness.

Smith (1998) has provided one of the staunchest critiques of modernism and has therefore been often identified as a 'perennialist'. However, his focus on ethnic persistence does not necessarily imply that *ethnies* are perennial entities, since he clearly identifies patterns of ethnic survival, contrasting them with instances of ethnic demise and extinction (Smith 2000; 2003). His novel approach, perhaps not yet a fully fledged theory, has come to the fore to bridge the gap: to overcome the dichotomy between perennialism and modernism, Smith (1986; 1998; 2004) has developed his own *ethnosymbolic* approach.

ETHNOSYMBOLISM

Ethnosymbolism underlines the continuity between premodern and modern forms of social cohesion, without overlooking the changes brought about by modernity. The persisting features in the formation and continuity of national identities are myths, memories, values, traditions and symbols. This is a complex set of elements that Smith tends to use interchangeably, often without sufficient specification to allow critical analysis or easy application. Myths of ethnic descent, particularly myths of 'ethnic chosenness', lie at its core. Of all these myths, the myth of a 'golden age' of past splendor is perhaps the most important.

Although Smith does not systematically focus on the *intellectuals*, he acknow-ledges their pivotal role as the creators, inventors, producers and analysts of ideas (Smith 1981: 109).[12] How is it that the intellectuals are central to ethno-symbolism? They mostly act as 'chroniclers' of the ethnic past, elaborating those memories which can link the modern nation back to its 'golden age'. Philolo-gists, archeologists, poets, literati and, most of all, historians are the key players in the ethnonational game (Conversi 1995; Hutchinson 1987). Leoussi (2004) adds visual artists, inspired by demotic, historical and ethnocultural themes. If one extends the category of intellectuals to include 'conveyors of ideas', rather than mere producers of ideas, one can see the key role of painters, musicians, sculp-tors, photographers, novelists, play-writers, actors, film directors and television producers in establishing a connection between the present times and a national 'golden age'. Smith recognises their strategic use of national *symbols*, as 'perhaps even more potent than nationalist principles' and ideology (2000: 72). Through them, the imagined community becomes vividly popular, emotionally awakened and periodically celebrated. Scholars, artists and poets help the modern nation to draw sustenance from a re-lived ancient past, providing the linkage with earlier *ethnies* or ethnic communities. Indeed, a historically deep ethnic foundation is a prerequisite to the survival of modern nations.

'Intellectuals' should not necessarily be understood as individuals belonging to a particular class and sharing a specific high culture. As initiators of nationalism, they first envision, define, codify and set the boundaries of the nation. Nationalist 'intellectuals' must be literate, but barely so: there is no need for particular *finesse* or sophistication. What matters is their capacity to express and combine a cred-ible national identity. This includes an ability, not simply to speak the language of their core constituencies, but to reinterpret and re-live their ancestral myths.

This leads us to ask how far the intellectuals can influence, mobilise and 'instrumentalise' public opinion. How can relatively lonely, isolated individuals have such wide appeal? How is it possible to convince people to believe in the immemorial, perennial essence of the nation? The answer is to be found in a second social category, the *intelligentsia* or the *professionals*. Smith (1991; 1996; 1998) identifies this category as a group of individuals exposed to some form of superior education. It is not strictly a class but rather a social category, since in theory individuals from all classes can belong to it. They have not merely the will and inclination, but also especially the power and capacity to apply and dissemi-nate the ideas produced by the intellectuals.[13] Therefore this stratum plays an even more crucial role in the success of nationalist movements. Once the intelligentsia begins to challenge officialdom by exploiting its strategic position, it becomes a key protagonist of expanding mass movements.[14]

In general, the intellectuals' role is seen by ethnosymbolists as providing a skeleton upon which to build a larger movement: 'bridges' must be built between past and present, between ethnic myths and their modern translation into viable, coherent identities and political programmes. If the focus is on the incipient stages of nationalism, then we could hardly conceive a nation without intellectuals. A first generation of amateur scholars is needed to envision the nation, to spawn an embryonic 'image' of the nation. Yet, nationalism can and does exist without them. Indeed, the worst nationalist excesses are often carried out in a wholly militarised environment, in which intellectuals may be routinely executed. Under such polarisation, their role – and the fate of culture in general – will be inevitably limited.

THE LIMITS OF ETHNOSYMBOLISM

Although ethnosymbolism remains broadly unchallenged on its own ground, some internal weaknesses may be signalled. I shall concentrate here on two of them.

The first weakness lies in its fragile conceptual foundations. Smith defines the nation as 'a named human population occupying an historic territory, and sharing myths, memories, a single public *culture* and *common rights* and *duties* for all members' (Smith 2004: 65, my emphasis). This is somewhat unclear. The inclusion of 'common rights and duties' in the definition seems to refer to *citizenship* rights, which can only be fully granted by the existence of a state or autonomous region. Around the world, there are cases that seem to substantiate Smith's definition: for instance, the Basque *fueros* were crucial in the formation of modern Basque national identity. The latter were 'common rights and duties' enshrined in bilateral agreements stipulated by the Crown with various localities (Conversi 1997). These rights ceased partly to exist ensuing state centralisation in 1876 (date of the final Carlist defeat). Of course, Basque nationhood persisted insofar as nationalist sentiments lingered on. It is even possible to affirm that nationalism was largely a response to the abolition of the *fueros*: the unilateral breach of such an agreement prompted an 'ethnogenetic' effect. I am not denying that a Basque *ethnie* existed before nationalism: indeed, the Basque case is a particularly rich illustration that a sense of shared ethnic distinction could be preserved for millennia without supportive state institutions. More limitedly, I am arguing that a new form of collective consciousness emerged as a result of the Spanish state's centralisation, forced assimilation and repression of ethnic dissent ('ethnogenesis' does not refer to the 'instant' creation of an *ethnie*).

A similar pattern could be found in Catalonia. In 1716 Philip V's Royal Decree of *Nueva Planta* ('New Order') banned the use of language and other autonomous institutions. Despite this centralist onslaught, a Catalan civil code persisted: indeed, an uncodified Catalan law remained in vigour till 1960, whereas the Spanish civil code (codified in 1889) was only applied as a complementary measure.

Connor (2004b) counter-argues that Smith's definition is far too inclusive to be effective, confusing nationhood with *citizenship* (and nation with state). Instead, Connor defines the nation as 'the largest group that can command a person's loyalty because of felt kinship ties; it is, from this perspective, the fully extended family' (1994: 202). I believe this to be a more straightforward definition. However, it may be even too rigid. For instance, Connor argues that there is no American or Indian nation (2004b: 37). The US Constitution's opening sentence, 'We the people', lends itself to two opposite interpretations: one ethnic, the other civic. The 'people' can be either the *ethnos*, sharing putative descent, or the *demos*, simply sharing citizenship and hypothetically equal rights, irrespective of their descent (Mann 2005: 55–69). Consequently, Connor's definition is not helpful here. In other words, the ethnic core of American 'patriotism' emerges both in extreme situations and in daily recurrences of 'banal nationalism' (Billig 1995).

A second weakness of ethnosymbolism relates to its apparent difficulty in explaining the variability of nationalist movements and their different motivations. Failing this task, ethnosymbolism risks remaining a descriptive endeavour. Until recently, ethnosymbolism had been relatively immune to criticism. Some authors have now come to describe it as a sort of scholarly romanticism (Özkirimli 2000: 216). How is it that ethnosymbolism is actually 'neo-romantic'? One 'romantic' postulate is ethnosymbolism's stress on the role of the intellectuals in the passage from *ethnie* to nation that I discussed above. The world has greatly changed since the first nineteenth-century nationalist stirrings. Do nations still depend on intellectuals to articulate their identities and aspirations? In my view, political elites are now key agents in nationalist movements, aided by the modern mass-media through which they obtain direct access to their constituencies. Indeed, outside the media's spotlight, a political movement would lose all chances to reach its 'natural' constituencies, unless, as sometimes happens, it uses terrorism as a reminder of its existence and goals. But, while terrorism is itself media-driven, it lies at the opposite spectrum of intellectual endeavour. Does this mean that intellectuals have become dispensable or inadequate? I would argue that intellectuals have become marginal in their public role, since the media-aided power of political elites to manipulate ethnic myths and traditions for their own ends has increased. This development is particularly prominent and dangerous in authoritarian and totalitarian regimes.

But it is not only totalitarian societies that aspire to the creation of a 'new man': media-driven societies can achieve the same outcome under apparently democratic conditions. Of all the media, the television has the power of achieving vast mobilising effects. For this reason, the political scientist Giovanni Sartori (1997) describes television as totalising to the point of *anthropogenesis* the creation of a 'new man', whom he calls '*homo videns*'.

The breakup of Yugoslavia is a litmus test. The country collapsed mostly because of the extreme distortion of pre-existing ethnonational myths blazed abroad by state-controlled media. Whereas primordialists tend to speak of a 'revival' of (mostly) Serbian pre-modern ethnic symbolism (Anzulovic 1999), a more prosaic interpretation is that these myths were strenuously deformed by state-controlled media, particularly Belgrade TV, the *Tanjug* News Agency and the newspaper *Politika* (Gallagher 2003; Malcolm 1994; Ramet 2002; Thompson 1999). A common misconception is that Yugoslavia 'fell apart' or suddenly 'broke up', due to the internal tensions caused by peripheral secessionism, particularly in Croatia and Slovenia. The conflict was instead induced by the militarily and politically dominant centre, mobilising pre-existing ethnosymbolic complexes through a 'rabidly distorted national control of almost all television and information on the conflicts' (Hardin 1997: 160).[15]

What I am trying to demonstrate is that a naked ethnosymbolic approach cannot do justice to the complexities of particular national circumstances. It is also limited in its power to explain how ethnic conflicts emerge and how nations are mobilised. Finally, ethnosymbolism has not addressed the wider context, nor the precipitates, nor the different outcomes of various ways of mobilising ethnic myths and symbols. So far, ethnosymbolism has largely disregarded the changes in and adaptations of these myths to the goals of elites. Hence, there is the risk of drifting towards an agency-less approach.[16] Furthermore, by dismissing outright the role of elite manipulation in the enormous emotional appeal of nationalism, ethnosymbolism leaves out of consideration the dynamics of power.

My critique does not question ethnosymbolism's deepest findings: even though it may be possible to claim that elites can, to a certain extent, engage in myth production, what most often appears to be the case is that they *deform* and *distort* existing myths beyond recognition. They can do so in specific and historically identifiable ways. But, in modern times, the control of the mass media is probably the essential precondition for such a change. Among other things, this limits or rules out the manipulative capacity of *non*-state actors. The implication is twofold: First, state and stateless nationalisms should be treated separately, because the latter cannot enjoy the monopoly of information and exert overwhelming control of the media. Second, in the radio–television age the role of the intellectuals remains more testimonial and occasional, as the state can easily dispense of their contribution.

I would like to believe that instrumentalism is not necessarily incompatible with ethnosymbolism. Indeed, in order not to remain on the surface and avoid 'descent into discourse', ethnosymbolism would need to be supplemented by a robust dose of instrumentalism, with special attention to mass manipulation. If Smith's approach could be ideally combined with Herman and Chomsky's (1988) scholarship on 'manufacturing consent', it could yield still unexplored and greatly more appealing results.

CONCLUSION

All the theories Smith has engaged with can shed light on different aspects of the rise of nations and nationalism. I have focused on two broad dichotomies: instrumentalism–primordialism and modernism–perennialism. Primordialism can offer testimonial insights into the nationalists' kinship-like vision of common descent. But instrumentalism is necessary to identify political dynamics, provided that it avoids determinist reductionism. Combining modernism and perennialism, ethnosymbolism focuses on the centrality of myths of descent in ethnic persistence. It also focuses on the role of the intellectuals and the intelligentsia as interpreters, rather than manipulators.

Has Smith achieved a universal account of ethnic conflict and nationalism? In my view, and on the basis of the preceding analysis, there remain two major obstacles to a universal application of ethnosymbolism: its uncertain conceptual basis, particularly in Smith's rather too inclusive definition of the nation; and its limited engagement with the problem of distortion of ethnic myths by political elites.

In defence of ethnosymbolism, this approach has been shown to be applicable and adaptable to a host of widely different epochs and latitudes. It can explain common features lying at the basis of a great deal of sociopolitical developments. But accepting that ethnosymbolism is one of the most sophisticated approaches to the study of nationalism does not bring us nearer to a general theory of nationalism. If Gellner's approach was trenchantly clear, it remained substantially removed from reality and, at best, over-simplified. In contrast, whereas the ethnosymbolic approach may perhaps be closer to reality, it remains conceptually opaque and politically un-nuanced.

The road that leads to the full understanding of nationalism in all its complexities is still a long one. Lacking a general theory, we have still to rely on several approaches, each of which will, in Smith's words, 'illuminate a corner of the broader canvas only to leave the rest of it in untraversed darkness' (1998: 220).

NOTES

1 For a recent discussion on this topic, see Banton (2004), Edwards (2004), Stone (2004).
2 Smith's choice of the term *ethnie* indicates the emphasis on a sense of collective identity as predating the rise of the modern nation-state, thereby dissociating the nation-state from

nationalism. The term is a French borrowing, which Smith encountered in the writings of the European federalist Guy Heraud (1963).

3 Brown (2000: 5) identifies 'three conceptual languages, which see nationalism as, respectively, an instinct (primordialism), an interest (situationalism) and an ideology (constructivism).'

4 Perennialism is not to be confounded with primordialism. The former refers to nations and is opposed to modernism, the latter refers to ethnic groups and is opposed to instrumentalism. For John A. Armstrong, '*Primordialism*, as the belief that nations have usually existed from time immemorial, has generally been discarded by scholars. However, *perennialism*, the belief that a few nations existed in antiquity or the Middle Ages, and revived subsequently, has more support ...' (Armstrong 2004, 9, my emphasis)

5 Smith (1991: 31) mentions the destruction of Carthage as a possible example of ancient 'genocide'. However, this and similar examples were of an entirely different sort: victors were exerting intimidating practices on the vanquished. In antiquity, it was not uncommon for winning armies to terrorise the populations into submission by providing chilling examples of the fate they might face in case they pondered over rebelling. This had nothing to do with the systematic targeting of entire populations, which can only be ascribed to modern times, with the rise of centralising states, the expansion of empire, scientific management, social engineering, military conscription, and large-scale war-making.

6 For a critique, see Smith (1986: 12; 1998).

7 Both Smith and Connor relate the nation inextricably to ethnicity, but they sharply disagree on the definition and the timing of nationalism (Smith 2004; Connor 2004b)

8 Smith (1998) devotes a chapter of *Nationalism and Modernism* as a critique of Gellner's 'culture of industrialism'.

9 The *Ruritanian* metaphor was not Gellner's coining. He took it from the writer Sir Anthony Hope Hawkins (1863–1933), who set his novel *The Prisoner of Zenda* (1894) in the fictional Kingdom of Ruritania.

10 'Early nineteenth-century Athens or Nauplia ... bore very little resemblance to Engels' Manchester, and the Morea did not look like the Lancashire dales' (Gellner 1997: 41).

11 A critique of the industrialisation–nationalism linkage can be shared by both modernists and non-modernists. The modernists see nationalism as a result of modernity, but most often locate the core of modernity in something other than industrialism, for example the modern state (Breuilly 1993), printing (Anderson 1983), or modern communications (Connor 1994, 2004a). Non-modernists insist more broadly on the pre-modern reality of nations (Horowitz 2004; Smith 2004).

12 Elie Kedourie places the intellectuals at the core of his Euro-centric approach (1960): nationalism spread via a mechanism of emulation touching first the local intellectuals and, subsequently, other elites. Its sources can be found in Fichte's combination of Kant's 'self-determination' and Herderian Romanticism, both of which allied with the political praxis of the French Revolution. Intellectuals of one country imitate those from another country, and the epicentre of everything lies in the midst of Europe (France and Germany).

13 The distinction between the two is not too sharp and they may overlap: in their lifetime some individuals have had the possibility both to create and disseminate their ideas. However, these are two clearly distinct activities or 'phases'. Generally, the tendency to be organised in professional corps indicates membership of the intelligentsia (Smith 1981: 109).

14 The milestone work on the intellectuals and the intelligentsia remains Miroslav Hroch (1985). With his three-stages model, Hroch shows how an incipient proto-elite of dreamers can flourish and become a mass movement. Phase A is the period of scholarly research, when poets, philologists, archeologists, historians, artists all contribute to the 'discovery', creation and formalisation of the national culture. Phase B is the period of patriotic agitation. Finally, phase C corresponds to the rise of a mass national movement.

15 For this purpose, I coined a concept hitherto inexistent in both International Relations and political theory: 'secession by the centre' (Conversi 2000, 2003). The dominant state-centred vision naively assumed that secession could only occur in the periphery, and that the centre was congenitally interested in maintaining the existing status quo. The rise of Serbian secessionism can be better seen as an attack on the Yugoslav Constitution and a denial of the 'rule of law' through the manipulation of ethnic myths and memories. It expressed no loyalty to the state, but only to the ethnic group, in high and consistent disrespect for political boundaries.

16 Agency-lessness is shared by postmodernism' s preference for broad descriptive portraits, although it is hard to identify a coherent post-modernist theory of nationalism. In his critique of postmodernism, John Stone (1998: 1) also indicates 'bringing power back in' as the most promising strategy.

REFERENCES

Anzulovic, Branimir (1999), *Heavenly Serbia: From Myth to Genocide,* New York: New York University Press/London: Hurst.

Anderson, Benedict (1983), *Imagined Communities,* London: Verso.

Armstrong, John A. (2004), 'Definitions, periodisation, and prospects for the *longue durée',* *Nations and Nationalism,* 10: 1–2, 9–18.

Banton, Michael (2004), 'Are ethnicity and nationality twin concepts?', *Journal of Ethnic and Migration Studies,* 30: 4, 807–14.

Billig, Michael (1995), *Banal Nationalism,* London: Sage.

Breuilly, John (1993), *Nationalism and the State,* Manchester: Manchester University Press/ New York: St. Martin's Press.

Brown, David (2000), *Contemporary Nationalism: Civic, Ethnocultural, and Multicultural Politics,* London: Routledge.

Connor, Walker (1993), 'Beyond reason: The nature of the ethnonational bond', *Ethnic and Racial Studies,* XVI, 373–89.

Connor, Walker (1994), *Ethnonationalism: The Quest for Understanding,* Princeton: Princeton University Press.

Connor, Walker (2004a), 'Nationalism and political illegitimacy', in Daniele Conversi (ed.), *Ethnonationalism in the Contemporary World: Walker Connor and the Study of Nationalism,* London: Routledge.

Connor, Walker (2004b), 'The timelessness of nations', *Nations and Nationalism* 10: 1/2, 35–7.

Conversi, Daniele (1995), 'Reassessing theories of nationalism. Nationalism as boundary maintenance and creation', *Nationalism and Ethnic Politics,* 1:1, 73–85.

Conversi, Daniele (1997), *The Basques, the Catalans, and Spain: Alternative Routes to Nationalist Mobilisation,* London: Hurst/Reno, NV: University of Nevada Press 2000.

Conversi, Daniele (2000), 'Central secession: Towards a new analytical concept? The case of Former Yugoslavia', *Journal of Ethnic and Migration Studies,* 26: 2, 333–56.

Conversi, Daniele (2003), 'The dissolution of Yugoslavia: Secession by the centre?', in John Coakley (ed.), *The Territorial Management of Ethnic Conflicts,* London: Frank Cass, 264–92.

Edwards, John (2004), 'Rational nationalism?', *Journal of Ethnic and Migration Studies,* 30: 4, 837–41.

Gallagher, Tom (2003), *The Balkans After the Cold War: From Tyranny to Tragedy,* London and New York: Routledge.

Gellner, Ernest (1964), *Thought and Change,* London: Weidenfeld and Nicolson/Chicago: University of Chicago Press.

Gellner, Ernest (1983), *Nations and Nationalism,* Oxford: Blackwell.

Gellner, Ernest (1997), *Nationalism,* London: Phoenix/New York: New York University Press.

Gentile, Emilio (2000), *Il Mito dello Stato nuovo,* Bari: Laterza.

Gregor, A.J. (1979), *Italian Fascism and Developmental Dictatorship,* Princeton: Princeton University Press.

Griffin, Roger (1991), *The Nature of Fascism,* London : Pinter / New York: St. Martin's Press.

Grosby, Steven (1995), 'Territoriality: The transcendental, primordial feature of modern societies', *Nations and Nationalism,* 1: 2, 143–62.

Hardin, Russell (1997), *One for All: The Logic of Group Conflict,* Princeton: Princeton University Press.

Hastings, Adrian (1997), *The Construction Of Nationhood: Ethnicity, Religion, and Nationalism,* Cambridge and New York: Cambridge University Press.

Hechter, Michael and Dina Okamoto (2001), 'Political consequences of minority group formation', *Annual Reviews of Political Sciences,* 4, 189–215.

Heraud, Guy (1963), *L'Europe des ethnies,* Brussels: Presses d' Europe.

Herman, Edward S. and Noam Chomsky (1988), *Manufacturing Consent. The Political Economy of the Mass Media,* New York: Pantheon Books.

Hobsbawm, Eric J. and Terence Ranger (eds) (1983), *The Invention of Tradition,* Cambridge: Cambridge University Press.

Hobsbawm, Eric J. (1995), *The Age of Extremes,* London: Abacus.

Horowitz, Donald L. (1985), *Ethnic Groups in Conflict,* Berkeley: University of California Press.

Horowitz, Donald L. (2004) 'The Primordialists', in Daniele Conversi (ed.) *Ethnonationalism in the Contemporary World: Walker Connor and the Study of Nationalism,* London and New York: Routledge.

Hroch, M. (1985), *Social Preconditions of National Revival in Europe: A Comparative Analysis of the Social Composition of Patriotic Groups among Smaller European Nations,* Cambridge: Cambridge University Press.

Hutchinson, John (1987), *The Dynamics of Cultural Nationalism. The Gaelic Revival and the Creation of the Irish Nation State,* London: Allen and Unwin.

Kedourie, Elie (1960), *Nationalism,* London: Hutchinson.

Kumar, Krishan (2003), *The Making of English National Identity,* Cambridge: Cambridge University Press.

Kuper, Leo. (1981), *Genocide: Its Political Use in the Twentieth Century*, New Haven: Yale University Press.

Leoussi, Athena S. (2004), 'The ethno-cultural roots of national art', *Nations and Nationalism*, 10: 1–2, 143–59.

Levene, Mark (2005), *Genocide in the Age of the Nation State*, London: I. B. Tauris.

Malcolm, Noel (1994), *Bosnia: A Short History*, New York: New York University Press.

Mann, Michael (2005), *The Dark Side of Democracy: Explaining Ethnic Cleansing*, Cambridge: Cambridge University Press.

Özkirimli, Umut (2000), *Theories of Nationalism: A Critical Overview*, Basingstoke: Macmillan.

Palmer, Alison (1998), 'Colonial and modern genocide: Explanations and categories', *Ethnic and Racial Studies*, 21: 1, 89–115.

Ramet, Sabrina P. (2002), *Balkan Babel. The Disintegration of Yugoslavia from the Death of Tito to the Insurrection in Kosovo*, Boulder, CO: Westview Press.

Rugman, Jonathan and Roger Hutchings (1996), *Ataturk's Children: Turkey and the Kurds*, London: Cassell.

Sartori, Giovanni (1997), *Homo Videns: Televisione e Post-Pensiero*, Bari: Laterza.

Smith, Anthony, D. (1972), 'Ethnocentrism, nationalism and social change', *International-Journal of Comparative Sociology*, XIII, 1–20.

Smith, Anthony D. (1981), *The Ethnic Revival*, Cambridge: Cambridge University Press.

Smith, Anthony D. (1986), *The Ethnic Origins of Nations*, Oxford: Blackwell.

Smith, Anthony D. (1991), *National Identity,* Harmondsworth: Penguin/Reno, NV: University of Nevada Press.

Smith, Anthony D. (1992), 'Chosen peoples : Why ethnic groups survive', *Ethnic and Racial Studies*, 15: 3, 436–56.

Smith, Anthony D. (1996), *Nationalism in a Global Era*, Cambridge: Polity Press.

Smith, Anthony D. (1998), *Nationalism and Modernism: A Critical Survey of Recent Theories of Nations and Nationalism,* London: Routledge.

Smith, Anthony D. (1999), *Myths and Memories of the Nation*, Oxford and New York: Oxford University Press.

Smith, Anthony D. (2000), *The Nation in History*, Cambridge: Polity Press.

Smith, Anthony D. (2003), *Chosen Peoples: Sacred Sources of National Identity*, Oxford and New York: Oxford University Press.

Smith, Anthony D. (2004), 'Dating the nation', in Daniele Conversi (ed.), *Ethnonationalism in the Contemporary World*, London: Routledge .

Stone, John (1998), 'New paradigms for old? Ethnic and racial studies on the eve of the Millennium', *Ethnic and Racial Studies*, 21: 1.

Stone, John (2004), 'Deconstructing rational choice: Or why we shouldn't over-rationalise the non-rational', *Journal of Ethnic and Migration Studies*, 30: 4, 841–53.

Thompson, Mark (1999), *Forging War. The Media in Serbia, Croatia and Bosnia-Hercegovina*. Luton: John Libbey Press.

Van den Berghe, P. L. (1981), *The Ethnic Phenomenon*, New York: Elsevier.

Chapter 2

THE ETHNIC ENIGMA: NATIONALISM, RACISM AND GLOBALISATION

John Stone and Polly Rizova

Arguments over the past few decades concerning the intrinsic nature of nations and nationalism have produced a fertile discussion about how modern individuals relate to 'community' and what they consider to be the legitimate forms of political representation. The meaning of national identity is a question that has become increasingly salient in the aftermath of the Cold War and concerns about globalisation in a non-ideological environment raise other important questions. As capitalism has spread, in one form or another, to virtually all societies on every continent, the issue of whether man can live by bread alone has taken on renewed significance. A resurgence of fundamentalist religious forces has often been interpreted as just one reaction to the amoral nature of seemingly unending materialism. Two other forces capable of filling the void in values are various forms of ethnic nationalism and the types of racial affiliations that have been so prominent during the 'irrational rationality' of the twentieth century. Before turning to the intertwining of these conceptually distinct, but often related, forms of identity, let us briefly consider the current situation in the debates over nationalism.

THE 'WHAT AND WHEN IS A NATION' DEBATE

One axis of the nationalism controversy concerns the superficially obvious, but in fact very complex, issue surrounding what constitutes a nation. The related question of when national consciousness can be said to have started has also led to diametrically opposed positions. On one side of the dichotomy is the claim that nationalism must be seen as a socially constructed belief system that emerged around the time of the great transformations embedded in the political and economic revolutions of the eighteenth and nineteenth centuries. Mass participation and some measure of literacy were an integral part of the process of mobilising modern individuals on the basis of a sense of community derived from beliefs about shared ancestry, history and culture. Hobsbawm and Ranger's

(1983) 'invention of tradition', Anderson's (1983) 'imagined communities' and the arguments associated with Gellner's (1983) analysis of 'high culture' and 'mass culture', view nationalism as a relatively recent social phenomenon, inextricably linked to the forces of modernity. According to this line of argument, one could invent a 'nation' in just the same manner as one could invent a 'race'.

The counterpoint to social constructionism is an emphasis on the historical evidence of certain national groups that appear to have persisted for centuries, if not millennia. How can such collectivities be seen to be the result of rather arbitrary circumstances coming together at some point in time which then create a new sense of national consciousness? To what has become known as *ethno-symbolism*, advocated most prominently by Anthony D. Smith, the antiquity of nations (Smith 2004a) and the deeply ingrained beliefs in chosen peoples (Smith 2004b) cannot be so simply dismissed. While Smith is far too sophisticated a sociologist to ignore any element of social construction, he argues in favour of placing the evolution of such belief systems in an appropriately historical and cultural context. Certain scholars of nationalism have proceeded further down this road to stress the 'primordial' essence of nationalism (Grosby 1994) and a few have gone still further to emphasise at least some bio-genetic causation (van den Berghe 1981). The most prominent advocate of this last position is Pierre van den Berghe who suggests that there are certain socio-biological factors – like nepotism and inclusive fitness – that must also be built into the causal explanation of the power and persistence of the nationalist message.

It would seem that many of the exchanges between the more permanent and the more flexible understandings of nationalism – in so many cases simplistic dichotomies are often a misrepresentation of what is, in reality, a continuum – depend on which examples of the phenomenon the scholar is attempting to analyse. Furthermore, it is imperative to know what aspects of the particular definition of nationalism are the object of scrutiny, for there is nothing inherent in a broad conception of nationalism that precludes both deep historical roots and a relatively recent process of mobilisation (see Leoussi 2006). The symbolic themes and the cultural bases of nationalist movements are often constructed from ancient myths and legends, but their coalescence into the building blocks of ethno-national movements (Connor 1994) is closely bound up in modern forces, like the spread of democratic political ideals, interacting with the complex dynamics of both the divisions within states and inter-state rivalries.

PARALLEL DISCUSSIONS IN THE FIELD OF RACE RELATIONS

Thus current attempts to define and understand the nature and dynamics of nationalism have reached a point that recognises a variable mix of factors that need to be considered. Modern nationalism, and in particular the forms of national consciousness that have become more salient in an era of globalisation, can also be considered against the related developments in the study of race relations. While race and nation sometimes are viewed as overlapping, virtually all modern societies are increasingly multi-racial in character. This is, in part, the result of changing patterns of international migration that have been stimulated by the economic forces of global capitalism and by political changes that have followed in the wake of the collapse of communism.

The demise of apartheid in the 1990s, and the continuing changes in the patterns of race relations in the United States, have produced a shift from stark divisions along a black–white boundary to a more subtle array of inter-racial relationships. African-Americans are no longer the largest minority in America, being overtaken by the continuing flow of Latino migrants from Mexico combined with immigrants from Central and South America, and in four states, according to the 2000 Census estimates, non-whites made up a majority of the population.[1] In this way the dynamics of race relations have become increasingly complex and variegated: hybridity, transnationalism, 'whiteness', poly-ethnicity, and a whole host of other topics, have entered into the contemporary discourse on American race relations. This suggests that the impacts of an ever-diverse set of new sources of migrants – whose distinctive origins are a result of the changes in the immigration laws in 1965 – are interacting with an increasingly global environment. The longer-term outcome is a matter of fierce debate, ranging from those who argue that the land border with Mexico raises an altogether new scenario as far as assimilation and adjustment to some 'core' notion of American culture and values is concerned (Huntington 2004; Etzioni 2005),[2] and those who maintain that some form of modified assimilation (Alba and Nee 2003; Bean and Stevens 2003) is a far more realistic evaluation of the empirical evidence.

When one adds a dramatically new dimension to the equation with the escalation of international terrorism, in the aftermath of the attacks on the World Trade Center in Manhattan and the Pentagon on 11 September 2001, and the implications that these events may be having for the Muslim diaspora, the situation both in America and in Europe becomes even more unpredictable. The complex interaction between terrorism, wars and the more 'normal' patterns of demographic change and global interpenetration demonstrate quite clearly that perceptions of 'race', ethnicity and nationalism are interrelated and constantly changing. This can be seen in the problems associated with the successful implementation of conflict-resolution measures, whether geared to racial, ethnic or national disputes, as it depends not simply on traditional inter-state diplomacy, or collective peace-keeping operations directed by the United Nations, NATO, African Union, or other multi-national organisations, but also on the flexible application of a whole range of institutional activities,[3] actions by NGOs and the selective adoption of economic pressure and military intervention. The success of intra-state or intra-federation conflict resolution equally depends on a diverse mix of policies designed to reduce both the perception and reality of group economic exploitation; the protection of linguistic, cultural and religious rights; a degree of political autonomy on core matters of group definition; and a sense of empower-ment and respect for difference in a shared environment. The ubiquity of conflict based on constantly changing boundary lines demonstrates just how difficult such a balance is to achieve and then maintain.

The democratic transition in South Africa represented another case where forces of nationalism and racism were intertwined with geo-political and other factors to produce an outcome that was surprising in terms of the standard models of social change, violence and revolution. Under apartheid, stark divisions of race relations were overlapping and interpenetrating a rich bundle of class and ethnic forces. Afrikaner nationalism represented the *ressentiment* that is often found in reactive responses to group humiliation at the hands of British imperialism (Greenfeld 1992). Imperial contempt for the group language, Afrikaans, hostility to the group's religion represented in the Calvinistic mutation that made up the doctrine of the Dutch Reformed Church, a history of dispossession from lands that were defined, however myopically, as the rightful inheritance from the Great Trek, all fused together to produce a powerful sense of identity. When this was superimposed on a feudal system of master–servant relationships defined along the colour lines dividing the powerful minority from the African majority, a seemingly explosive amalgam of race and nation came together.

Cross-cutting cleavages that in many situations seem to ameliorate group con-flict appeared to be absent. Thus, the existence of substantial minorities that did not fit within either of the two major group boundaries did not generate bridges between the polarised hierarchy. The Cape Coloured community, transparently a hybrid category whose Afrikaans language revealed the origin of many members of this group, demonstrated how race trumped language in the steady evolution of Afrikaner nationalism. Quite why this should have been the case is somewhat surprising since the 'threat' to the distinct survival of the Afrikaner community lay, initially, as much from the cosmopolitan influences of the English language, the global commercialism of the *uitlanders* and, of course, the military might of the British Empire. However, given the subsequent post-Boer War compromise among the South African whites, that relegated the African influence in the polit-ical system to that of a conquered nation, the division between black and white became the hallmark of apartheid. In much the same way, the South African Indian community, located predominantly in Natal and despite the early (unsuc-cessful) attempts of Gandhi to mobilise opposition to the regime, added little to ameliorating the crude divisions along the colour line and moved its support behind the non-racial ANC as the only practical strategy to oppose apartheid.

The resolution of the apartheid struggle in a relatively peaceful manner provided important insights into the shifting nature of geo-politics. An analysis of the factors that brought about this unexpected outcome highlighted a series of developments that systematically undermined the ability of the white elite to sustain a racial state in an economy that had always been dependent on international allies. With the end of the Cold War, the perceived strategic importance of South Africa ceased to be seen as critical to the protection of Western interests in the struggle against Communism. This brought enormous pressure on the regime to re-think the options and to decide that the maintenance of a racial state was no longer worth the price that would have to be paid to sustain it. The collapse of apartheid in the early 1990s and its replacement by a non-racial democracy was another development realigning the global perception of the colour line. What was the resolution of a long and bitter struggle had an important symbolic impact not only in Africa, but also in Europe and the United States by the end of the century.

EUROPEAN–AMERICAN CONTRASTS AND SIMILARITIES

As the United States evolved into a far more complex array of disparate groups and forces, this was also true for the emerging scene in Europe. The component states of the enlarged Union do not share a myth of immigrant origin to act as a benchmark for recent racial and ethnic shifts. But as the structure of state units has begun to slowly dissolve and blur, at least on the internal political boundaries of the member states of the EU, this has had significant implications for ethnic and racial relations within the Union, as much as it has for the composition of the constituent parts of the evolving super-state. Flows of migrants that were previously difficult, if not impossible, to sustain have changed the ethnic and racial mix of societies that had traditionally been diversified by migration from the former colonies, rather than by extensive inter-European movement. Two illustrations of these dynamic developments can be seen in the steady, if uneven, progress towards peace in Northern Ireland, and the reversal of both Ireland and Italy from being societies of emigration to ones that are experiencing the economic, social and political impact of immigrants.

In the first case, the emergence of Brussels as the neutral pole between London and Dublin has helped to mitigate the worst fears of both the Protestant and Catholic communities in Northern Ireland that the only resolution of 'the troubles' must be the 'victory' of one side over the other (that is, that the conflict is a zero-sum game). The new political and administrative structure of the European Union suggests that a compromise could work and develop into a genuine 'win-win' outcome. Of course, other factors have played an important role in this realignment in as much as post-11 September concerns about terrorism have questioned the legitimacy of the traditional support found among many Irish-Americans for the IRA. Furthermore, the economic transformation of the Irish Republic into a 'Celtic Tiger', exhibiting sustained economic growth and high levels of economic prosperity, has also been a critical factor in turning a traditional society of emigration into a society attracting many immigrants. Much the same side effects, emanating from the similar economic prosperity of the Italians in the later decades of the twentieth century, have also produced an entirely predictable, yet ironic, reversal of attitudes towards 'outsiders', many of whom arrived under the aegis of the greater European project (O'Dowd 2005).[4]

Perhaps the largest single challenge facing the future of the EU, following the failure of the political leadership in both France and Holland to secure the ratification of the new draft European Constitution in 2005, is the relationship with Turkey. Incorporating a 'secular' Muslim state with a population the size of Germany raises a barrage of new questions about the emerging ethnic and religious shape of the continent. Not only would such a move further challenge the Christian monopoly on religious identity, but the internal power dynamics of the substantial Islamic communities, numbering between 15 and 20 million people in aggregate, and located in significant proportions in France (9 per cent); Germany, Austria, Belgium and Switzerland (4 per cent); Britain, Denmark, Greece and Sweden (3 per cent), would almost certainly be profoundly affected. While some observers have argued that Muslims and Mexicans fulfil essentially the same functions on the two continents (Zolberg and Woon 1999), we need to ask to what extent this is a reasonable assessment. Are the consequences of a minority which is marked out by a distinct world religion, Islam, much the same as those for a minority whose primary boundary is linked to a different world language, Spanish? Bilingualism is easier to acquire and a much more flexible option than membership in more than one monotheistic religion. Does a long and continuous land border pose more of a perceived threat to the United States than the religious affiliations of citizens whose faith is currently being challenged by strong fundamentalist movements? It also raises other provocative questions: will Islamophobia help to reduce the long-standing tensions associated with other types of boundaries by shifting hostile attention away from non-Islamic minorities? Will Latinophobia have a similar impact on African-Americans' status in the United States? This last question appears rather implausible given the relatively rapid assimilation of many Latino groups, notably the Cubans in Miami (although in this case the obsession with Castro has certainly given them an edge over other immigrant/refugee groups like the Haitians), and the persistence of racial discrimination between American whites and blacks in health care, housing, education, employment, income, wealth and social mobility (Loury, Modood and Teles 2005; Shapiro 2004).[5]

GLOBALISATION'S IMPACT ON ETHNONATIONALISM AND RACE RELATIONS

Such questions remain at the core of the ethnic enigma for the twenty-first century. No matter the perspective chosen by scholars of nationalism, there is general agreement that the demise of the state is a long way off, despite the negative impact of much nationalism in the twentieth century (Smith 1998).[6] Clearly, globalisation has reconfigured the strength of certain boundaries, reinforcing some and weakening others, in much the same manner that the forces of decolonisation, and the ramifications of the end of the Cold War, helped to restructure the world's racial system. The long-term implications of such changes, however, are subject to similar problems of interpretation. Just as many scholars maintained that de-colonisation was replaced by neo-colonialism, so contemporary critics of the global economy point to the massive imbalances in wealth and influence symbolised by the leading multinational corporations whose assets dwarf the Gross National Product of many 'independent' states. There is considerable evidence (Stone and Rizova 2007)[7] to support the basis of such claims, although the actual implications for national identity and race and ethnic relations are much more difficult to predict. It is the *processes* enhanced by globalisation and, more particularly, the changes in international migration – both legal and illegal – that are as influential as the corporate institutions *per se*. This is because, in most situations, it is the movement of diverse peoples that is often seen as a more visible challenge to both national boundaries and to the ethnic-racial balances of power within states.

Another development is the way in which incidents that several decades ago would have been defined largely as national, that is, intra-state, matters, are now being translated onto a wider and more complicated set of arenas. The racial ramifications of Hurricane Katrina, with television reports revealing the predominantly black faces of the people stranded on buildings and in the sports arena for days at a time before any rescue action was taken, quickly became a global metaphor for the Bush administration's priorities with respect to poor blacks in America, and by extension to the wretched of the earth. As this took place at the same time that the United States was waging war in Iraq, an intervention into the affairs of a Muslim state and one deeply resented by most Muslims around the world, the global ramifications of what was essentially the response to an internal natural disaster quickly became translated into wider ethnic and racial significance.

Within a few weeks of these events, the burning vehicles and buildings in the slums around Paris, triggered by the deaths of two young French Muslims fleeing the police, and the government's attitude towards the behaviour of minority youth that the Interior Minister initially characterised as the action of 'scum', set off a chain reaction of arson attacks around France, followed by other further incidents in Belgium and Germany. Attempts to frame such violence in terms of the agitation of fundamentalist clerics, rather than as a clear demonstration of the failure of French policies of immigrant assimilation, seemed increasingly implausible as the minority religious leaders consistently spoke out against the riots (*Le Monde* 4 November 2005).

While evidence of patterns of global support for ethnic and racial struggles is by no means new, the speed with which such incidents of ethnic and racial violence are translated onto a world stage adds a new dimension to the dynamics of contemporary conflicts. Thus nationalism and racism, far from declining or becoming obsolete, have changed shape and must be viewed against a global backdrop. So while global capitalism has on the one hand broken down barriers of national autonomy, on the other it has generated new forms of diversity as a result of the need to free up the movement of labour as much as capital. This in turn has revived the debates on the meaning of community and who can be regarded as legitimate members of what are frequently enlarged political units. As borders within the EU have become more porous and sometimes invisible, the corollary is the hardening of the collective boundaries, or exterior shell, to produce what has been termed a 'Fortress Europe'. This, in its turn, leads to pressures to avoid or circumvent the barriers and to a major issue over illegal immigration, the smuggling of people and an internal backlash against what is often perceived, and frequently cultivated by politicians wishing to capitalise on xenophobic fears, as a threat of an 'invasion' by aliens. The global reach of Al-Qaeda cells, with dramatic and lethal terrorist bombings from Madrid to Bali and from London to Amman, also creates a related demand for enhanced security measures and for the serious implementation of many border controls that are increasingly difficult to seal. All the evidence, however, suggests that such restrictions are ineffective and that the number of illegal immigrants coming to the United States, for example, now outnumber the foreigners who come with visas (Passel and Suro 2005).

CONCLUSION: IS THERE A SOLUTION TO THE ETHNIC ENIGMA?

This brief and highly selective overview of some of the major trends in ethnicity, nationalism and race relations confirms the conclusions of those emphasising the persistence of identification with both nation and race in the new century. The belief that modernity, and the moves towards a globalised, capitalist world economic system, would both undermine attachments to nations, or eradicate racial definitions, has been shown to be implausible. Modern materialist society seems to lack the cohesiveness and value systems that so many of the people of the world crave. Paradoxically, the humanistic and universal values of Enlightenment thinking fail to provide for many the vital forms of identity that modern individuals seek to shield themselves from the uncertainties of rapid and discontinuous social change. The quest for *Gemeinschaft* within *Gesellschaft* seems to be a better description of modernity than the classical models suggesting a systematic movement in only one direction. Expression of crude racist ideologies may have been ameliorated in a world where the balance of power has started to shift away from Euro-American domination but there is persistent evidence of massive disparities in wealth and influence that still follow traditional patterns of racial hierarchy.

The revival of fundamentalist versions of all religions can be seen in this context, as indeed the tendencies of intellectuals to misunderstand or fail to grasp their importance. There is a greater appreciation that 'globalisation is a much longer [older] phenomenon than most theorists of the subject are willing to acknowledge, and the agents and processes are not simply secular but include religion and warfare, both of which encourage differentiation' (Hutchinson 2005: 188–9). Furthermore, while states have been forced to cooperate in larger political and economic groupings for certain purposes, there is little evidence that the active units within such coalitions, or inside loose federations, are free from the system of national states. In conclusion, it would seem that the future shape of global relationships, at individual and collective levels, will continue to be influenced by both nationalism and race relations, and their frequent interaction, for many decades to come.

NOTES

1 In 2005, Texas joined California, New Mexico and Hawaii as states with a majority non-white population. In the first three, Latinos form the majority group and in Hawaii Asian Americans constitute the largest single group. Five other states have populations with at least 40 per cent non-white populations: Maryland, Mississippi, Georgia, New York and Arizona (US Census, 2000).

2 Etzioni points to the ideological nature of the Huntington book and particularly to its highly selective use of evidence. On the critical assertions of an imminent threat of secession in the South-West, the persistence of bilingualism, an absence of the Protestant work ethic and a lack of intermarriage, Huntington is either factually incorrect or misses the positive contributions that Mexican values and culture can provide to America.

3 In his assessment of Jagdish Bhagwati's *In Defence of Globalisation* (2004), George Scialabba refers to 'this alphabet soup of agreements, rules and organisations ... [that] defenders and opponents mean by globalisation' [*Boston Globe* 22 August 2004]. These include both

   global institutions such as the IMF and World Bank, and trade regulations and rules established under the WTO, NAFTA, and so on.
 4 Using Norbert Elias's Established-Outsider model, O'Dowd has analysed these changes in
   attitudes by a content-analysis of newspaper reports in both Ireland and Italy. The systematic stigmatisation of new immigrants is part of a familiar process of cultivating boundaries
   between the outsiders and the established core communities in both societies.
 5 The evidence of persistent black-white segregation in the US is overwhelming. Whether
   one looks at schooling, where more than a half century after the 1954 Brown versus Board
   of Education ruling, public schools have been essentially resegregated; or at the housing
   market that has also maintained its description as American Apartheid. See, for example,
   the report *More than Money,* Harvard Civil Rights Project (2004); Kozol (2005). Of course,
   in America, residence and opportunities for good public schooling are inextricably linked.
 6 By 1945, any naive views about the potential for nationalism to liberate groups from
   oppression had been dispelled. As Smith puts it: 'In the convulsions that followed [the
   inter-war years], first in Europe then across the world, the rampant red line of nationalism
   blended with the darker forces of fascism, racism and anti-Semitism, to produce the hor-
   rors of the Holocaust and Hiroshima' (Smith 1998: 2).
 7 In the middle of the first decade of the twenty-first century, Wal-Mart offers the archetype
   of the multinational corporation that has followed the ruthless logic of global capitalism.
   It is the world's largest retailer with annual sales of $285 billion, employs 1.6 million people
   worldwide and has manufacturing facilities in Mexico, Argentina, Brazil, China and
   Korea, as well as in Germany, the United Kingdom and Canada (Dicker 2005).

REFERENCES

Alba, Richard and Victor Nee (2003), *Remaking the American Mainstream: Assimilation and
    the New Immigration,* Cambridge, MA: Harvard University Press.
Anderson, Benedict (1983), *Imagined Communities: Reflections on the Origins and Spread of
    Nationalism,* London: Verso.
Bhagwati, Jagdish (2004), *In Defence of Globalisation,* Oxford: Oxford University Press.
Bean, Frank and Gillian Stevens (2003), *America's Newcomers: The Dynamics of Diversity,*
    New York: The Russell Sage Foundation.
Connor, Walker (1994), *Ethnonationalism: The Quest for Understanding,* Princeton: Princeton
    University Press.
Dicker, John (2005), *The United States of Wal-Mart,* London: Penguin.
Etzioni, Amitai (2005), 'The Real Threat: An Essay on Samuel Huntington', *Contemporary
    Sociology,* 35: 5, 477–85.
Gellner, Ernest (1983), *Nations and Nationalism,* Oxford: Blackwell.
Greenfeld, Liah (1992), *Nationalism: Five Roads to Modernity,* Cambridge, MA: Harvard
    University Press.
Grosby, Steven (1994), 'The Verdict of History: The inexpungeable ties of primordiality – a
    Response to Eller and Coughlan', *Ethnic and Racial Studies,* 17: 1, 164–71.
Hobsbawm, Eric and Terence Ranger (1983), *The Invention of Tradition,* Cambridge: Cambridge
    University Press.
Huntington, Samuel (2004), *Who Are We?: The Challenges to America's National Identity,*

New York: Simon and Schuster.

Hutchinson, John (2005), *Nations as Zones of Conflict*, London: Sage.

Kozol, Jonathan (2005), *The Shame of the Nation: The Restoration of Apartheid Schooling in America*, New York: Crown Publishers.

Leoussi, Athena S. (2006), 'Nationalism', in George Ritzer (ed.), *The Blackwell Encyclopedia of Sociology*, Malden, MA: Blackwell.

Loury, Glenn, Tariq Modood and Steven Teles (eds) (2005), *Ethnicity, Social Mobility and Public Policy: Comparing the US and UK*, Cambridge: Cambridge University Press.

O'Dowd, Amie (2005), 'Establishing Boundaries: A Comparative Analysis of Immigrants as Outsiders in Ireland and Italy', unpublished Ph.D. thesis, University College, Dublin.

Passel, Jeffrey and Roberto Suro (2005), *Rise, Peak and Decline: Trends in US Immigration 1992–2004*, Washington, DC: Pew Hispanic Center Report.

Shapiro, Thomas (2004), *The Hidden Costs of Being African American*, New York: Oxford University Press.

Smith, Anthony D. (1998), *Nationalism and Modernism: A Critical Survey of Recent Theories of Nations and Nationalism*, London: Routledge.

Smith, Anthony D. (2004a), *The Antiquity of Nations*, Cambridge: Polity Press.

Smith, Anthony D. (2004b), *Chosen Peoples: Sacred Sources of National Identity*, Oxford: Oxford University Press.

Stone, John and Polly Rizova (2007), 'Rethinking Racial Conflict in an Era of Global Terror', *Ethnic and Racial Studies* (forthcoming). Special Issue edited by Ian Law and Bobby Sayyid.

van den Berghe, Pierre (1981), *The Ethnic Phenomenon*, New York: Elsevier.

Zolberg, Aristide and Long Woon (1999), 'Why Islam is like Spanish: Cultural Incorporation in Europe and the United States', *Politics and Society*, 27, 5–38.

Chapter 3

WARFARE, REMEMBRANCE
AND NATIONAL IDENTITY

John Hutchinson

The study of warfare is central to an understanding of nation-formation. It is hardly an exaggeration to say that nationalism, in both its civic and ethnic varieties, was born in war: the former during the defence of the French republic against the armies of the European monarchies in 1792; the latter, articulated in Fichte's 'Addresses to the German Nation', after Napoleon's humiliation of Prussia. Most nation-states that came into existence before the mid-twentieth century were created by war or had their boundaries defined by wars or internal violence (Howard 1991: 39–41). The struggle for political citizenship has often been linked to a willingness to sacrifice for the nation, as captured in the Swedish slogan 'One soldier, one rifle one vote' (Enloe 1980: 50–1), thereby, some feminists would argue, gendering the nation. Warfare has offered the greatest opportunities for national minorities, as historically the greatest periods of nation-formation have followed the military collapse of empires. But since many genocides have occurred in warfare, it has also created the greatest threat to such minorities, who have often been stigmatised as fifth columnists or worse.

These are large and complex topics, the subject for a book rather than a brief chapter. More fruitful here is to explore how one of the major theoricians of nationalism, Anthony D. Smith, understands the relationship between warfare and nations. I define warfare here as politically organised campaigns of violence between two or more collectivities. I will use Smith's work to examine the following issues: firstly, the idea of the nation as a community of sacrifice; secondly, the importance of memory in the reproduction of nations; and thirdly, changes in the nature of warfare and their potential to subvert national solidarities. In discussing these topics, I will draw, in particular, on Smith's seminal article (1981a) and his 2003 monograph.

WARFARE AND NATION-FORMATION

Smith conceives of the nation in Durkheimian terms as a sacred community that elicits mass sacrifice in its defence, although he observes that nationalism and its referent, the nation, combine both secular and 'religious' qualities. It is secular because the goals of nationalists are this-worldly, oriented to the welfare and progress of a distinctive people settled on an ancestral homeland, who organise themselves collectively, usually through a state. It also assumes a quasi-religious character, in inaugurating commemorative ceremonies and rituals which bind their members into a historical community through participation in which its members guarantee their immortality (Smith 2003: ch. 3). In examining the formation of nations, warfare is given a significant (though not essential) role. In earlier writings (1981a and b) Smith identifies as causal factors the rise of competitive interstate systems during the premodern and modern eras, and such associated processes as state centralisation, mass mobilisation, and colonisation. Interstate warfare serves to elaborate and harden ethnic group self-images and group stereotypes and thereby form over time a common national consciousness, though it may pose a threat to multinational states or sharply stratified societies (Smith 1981a: 390–7). State mobilisation unites individuals from different localities for a common cause, and the struggle for territory serves to define the boundaries of a collectivity. Perhaps most salient are the cultural effects of warfare – we/they stereotypes are created by the competing propaganda of rival states, and heroes and epochal events provide role models and reference points especially when taken up by poets, artists and writers who embed these in the collective consciousness (Smith 1981b: 74–8).

Smith distinguishes between the wars of premodernity and modernity, which shape the experiences of *ethnie* and nations respectively. Myths of origin, an attachment to a territory, a sense of cultural distinctiveness are common to both; but in addition nations possess a mass public culture and, through processes of democratisation, common rights and duties. The wars of premodernity and modernity differ. Smith, of course, is aware of mass mobilisation of populations in ancient and medieval periods, for example during the Roman–Jewish War from 66 to 72 CE, and during the Mongol expansion. On the whole, before the eighteenth century, wars generally fought by mercenaries or small professional armies or an aristocratic warrior stratum tended to be limited in their social effects, and their consequences for later nation-formation are indirect. Protracted and recurrent conflicts in the premodern period (for example, the Hundred Years War between the English and French) can have long-term effects, and memory of struggles (personified in such figures as Jeanne d'Arc) may shape the modern nation. Nonetheless, the effects of modern war-making are much more direct: the introduction of conscription in the nineteenth century and development of total wars during the twentieth century that integrated civilian and military fields for the struggle engendered a mass national consciousness.

Subsequently, Smith tends to shift his focus to the role of memory and of cultural meanings (see Smith 2003), influenced by George Mosse's research into the rise of large-scale commemorative ceremonies and symbols in Germany during the nineteenth century (Mosse 1975; 1991). These are at first activities of the middle classes who celebrate the individual heroism of 'fallen soldiers', but as wars become industrial, involving the masses by the early twentieth century, so Smith, following Mosse, notes a shift from individual heroism to the celebration of the national people. The institutionalisation of commemorations around monuments to the dead provides a central reference point for subsequent nationalists. In *Chosen Peoples* (2003: ch. 9) Smith elaborates on the different models of exemplary sacrifice for a higher cause (of a life of ease, of things held dear, and of life itself) thrown up by warfare that inspire future generations. Such sacrifice creates a compact between the living and the dead, reversing the attrition of individual egotism and class divisions, and forms a moral community of the nation.

This, however, is only one of several perspectives on the relationship between warfare and nationality. Those who argue that warfare is functionally necessary for the reproduction of nations would consider that Smith emphasises too much the sacrifices evoked by the nation rather than the violence it instigates. For modernist theorists, who consider the nation as a political construct, Smith reifies 'memory', failing to foreground that such memory is a product of competing interests and to address the significance of the wider political processes by which states incorporate populations into the nation. Finally, from a postmodernist perspective Smith pays insufficient attention to changing forms of warfare and how the rising cost of warfare in the nuclear age makes nationalism and the nation unviable.

SACRIFICE AND THE NATION

The idea of self-sacrifice is tied to Smith's conception of the nation as a moral community, and to his sharp criticisms of interest-based approaches to nationalism that fail to explain why so many people are prepared to die for the nation. He is not alone in being struck by the emotional hold of the nation. Benedict Anderson remarked (1991: 132) on the great wars of the twentieth century as 'extraordinary not so much in the unprecedented scale in which they permitted people to kill as in the colossal numbers persuaded to lay down their lives ...'. 'Blood sacrifice' for the nation either in the case of a liberation war (as in the German territories in 1813), or in a civil war (USA) or indeed a post-independence war (Australia's Gallipoli campaign) has often been viewed as an essential rite of passage. Indeed, for many nineteenth-century nationalists the very rights to national independence and warfare became indissolubly linked. This was articulated by a German delegate to the Frankfurt Assembly in 1848: 'Mere existence does not entitle a people to political independence: only the force to exert itself as a state against others' (cited in Howard 1991: 39–40).

However, the last quotation is at best ambiguous: is it the will to sacrifice that constitutes the nation or a cult of force? The rise and spread of nationalism over the past two centuries has been accompanied by great violence. Smith's emphasis on sacrifice is open to criticism from those who believe the nation is founded on organised violence and that mass death in war is not a demonstration of collective will but rather of the coercive powers of the state.

Carolyn Marvin and David Ingle in *Blood Sacrifice and the Nation: Totem Rituals and the American Flag* argue in Durkheimian fashion that in the modern world where authority has passed from Church to State, blood sacrifice in warfare has replaced religion as the central legitimising social and political ritual. The violence of human beings that is an inherent threat to social order is tamed by diverting it against outsiders in willed sacrifice of the young for the nation. This sacrifice, in turn, creates and recreates the sense of a unique bounded group and binds the living in moral obligation to the dead to the upkeep of social order. Great commemorative ceremonies, focused on the flag which stands for the body of the nation, have created a surrogate civil religion. But the ugly secret (or totem taboo) behind this religion is that the voluntarism of the young is an illusion because of the system of military conscription in most industrialised states. Although to elicit sacrifice and solidarity wars need to be portrayed as in the nation's defence, in reality the nation-*state* (conceived of in Weberian terms as a centralised coercive apparatus) acts as a deity demanding the mass death of the young on a regular basis. This totem sacrifice 'leads us to define the nation as the memory of the last sacrifice' (Marvin and Ingle 1999: 5). In periods without such wars the nation falls into a malaise.

Marvin and Ingle reject the idea that warfare in the contemporary world is an outgrowth of ethnic hatreds; rather violence is the means by which nations re-energise themselves (Marvin and Ingle 1999: 3). Smith, although acknowledging the powerful emotions evoked by 'blood sacrifice', would rightly reject both this reduction of the nation to an embodiment of primitive cycles and the idea of a will to violence as inherent in nationalism. Rather the nation is potent to the extent that it seems to provide answers to problems of meaning through its myths, memories and, above all, culture. As Smith argues, warfare by itself may strengthen and reinforce group identities but cannot by itself create them. For a population to defend itself militarily, there already has to be a sense of common values and interests around which they can be mobilised. In short, warfare is only one of several factors that contribute to nation-formation; religion is another, and this undermines the idea that cohesion is only possible through regular bloodshed.

In young nations such as the USA and Australia that lack strong ethnic and historical traditions, specific wars are often cited as rites of passage during which a national consciousness develops. Countries which have been unified by force (for example, Germany) or where the nation is associated with an imperial mission may define themselves by reference to military power. But it is implausible to view regular warfare as a requirement for national cohesion, since there are many examples of solidary nations without experience of recent wars such as Switzerland or Sweden, but for which the memories of warfare, as enshrined in commemorative rituals and popular culture, remain. This suggests that what is important is the existence of institutionalised memories of warfare, and that there is no inherent linkage between nationalism and mass violence.

But to what extent is the will to sacrifice itself a myth, as Marvin and Ingle argue? Given that Smith's focus is on *interstate* wars, is the emphasis on large-scale self-sacrifice not a weakness in his interpretation? Political 'realists' such as Charles Tilly (1995) and Michael Mann (1993: ch. 7) argue that individuals do not fight in state armies because of national sentiments, rather they are formed into nations by coercive states. From this perspective the driving force is an increasingly competitive and militaristic state system that, as societies industrialise, compels polities to intervene ever more in social life and circumscribe (territorially enclose) their populations in order to mobilise all their resources against their rivals. Nationalism is the ideological cement that 'justifies' this caging of peoples, and the key institutions are the mass education system and military conscription, that together indoctrinate their populations for sacrifice to the (nation-)state (Posen 1995).

In support, they could claim that although there are many examples of young men volunteering for national conflict, they represent a small minority of the population and their motives for doing so are mixed. Young men might enlist out of a sense of adventure, like many Australians in the First World War, and to see the world. Among the volunteers in Britain and Germany at the beginning of the First World War, the expectation was not necessarily one of sacrifice but rather participation in a short campaign that would be over by Christmas. In reality, most wars have been of professional and conscripted armies, and by 1916 the slaughter on the western front was such that even in Britain there was a switch from voluntary enlistment to conscription. Desertion has been a problem, even in the armies of the French republic and later of Napoleon. What kept men fighting has been a sense of loyalty to their comrades and draconian penalties rather to the abstract entity of the nation (Forrest 2002: 8, 177–80). Should armies of the state be crushed, as was suffered by France in 1940, there is often very little in the way of resistance to the occupying power.

There is something in these arguments, but they apply much more strongly to wars fought outside the national soil. Political leaders in war almost invariably appeal to the idea of a threatened *home*land, and to the idea of the nation as a family, which implies the resonance of such collective sentiments (Stern 1995: 113–16). Such appeals are likely to be effective, as Marvin and Ingle argue, where the war is perceived to be defensive rather than one of aggression. Although loyalty to comrades in battle may be more 'real' than to an abstract nation, it is hard to see that this would be a sufficient motivating force over an entire war. What is striking is the endurance not only of soldiers but of peoples faced with starvation or bombing when the homeland is under threat. Collapse of the state generally brings war to an end, for only a heroic few will join underground movements if the occupying power is efficient and ruthless. But to be effective an occupation requires co-option of national elites such as in Second World War France where the Petain-led collaborative Vichy regime sapped the will to resist. All the same, this points to the fact that sacrifice is as much myth as reality.

COLLECTIVE REMEMBRANCE AND NATIONAL FORMATION

For Smith it is indeed the memory (equated in his framework with myth) rather than the experience of warfare that is important. Without memory, he writes, there is no identity, and warfare is significant as one of the major contributors to the stock of collective myths and memories. These recall not just recent and modern conflicts but also those associated with the foundation of the nation or with a national golden age (for example, England's defeat of the Spanish Armada in the age of Shakespeare). As John Armstrong (1982: ch. 3) might add, particularly formative are the identities created when populations such as the Poles, Serbs and Croats, Castilian-Spanish and Russians find themselves on the faultline between conflicting religions. Over centuries they come to regard themselves as border guards of their respective civilisation. Such identities have been carried into the modern period through religious institutions, aristocracies (linked to heritage of military service), popular poetry and legend, imparting at times a messianic character to their nationalism, and at times a concern with purification (of the alien 'other').

Smith combines this emphasis on the potency of the premodern in the present with an acknowledgement of the qualititative change introduced by the historicist revolution when, under the influence of secular neo-classicism and romanticism, history came to rival religion as the source of meaning. One manifestation was the novel ideology of nationalism with its rituals based on the idea of the fallen soldier.

Is there, however, not a tension here between Smith's emphasis on the weight of premodern ethnic memory on the nation and his acknowledgement of the relative novelty of public commemoration? (There were, of course, forms of public memorialisation, for example in the Greek city states, but in the modern period the cult of heroes is part of a self-conscious ideology.) For construction-ists, such as John Gillis (1994), the rise of ideologised 'sites of memory' represents the discontinuity between premodernity and modernity: they are a symptom of the death of the traditions as a living force in communities, uprooted by secu-larisation and industrialisation. Psychologists, moreover, inform us that memory is not an objective datum but a selective process, *remembrance*, which includes forgetting as well as recollection, and that each act of recalling is shaped by the context in which it occurs (Winter and Sivan 1999). John Gillis argues thus that commemoration has been a political process: what was memorialised reflected the interests of the official elites who made invisible the contributions of women, workers and ethnic minorities. Such national memories, to become hegemonic over locally based traditions, required a colonisation of subordinate groups, though as workers and other minorities became politicised they produced alter-native representations of the nation.

In this interpretation warfare may supply myths and images, but the question that needs to be asked is who controls what is recorded and celebrated in official ceremonies. The past has no intrinsic hold on populations, rather 'memory' is a plasticine to be moulded according to the changing needs of the present. A more radical criticism (of a postmodernist kind) is to question the notion of identity itself, which masks the plural and competing self-perceptions to be found both within individuals and populations. The very notion of group identity is a mysti-fication, for in reality all populations have multiple 'memories'.

This critique of collective memory is valuable, though both Smith and Mosse speak explicitly of the *myth* of the war experience. But an interpretation of national myths as means by which groups achieve political hegemony and social status fails to give sufficient recognition to the spontaneous character of myth-construction by participants in war and to account for the resonance of public commemoration. When examining the legends emerging out of the First World War, the myths of the war experience are often initially created by participants themselves as an attempt to overcome the horror of mass death by celebrating the ideas of comradeship and redeeming the war 'as the war to end all wars' (Mosse 1991: ch. 3). The postwar ceremonies that attempted to provide a permanent memorial to the dead achieved a resonance because the suffering was so extensive as to be perceived as collective. Participating in collective rituals recalled the dead to life, gave purpose to otherwise random deaths, and restored agency to those who otherwise felt as victims.

Official commemorations could backfire. Kaiser Wilhelm II's attempts to co-opt national sentiments to the service of an autocratic Prussian state resulted in communitarian nationalist movements such as the *Wandervogel* (Mosse 1981: ch. 9). The nature and political effects of war myths vary considerably according to whether the nation was a winner or loser. In the case of winning nations, one might expect more of a consonance between official and private memories. In modern Britain, the myths of the Second World War have provided a powerful repertoire to which different political projects have appealed. For Conservatives they evoke a sense of grandeur (of Great Britain), military heroism and the foresight of a great conservative prime minister, and for Labour the democratic spirit of the people, the collective values and institutions mobilised for victory that inspired the introduction of the Welfare State. Defeat, on the other hand, has tended to undermine the legitimacy of political leaders (and perhaps states) and encouraged a search for scapegoats. But what cannot be gainsaid is the very long life of traumatic collective memories, maintained by family stories, handed down from old to young (whose linkages have been extended by longer lifespans), by pilgrimages to battle and grave sites, museums – all manifested in the popularity of many contemporary works of literature based on the First World War (Winter and Sivan 1999).

Even so, constructivists might cite the revival of myths that bear little immediate relationship to the traumatic experiences of populations and whose selection might seem to be a product of political interests. One example is the rise in nineteenth-century France, as national symbol, of Jeanne d'Arc, heroine of the Hundred Years War against the English, but downgraded by the Monarchy and Church for her peasant background, assumption of unconventional gender roles and associations with heresy. In the 1830s she was revived as a symbol of the democratic nation, betrayed by Church and Monarchy, by republicans wishing to ground the Revolution in historic French values. In response, Catholics and monarchists, anxious to legitimise their cause in an increasingly democratic society, sought to appropriate her as the authentic spirit of French people devoted to Church and King. She was subsequently claimed in the twentieth century by almost every major political movement – Action Française, Communists, Vichy, fascists, Gaullists and Le Pen's Front National (Gildea 1994: 154–65).

This, however, is an illustration of the capacity of 'memory' once formed to take on a life of its own, and of the importance of France's medieval past (when it was a preeminent force in European culture and politics) as a reference point to French people. The fact that different factions struggled to 'own' Joan rather than construct rival figures and seek to make these hegemonic indicates the capacity of this fourteenth-century myth to provide for an embattled country multiple meanings in troubled times to broad sections of the French people. At times of overwhelming crisis as in the First World War, great ceremonies devoted to the national saint united the French in their struggle to rid their soil of German invaders.

What remains to be explored is how the different types of war memories suggested above, such as the 'traumatic' and the 'framing', interrelate. Even though the 'trauma' may be transmitted down the generations (as one sees in the grand-children of Holocaust survivors), it takes on multiple meanings over time and may soon itself become an organising myth for the nation. Yet, ancient 'framing' myths (for example, of the Crusades) can excite visceral reactions in the present. This, however, is too complex a topic to be addressed here.

WARFARE AND THE FUTURE OF NATIONS

Does this generally positive relationship between warfare and nation-formation still pertain? In practice, 'warfare' varies enormously over time and space – it can refer to conflicts involving such different actors as empires, tribal confederations, modern states, guerilla movements; to many different types of military technolo-gies, fighting units, civil–military relations, and economic and fiscal regimes. For many scholars the supportive relationship between warfare and nation-formation is limited to a specific period – to the popular mobilisation of the nineteenth century. Changes in military conflict during the twentieth and twenty-first centuries now represent a threat to the classical nation state. Nations must increas-ingly find other sources of cohesion.

In Mosse's analysis, the myth of the fallen soldier was a product of the revalu-ation of the status of soldier during the French revolutionary era when citizen volunteers, initially educated middle-class youth, replaced mercenaries or drafted peasants in national armies. Although armies soon engaged a broader social stratum, it was the educated middle classes, influenced by romanticism, who commemorated the war as an event of willed sacrifice in poetry and song, and who inspired the construction of mass ceremonies and monuments to perpetuate the myth. The nature of warfare changed in 1914 to a mass technological phenom-enon, dominated by artillery and machine guns, anonymous and alienating except for the camaraderie of the trenches, and it was one that produced death on an industrial scale. Although Paul Fussell (1975) suggests that this experience destroyed the cult of romantic heroism, on which nationalism was dependent, and intensified a modernist disillusion with bourgeois Christian civilisation, Mosse maintains, as we saw above, that mourning was accompanied by a more positive note. It was the Second World War that radically undermined the myth – this was truly a total war that blurred the vital distinction between fighters and civilians, and was characterised by the complete destruction of cities, the mass murder of peoples and the introduction of (nuclear) armaments that threatened the annihilation of nations (Mosse 1991: ch. 10).

For many Europeans after 1945 nationalism was the cause of the two world conflicts that had almost destroyed their civilisation, and warfare could no longer be seen as a regenerator of heroic values but as a threat to nations. In this light one can understand the rise of the European Union as a supranational project to transcend the nation-state and transform the continent into a zone of peace.

These arguments are overdrawn. Mosse's arguments are heavily focused on Germany where, like Japan, there has been a strong collective guilt about the war. In France to overcome the shame of occupation and collaboration, de Gaulle encouraged the myth of resistance and developed France as a nuclear power. It is arguable that the experiences of two world wars in Europe have undermined identification more with the nation-*state* (and the elites who failed the nation), rather than the nation. Even so in *victor* nations such as Britain, the USA and Russia the war has been remembered as demonstrating the heroism and endurance of the people.

Nonetheless, what of the argument that as armaments become ever more lethal through the proliferation of nuclear weaponry worldwide, so collective identification with the nation will decline in favour of regional (EU) and global organisations that alone can protect security? Warfare between the great powers now becomes unthinkable and the mass conscript army, one of the central institutions of the national state, is no longer necessary, since war can be carried out by experts and highly trained professionals. This is questionable. Although this might appear to have force in much of the demilitarising European subcontinent (although Britain's war with Argentina over the Falklands offers an exception), wars between Croatia and Serbia, Israel and Arab states, India and Pakistan, and Vietnam and China have generated national sentiments.

Meanwhile, intrastate wars proliferate. Although Smith focuses on interstate wars because of the capacity of the state to intensify and extend the effects of conflict, arguably it is guerilla wars that are more nationalising, since rebels are more dependent on the support of the community for their success. This embeds memories of resistance and heroism at the popular level and to a degree beyond the easy manipulation of political elites. In the postwar and contemporary period the legends of liberation wars in Africa and Asia (notably China and Vietnam) have provided the foundation myths of the new states and given political legitimacy to the leaders of these struggles. There is no end in sight to such wars, as we see in the long attritional struggles between Chechens and Russia and Tamils and Sinhalese. Indeed, globalisation has made possible the rise of new worldwide terror campaigns in pursuit of ethnoreligious objectives against the West, that are in turn creating a nationalist backlash against enemies within – Muslim immigrants who are viewed as a potential fifth column (Hutchinson 2005: ch. 5).

With globalisation, too, has come a spiralling of conflicts of many different kinds that have caused a renewal of nationalism in much of the world. One of the many sources of tension is the effects of climate change as tensions intensify between neighbouring states over water. Even if warfare were to fade (and unfortunately there is little sign of this), the 'memories' of warfare continue to be mined in the everyday culture of nations enjoying long periods of peace. Memories of the Second World War have become the staple of banal nationalism in victor states, as novels, television programmes and films recycle heroic incidents as entertainment to new generations. In other contexts such memories are far from 'banal', exciting a deep sense of resentment as we observe in recent demonstrations in China and Korea against Japanese 'war crimes'. Ironically, the significance of 'memory' for collective identity is demonstrated not just by such popular anger, but also by the unwillingness or inability of Japanese governing elites to acknowledge the sins of the past. The subject of suppressed martial pasts and their consequences is another worthy subject for an ethnosymbolic analysis.

REFERENCES

Anderson, B. (1991), *Imagined Communities*, London: Verso.
Armstrong, J. (1982), *Nations before Nationalism*, Chapel Hill: University of North Carolina Press.
Enloe, C. (1980), *Ethnic Soldiers*, Harmondsworth: Penguin.
Forrest, A. (2002), *Napoleon's Men: The Soldiers of the Revolution and Empire*, London: Hambledon Continuum.
Fussell, P. (1975), *The Great War and Modern Memory*, Oxford: Oxford University Press.
Gildea, R. (1994), *The Past in French History*, New Haven: Yale University Press.
Gillis, J. (ed.) (1994), *Commemorations*, Princeton: Princeton University Press.
Howard, M. (1991), *The Lessons of History*, Oxford: Oxford University Press.
Hutchinson, J. (2005), *Nations as Zones of Conflict*, London: Sage.
Mann, M. (1993), *The Sources of Social Power, Volume 2*, Cambridge: Cambridge University Press.
Marvin, C. and Ingle, D. (1999), *Blood Sacrifice and the Nation: Totem Rituals and the American Flag*, Cambridge: Cambridge University Press.
Mosse, G. (1975), *The Nationalisation of the Masses*, New York: New American Library.
Mosse, G. (1981), *The Crisis of German Ideology*, New York: Howard Fertig.
Mosse, G. (1991), *Fallen Soldiers*, Oxford: Oxford University Press.
Posen, B (1995), 'Nationalism, the mass army and military power', in J. Comaroff, J. and P. Stern (eds), *Perspectives on Nationalism and War*, Amsterdam: Gordon and Breach Publishers.
Smith, Anthony D. (1981a), 'War and ethnicity: the role of warfare in the formation, self-images, and cohesion of ethnic communities', *Ethnic and Racial Studies*, 4 (4), 375–97.
Smith, Anthony D. (1981b), *The Ethnic Revival*, Cambridge: Cambridge University Press.
Smith, Anthony D. (2003), *Chosen Peoples*, Oxford: Oxford University Press.
Stern, P. C. (1995), 'Why do people sacrifice for their nation?', in J. Comaroff, J. and P. Stern (eds), *Perspectives on Nationalism and War*, Amsterdam: Gordon and Breach Publishers.
Tilly, C. (1995), 'States and nationalism in Europe, 1492–1992', in J. Comaroff, J. and P. Stern, (eds), *Perspectives on Nationalism and War*, Amsterdam: Gordon and Breach Publishers.
Winter, J. M. and Sivan E. (1999), 'Setting the framework', in J. M. Winter and E. Sivan (eds), *War and Remembrance in the Twentieth Century*, Cambridge: Cambridge University Press.

Part II

MUSIC AND POETRY IN THE
ETHNOSYMBOLIC APPROACH

Chapter 4

MUSIC AND NATIONALISM: FIVE HISTORICAL MOMENTS

Jim Samson

CHOPIN AND THE *VOLKSGEIST*

In 1829, the poet and critic Kazimierz Brodziński published his short pamphlet *O tańcach* (*On Dances*) in Warsaw. Its implicit nationalist agenda caught the moment well, for there was an atmosphere of mounting political tension in Warsaw just on the eve of the December uprising of 1830. Brodziński was an influential figure in Warsaw's intellectual life, closely involved with the National Theatre, the Towarzystwo Przyjaciół Nauk (Society for the Friends of Learning), the Masonic lodge and the University, where he lectured on literature. Among his colleagues at the University was the composer Józef Elsner, known to us today as Chopin's teacher, but a key figure in the complex world of Warsaw's formal musical culture (Frączyk 1961). Indeed, Brodziński had earlier translated parts of Johann Nikolaus Forkel's well-known *Allgemeine Geschichte der Musik* of 1788–1801 specifically for use in Elsner's teaching, including those sections dealing with the rhythmic and melodic characteristics of so-called 'national' musics. This was the subject to which he returned in *O tańcach*. However, there was an ideological space between Forkel's treatment and Brodziński's. Forkel's account of increasing stylistic diversity within a single 'universal' history reflected well enough the creative praxes of late-eighteenth-century composers, for whom so-called 'national' styles were largely a matter of adding local colour to an established *lingua franca*. Brodziński took a rather different line, attributing a deeper meaning to national dances, assigning them a generative role in creativity, and following Herder in viewing them as somehow emblematic of the spirit of the nation.

Chopin had just completed his studies in Warsaw when *O tańcach* appeared, and he was certainly familiar with Brodziński's thought. For one thing, the Chopins were immediate neighbours of the poet in the Kazimierzowski Palace. Then Mikołaj Chopin, the composer's father, was a regular at the meetings of the Towarzystwo Przyjaciół Nauk. But most telling of all, Chopin himself commented, in a letter to his friend Jan Białobłocki, that he had attended

Brodziński's lectures at the University (Sydow 1955: 37). It seems possible, then, that Brodziński may have played some part in shaping Chopin's understanding of what he himself would later call 'our national music' (Sydow 1955: 210). There is plenty of evidence, including the evidence of the music itself, that in his final year in Warsaw Chopin's attitude to composing and performing changed subtly but irreversibly, and that these changes crystallised into something qualitative when he left Poland in November 1830. This was by no means only, or even primarily, about national dances. But it may well be that the combined effects of Brodziński's intellectual agenda (notably on the deeper significance of the dances), the political reality of the uprising (which broke out exactly a month after Chopin left Poland for good), and the effects of displacement (always a powerful catalyst to nationalist sentiments), worked to transform his approach to the polonaise and the mazurka during the Vienna and early Paris years.

The names of the dances tell us something already: 'polonaise', a high-status national dance of long standing (though with regional origins); 'mazurka', a popular regional dance. Now it is of the greatest significance that Chopin turned his back on the polonaise for several years following the suppression of the uprising, and that he released none of the solo polonaises from the Warsaw period for publication. It is as though he wanted to dissociate himself from an earlier understanding of national music, as something linked with the nation but available to all. Prior to 1835 the polonaise was, after all, favoured by W. F. Bach, Telemann, Beethoven, Hummel and Weber, and in their hands it had no more to do with Polish nationalism than had the écossaise with a struggle for Scottish independence. When Chopin returned to the polonaise in the mid 1830s – the Op. 26 pieces are the first he himself issued for publication – he redefined the genre totally. He made it anew, and he claimed it for Poland.

In contrast, the mazurka had only just made its way from region to nation when Chopin took it up. Although it appeared frequently in early lute and organ tablatures, it conspicuously lacked any significant history in art music, and for that very reason it was available for nationalist appropriation right from the start. With Opp. 6 and 7, the first mazurkas he composed after leaving Poland and the first he himself published, Chopin signalled a new-found ambition for the genre. By presenting these mazurkas in sets of four or five pieces, he consolidated the genre, and in a sense defined it for art music. He even spelt out that these pieces were 'not for dancing', which tells us something about how he viewed his earlier efforts (Sydow 1955: 161). From Op. 6 onwards, Chopin thought of the mazurka as a site for sophisticated dialogues between so-called 'folk music' and contemporary art music, and at the same time as a locus for both compositional innovation and subjective expression. Indeed it was precisely because Chopin's nationalism was harnessed to an Idealist aesthetic, investing in both subjectivity and organicism (the work was an expression of the self, but it was also a unified whole, and thus transcended the self), that it was capable of achieving canonic status.

A case can be made for regarding these mazurkas as the first canonic repertory of European nationalism, predating the relevant works of Glinka by several years, and inaugurating a century of romantic nationalism in art music. There was of course a prehistory to this, in Russian Poland, as in Russia itself. Traditional music had first to be married to the nation (the ethnologist Oskar Kolberg was instrumental in Poland, and Chopin was familiar with his early collections with piano accompaniment), then appropriated by art music, and only then absorbed by a European project of greatness. The publication of Opp. 6 and 7 constituted a significant historical moment, then. These mazurkas registered (in intention and reception) a principle of authenticity which ceded privileged understanding of the traditional repertory on the basis of nationality; hence the implicit competition that is a mark of ethnonationalism (Bohlman 2004: 119). At the same time, and this is the paradox underlying nationalist art music, they stake their claim on our attention today as a respected contribution to a generalised high-prestige bourgeois culture; for all their aspiration to speak for the nation, they remain in reality a variety, a species, of that wider culture.

INSTITUTING GERMANY

In 1842 the foundation stone for the extension (*de facto* completion) of Cologne Cathedral was laid. The entire project was powerfully symbolic of German national consciousness, expressing that 'spirit of German unity and strength' to which King Friedrich Wilhelm IV referred on the occasion. Indeed, had architect Sulphis Boisserée been given his head the walls of the aisles would have been filled with monuments, to serve as a kind of national Valhalla. As Anthony D. Smith has argued, monuments celebrate the *Volksgeist*; myths and symbols keep it alive (Smith 1999). Beyond its monumentalising role, the Cologne project registered the elevation of the Rhine as a potent symbol of nationhood, the more so in that it linked north and south: the Prussian Rhine Province and the Bavarian Rhine Palatinate. Rhenish romantic nationalism reached its apogee in the remarkable outpouring of Rhenieder in the 1840s, in the work of the Nazarene painters, in Schumann's 'Rhenish' symphony, and ultimately in Wagner's tetralogy *Der Ring des Nibelungen*, whose poem was begun later in the decade (Porter 1996). The folk ethos and nature worship so central to German nationalism was embodied in such Rhenish themes, and it found a wider context in the collections of 'Germanic' folklore and myth made by the Heidelberg *literati*. Music, then, played its part in creating those poeticised images of the forest, the hunt, the ubiquitous hero-wanderer, and the animised Rhine itself (the Lorelei and Nibelungen) that worked to generate an image of Germany.

In 1843, a year after that foundation stone was laid at Cologne, the Leipzig Conservatory was established. Mendelssohn was the first Director of what would soon become one of the great teaching institutions in the world, and one that would do a great deal to promote German symphonism as a kind of universal ideal. As conductor of that other great Leipzig institution, the Gewandhaus concerts, Mendelssohn had already played a key role in canon formation, conceiving his famous historical concerts 'according to the chronological order of the great masters from one hundred years ago to the present day'. And when he and Schumann established a syllabus for the teaching of music history at the conservatory, they effectively periodised this emergent German canon: Bach and Handel; Haydn, Mozart and Beethoven; Schubert; Mendelssohn and (note the significant exception) Chopin. Other taste-creating institutions fell into line. It was also in 1843 that the proselytising *Signale für die Musikalische Welt* was founded in the city. Then, as though to set the seal on Leipzig's reputation as a centre for German 'classical' music, the leading music publisher in the city, Breitkopf and Härtel, instigated a few years later what one commentator has called 'the first serious and systematic attempt to establish the works of musical authors in a canonic way' (Brett 1988: 86).

In 1844, a year after the Leipzig Conservatory opened its doors, Franz Liszt arrived in Weimar, following a succession of tours of the German cities. He too had done his bit for German nationalism. He had given fund-raising concerts for the Cologne project, and he had contributed to the monumentalising of an emergent Austro-German canon with donations to the Mozart Foundation and to the Beethoven monument about to be erected in Bonn. Yet if these latter gestures celebrated Viennese classicism, Liszt invoked a rather different classicism on arrival at Weimar, at the beginning of what would be a long connection with the Weimar court. He enjoyed Weimar's association with Bach, of course. But his major inspiration was the Weimar classicism of Goethe and Schiller, and his larger aim was to achieve a working relationship with the Grand Duke Carl Alexander that might prove as fruitful for the arts in general as that between Goethe and Carl August. In January 1844 he wrote to his mistress Marie d'Agoult: 'Weimar under the Grand Duke August was a new Athens. Let us now think of building the new Weimar. Let us openly and boldly renew the traditions of Carl August' (Williams 1998: 206). Through his association with Weimar, Liszt worked to fuse tradition and innovation, and he associated the latter as well as the former with the spirit of German nationalism.

In 1845, a year after Liszt's arrival at Weimar, Franz Brendel replaced Schumann as editor of *Neue Zeitschrift für Musik*. Brendel was a close associate of Liszt, and

NZfM was to become a major forum for Weimar cultural politics, effectively institutionalising the fusion of historicism and modernism peculiar to that politics. In contrast to the conservation fostered in Leizpig, the Weimar circle argued for a 'music of the future', but importantly they saw this as inseparably linked to a revisionist look at the classical heritage. 'To honour these patriarchs', Liszt argued, 'one must regard the forms they used as exhausted and look on imitations of them as mere copies of slight value' (Ramann 1882: 24–5). As a result, both sides of the emerging polemic between 'absolute' and 'poetic' music were equally committed to a classical past, and specifically to an Austro-German classical past. It was Brendel, after all, who would in due course coin the term 'Neue Deutsche Schule'. Liszt and Brendel took Hegel's historicist thesis and even some aspects of his classification of the arts as the starting-points for an aesthetic of music that foregrounded its links with the poetic, and they further validated their position through an understanding of Beethoven which stressed the poetic ideas (*Grundideen*) presumed to have motivated his music. For Liszt, this 'poetic solution' for instrumental music was an idea whose time had come. Essential to the character of his new genre, the symphonic poem, was a programme rooted in world literature and known legend, a familiar, high-status topic on which the music could discourse. Of course, one other composer stood alongside Liszt and his circle in their campaigns for the music of the future, and he too established a new genre that played its part in instituting German nationalism. He even gave it a new performance site, and one that would in due course stand as the supreme symbol of *Kunstreligion*. It was in Wagner's music drama, and in Bayreuth, that Liszt's epopoeia, fusing music and the poetic to achieve a higher art, came closest to successful realisation.

EAST-CENTRAL EUROPE: NATIONALISM OR MODERNISM?

In 1905, Bartók began collecting folksong in Hungary, marking the beginning of a distinguished career as an ethnologist, which he regarded as no less important than his career as a composer. For the rest of his life he engaged in detailed classifications of this music, as also the traditional music of North Africa, Turkey and Romania, paying particular attention to recording its many variants. We should note that by 'folksong' Bartók meant traditional rural music associated with the peasant class, very different from the semi-professional Rom (gypsy) music admired by Liszt. His attack on Rom music was in part a modernist attack on the conservative position on nationhood in Hungary, a position that basically excluded the peasants and their music, and in part a contribution to a much broader discourse of social Darwinism. For Bartók, Rom music was culturally degenerate, contaminated and inauthentic; it was a bad hybrid, unlike the good hybrid that might result from his own attempts to integrate peasant idioms within a contemporary art music (Brown 2000: 119–42). We need to be careful, though, when attributing motives to these attempts at folk–art fusions. From the start Bartók was by no means primarily interested in using peasant music simply to publicise Hungarian nationalism; significantly, his earlier expeditions and the arrangements that resulted from them promoted rather more the music of Slovakian and Romanian ethnic minorities within Greater Hungary. And that in turn speaks of a larger point about East-Central Europe.

Nationalism was undoubtedly the trigger for a musical awakening in this region in the late nineteenth century. We could rehearse for East-Central Europe the appropriation of folk music as a symbol of prospective nations, much as we did in relation to Chopin. Equally, we could track the institutionalisation of national music in formal culture, rather as we did for Germany (though in this region, even more than in Germany, the institutions also served to highlight exclusions and dispossessions). However, in the end the awakening in East-Central Europe was fully registered across the region only when nationalism was subsumed by the rather different and larger aesthetic projects of the modernist generation: the realism of Janáček, the conquest of the exotic in Szymanowski, the East–West synthesis of Enescu and of Bartók himself. It was, in short, not nationalism but the legacy of nationalism that gave to the music of this region its very particular character. And this is made clear above all in the changing approach to folk music by the modernist generation. Far from a symbolic adjunct of nationalism, it became an essential ingredient of modernism.

In particular there was an enhanced respect for peasant music. This was evidenced by a new realism in the interpretation and analysis of its traditions; compare the 'scientific' approach to collection adopted by Bartók and Kodály with the revisionist approach of nineteenth-century collectors. But it was no less apparent in the changing nature of folk appropriations by art music. Unlike the rationalised folk and popular music of romantic nationalism, these peasant traditions were valued precisely because they had fallen largely outside the dominant Western processes of rationalisation, and could therefore be used critically to radical, progressive ends. Something of the symbolic values associated with folk music remained, of course, in particular its identification with a collective 'natural' community. But it was no longer a national community which was evoked. And this is why Bartók's project is less a nationalist than an authentically modernist one: to span the gulf between an ahistorical epic 'natural community', where the individual might be thought to speak for the community as a whole, and the contemporary world of Western modernity, where the individual is deemed to be alienated, his/her sense of the social whole partial and fragmented.

In stylistic terms this amounted to an interpenetration of East-European peasant idioms and the handed-down genres, formal types and tonal schemata of a sophisticated Western art-music tradition. Folk music was not used here as an agent of romantic nostalgia, as in the early nineteenth century, nor of national heritage gathering, as in the later nineteenth century. Rather it was a means of confronting what Adorno once described as that 'rupture between the self and the forms' that characterises modernity. The folk material, and the 'natural community' it signifies, are brought into direct confrontation with the dead forms, so to speak, of an increasingly fragmented Western art-music tradition. To extend Adorno's argument, the resulting fusion does not conceal alienation under the mask of a false reconciliation of the epic and the modern. Rather, in using the folk material as a critique of the used-up forms of Western art music, alienation is thrown into relief. Thus, Bartók's attempted synthesis of these two very different musics may indeed forge a new and integrated musical language, but in doing so it does not hide the fractured character of the components of that language. In short, the modernist credentials of this music are never in doubt.

We might locate this species of modernism between two extreme positions, which is another way of saying that we might 'place' the modernism of Bartók somewhere between that of Schoenberg and that of Stravinsky. The most progressive Austro-German response to the rupture between the self and the forms was to compel the material to yield up its own solution, to deal with the problem from within, as it were. Paradoxically, the norms were too much a part of – too much owned by – the tradition to be easily modified: they could only be abandoned. The most progressive Russian response, on the other hand, was to deal with the problem from without, imposing outmoded forms upon the chaos and diversity of the material, as a kind of ironic game with masks. Here, again paradoxically, it was only because Russia had established and maintained some distance from the forms already in the nineteenth century that they became available to this kind of play. The significance of the modernists of East-Central Europe is that to some extent they mediated this opposition: not rejection, not ironic play, but creative critique.

NEO-NATIONALISM IN NORWAY

In 1924 the composer David Monrad Johansen gave a lecture on Norwegian national music to the Society of Music Teachers in Oslo. The lecture was later published in a series of articles in the national newspaper *Aftenposten* (Johansen 1924), and as music critic of that paper in the late 1920s and 1930s, Johansen repeatedly returned to the subject, creating a twentieth-century parallel to the extended article written in 1866 by the Norwegian composer Otto Winter-Hjelm (Winter-Hjelm 1866). It is reasonable to ask why there should have been this belated focus on the national dimension of Norwegian music between the wars, amounting to a prescriptive view of what constituted a 'correct' musical style (Vollsnes et al. 2000). It is not too much to claim that through Johansen and his circle 'the presence of something Norwegian' became the principal criterion of value in music criticism at this time. Partly the issue may have been a sense of inferiority and periphery, but perhaps even more crucial was the consciousness of a threat from outside, whether it was the fear of war or, more particularly, the fear of communism. Accordingly, the clarion call was for a return to the values associated with the Norwegian peasant and his culture, associated as they were with ideas of an 'old Norse' culture, since only those values were deemed capable of fending off the threat from without. As Johansen saw it, Norwegian music should ideally capture something of the toughness of the Vikings, or alternatively, the toughness of the Norwegian climate, both healthy antidotes to what he saw as the decadence of contemporary European culture and politics.

Johansen's manifesto for national renewal involved both the expulsion of existing cultural values (which he saw as part of the heritage brought to Norway by the Danes) and at the same time the recovery of something ancient. In this he was a true successor to Arne Garborg, whose formation of the dialect language (*Nynorsk*) in the late nineteenth century had famously articulated a collective national identity on Herderian lines. Ståle Kleiberg has argued that there is a close parallel between Garborg's project and Johansen's (Kleiberg 2001: 142–62). A Norwegian musical style would ideally be based on the particularities of the Norwegian language, landscape and topography if it were to stand muster as authentically national. More specifically, it would turn to Norwegian folk music, as varied as the many dialects that constituted *Nynorsk*, and create from this stylistic variety a kind of synthesis. Unlike the modernists of East-Central Europe, then, Norwegian composers approached folk music as though replaying the story of nineteenth-century romantic nationalism, and the result was a musical language of broadly conservative tenor. At the same time, and this was widely debated in the 1930s, they were aware of the need to create a national music which would be something more than an extension of Grieg. Hence the limited engagement with yesterday's 'modern' music, notably by way of French harmonic techniques, a kind of 'Norse impressionism'. Johansen in particular made a close study of Debussy (Kleiberg 2001: 142–62). His notebooks included detailed analytical observations on the *Préludes*, and some of the techniques used in works such as the Suite No. 1 for piano, *Nordlandsbilleder* (*Pictures from the Northland*), confirm that Debussy was indeed the channel through which he attempted to modernise a folk-based idiom.

Johansen's was not a lone voice in debates about Norwegian nationalism. Other composers, notably Geirr Tveitt, Eivind Groven, Bjarne Brustad and Harald

Sæverud, were united in their commitment to the idea of nationalism, though they differed widely in their musical styles and in their attitudes to modern tendencies from Europe, which by the interwar years meant not so much Debussy as a moderately toned neo-classicism. Thus Sæverud, probably the best-known and most popular composer from the interwar period, tried to bring together folk-inspired and neo-classical elements in works such as his Fourth Symphony (1938) and *Slåtter og stev fra Siljustøl* (*Slåtter and Stev from Siljustøl*) (1939). Geirr Tveitt, too, developed a musical language derived in part from folk music, but responsive at the same time to contemporary idioms, ranging from an early flirtation with Ravel (*Baldurs draumar* [*Baldur's Dreams*]) to an engagement with Bartók and Prokofiev. There were more sceptical voices too. In several articles dating from the 1930s, for example, the composer and critic Pauline Hall criticised what she regarded as an over-facile view of the relation between nationalism and folk music. In 'Norsk Musikklic I dag' ('Norwegian Musical Life Today'), published in *Nordmandsforbundet* in 1935, she argued that the modes through which Norwegian composers were accustomed to assert national values were 'as much French as Norwegian', calling into question the principle of authenticity that had proved so important to an aesthetic of romantic nationalism.

Committing to that aesthetic in the interwar period created various dilemmas around the issue of musical style for Norwegian composers. How were they to maintain a folkloristic basis for their music and at the same time aspire to contemporary relevance? Moreover, these aesthetic tensions extended into the political arena, culminating in major divisions during World War II. For a composer such as Sæverud, music was a medium through which to make a stand for Norwegian values at a time of German occupation (see in particular his *Kjempeviseslåtten* [*The Ballade of Revolt*] and his fifth, sixth and seventh symphonies). For Johansen and Tveitt, on the other hand, the assertion of national identity led to very different conclusions. As Daniel Grimley has remarked, 'metaphors of landscape, language and cultural purity inevitably assumed a far darker significance in the 1930s' than in the nineteenth century (Grimley 2006). The association of cultural nationalism and political fascism was not an unfamiliar one in the interwar period. During the war, Johansen supported the Quisling government during the German occupation, and Tveitt (whose *Baldurs draumar* was an explicitly political work) was for a short time leader of the Nazi-appointed Kulturting (Cultural Council), having been a member of the Wilhelm Hauer's 'Deutsche Glaubensbewegung' during his stay in Germany in the 1930s (Emberland 2003). Such political affiliations seem ultimately to have cost these composers less dearly than one might have expected, though for a brief period after the war Tveitt was expelled from the Norwegian Society of Composers, despite having distanced himself from the regime from 1941 onwards. Significantly, the postwar era in Norway wiped the board clean, silencing historical voices or deciding not to hear them. And where official cultural policy was concerned, the nationalist agenda was finally put to rest.

GLOBAL BALKANS

In June 1991 the wars of Yugoslav succession began. They were the culmination of a major resurgence of ethnonationalism in the Balkans generally, and they coincided almost to the day with the collapse of the last communist regime in the region, that of Albania. In a climate of war, the political appropriation of cultural forms is hardly to be wondered at. However, in the Balkans, with its mix of ethnicities and religions, indigenous cultural forms, where they can be identified at all, were nothing if not diverse. Historically, music had long been used to exhibit, and even to encode, membership of particular cultural communities, with the resulting musical identities subject either to constant transformation or defiant preservation as they came into mutual contact. We may add to that the more general diversity associated with the global culture of the late twentieth century, to which the Balkans was not immune. Many musics jostled for attention in the 1990s, crossing over in novel ways, and resisting easy affiliation to particular political and social units. In such a context collective cultural identities were hard to maintain, the more so because a global culture homogenises (music, of course, but some would say listeners too) even as it diversifies. All the same, ethnonationalist agendas did their work, resulting in the appropriation of some repertories, the revival of others and the transformation of yet others. In examining some of these processes our focus shifts from art music to oral traditions, including popular music.

The appropriation of folk music often amounted to a straightforward extension of the policies of Communist regimes following World War II. Consider the carving up of indigenous music such as the singing *na glas* characteristic of the entire range of the dinaric alps into separate national properties, or the embrace by 'Romanian folk music' of the unique singing 'à tue-tête' characteristic of the Pays de l'Oach (Bouët, Lortat-Jacob and Rădulescu 2002). But in some cases traditional genres were strategically revived in direct response to nationalist tensions, as in the renewed enthusiasm for Serbian folk epics accompanied by gusla during the 1990s, and even the composition of entirely new epics based on the 'heroic' events of the recent past. In other cases 'folk music' was radically transformed, shading into 'popular music', and again with a strong nationalist agenda. Thus the genre of *novocomponovana narodna muzika* (newly composed folk music), common to the whole region from the 1960s onwards, took a very specific direction in Belgrade in the 1990s through what has become known as 'turbo-folk'. This amounted to an odd fusion of 'orientalised' traditional folk melodies and techno-pop, a flashy, escapist alternative to Western pop and rock that came to stand for conservative, nationalist values, well attuned to, and promoted by, the Milošević regime (Djuric and Tarlac 2002; Gordy 1999). Turbo-folk conquered almost all in this context of mass propaganda and censorship, of upbeat television stations such as TV Pink and TV Palma. But the counter culture had its music too; witness the international rock 'n' roll idiom promoted against all the odds by the Belgrade radio station B92 (Collin 2001).

Even the music of the Orthodox Church became the focus for debates about the nation in the 1990s. In Bulgaria, despite a paucity of sources, there was a clear imperative to claim something distinctively national. In Serbia, some argued for a traditional (that is, harmonised) chant 'owned' by the nation, while others – the so-called 'newly baptised' or Neophytes – sought a return to earlier, supposedly pure Greek models. Such debates rehearsed again the sort of polemic found in Greece itself in the later nineteenth century, when there was a perceived need to preserve the chant from corruption from East as well as West. Protectionism of this kind recurred in other spheres of Greek music in the early twentieth century. There was the censorship of *rebetico* in the 1930s (as tainted with oriental values), and in art music the opposing claims to 'Greekness' of the Kalomiris circle and the Ionian school of composers. So it is telling that in the 1990s Greek musicians began to show renewed interest in their post-Byzantine Ottoman inheritance, not least through initiatives of the musicologist Christodoulos Halaris (Feldman 1996: 17). In this part of the Balkans at least, music built bridges during the 1990s, and in more than one direction, as studies of the music and dance on the Greek–Macedonian border suggest (Manos 2002).

The revival of interest in *rebetico* and *smyrneika* in Greece, and among Greek communities worldwide, found a parallel in the revival of *sevdalinka*, with its blend of Ottoman and Slavic elements, in Bosnia. Even in commercialised form (accordion rather than saz), an Ottoman trace was naturally more easily attuned to the political status quo in Bosnia than in Greece. An even more potent demonstration of this was the astonishing transformation of *Ilahje* in the aftermath of the war. In the 1990s, these simple, and essentially private, devotional songs belonging to Sufi traditions of Islam were transformed into public statements, in which the *Ilahje* repertory (much of it newly composed) would be accompanied by orchestra and associated with big, glitzy events in an obvious assertion of Bosnian national identity. This is perhaps the most radical of all examples of how an 'innocent' music might be pressed into national service. Yet throughout the 1990s the forces of globalisation, in Bosnia as elsewhere in the Balkans, worked constantly to counter such appropriations. Much of this was intransitive, a by-product of world music's 'interactive zone', to borrow a term from so-called World Historians (McNeill 1998: 21–40). But in some cases it was part of a creative intention. There is some evidence from ethnographical studies, notably Svanibor Pettan's film (Pettan 1999), that Kosovo Rom musicians in the 1990s deliberately adopted transnational idioms, including Western popular music, if not to promote a universalist ideology, then at least to maintain neutrality at a time of prevailing ethnic tension.

There are signs today that the culture of periphery traditionally associated with the Balkans may be giving way to a much more fluid circuitry, a network of interactive forms in which local and global elements are in constant flux. Faced with such diversity, the individual as well as the institution can appropriate cultural forms, establishing unusual alliances, breaking down old borders, and erecting new ones, building new bridges and destroying old ones. This weakens the grip of cultural nationalisms, and the collective identities they assert. Yet that grip remains hard to break; witness the Eurovision Song Contest. Even in the 'new Europe', this region still remains the most obvious casualty of a liberal view of history that gained momentum in the West in the nineteenth century, taking its stand on modernity and progress, on the quest for freedom, and on the idea of European exceptionalism. Progress, freedom, and exceptionalism: each of these produced its own dependent negative image, and it is for that cluster of negative images that the Balkans has come to serve as an all too convenient exemplar.

REFERENCES

Bohlman, Philip (2004), *The Music of European Nationalism: Cultural Identity and Modern History*, Santa Barbara, Denver and Oxford: ABC-CLIO.

Bouët, Jacques, Bernard Lortat-Jacob and Speranța Rădulescu (2002), *À tue-tête: Chant et violon au Pays de l'Oach, Roumanie*, Nanterre : Société d'ethnologie.

Brett, Philip (1988), 'Text, context, and the early music editor', in Nicholas Kenyon (ed.), *Authenticity and Early Music*, Oxford: Oxford University Press.

Brown, Julie (2000), 'Bartók, the gypsies, and hybridity in music', in Georgina Born and David Hesmondhalgh (eds), *Western Music and its Others: Difference, Representation, and Appropriation in Music*, Berkeley: University of California Press.

Collin, Matthew (2001), *This is Serbia Calling*, London: Serpent's Tail.

Djuric, Vladimir and Goran Tarlac (eds) (2002), *Pesme iz stomaka naroda: Antologija o turbo-folku* [*Songs from the Stomach of the People: A Turbo-folk Anthology*], Belgrade: Studentski kulturni centar.

Emberland, Terje (2003), *Religion og rase, nyhedenskap og rasisme i Norge 1933–1945*, Oslo: Humanist Forlag.

Feldman, Walter (1996), *Music of the Ottoman Court*, Berlin: Verlag für Wissenschaft und Bildung, 17.

Frączyk, Tadeusz (1961), *Warszawa młodości Chopina*, Warsaw: Polskie Wydawnictwo Muzyczne.

Gordy, Eric D. (1999), *The Culture of Power in Serbia*, Pennsylvania: Penn State Press.

Grimley, Daniel (2006), *Grieg: Music, Landscape and Norwegian Identity*, Woodbridge: Boydell and Brewer.

Johansen, David Monrad (1924), 'Nationale verdier I vor musik', *Aftenposten*, 5–9 July 1924.

Kleiberg, Ståle (2001), 'Following Grieg: David Monrad Johansen's musical style in the early Twenties, and his concept of a national music', in Harry White and Michael Murphy (eds), *Musical Constructions of Nationalism: Essays on the History and Ideology of European Musical Culture, 1800–1945*, Cork: University of Cork Press.

Manos, Ioannis (2002), *Visualising Culture – Demonstrating Identity: Dance performance and identity politics in a border region in northern Greece*, Diss. Hamburg: University of Hamburg.

McNeill, William (1998), 'The changing shape of world history', in Philip Pomper, Richard H. Elphick and Richard T. Vann (eds), *World History: Ideologies, Structures, and Identities*, Oxford and Malden: Blackwell.

Pettan, Svanibor (1999), *Kosovo through the Eyes of Local Rom (Gypsy) Musicians*, Krško (self-published video).

Porter, Cecelia Hopkins (1996), *The Rhine as Musical Metaphor: Cultural Identity in German Romantic Music*, Boston: Northeastern University Press.

Ramann, Lina (ed.) (1882), *Franz Liszt. Gesammelte Schriften*, Leipzig: Breitkopf and Härtel, 1881–99, vol. 4 (1882), 24–5.

Smith, Anthony D. (1999), *Myths and Memories of the Nation*, Oxford: Oxford University Press.

Sydow, B. E. (ed.) (1955), *Korespondencja Fryderyka Chopina*, Warsaw: Polskie Wydawnictwo Muzyczne, vol. 1.

Vollsnes, A. O., A. Holen and S. Kleiberg (eds.) (2000), *Norges Musikkhistorie*, 4 vols, Oslo: Aschehoug.

Williams, Adrian (ed.) (1998), *Franz Liszt: Selected Letters*, Oxford: Clarendon Press.

Winter-Hjelm, Otto (1866), 'Om norsk kunst og nogle Komposistioner af Edvard Grieg', *Morgenbladet*, 14 and 16 September 1866.

Chapter 5

THE SOUND OF ENGLAND
David Martin

———⊂⊃———

LOCATING THE NATIONAL INFLECTION

Nikolaus Pevsner, a refugee, had no difficulty in locating the Englishness of English architecture, or the Marxist Perry Anderson in locating an unfortunate ideological modesty in English letters and historiography (Pevsner 1956). Pevsner celebrated the horizontality of English Gothic and the domesticity of later English architecture while Anderson complained that the ideology-shaped gap in the English mind had been filled by the wrong kind of 'white' refugee (Anderson 1969; Martin 1970: 77–84). If such confident characterisations can be made, then perhaps other characterisations are possible about the Englishness of English music.

My focus is on the English musical renaissance beginning in 1880 as it recovers and transmutes earlier musical expressions of Englishness from 1350 to Purcell's death in 1695. In particular I look at how that Englishness was received by the generations located between 1920 and 1960. Probably most people accept the idea that with different inflections over time English or French music exhibits a particular ensemble comprising tone, colouring, phrase length and rhythm. French seventeenth- and eighteenth-century music, for example, is distinct in its rhythms and decoration, and its phrases are surprisingly short-breathed given the genius of the French language. So far as the music of the English renaissance goes there is a rhapsodic tendency admixed with modal elements such as you find in Vaughan Williams' *Fantasia on a Theme of Thomas Tallis* or *The Lark Ascending*, or folk song elements such as you find in his *Greensleeves* or *Five Variants on Dives and Lazarus*. The distinctive sound world thus created and then 'received' by transmission, in this case through the schools and the BBC in its Reithian period as a cultural guardian (also a time when it promoted modern music), is an example of the 'ethno-symbolism' richly conceptualised by Anthony Smith in such works as *National Identity* (1991) and *The Ethnic Origins of Nations* (1986).

That, however, is merely to convey the broadest notion of identifiable spatial and temporal location in music. The issue posed here is more restricted. English

music holds its own from 1350 to 1700, and from 1880 onwards there was a significant renaissance. But from 1700 or so, give or take composers like Arne, Croft and
Stanley, or in the early nineteenth century Samuel and Samuel Sebastian Wesley,
Sterndale Bennett and John Field, there was a gap in which England became a
musical colony of Central Europe. Handel was a special case as a cosmopolitan
composer permanently domiciled in London; and J. C. Bach lived in London
long enough to be called the 'London Bach', but these long-term migrants do
not alter the picture of a country prone to consume foreign music rather than
producing music on its own account.

The English renaissance from 1880 onwards occurred in a country briefly
at the heart of the largest empire the world has ever seen. England had also
produced the first industrial revolution and arguably the first example of popular
nationalism (initially English then British) to take place under single governance.
Yet music in this advanced, powerful and united nation succumbed to the music
of an advancing, potentially powerful but still disunited Germany. Probably most
English people would happily have gone on making music that simply offered
popular entertainment or piety, and was at a higher level written by foreigners,
but English musicians needed to find an independent voice, however much they
admired German music and were grateful to Germany for their training. For that
they had a model in a romantic tradition showing how national affirmation might
be achieved through music, for example in Dvorak and Smetana, or Moussorgsky.
However, unlike the Czechs, and certainly unlike other nations involved in the
Slavic renaissance, the English had no need of a recourse to a myth of the 'land',
with its invocation of people, language, epic and/or faith as in Janacek's *Glagolitic
Mass* (or in Sibelius's potent response to the *Kalevala*). Nevertheless, those who
initiated the English renaissance had precisely such recourse, leaping back over
capitalist achievement as well as ignoring a long period of military success under
Protestant aegis. Instead they invoked the period of defeat under the Catholic
Stuarts before 'Dutch William' and the founding of the Bank of England (with
the involvement of the Huguenots) in 1694. That leap back of two centuries (and
more, taking into account nostalgia for the Elizabethans) required a devaluation
of Handel as an icon of imperial confidence and Victorian piety. That was because
Handel represented a different myth of England, emerging post-1689 with the
'Glorious Revolution', one in which a philo-semitic New Israel appropriated the
Biblical narrative to itself. This clash of myths, one before and one after 1689, did
not afflict the nascent USA because 1776 firmly fixed the 'first new nation' in
the trajectory of progress, Protestantism, capitalism and its own version of the
New Israel. When Americans eventually declared their musical independence,
indigenous resources had to be located on the American continent (Appalachia
and New Orleans), not in a quasi-Catholic, Laudian or Elizabethan past. That is

why the USA is not distracted by a tussle over myths which in Britain still affects our relation to the European continent, especially everything implied by the Treaty of *Rome* in 1957.

THE COMPLEMENTARITY OF THE RADICAL AND NOSTALGIC

There is more than a hint of merrie Catholic England and mumming in all this, as well as the kind of ambivalence towards the Protestant version of progress and capitalism represented by R. H. Tawney's *Religion and the Rise of Capitalism* (1975 [1926]). Of course, the pre-industrial past was in reality a mixture of mud and banditry but it could still carry musicians' unease with contemporary materialism and utilitarianism and the philistine Evangelicalism attacked by Matthew Arnold in *Culture and Anarchy* (1869). Why was there no composer from the ranks of Evangelicalism and Nonconformity to complement all the politicians, reformers and makers of jam, flour, chocolate and mustard?

From the viewpoint of Marxist historiography such a retrospective vision of 'pastoral and idyllic relations' was another of those 'invented traditions' that could be manipulated to fool the people, at least part of the time (Hobsbawm and Ranger 1992). Yet this vision, insofar as it rejected the utilitarian ethos and sought a rounded humanity, was also one they sympathised with. Radical historians could quite happily celebrate the gamey, feisty England (and Wales) suppressed by Puritan seriousness and Methodist work-discipline (Thompson 1963). The tangled roots of this feeling lay not only in the socialist William Morris with his revival of arts and crafts to civilise an industrial age, but also in intensely religious figures like John Ruskin who adored the Gothic and sought an England where rewards and satisfactions should be '*Unto this Last* as to this first', as the Gospel puts it. In a similar way Pugin, as a Catholic architect, saw the classicism of the eighteenth century as cold, Protestant and inhuman. The pre-Raphaelites also looked back to earlier kinds of labour, to the medieval guilds as well as the Christian humanism and courtesy of the Renaissance. In short, the radical and the nostalgic were in some respects not far apart and their shared yearning generated a cultural rather than a chauvinistic nationalism, especially when a pacifist wave allied to socialist idealism swept much of Britain (especially Wales) between the two wars. Britten was a pacifist on the left, as witness *Owen Wingrave* (1971) and *The War Requiem* (1962) with its mixture of liturgy and Wifred Owen's poems on 'the pity of war'. So was Tippett, a gnostic mystic and eclectic whose idealistic protest comes out in his *A Child of Our Time* (1939–41), with negro spirituals replacing chorales. At the same time, though Britten and Tippett continued the 'sound of England', they were also, as children of the 'realist' thirties, iconoclastic towards it as the escapist fantasy of an older musical generation.

At any rate, England's declaration of musical independence against the 'Central Powers' of music drew on precisely the radical and/or retrospective nostalgia that informed romantic nationalism throughout Europe, and had a special intensity in the nations of eastern Europe, except that the eastern Europeans sought and achieved musical independence well before England, just as they achieved national independence much later. This was the kind of backward look, mingling faith and language that inspired Herder in Germany and a little later Wordsworth in England. However, in Germany the rural mythic and/or the retrospective look as realised in lieder, in Beethoven's sixth symphony and in Wagner's primeval myth-making or evocation of the German Middle Ages in *Lohengrin*, *Tannhauser* and *The Mastersingers*, looked *forward* musically. Earlier musical modalities were not revived as they were in England, except at the margin. From the time of Beethoven, a composer constructed as a revolutionary icon (up to Klimt, for example), there also emerged an 'absolute music' divorced from what had been a universal union of voice and verse. This union maintained itself in England, and was characteristic of the English renaissance. So much was England out of phase that the English romantic national renaissance almost coincided with the Second Viennese School.

We should notice the exceptions. Elgar was eclectically open to the continent even as he established an 'English music', and even Vaughan Williams went to Ravel for musical enlightenment. Britten, while a 'conservative' composer, evoked a darker and not very merry pre-industrial England, and was open to continental influences, for example the serialism at the heart of *The Turn of the Screw*. Tippett was eclectic, and, by the time of Maxwell Davies and Harrison Birtwhistle, there was no issue of independence because the Austro-German dominance ended with the Second Viennese School, to be followed by a pan-European pluralism. Alexander Goehr, for example, is strongly influenced by Messiaen.

For English music, place and (maybe) sacred site matter whether it is a sacred landscape from Dorset to Malvern and Shropshire along the marches of Saxon and Celt, or the darkened vision of East Anglia and its seascape found in Britten's *Peter Grimes*. John Casken has testified on Radio 3 (2 May 2005) to the power of the northern landscape of Yorkshire and the Pennines in his music (Casken 2005).[1] Gustav Holst's evocation of Hardy's Wessex in *Egdon Heath* and *Mai Dun* looks back to the surly, resistant, primeval and neolithic. The only important invocations of urban England are of London: Dyson's *London thou art the flower of cities all*; Elgar's *Falstaff*; Vaughan Williams' *London Symphony*; Walton's *A Song for the Lord Mayor's Table*; and Holst's *Hammersmith*. But even these exceptions mostly invoke a long-vanished London.

What now follows is a survey of some musical traditions in England roughly contemporary with or prior to the English renaissance with which the English renaissance might have had negative or ambivalent relations (Handel, Protestant choralism and Gilbert and Sullivan) or positive relations (the Anglican Church, especially Anglo-Catholicism, and the revived Catholic tradition).

Such a survey has to include the parallel renaissance of Celtic culture, which had musical as well as literary and painterly aspects. Indeed, at an earlier stage Celtic romanticism in the trail of 'Ossian' and Sir Walter Scott was leased out to European romantics: Beethoven, Schubert, Mendelssohn, Bruch, Brahms and even Wagner (*Tristan*) among the Germans, as well as the French, for example Chausson. After all, Celtic cultures had the appeal of proto-nations full of pre-capitalist vitality which meant they could provide an artistic alias for English artists and musicians repelled by Protestant utilitarianism. Arnold Bax spoke of his Irish persona in spite of having no Irish connections. Perhaps it is significant that the 'sacred landscapes' evoked by English nostalgia abutted the borders of the Celtic realm, for example the Severn Valley and Gloucester, birthplace of Herbert Howells, Vaughan Williams and Ivor Gurney. This pro-Celtic sentiment has persistently tried to elide the Anglo-Irish and Ulster Protestant cultures to which so many Irish writers in fact belonged. In a spring 2005 exhibition at the National Portrait Gallery in London on the theme of the Irish cultural conquest of England, the massive Anglo-Irish Protestant contribution was carefully not commented on.

In the final sections of this chapter on the English declaration of musical independence from colonisation by the Austro-German canon I suggest some cross-national comparisons, but it is worth noticing here what one might call French and Italian exceptionalism. France retained her musical independence throughout, though suborned more than once by Italian hegemony and by German hegemony in the late nineteenth century. Not even the most Wagnerian of French composers, for example Chausson, was other than 'essentially' French. Italy retained its independence by concentrating on a popular operatic tradition, with nationalistic resonances, from Rossini and Verdi to Puccini.

PARALLEL TRADITIONS: CONNECTED OR DISCONNECTED?

Some aspects of English music-making need to be canvassed which have contrasting relations to the English renaissance. These are the Savoy operas of Gilbert and Sullivan, the Community Singing Movement, the Church traditions as they relate to the English renaissance (and 'arts and crafts'), English 'art song', and the popular English (and Welsh) choral traditions, together with the complementary brass band movement.

The Savoy operas are very English in containing folkish elements like *The Yeomen of the Guard* or *Iolanthe* and a kind of robust political satire distinctly askew the *gemütlich* sentiment of continental, especially Austrian, operetta. James Day in his *Englishness in Music* devotes a chapter to Gilbert and Sullivan, but they were somehow not treated as part of the circumambient atmosphere of the English renaissance as promoted by the BBC or even (so far as my limited experience goes) the schools (Day 1999).

The Community Singing Movement was also set in a social niche at some distance from the art music likely to be received as part of the English renaissance, perhaps because it was popular in the wrong sense. Some of its events took place in the Albert Hall and were promoted by the *Daily Express*, a conservative newspaper with imperial leanings. *The Daily Express Community Song Book* was an eclectic production of hymns, national songs (Scots, English and Welsh), Victoriana and Edwardiana of the kind successfully revived by Robert Tear and Benjamin Luxon in the 1970s.

There is a repertory here which needs to be given an airing as part of Englishness even if not part of the English renaissance, beginning with choral songs like *Non Nobis, Domine, The Agincourt Song* and *The Ballad of London River* (at one time known to every schoolchild educated by the London County Council). This is where one might locate all the shanties and songs of the sea, many of them of the eighteenth century, that celebrated Britain's seafaring tradition, like *Hearts of Oak, The Bay of Biscay, Toll for the Brave* and (later) *Rocked in the Cradle of the Deep* and *Down among the Dead Men. Home Sweet Home* and *Tom Bowling* (the brave sailor) also belong here as intense expressions of sentiment about England, and both are included in the Last Night of the Proms.

By contrast with all the above, the Anglican Church, equally in the industrial north and the Arcadian haunts of the Welsh marches, East Anglia and Wessex, was very deeply implicated in the English renaissance. The Anglican tradition has been virtually continuous since the 1540s but was reinstated as part of the English renaissance with new hymnals, such as *The English Hymnal*, and the revival of folk song and of the traditional carol (as distinct from the Christmas hymn) as filtered through the imagination of the English renaissance by Vaughan Williams, Charles Wood, Martin Shaw, Geoffrey Shaw and David Willcocks. The sound of the traditional English carol (supplemented today by the music of John Rutter and sundry items of Americana) evokes England to an extraordinary degree, especially as broadcast from King's College, Cambridge, on Christmas Eve. There is also the ceremonial tradition (which overlaps Purcell and Handel as court composers), best known perhaps by Parry's anthem *I was Glad* sung at the beginning of the coronation ceremony. Behind this lies a more intimate world of masters of choristers and organists whose influence elicits complaints by the partisans of continental opera about the power of the organ loft in English music. Here one invokes the music of the Victorian organ, itself a very pragmatic and English composite of influences as characterised, for example, by Andrew McCrea (McCrea 1998).

The Anglican tradition has a plangent repertory contributed to by Britten, Walton, Herbert Howells, Vaughan Williams, Stanford and Parry, while Catholic church music was composed by Elgar, Rubbra, Lennox Berkeley, Anthony Milner and Malcolm Williamson. The resonance of boys' voices and counter-tenors finds its echo in the androgynous figures and sounds of Britten's operas. The Anglican sound is crystallised in the distinctive shapes and harmonies of Herbert Howells, a devout agnostic, like some of his peers, and like Vaughan Williams (and Gurney) from the 'western' county of Gloucestershire. Gloucester is one of those cathedral cities which host the Three Choirs Festival, and Howells (with Herbert Sumsion) can symbolise the spirit of that with his 'services' and anthems such as *Like as the Hart* or *Take Him, Earth, for Cherishing*. In the context of this genre in cathedrals and collegiate churches the notae of Englishness are very clear, since nothing like it exists anywhere else. Like the Anglican Church it is *sui generis*. By contrast, the Catholic liturgical and musical revival at Westminster Cathedral from R. R. Terry to George Malcolm cast its net much more widely, though the musical treasures of Catholics and Anglicans are now shared, with quite a pronounced contribution from French liturgical settings.

It is worth elaborating a little on a para-Church religious imagination and sensibility. The union of voice and verse (celebrated in Milton's *Blest Pair of Sirens*, *Voice and Verse* itself set by Parry) was mixed with a mystical strain sometimes picking up on seventeenth-century poetry, and especially the neo-Platonist side of English sensibility from Vaughan and Traherne to Wordsworth and Bridges. An example would be Finzi's setting of Traherne in *Dies Natalis*. The English Church provided commodious shelter for this vein of religious imagination for urban working-class people as well as the middle class, appealing to sensitive souls bruised by a fact-obsessed and macho world or fleeing from over-personal salvation thrust upon the young in some Protestant chapels. This imaginative version of pietas centres on location, sacred rite and sacred site rather in the manner of the Welsh poet and artist David Jones or the sculptor Eric Gill. The political radicalism embraced by Alan Bush or the hatred of Christianity professed by Frederick Delius, composer of a Nietzschean *Mass of Life*, is very rare.

I doubt if Alan Bush was 'received' at all. He broke with the tradition that united political and religious aspiration, all the way from Beethoven's Ninth Symphony to Mahler's Resurrection Symphony. In twentieth-century England that politico-religious unity was not strained as it was on the continent, and the English Church by maintaining 'porous' borders created a context where composers might explore 'alternative' religious traditions, for example the gnosticism of Holst's setting of apocryphal gospels in *The Hymn of Jesus*, Vaughan Williams' settings of both

Bunyan and pantheistic outpourings from Walt Whitman, and Tippett's *Vision of Saint Augustine*. The fact that the agnostic Vaughan Williams set so central a Protestant text as Bunyan's *Pilgrim's Progress* is interesting because in his hands it becomes an invocation of an English Eden in *The Shepherds of the Delectable Mountains* as contrasted with the amoral capitalist market of *Vanity Fair*. On the continent by contrast this open space for autonomous religious feeling was less available. One might be secular like Bartok or return explicitly to your national Church, as Poulenc and Stravinsky did.

Art song complemented the mystical element in the English renaissance, and like church music illustrates the relative concentration of English music on the vocal. Here I draw on Stephen Banfield's study, *Sensibility and English Song* (1985). Like music for the English Church, English art song doesn't travel all that well. Yet even in the doldrums of English music before 1880 when commercial balladry and conventional cosmopolitan styles of setting inferior poetry dominated, there were exceptions. In 1869 Sullivan produced his song cycle *The Window, or the Songs of the Wrens* anticipating the resuscitation of English song by Somervell, Parry and Stanford. Elgar produced one major contribution, *Sea Pictures* (1899) and Delius injected a fresh harmonic stimulus.

Stephen Banfield identifies a lyrical musical romanticism which in the early twentieth century provided an inflection of romantic themes embraced by music in early nineteenth-century Vienna, and by poetry in early nineteenth-century England. The Wanderer, the Wayfarer, the Vagabond and the Shropshire Lad embodied dreams of experiencing everything, in sorrow and in joy. Vaughan Williams represents this English musical voice looking back to the Tudors, to plainsong and a kind of meditative stasis, and to folksong, though he initially hesitated about folksong because England had no peasantry such as could provide a reference point in central and eastern Europe. The mood was expressed orchestrally in the *Norfolk Rhapsodies* and *In the Fen Country* (1904) before Vaughan Williams set Housman in the song cycle *On Wenlock Edge* (1909).

Housman and Hardy were both poets who attracted musical settings and expressed an ironic sense of fate in a local pastoral setting. Walter de la Mare also attracted musicians with his vein of childhood fantasy. Ireland, Warlock and Gurney were major exponents of English song, and the themes were the familiar ones of place, love, death, time, tradition, loss, destiny and spiritual ecstasy. One of the last exponents of this lyrical romanticism was Gerald Finzi in his settings of Thomas Hardy.

The lyricism associated in particular with the Georgian poets, and admixed with elements of Celtic Revival, survived 1914–18 and through the inter-war period until Benjamin Britten initiated its demise with *Our Hunting Fathers* in 1936. Britten also explicitly rejected the Germanic canon, in particular 'absolute music' from Beethoven to Brahms, though its dominance had in any case already fragmented in many directions. He reoriented the English sound with a sense of place which included the cruel sea and images of exclusion, violence and sacrificial victims. One masterpiece on the theme of innocence and sacrifice is his Second Canticle, *Abraham and Isaac* (1952) with its premonitions of the same theme in *The War Requiem*. His music had neo-Baroque elements, asperity, technical brilliance, variety, and included social commentary, for example in his settings of Auden in *On This Island* (1937). His choice of poets also reflected the long tradition, going back to Parry in his *Songs of Farewell*, drawing on the religious strain of feeling represented by English medieval lyrics, Donne, Smart, Blake and T. S. Eliot. After Britten, the musical language of song became noticeably 'difficult' appealing only to a small niche market, even in composers like Malcolm Williamson who adopted a relatively popular style and set a great deal of English poetry (such as *A Vision of Beasts and Gods* [1958] with words by George Barker) or Peter Maxwell Davies. Maybe Britten's summation had finally exhausted the English sound.

Handel, Mendelssohn and the great choral traditions of the industrial North and Wales, like G. and S., also belong in a provincial (and Nonconformist) niche, and one which was dismissed, with the Victorian cantata and oratorio market, as inimical to the English renaissance, and indeed to professionalism in music. Today, the northern choirs have been mostly superseded by metropolitan professional groups of an astonishingly high standard who have spearheaded the Baroque revival and revived a different Handel from the idolised 'Evangelical' figure of the past.

This choral tradition in the North existed alongside the brass bands ubiquitous throughout industrial and mining areas beginning with the Stalybridge Old Band founded in 1814 in Lancashire. Where the choral societies might be associated with churches and especially chapels (with their temperance halls) the brass bands might practise in a room above a public house. There was also a tradition of urban folk song revived in the second half of the twentieth century by an interested intelligentsia but not much associated with the English renaissance.

THE CELTIC AND OTHER 'SURROUNDS'

We now need to think about the English musical renaissance in relation to nationalist renaissances in the 'surrounds' of Anglo-Saxon England. The Celtic and English renaissances commingle and define themselves against each other, and the kind of evocation of Celtic Cornwall or Ireland by Arnold Bax (Master of the King's Music 1942–53) sits between the two. Here Stephen Banfield's argument in his chapter 'The Artist and Society' in Nicholas Temperley's edited volume *The Romantic Age, 1800–1914* is relevant (1981). Having earlier discussed the lacuna (Handel apart) between Purcell and Elgar, Banfield highlights an opportunity missed by the Celts as they take over the role of 'other' from the Jews. Matthew Arnold felt that the Celt was 'the perfect foil for the fact-obsessed Anglo-Saxon philistine' but whereas Celtic and Norse literature had helped spark off English literary romanticism in the early phase, so far as music went it was in the later phase pushed aside by the Wagnerian invasion (so loudly trumpeted by the Anglo-Irish Protestant, Bernard Shaw). Like Arnold, says Banfield, Parry was unable to relinquish his aristocratic classicism to pick up this theme and redress it in native clothes although Hamish MacCunn as Wagner's most noteworthy British follower tried to do so in his choral ballads and overtures on Scottish themes.

Moreover, 'Elgar began to explore fresh northern subjects in *King Olaf, The Black Knight, The Banner of St. George* and *Caractacus*; and *Gerontius* eventually appeared bearing a curious similarity to both Parsifal and Amfortas ...' (Banfield 1981: 26). That was a context in which the Celt stood for the imaginative life and provided an alias for the artist's alienation from English bourgeois society. Banfield goes on to mention the many Irish-, Scottish- and Cornish-inspired works of Bax, the Arthur Machen-inspired primaevalities of John Ireland, and Warlock's Yeats song cycle *The Curlew*. He also touches on the issue of class that affected men like Parry on one side of the divide and Elgar on the other and the sense that artists had of being *déclassé* as well as alien to the ethos of established English society. Successful English composers had mostly to rely on private incomes or, in the case of Walton and Bridges, on patrons.

The interesting point here is that whereas Handel rallied an anxious, burgeoning empire (Martin 2002), the composers of the English renaissance emerged at its apogee and with the First World War experienced major intimations of its collapse. Moreover, the profoundly religious themes that engaged the composers of the English renaissance came at a time just prior to a major secularisation in the thirties, later reinforced in the sixties. Elgar's most profound music included the Catholicism of *The Dream of Gerontius* and the recasting of its themes in terms of artistic isolation in his setting of Arthur O'Shaughnessy's ode *The Music Makers*.

A neglected theme so far has been the powerful influence of the folk-song revival as creating the ambience of Englishness particularly for the first half of the twentieth century. However, Englishness was also represented in a different class milieu by the 'folk-like intimacy' of the Victorian and Edwardian music hall. Richard Middleton in his discussion of 'Music of the Lower Classes' in Temperley's edited book comments that 'this role of the folk song [was later] taken over largely by Afro-American sources, which from ragtime onwards have dominated the significant development in Britain as elsewhere ... The century which started with the decline of rural folk song ended with the musical emergence of that twentieth-century folk hero, the Negro' (Middleton 1982: 91).

TWO TREATMENTS OF THE SOUND OF ENGLAND

Clearly Englishness in music is related to time, place and social milieu, whether we speak of *Sumer is I-cumen in*, Dunstable, Morley's *Triumphs of Orianna*, a song like *Linden Lea* or light music by Eric Coates and Percy Grainger. I begin with two treatments of this theme, my own in *Poetry Nation Review* (1978) and James Day's book *Englishness in Music* (1999). These treatments, Sullivan apart, have in common what their authors take to be the proper scope of their subject from Elizabethan times to Britten.

In the *Poetry Nation Review* article I identified a thematic index I could illustrate with a poetic evocation of topography and the biblical phraseology native to English musical sensibility (1978: 15). First of all there is music herself as St Cecilia as well as the 'quiring of young eyed cherubims' and the singing spheres. Then there is religion in Nonconformist hymn or Anglican verse anthem and psalm, or Catholic mass and motet from Byrd to its revival by Vaughan Williams and Britten. Next there is Nature, as a creation to be observed and admired, or adored in various versions combining neo-platonic mysticism and Romantic absorption with visions of English earth and a Virgilian piety of cultured field, tilled by a free people. Englishness is very closely bound up with a national theophany as 'the sounds of music creep in our ears', and nature, music and piety can all be fused together. This is the union of May and Magnificat celebrated by the Jesuit poet Gerard Manley Hopkins and central to an English and sometimes an Anglo-Welsh myth. I am aware, of course, that in summarising in this way I am also summoning up the 'myth-symbol complex' as received by me in particular and people of my generation, but that is precisely what I am trying to get at. It all has to do with 'This island now' and Albion, Arthur and Alfred, as well as the sea in Elgar's *Sea Pictures*, Vaughan Williams' *Sea Symphony*, Stanford's *Songs of the Sea* and the tragic seascapes of Britten's *Peter Grimes* and *Billy Budd,* both operas infiltrated by Christian images of the scapegoat. The English myth also includes the 'far flung battle line' of empire, London, 'the flower of cities all' and the threnodies brought about by the First World War, English equivalents of Shostakovich's searing accounts of the experience of Leningrad in the Leningrad Symphony. Peace is a major politico-religious theme not only in Britten and Tippett (*The Knot Garden*) but in Vaughan Williams' *Dona Nobis Pacem* (1936). These are visionary worlds very different from Handel's *O lovely peace with plenty crowned* or Purcell's *Fairest Isle all isles excelling* or the choral hymn based on Shakespeare's *This royal throne of Kings.* It is closer by far to the apprehension of death in Housman's *For I hear the steady drummer/Drumming like a noise in dreams* set by Butterworth, killed at the Somme in 1916.

The musical prayer for peace is part of a national liturgy and in a quasi-secular age unites Protestant seriousness with catholic ecstasy. The wider political background is (to exaggerate) no autocracy, no revolution, no courtly opera, no absolute music. There are symphonies by Elgar, Vaughan Williams, Walton and Havergal Brian, and (of a kind) Britten, but it is worth noting that Stanford, the Anglo-Irish Protestant agnostic, is not known for his Irish Symphony but for his songs, services and anthems.

James Day in his *Englishness in Music* opens up arguments about national character and stereotypes as they are built into what Anthony D. Smith calls 'the myth-symbol complex'. Myths and stereotypes are not only susceptible to manipulation, but also contain grains of truth (1999). Day begins with language, claiming that when it comes to music the language informs its inflections, rhythms and phrase lengths. So too do the rhythms of folk music along the lines exploited by Bartok. On the other hand what we suppose to be 'essentially national' is in practice easily susceptible to translation so that the British national anthem can be transmogrified in American or Swiss guise, while *The Stars and Stripes* began life as *Anacreon arise!* sung by a London glee club in the 1760s. Elizabethan music like Elizabethan poetry was influenced by the vogue for things Italian and Purcell was influenced by the court vogue for things French.

Day argues for the ethos of a people in terms of five headings: love, death, character, ceremony and God. And that is so, he says, in spite of changes in national character, in spite of characteristic contradictions and differences all the way between the medieval notion of the political nation of the nobility and 'the people' as understood in the twentieth century. That leads him to an inventory almost identical to what was covered in my own *Poetry Nation Review* article. His inventory is 'The Fair Orianna and the Golden Age', 'Henry Purcell: the Complete Restoration Man', 'An Honorary Englishman: Georg Friedrich Handel' followed by two chapters on the English paying for the music of other nations and the issue of sublimity or utility which dogged the age of Mendelssohn. The final chapters concern Edward Elgar 'Knight, Gentleman and Soldier', Vaughan Williams 'The Rebel Conformist' and Benjamin Britten, together with the turbulence imported into English and British music in the interwar period. Day might also, by way of elongating the Celtic theme, have focussed on James Macmillan as a Scottish Catholic (and left-wing) composer, or Peter Maxwell Davies, a northern Mancunian agnostic, who went much farther north to the Orkney Islands to write much music with a Catholic ambience, including a work on the medieval pacifist saint, *Saint Magnus* (paired with Bonhoeffer). Other illustrations of a broad religious trait are provided by Malcolm Williamson (Catholic convert and

Australian but Master of the Queen's Music from 1975 to his death in 2004), Jonathan Harvey, Jonathan Dove and John Taverner (who became an Orthodox with a strong retrospective vision). Taverner is often classified with the 'holy minimalists' like Arvo Part or John Adams who are among the few accessible voices of serious music, contemporary, but not in the 'avant-garde' sense 'modern'.

COMPARATIVE ELEMENTS EAST AND WEST

In his own contribution on 'Nations and Nationalism' to his edited volume *The Cambridge History of Nineteenth-Century Music* (2002) Jim Samson uses an analysis of Britain vis-à-vis Russia based on centre and periphery (or edge) of a kind that has also served to make sense of geo-political alignments where the outer ring faces off the inner ring of the Central Powers, with or without France. Russia was land-locked, backward, vast and continental, perpetually agonising over its relationship to the West; Britain was a small, imperial and industrially advanced island inclined to try European ideas for size and not agonising enough. For Samson, Britain reduced aesthetics to ethics and Russia vice versa whereas Germany (and France) kept them in creative tension. Nineteenth-century Britain devoted itself to the canonical and popular repertoire, and cultivated a market of listeners and performers at the expense of composition. As a result 'only through the idiomatic demands of word-setting was there any real resistance to continental styles'. Samson goes on, in terms highly relevant to this essay, 'The timely adoption of Elgar as a national figure, together with the creative reclamation by later composers of folksong and the Tudor-Elizabethan inheritance in a circular and self-referential quest for Englishness belongs essentially to twentieth-century history' (Samson 2002: 591–2). By contrast, Russia in the course of the nineteenth century engaged in a creative dialogue with Western Europe to bring about a distinctive music able to serve as a model to other nations concerned to challenge Austro-German hegemony, above all in the sphere of song, for instance Moussorgsky, Rachmaninoff and Tchaikovsky.

Where does that leave our 'quest for Englishness' in English music over the centuries? Leaving aside the question of Handel, it confirms the colonial status of Britain (England) vis-à-vis Europe, and above all Germany for two hundred years from 1695 to the late nineteenth century. That long gap apart, music on this island, though picking up various continental influences (indeed part of them prior to the Reformation when the low countries were its close cultural neighbours), generated some elusive insular character which others believed they could intuit. That character was carefully cultivated and reinstated by the composers of the English renaissance, above all with reference to Purcell and the Elizabethans. Maybe Spain most resembles England (or Britain) in being a world-empire with a world-literature, but musically confined to a Golden Age and a late nineteenth-century Spanish renaissance.

Englishness was very much retrospective in, for example Vaughan Williams' *Five Tudor Portraits* and *Mass in G Minor*. That apart, one is reduced to pointing to examples such as Gibbons's verse anthems, Dowland's melancholy muse, Purcell's *Harmonia Sacra,* a song like *Cherry Ripe* and Elgar's invocation of the Malvern Hills in his *Introduction and Allegro*. One intuits a strong relationship to the distinctiveness of the English Church and the English language, giving rise to a thematic index of faith, death, love (secular and sacred), childhood and spring. Britten in his intense response to spring and his relation to childhood was very much part of the English tradition.

I have been suggesting that maybe there is something a little strange about so retrospective a vision at the heart of the romantic versions of the English renaissance. I have also indicated that for the left this 'reinvented' tradition, like its ceremonial accompaniments in the reorganised Coronation ceremony, reflected the modes of manipulation and sponsorship deployed by a dominant culture. Yet, as suggested near the outset, the anti-capitalist, anti-Protestant and anti-utilitarian bent of the English renaissance was a nostalgia harboured and fostered by the left itself, especially in its soft versions. Furthermore, though the point cannot be expanded into a proper critique, it is equally strange that a myth attributed by the left to a specifically English brand of cultural sponsorship should be so widespread across a large range of cultures all over Europe.

CULTURAL CLOSURE AND CULTURAL INACCESSIBILITY

All this would be academic had the losses in education and in the media of the shift post-1960 not been so severe. Part of the cultural elite accepted the left-wing critique to the point where institutional protections gave way, above all in the Schools of Education, before the utilitarianism so detested by both radicals and cultural conservatives. The words 'authoritarian' and 'elitism' did servile duty here, because whereas the opening up of culture aided by new communications post-1920 sought to extend and thus nullify the differential access enjoyed by elites, its closure post-1960, also aided by new communications, depended on a rejection of the very idea of excellence because tainted by differential access. Even in English literature conceived as a focus of identity and culture by F. R. Leavis, there was a loss of confidence in its intrinsic value and capacity to civilise, while 'art music' was all but overwhelmed. The endless battering of the radicals served only to throw open the gate to the Benthamites and successors of Arnold's philistines, on whose criteria any analysis such as this should be statistical rather than aesthetic and the 'Liverpool sound' should define the 'English sound' post-1960 just as *Abide With Me, Let's All Go Down the Strand, Birdsong at Eventide* and ballads like *I Hear You Calling Me* should define it before 1920.

The stances taken up post-1960 were hostile to history, place, continuity, nation and religion as well as to objectivity, learning and educated judgement in music and the arts. The promise of cultural expansion, on the way to being made good post-1945, in particular through the schools and the BBC, was retracted on the ground that what counted as worthwhile was merely a matter of opinion. To quote Bentham, 'Pushpin is as good as poetry'.

However, the halting of the cultural escalator and cultural closure explains too much and too little. The demise of a sound of England with Britten is part of the broader problem of accessibility with regard to 'modern' music. The audience for such music in a world dominated by market forces is tiny, whereas that for the composers up to Britten was extensive. Nor has the 'modern' in the 'avant-garde' sense become more accessible with familiarity. As indicated earlier it is only the 'holy minimalists' who have broken through the impasse, and the religious aspect is in itself significant, but that has nothing to do with any identifiable sound of England.

NOTE

1 Casken commented: 'I've always lived in the north ... I look out on northern landscape and weather ... It's in my voice. It does somehow get into my music.' For an example from the south, see Halsread 2006.

REFERENCES

Anderson, Perry (1969), 'Components of the national culture', in Alexander Coburn and Robin Blackburn (eds), *Student Power*, Harmondsworth: Penguin.
Banfield, Stephen (1981), 'The artist and society', in Nicholas Temperley (ed.), *Music in Britain: The Romantic Age 1800–1914*, Oxford: Blackwell, pp. 11–28.
Banfield, Stephen (1985), *Sensibility and English Song*, Cambridge: Cambridge University Press.
Casken, John (2005), Interview on 'In Tune', BBC Radio 3, 2 May 2005.
Day, James (1999), *Englishness in Music*, London: Thames.
Halsread, Jill (2006), *Ruth Gipps: Anti-modernism, Nationalism and Difference in English Music*, Aldershot: Ashgate.
Hobsbawm, Eric and Terence Ranger (eds) (1992), *The Invention of Tradition*, Cambridge: Cambridge University Press.
Martin, David (1970), 'Black, red and white', *Encounter*, February 1970: 77–84.
Martin, David (1978), 'The sound of England', *Poetry Nation Review*, 8, vol. 5, no. 4: 7–10.
Martin, David (2002), 'Sacred and secular in Handel's reception', in David Martin, *Christian Language and Its Mutations*, Aldershot: Ashgate, 69–81.

McRea, Andrew (1998), 'British organ music after 1880', in Nicholas Thistlethwaite and Geoffrey Webber (eds), *The Cambridge Companion to the Organ*, Cambridge: Cambridge University Press, 79–98.

Middleton, Richard (1982), 'Popular music of the lower classes', in Nicholas Temperley (ed.), *Music in Britain: The Romantic Age 1880–1914*, Oxford: Blackwell.

Pevsner, Nikolaus (1956), *The Englishness of English Art* (Reith Lectures, BBC 1955) London: Peregrine Books.

Samson, Jim (2002), 'Nations and nationalism', in Jim Samson (ed.), *The Cambridge History of Nineteenth-Century Music*, Cambridge: Cambridge University Press.

Smith, Anthony D. (1986), *The Ethnic Origins of Nations*, Oxford: Blackwell.

Smith, Anthony D. (1991), *National Identity*, Harmondsworth: Penguin.

Tawney, Richard H. (1975 [1926]), *Religion and the Rise of Capitalism*, Harmondsworth: Penguin.

Thompson, Edward P. (1963), *The Making of the English Working Class*, London: Gollancz.

Chapter 6

MYTH, HISTORY AND NATIONALISM: POETRY OF THE BRITISH ISLES

David Aberbach

Just as poetic myth as part of nation-building has been neglected in studies of nationalism, so also nationalism has been ignored in studies of myth.[1] The work of Anthony D. Smith (for example, 1999; 2003) is notable, among many reasons, for helping create an intellectual framework bridging studies of poetry and myth in the arts with more traditional studies of nationalism in History and the Social Sciences. This chapter explores uses of myth and history in the poetry of the British isles, particularly works by Scott, Tennyson and Yeats.[2] In doing so, it illustrates the general significance to cultural nationalism of poetry – the royal road to a nation's identity.

English poetry, rooted in myth and history transformed to myth, largely defined the modern concept of national identity (Hastings 1997). Medieval England absorbed much foreign influence through invasion and conquest: by Germanic tribes (fifth century), the Danes (ninth century) and the Normans (1066). Its adoption of Christianity by the seventh century and the growth of Old English, which has the oldest Western European literature in the vernacular, ensured Britain's cultural distinctiveness.

The poetry of the British isles seems to reach artistic peaks in moments of heightened national self-awareness, when independence is threatened or lost, whether because of foreign invasion or internal wars or disasters. The battle of Maldon fought against the Viking invaders in 991 is commemorated in a magnificent Old English poetic fragment culminating in the death of the old warrior Byrhtwold. Raising shield and shaking spear, he emboldens his men with dying breath:[3]

> Strength fails, spirit must be firmer,
> heart bolder, courage greater.

Britain's greatest crisis after the Norman invasion, the Black Plague in the mid-fourteenth century, in which an estimated one-third of Europe's population died, was followed by literary flourishing, including works of Chaucer, Langland's

Piers Ploughman and *Sir Gawain and the Green Knight*. The Reformation and the conflict with Spain are the background to much Elizabethan poetry, notably Spenser and Shakespeare. The deposition and execution of Charles I and the Civil War in the 1640s, Cromwell's rule and the restoration of the monarchy in 1660, were crucial influences on Milton's poetry, above all *Paradise Lost*. The French Revolution and Napoleonic wars marked English poetry in the Romantic period as did the two world wars in the twentieth century.

These crises and others appear in the poetry of England, Ireland, Wales and Scotland both as separate and shared histories, each country distinct in time of conflict with one another but in peacetime united as parts of Great Britain. There is a significant literature in Welsh, Scottish Gaelic and Irish Gaelic, in which relations with England are a common thread. In 'The True-Born Englishman' (1701), Defoe savagely mocks what he sees as the violent indecent yokings-together that created 'the mongrel half-bred race' of English identity:

> In eager rapes, and furious lust begot,
> Betwixt a painted *Briton* and a *Scot*:
> Whose gend'ring offspring quickly learnt to bow,
> And yoke their heifers to the *Roman* plough:
> From whence a mongrel half-bred race there came,
> With neither name nor nation, speech or fame
> In whose hot veins new mixtures quickly ran,
> Infus'd betwixt a *Saxon* and a *Dane*.
> While their rank daughters, to their parents just,
> Receiv'd all nations with promiscuous lust.
> This nauseous brood directly did contain
> The well-extracted blood of Englishmen ... (336–47)

This jaundiced swipe at English national identity, which recalls the prophetic denunciations of Israel as harlot (for example, Hosea 1–2, Ezekiel 23), can paradoxically signify the nation's strength: Colley describes these lines as a 'powerful demonstration of English confidence. Far more than the Welsh and Scots felt able to do, the English could – occasionally – ridicule themselves because they had a strong sense of who they were and of their own importance' (1992: 15–16).

The British isles might have lain down a slut, as Defoe suggests, but rose a woman of valour. After centuries of turmoil and mixing, some of the greatest poets writing in English were Scottish (Byron), Irish (Yeats), and Welsh (Dylan Thomas). Monogamous nationalism exacted a price, though. By the nineteenth century, poetry in Welsh and Gaelic was greatly diminished by English intrusion and emigration. Nevertheless this poetry retains its power to inspire a strong, even militant national identity.

MEDIEVAL WALES AND SCOTLAND

Memories of Welsh and Scottish independence survive in medieval poetry. Scottish poems, such as John Barbour's *The Bruce* (c. 1370) and Blind Harry's epic *Wallace* (c. 1460), record Scottish courage and defiance. Though Scotland and England have shared a monarch since 1603 and a Parliament (1707–1999), Scotland preserves in poetry the memory of its revolt against England under Robert the Bruce and its triumph over England in 1314 in the battle of Bannockburn, after which (in 1328) England recognised Scottish independence.

Long before the loss of Welsh independence in 1282, there was a remarkable tradition of Welsh poetry, notably the *Hengerdd* (old song). Welsh history, particularly the medieval struggle against the Normans, stimulated some of its greatest poetry, affirming Welsh national identity in Welsh, such as Cynddelw Brydydd Mawr's elegy for Madog ap Maredudd, prince of Powys, who died in 1160:

> Door of a fort he was, companion shield,
> Buckler on battlefield, and in brave deeds:
> A tumult like flame blazing through heather,
> Router of enemies, his shield stopped their way;
> Lord sung by a myriad, hope of minstrels,
> Crimson, irresistible, unswerving companion. (Conran 1967: 118)

In the twelfth and thirteenth centuries, Wales was transformed from an autonomous state under Welsh rule into a feudal vassal of England. Gruffudd ab yr Ynad Coch wrote a haunting lament for Llywelyn ap Gruffudd, the last prince of independent Wales, killed by the English in 1282:

> Mine now to rage against Saxons who've wronged me,
> Mine for this death bitterly to mourn.
> Mine, with good cause, to cry protest to God
> Who has left me without him. (Ibid. 128)

In Wales, the annual Eisteddfod (bardic festival), which dates from 1176, when Wales was still independent, has a strong nationalist character. It preserves memory of past, and hope of future, Welsh independence.

ENGLISH MYTH: FROM SHAKESPEARE TO TENNYSON

Myth and mythical history dominate much English poetry. English nationalism commonly flares up in crisis. Poetry often results. Shakespeare's histories, for example, date mostly from the 1590s, after the defeat of the Spanish Armada in 1588, 'the years of the Spanish war at its fiercest' (Hastings 1997: 207). Henry V's speech at the battle of Harfleur is a classic of nationalist propaganda:

> And you, good yeomen,
> Whose limbs were made in England, show us here
> The mettle of your pasture; let us swear
> That you are worth your breeding; which I doubt not;
> For there is none of you so mean and base
> That hath not noble lustre in your eyes.
> I see you stand like greyhounds in the slips,
> Straining upon the start. The game's afoot:
> Follow your spirit; and, upon this charge
> Cry 'God for Harry! England and Saint George!' (III, i, 25–34)

Again, on the night before the battle of Agincourt (1415) Henry V inspires his men with a fighting national spirit:

> We few, we happy few, we band of brothers;
> For he to-day that sheds his blood with me
> Shall be my brother; be he ne'er so vile
> This day shall gentle his condition:
> And gentlemen in England, now a-bed
> Shall think themselves accurs'd they were not here,
> And hold their manhoods cheap whiles any speaks
> That fought with us upon Saint Crispin's day. (IV, iii, 60–7)

There is little proof that Henry V actually said anything like this, but this is what he *should* have said.

In a later age of crisis, when France threatened to invade, Coleridge in 'Fears in Solitude' (1798) declared love for Britain almost as a divine being. The madonna-like national image in this poem is as far removed from reality as Defoe's slut, yet such national feelings in crisis are common. In quieter, more stable periods, English poets often seem more vulnerable to doubts. As the British empire reached the height of its power in the nineteenth century, some English poets, such as Tennyson and Kipling, became uneasy. They feared the corruption of power and imperial decline. In some cases, their poetry was a form of spiritual revitalisation, providing moral guidance through British historical figures and events. Tennyson, Poet Laureate from 1850 to 1892, wrote a series of historical dramas, *Queen Mary* (1875), *Harold* (1876) and *Becket* (1884), each illustrating the strengthening effect of crisis. In poems such as 'Puck's Song' (1906), Kipling called up defining historic moments associated with spots in the English landscape:

> See you our stilly woods of oak,
> And the dread ditch beside?
> O that was where the Saxons broke
> On the day that Harold died.

> See you the windy levels spread
> About the gates of Rye?
> O that was where the Northmen fled,
> When Alfred's ships came by.

POETRY AND MYTH IN SCOTTISH NATIONALISM

The Scottish poets Macpherson, Burns and Scott have had especially strong influence on Scottish nationalism, drawing on Scotland's rich store of history and myth either to support independence from or union with England. Burns' use of myth is less apparent than that of Macpherson and Scott. The poetic fragments of the legendary third century CE bard, Ossian, however fraudulently presented by Macpherson in the late eighteenth century (Samuel Johnson derided them as 'impudent forgeries'), roused Scottish nationalism.[4] Macpherson's poetry, like that of Burns, is poetry of Scottish defiance after its defeat by England at Culloden in 1746. The controversy over Ossian was not just over scholarly authenticity, but also over national authenticity: did Scotland have a national identity distinct from that of England? The fame of Ossian, amounting to a craze, in eighteenth- and nineteenth-century continental Europe, brought the past alive in the nation's hopes.

Scott is unusual as at different times he hoped for Scottish independence from England and supported union with England. His deep-bred Scottish nationalism was at times neutered by his commitment to Britain and Tory politics. Scott was raised in late eighteenth-century Edinburgh in an atmosphere of resentment at the Treaty of Union of 1707 and the Scottish defeat and humiliation in the uprising of 1745–6, the atrocities of the English army, the consequent English military presence, the proscription of Highland customs and the Highland clearances. As a child, Scott absorbed Scottish culture – the language, stories, songs, the great medieval poems and ballads, and folk culture – from people who, in some cases, had seen or taken part in the Scottish revolt. In the introduction to Canto III of *Marmion* (1808), Scott called up childhood memories of Scottish lore and heroism:

... ever, by the winter hearth,
Old tales I heard of woe or mirth,
Of lovers' slights, of ladies' charms,
Of witches' spells, of warriors' arms;
Of patriot battles, won of old
By Wallace wight and Bruce the bold;
Of later fields of feud and fight,
When, pouring from their Highland height,
The Scottish clans, in headlong sway,
Had swept the scarlet ranks away.

Scott could easily have become a revolutionary but was born too late. In 1813, after he stopped writing poetry, he confessed:

> I am very glad I did not live in 1745 for though as a lawyer I could not have pleaded Charles's right and as a clergyman I could not have prayed for him yet as a soldier I would I am sure against the convictions of my better reason have fought for him even to the bottom of the gallows. (Scott 1932, III: 302)

In time, the bitterness of the Scottish defeat shrank. Scotland kept its own Church and legal system, which came to symbolise Scottish independence. Scott trained in law, as did many Scottish historians, philosophers, literary artists and essayists. The Scottish Enlightenment was an outburst of new-found confidence of a rational, modern people. Crucial in Scotland's psychological transformation was that for an entire generation in the Napoleonic wars the English and the Scots had a common enemy – the French – and fought bravely and successfully side by side. The Union on paper was sealed in blood. Scott's career as a poet was almost entirely confined to the Napoleonic period, when French invasion of Britain was a constant threat. According to Sutherland, Scott's choice in *Marmion* of the Scottish defeat by England at Flodden in 1513 – 'the greatest catastrophe in Scottish history' – 'seems to have been in the service of a higher patriotism towards Britain' (1995: 125). There is an 'extinction of Scotland' in *Marmion*. In the first Epistle, for example, instead of 'Scotland' and 'Scottish', 'Britain' and 'British' appear twelve times (and 'English' once), and the poem is pure English, with no trace of Scottish dialect (Sutherland 1995: 126). Had *Marmion* been published in 1758 rather than 1808, the stress would probably have been on Scottish nationalism and English villainy.

The omission of Scotland seems to reflect the unification of the British isles by war with France. Yet, Scott regretted Scotland's loss of independence. His wavering to and from Scottish nationalism continued after he turned from poetry, poleaxed by Byron's success in *Childe Harold* (1812), to the novel: the hero of *Waverley* (1814) is both Jacobite and Hanoverian and fights on both sides.

Scott's Romantic Scots nationalism was watered down both by Enlightenment internationalism and by self-interested (but not bogus) loyalty to Great Britain. The strands of Scottish nationalism and commitment to Great Britain are intertwined in Scott's life and works, which themselves became an act of union. From childhood, Scott was drawn more to coarse and primitive but alive Scottish language than to the genteel, elegant English of the Enlightenment. He admired the work of Fergusson and Burns to revive Scottish poetic language. One of Scott's earliest publications, before he became a poet and novelist, was his collection of Scottish ballads, *The Minstrelsy of the Scottish Border* (1802), influenced by Bishop Percy's ballad collection, *Reliques of Ancient English Poetry* (1765) and by the German Romantics, by Herder and Goethe. Poetry as a tool of national survival and regeneration is implicit in Scott's *The Lay of the Last Minstrel* (1805). The evil dwarf magician is driven away when the minstrels join together to sing songs of the past. Though the poem is set in sixteenth-century Scotland, it reflects Scottish national feeling of the late eighteenth and early nineteenth centuries, when the minstrel was needed as 'an apostolic link with that period [the sixteenth century]' when, as Scott (anticipating Heine) put it in his 1824 essay on 'Romance', 'poets were the historians and often the priests of their society' (Sutherland 1995: 100).

Scott's narrative poems helped to define Scottish national identity within Great Britain. Scottish customs, speech, dress and landscape first became widely known through Scott's narrative poems. *The Lady of the Lake* (1810) set off a wave of Scottish tourism at a time when the Grand Tour of continental Europe was impossible because of the Napoleonic wars. At the same time, as a successful writer, Scott became a leader of the British Establishment. His politics were High Tory and he eventually became a baronet and – his financial coffin – laird of Abbotsford. During the war with France, he joined the Edinburgh Volunteers Light Dragoons (Burns, similarly, after early sympathy with the French Revolution, joined the Dumfries Volunteers), his military zeal at odds with his writings, in which war is cruel and senseless. He supported Henry Dundas, Scotland's virtual ruler, despised by Scottish nationalists as a traitor. His conservatism was such that, panicked at the thought of popular revolt, he defended the Peterloo massacre in 1819. When George IV visited Scotland in 1822, Scott escorted and introduced him as the monarch of the Highland clansmen. Scott's complex form of nationalism was not unlike that of the exiled Jews after the loss of territorial sovereignty who, while remaining scrupulously loyal to the countries where they lived, preserved a healing memory of past glory, of noble battles and great men and women – but in culture, not aimed at political action. Daiches sums up the therapeutic ambivalence to Scottish nationalism in Scott's writings:

Scott's aim in much of his writing was a healing one: to present the glamour of Scottish history and landscape, with the heroic violence that made part of the glamour modulated quietly into the past tense so that Scotland could be seen now as part of a peaceful and enlightened Britain. (1971: 83)

THE BRITISH EMPIRE AND TENNYSON'S REVIVAL OF ARTHURIAN LEGEND

Tennyson's revival of the legends of the fifth-century King Arthur coincided with the emergence of Britain as the most powerful empire in history. These legends are taken for granted as part of 'British national consciousness'. Yet, as in the case of many other mythologies, such as the *Kalevala*, this literature, much of which derived from oral tradition, was largely forgotten until the Victorian age. The rediscovery of Arthur and the Round Table was mainly the work of Tennyson, in his epic poem and life work, *Idylls of the King*. The poem was begun in the 1830s and not published in its complete twelve-part form until 1885. Prior to the imperial age, Milton and Wordsworth had rejected Arthur as an inappropriate subject for an English national epic. Sir Thomas Malory's fifteenth-century epic, *Morte d'Arthur*, Tennyson's chief source, was never widely popular. Consequently, the stories were unknown to the English-reading public. On publication of the first edition of Tennyson's *Idylls*, in 1859 (comprising 'Enid', 'Vivien', 'Elaine' and 'Guinevere'), the *Saturday Review* described the material as 'a forgotten cycle of fables which never attained the dignity or substance of a popular mythology' (Shaw 1973: 83). The stories of Arthur did not stay forgotten for long: the *Idylls* sold 10,000 copies in the first week (Shaw 1973: 82).

Tennyson was influenced by nineteenth-century research into ancient texts as part of the recovery and invention of tradition and by the suggestion of Albert, the Prince Consort (himself a German prince), that 'the Arthurian cycle was the equivalent of Germany's national epic, the *Niebelungenlied*' (Jordan 1988: 157). Occasionally, Tennyson could strike a militant, even chauvinist note, for example in the poems he wrote after the French *coup d'état* of 1851 ('RISE, Britons, rise, if manhood be not dead'). Yet, he was chiefly an introspective, spiritual poet ('the saddest of poets', as T. S. Eliot described him). Tennyson used the stories of Arthur, Queen Guinevere, Arthur's sword Excalibur, the Knights of the Round Table, Merlin the magician, and the Holy Grail not to justify imperial conquest but, as in the poetry of the biblical prophets, to highlight spiritual ideals. There are unforgettable mythic images, such as Sir Bedivere's return of Excalibur to the Lady of the Lake as Arthur lies dying:

Then quickly rose Sir Bedivere and ran,
And, leaping down the ridges lightly, plunged
Among the bulrush-beds, and clutch'd the sword,
And strongly wheel'd and threw it. The great brand
Made lightnings in the splendour of the moon,
And flashing round and round, and whirl'd in an arch,
Shot like a streamer of the northern morn,
Seen where the moving isles of winter shock
By night, with noises of the Northern Sea.
So flash'd and fell the brand Excalibur:
But ere he dipt the surface, rose an arm
Clothed in white samite, mystic, wonderful,
And caught him by the hilt, and brandish'd him
Three times, and drew him under in the mere.
                                   ('The Passing of Arthur', 301–14)

Tennyson defines heroism in biblical, not pagan, terms. Arthur's wise mentor, Merlin, is a prophet-like bard. Conquest of enemies counts for less than conquest of the self, of the inner defiling monster of ethical frailty (particularly Guinevere's sexual betrayal of Arthur) which ruins the social order. As in his best-known long poem, *In Memoriam*, loss and the prospect of loss fill his national epic and call into question Victorian power and confidence. The *Idylls*, like the *Nibelungenlied*, is concerned less with the pride and confidence of a new power than with the dark-edged dignity of an order in decline. As national poems, both foreshadow the weakening of the monarchy and in the case of Germany, its fall.

YEATS AND IRISH LEGEND

Part of the attraction of Irish legend to those who wanted independence from England was that it preceded the English conquest. England had controlled parts of Ireland for centuries but gained absolute rule only in the seventeenth century. In the Act of Union of 1801, England and Ireland became the 'United Kingdom of Great Britain and Ireland'. The consequent decline of Ireland led to the rise of Irish nationalism, the revival of Irish language and an outstanding literature, dominated in poetry by Yeats. Influenced by Irish cultural nationalists such as Standish O'Grady, John O'Leary and Douglas Hyde, Yeats became a connoisseur of Irish legend. He edited several volumes, including *Fairy and Folk Tales of the Irish Peasantry* (1888), *Stories from Carelton* (1889) and *Representative Irish Tales* (1890), and used this material in his own poetry. Yeats discovered in this ancient literature, much of which came from oral Gaelic traditions among the western

Irish peasantry, a pristine national spirit more powerful than British culture, which could be seen as corrupted by the power of the empire. Yeats wrote of the Irish legends he edited:

> All that is greatest in our literature is based upon legend – upon those tales which are made by no one man, but by the nation itself through a slow process of modification and adaptation, to express its loves and its hates, its likes and its dislikes. (Pritchard 1972: 36)

Yeats saw himself not just as a teller of legends but as a legendary figure himself. According to Ellmann, Yeats believed that '... the artist was to conceive of himself as a representative figure, to identify himself with all men, or with Ireland, or with some traditional personage. In this way the correspondences of old legends with modern life could be established, and so, as Yeats proposed, a dead mythology might be changed to a living one' (Ellmann 1968: 18).

In an early poem, *To Ireland in the Coming Times* (1892), Yeats declares his kinship with Irish national poets of the past. He uses Irish myth to unlock the national unconscious:[5]

> Nor may I less be counted one
> With Davis, Mangan, Ferguson,
> Because, to him who ponders well,
> My rhymes more than their rhyming tell
> Of things discovered in the deep,
> Where only body's laid asleep.

To Yeats, as to Shelley, poetry is meant to educate, to remind its listeners of their heroic past and unite them in hope. Heroes such as Oisin and Cuchulain are archetypes of heroic resistance. In Yeats' 'The Wanderings of Oisin' (1888), the chained woman whom Oisin liberates resembles Ireland in English chains, and Oisin's 'battles never done' recall the never-ending Irish struggle for independence (Ellmann 1968: 18–19). Similarly nationalistic is Yeats' 'Cuchulain's Fight with the Sea' (1892), which draws on one of the most famous images in Irish legend:

> Cuchulain stirred,
> Stared on the horses of the sea, and heard
> The cars of battle and his own name cried;
> And fought with the invulnerable tide.

Like Tennyson's Arthur, Yeats' creation of Cuchulain was greatly influenced by the *Nibelungenlied* (both the medieval poetry and Wagner's music) as a pure expression of national spirit. Yeats in 'September 1913' unfairly contrasted what he then regarded as the failure of Irish nationalism, its descent into pettiness, with heroes of Irish history such as Edward Fitzgerald (1763–98), Robert Emmet (1778–1803) and Wolfe Tone (1763–98), all martyrs for Irish independence. After the 1916 revolt, Yeats implicitly admitted in 'Easter 1916' that he was wrong about the Irish lack of spirit: 'a terrible beauty is born'.

By the end of his life, in 'The Statues' (1938), Yeats was skilfully using Irish legend for contemporary needs. Echoing Blake's 'The Tyger', he writes in wonder of the Irish martyrs in the 1916 uprising who had a cult of Cuchulain – their fight being equally heroic and, in the short run, futile – remembered by the Irish government with a statue of Cuchulain in the Dublin Post Office where the rebels held out for a few days against far superior British firepower:

> When Pearse summoned Cuchulain to his side,
> What stalked through the Post Office? What intellect,
> What calculation, number, measurement, replied?
> We Irish, born into that ancient sect
> But thrown upon this filthy modern tide
> And by its formless spawning fury wrecked,
> Climb to our proper dark, that we may trace
> The lineaments of a plummet-measured face.

The contradictions inherent in Yeats' poetry made it hard for the Irish to see him in his lifetime as a true national poet. Even as he extolled the virtues of Gaelic and the peasantry, he wrote in English (indeed, in the English Romantic tradition) and lived in cities; and much of his poetry stands out less in its Irish nationalism than in its universalism. Yet, with the passage of time, it has been possible even for the Irish to accept Yeats as a master of Irish legend and representative of national identity and hopes (Hutchinson and Aberbach 1999).

CONCLUSION

What can we learn from poets about nation-building? Poets use myth and mythical history as a shifting tapestry of national identity. They explore or invent the unique character of the nation, emphasising what seems most original and distinctive, and most likely to enable the nation to hold together and resist oppression, to endure and prosper. They recreate national heroes, give hope in victory, wisdom in failure, unity in defeat. They instil pride in national accomplishments even when the nation is defeated and powerless. They stress core ideals to give legitimacy and power to a nation, to 'the great Idea', as Whitman put it, 'that is the mission of poets' ('By Blue Ontario's Shore', 11).

NOTES

1 In many important studies of nationalism (for example, Gellner 1983; Seton-Watson 1977; Armstrong 1982; Hroch 1985; Hobsbawm 1990; Breuilly 1993) 'poetry' and 'myth' do not appear in the index, and poets are rarely mentioned. Influential literary critical studies of symbol formation (for example, Ellmann 1968; Bloom 1969; Frye 2000) tend to emphasise individual rather than national significance. The entries on 'myth' and 'myth criticism' in the *Princeton Encyclopedia of Poetry and Poetics* (Preminger et al. 1993) do not mention nationalism.

2 On the poetry of nationalism, see Hutchinson and Aberbach (1999) and Aberbach (2003).

3 The translation is by David Aberbach, admittedly one of Sir Randolph Quirk's less illustrious pupils of Anglo-Saxon at University College, London, but thankful nevertheless that some vague (perhaps mythical) memory of Sir Randolph's classes might remain. Corrections would be gratefully accepted.

4 Ossian greatly inspired nationalism in the century after the French revolution. The Hungarian poet Petofi, in 'Homer and Ossian' (1847), for example, recalls the glory of the dead, defeated warriors depicted by Ossian as an inspiration to those who, like the Hungarians against the Russians, rebelled against tyranny (Petofi 1974: 93).

5 Yeats' younger contemporary, Patrick Pearse, had a similar mystic identification with the nation, in 'I am Ireland':

I am Ireland:
I am older than the Old Woman of Beare.

Great my glory:
I that bore Cuchuloainn the valiant.

Great my shame:
My own children that sold their mother.

I am Ireland:
I am lonelier than the Old Woman of Beare. (in Kennelly 1970: 295)

REFERENCES

Aberbach, David (2003), 'The poetry of nationalism', *Nations and Nationalism*, 9, 22: 255–75.

Armstrong, John A. (1982), *Nations Before Nationalism*, Chapel Hill: University of North Carolina Press.

Bloom, Harold (1969 [1959]), *Shelley's Mythmaking*, Ithaca, NY: Cornell University Press.

Breuilly, John (1993 [1982]), *Nationalism and the State*, 2nd edn, Manchester: Manchester University Press.

Colley, Linda (1992), *Britons: Forging the Nation 1707–1837*, New Haven and London: Yale University Press.

Conran, Anthony (ed. and tr.) (1967), *The Penguin Book of Welsh Verse*, Harmondsworth: Penguin.

Daiches, David (1971), *Sir Walter Scott and his World*, London: Thames and Hudson.

Ellmann, Richard (1968 [1954]), *The Identity of Yeats*, London: Faber.

Frye, Northrop (2000 [1957]), *Anatomy of Criticism: Four essays*, Princeton: Princeton University Press.

Gellner, Ernest (1983), *Nations and Nationalism*, Oxford: Blackwell.

Hastings, Adrian (1997), *The Construction of Nationhood: Ethnicity, Religion and Nationalism*, Cambridge: Cambridge University Press.

Hobsbawm, E. J. and Terence Ranger (eds) (1983), *The Invention of Tradition*, Cambridge: Cambridge University Press.

Hobsbawm, E. J. (1990), *Nations and Nationalism Since 1780*, Cambridge: Cambridge University Press.

Hroch, Miroslav (1985), *Social Preconditions of National Revival in Europe*, B. Fowkes (tr.), Cambridge: Cambridge University Press.

Hutchinson, John and David Aberbach (1999),'The artist as nation-builder: William Butler Yeats and Chaim Nachman Bialik', *Nations and Nationalism*, 5, 4: 501–21.

Jordan, Elaine (1988), *Alfred Tennyson*, Cambridge: Cambridge University Press.

Kennelly, Brendan (ed.) (1970), *The Penguin Book of Irish Verse*, Harmondsworth: Penguin.

Petöfi, Sandor (1974), *Rebel or Revolutionary?*, ed. B. Köpeczi, Budapest: Corvina Press.

Preminger, Alex and T. V. F Brogan et al. (eds) (1993), *The New Princeton Encyclopedia of Poetry and Poetics*, Princeton: Princeton University Press.

Pritchard, William H. (ed.) (1972), *W. B. Yeats: A Critical Anthology*, Harmondsworth: Penguin.

Scott, Sir Walter (1932–7), *The Letters of Sir Walter Scott*, H. J. C. Grierson et al. (eds), 8 vols, London: Constable.

Seton-Watson, Hugh (1977), *Nations and States*, London: Methuen.

Shaw, M. (1973), 'Tennyson and his public', in D. J. Palmer (ed.), *Tennyson*, London: G. Bell and Sons.

Smith, Anthony D. (1999), *Myths and Memories of the Nation*, Oxford: Oxford University Press.

Smith, Anthony D. (2003), *Chosen Peoples: Sacred Sources of National Identity*, Oxford: Oxford University Press.

Sutherland, John (1995), *The Life of Walter Scott: A Critical Biography*, Oxford: Blackwell.

Part III

ANTIQUITY IN THE
ETHNOSYMBOLIC APPROACH

Chapter 7

THE SUCCESSOR TERRITORY

Steven Grosby

———◁▷———

I wish to examine one factor in the formation of nations: the 'successor territory'. My reasons for doing so are two. First, I intend this investigation to contribute to understanding the ways by which certain symbols are pivotal to the existence of nations. In analysing one such symbol, the image of the 'successor territory', I will turn to its manifestation in the formation of ancient Israel. While ancient Israel offers a clear example of the 'successor territory', it is by no means limited to it. As the 'successor territory' is found repeatedly throughout history, it is offered here as a category fundamental to the 'ethnosymbolic' analysis of nationality.

Second, I want to correct an assumption (Grosby 1991) concerning the dating of the image of the territory of ancient Israel as distinct from the conception of the 'promised land'. The latter is likely inseparable from the Deuteronomistic literary complex (Deuteronomy through 2 Kings); however, the former is considerably older.

THE SUCCESSOR TERRITORY AND TEMPORAL DEPTH

The category of the 'successor territory' refers to the fact that territorial designations tend to persist over time; where recognition of the territorial boundaries of one society continues throughout different historical periods as a point of reference in the formation of a subsequent society, thereby asserting the temporal depth of that latter society. The classic example of this phenomenon is the biblical description of the 'land of Israel' as successor to the ancient Egyptian province of 'Canaan'. While scholars (Mazar 1930, 1986; Alt 1953; de Vaux 1978; Aharoni 1979) have discussed the evident relation between the boundaries of the territory of Canaan and those of the land of Israel, the first person to employ the phrase 'successor territory' appears to have been the biblical historian and geographer Zecharia Kallai (1998).[1]

The name of the historically subsequent society, the territory of which is understood by its members to be the 'successor' of the land of a former society, may not be the same as that of the former society; and its boundaries may not correspond precisely to those of the former society. Nonetheless, territorially designating formulae, often conveyed by reference to topographical features, tend to persist, thereby connecting through time one society to another. For ancient Israel, territorial formulae such as 'from Lebo-Hamath [Lebanese Beqa'] to the wadi of Egypt' (1 Kings 8: 65) and 'from Lebo-Hamath to the Sea of Arabah [Dead Sea]' (2 Kings 14: 25; Amos 9: 14) conveyed an understanding of Israel as the territorial successor to Canaan. These territorial designations are not merely bearers of historical memory; rather, they are focal points around which that memory is organised. Perhaps obscured by formulations like '*la longue durée*' is this factor implied by the phrase 'successor territory': spatially organised patterns of conceptions that are sustained over time by relatively fixed territorial designations.[2]

We get a good idea of the persistence of territorial designations from an observation of Frederic Maitland (1897: 12–13) on the early medieval vill (village, township) in his analysis of William the Conqueror's *Domesday Book*.

> A place that is mentioned in Domesday Book will probably be recognised as a vill in the thirteenth century, a civil parish in the nineteenth century ... about a hundred and ten vills that were vills in 1086 are vills or civil parishes at the present day, and in all probability they then had approximately the same boundaries that they have now.

Maitland was aware that this notional continuity could be complicated by the legal portability of land, that is, land could be legally divided and reorganised. Despite this and other complications, Maitland (1978: 14–15) concluded that in general the vill of *Domesday Book* remains a vill in later days.

This persistence, over a period of eight centuries, of the territory of the English vill in no way denies its diverse origins and purposes, ranging from ecclesiastical division to organisation for taxes; nor does it deny the varying significance for the individual of being a member of the village community from the eleventh century to today – a variability magnified by increased mobility and potential for recognition and acceptance of a wider range of traditions. Such diversity of purpose and variability of significance are to be taken for granted; it is the persistence of the territorial designation that must be acknowledged and pondered.

An analytical tradition has sought to account for the persistence described by Maitland as a consequence of face-to-face relations, thereby restricting it, as an anthropological and historical phenomenon, to the *Gemeinschaft* of the village. There is merit to this analytical tradition, as spatial familiarity is certainly limited, and continually reaffirmed, by the immediacy of the experience of face-to-face relations. Nonetheless, there is a methodological complication.

Attachments to territory, in some measure constitutive of one's understanding of the self, are expressed through delimited patterns of conceptions (such as local customs, idioms, and dialects) with topographical reference. This 'topophilia' (to resort to the felicitous neologism of Yi-Fu Tuan [1974]) is symbolically expressed as *landscape*, as portrayed, for example, in Thomas Hardy's arresting description of Egdon Heath in *The Return of the Native*. While attachments to local community and its topography are resilient because of the sustained immediacy of the individual's relation to his or her environment (both to the other individuals of the face-to-face relations and to the features of local topography), their significance to the individual is a consequence of those attachments becoming objects of contemplation through symbolic representation, for example the statue of Athena in the ancient Athenian agora or, topographically as landscape, for example, the Jerusalem valley of Hinnom (Hebrew, *Ge [ben] hinnom*), where fires that were originally for executed criminals and garbage were later associated with, and thereby transformed into, the burning torments of Hell (Greek, *Gehenna*).[3] Only when that experience is lifted out of the ebb and flow of life and achieves the relatively independent, objective form of a tradition (which may not be materially embodied) do the behavioral attachments of familiarity become an object of shared appreciation, and, as such, capable of persistence over time (the precondition for any subsequent transformation), thereby joining one generation to another. Thus, the direct experience of a locality must be distinguished from the significance attributed to that area, where the latter becomes a space with (an unavoidably variable) meaning: a territory.

As objects of contemplation through symbolic representation, traditions of appreciation, including of the *Gemeinschaft*, are susceptible to re-evaluation and transformation, even if, for the local community, relatively less so. They may even be rejected. This elementary, methodological complication often becomes a trivial exercise of confusion when this susceptibility is portrayed as capricious 'invention', for the 'artificiality' of the symbolic objectivation and transformation of experience – artificial only in the sense that imagination has ineluctably intervened into the immediacy of experience – need not be arbitrary. All civilisations and historical periods bear witness to the persistence, albeit unavoidably variable, of territorially local attachments, for example, the English vill, the Arab *watan*, the ancient Greek πατρίς, the Japanese clan, and the homelands of the African Bushmen and Swazi.[4] How could it be otherwise?

The persistence of the image of a territory is not restricted to such local communities as the English vill. It is also a necessary factor in the existence of a nation. It is the most obvious, historical and anthropological factor that justifies the ethnosymbolic analysis of nationality.

Moreover, there is evidence for the stability of images of extensive, yet bounded, territories in antiquity; thus, Anthony Smith (2004: 20) is correct to observe that nations may be found in pre-modern epochs. In antiquity, that stability, conveyed through territorial formulae, was enhanced when those formulae were 'fixed' because they referred to natural, topographical features as boundaries, for example, for ancient Israel, the Mediterranean Sea, Jordan River and Mount Halak.

Not only is the classic example of this persistence to be found in the traditions of the ancient Israelites and subsequently Jews, but also in its influence on the history of the Occident (Hastings 1997; Sutcliffe 2003: 43–7; Grosby 2005). The reanimation of the Israelite tradition of the image of the national territory of the promised land during the Middle Ages (for example, during the reign of the French Philip the Fair, the sixteenth-century Dutch 'new Israel', by Althusius in his *Politica*, by the English and American Puritans) required that this tradition be transformed through the 'emptying' of its original topographical content and replacing it with another. This European reanimation of Israelite tradition clearly served the 'interest' of political independence from imperial ambition. However, it is a fundamental error to collapse that tradition into such an interest, as if the former, even though transformed, had no independent existence.

The importance of the example of ancient Israel is that the persistence of tradition is not only not confined to local community, but that even in antiquity territorial attachments were capable of being expanded in the absence of modern vehicles of imaginative extension, for example, modern means of communication. For ancient Israel and subsequently Judaea, this expansion was evidently a consequence of military alliances in war (Judges 4–5, the Maccabees), the formation of a state (1 Samuel 8) with its territorially unifying law and institutions (Deuteronomy 17: 8–12, the Sanhedrin), a relatively high degree of literacy (see Schniedewind 2004) and, of course, religion. None of these factors are unambiguously national; thus, a state may be imperial and a religion may be universal. Crucial for the formation of the nation is the symbolic limitation on the range of expansion. The persistence of the symbolic independence of a *limiting* tradition for the constitution of nationality is nowhere more obvious than the phenomenon of the 'successor territory'.

ANCIENT ISRAEL AS SUCCESSOR TERRITORY

The Hebrew Bible explicitly asserts a relation between the land of Canaan and, as its territorial successor, the land of Israel, for example, at Genesis 9: 25–7; 10: 15–20; Numbers 34: 2–12.

Blessed be Yahweh, the God of Shem [Israel]; let Canaan be his slave. (Genesis 9: 26)

The boundaries of Canaan extended from Sidon as far as Gerar, near Gaza, and as far as Sodom, Gomorrah, Admah, and Zeboiim, near Lasha. These are the descendants of Ham [ancestor of Canaan], according to their clans and languages, by their lands and nations (*gôyim*). (Genesis 10: 19–20)

When you enter the land of Canaan, this is the land that will fall to you as your inheritance, the land of Canaan according to its boundaries. Your southern sector will extend from the wilderness of Zin alongside of Edom. Your southern boundary will start on the east of the tip of the Dead Sea. Your boundary will then pass to the south of the ascent of Akrabbim and continue to Zin, and its limits will be south of Kadesh-Barnea, reaching Hazar-adar and continue to Azmon. From Azmon the boundary will turn to the Wadi of Egypt and end at the [Mediterranean] Sea. For the western boundary, you will have the coast of the [Mediterranean] Sea; this will be your western boundary. This will be your northern boundary: draw a line from the [Mediterranean] Sea to Mount Hor; from Mount Hor draw a line to Lebo-Hamath, and let the boundary reach Zedad. The boundary will then run to Ziphron and end at Hazar-enan. That will be your northern boundary. For your eastern boundary, draw a line from Hazar-enan to Shepham. From Shepham the boundary will descend to Riblah on the east side of Ain; from there the boundary will continue downward and reach the eastern slopes of the Sea of Chinnereth [Sea of Galilee]. The boundary will then descend along the Jordan [River] and end at the Dead Sea. This will be your land according to its boundaries on all sides. (Numbers 34: 2–12)

But what of the word Canaan itself? The origin of the term is obscure.[5] Its first appearance, as 'Canaanites' (or 'men of Canaan'), is from a mid-eighteenth-century BCE tablet from Mari.[6] Later, from Alalakh in northwest Syria, two inscriptions further clarify the term 'Canaan'. The first, brief reference is 'Šarniya, a son of the land of Canaan.' The description here of Šarniya should not be understood as merely indicating his place of origin; rather, he is a 'Canaanite' because he is from – a native of – Canaan. The territorial referent in the sociologically relatively amorphous ethnic group should not be overlooked. (Note the biblical *'ezrach ha'arets*, 'native of the land', as a designation for Israelite.[7]) The second, longer reference appears in the stele of Idrimi (c. 1500 BCE).

I took my horse and my chariot and groom and went away; I crossed over the desert and entered among the Sutû warriors. I spent the night with them ... The next day I went forth and came to the land of Canaan. The town of Ammiya is located in the land of Canaan. In the town of Ammiya there dwelt people from the city of Halab, people of the land Mugiš, people of the land of Ni'i, and people of the land of Ama'e.

From these and other inscriptions, one concludes that by the fifteenth century BCE Canaan was a recognised territory; and, furthermore, that territorial designations such as Canaan, Mugiš, and so forth could also designate the inhabitants of those territories. This conflation of referents between a territory and, thus, its people is characteristic of 'ethno-geographic' collectivities, such as often the Israelite *šēbet* ('tribe'), the *gāyum* of ancient Mari (Malamat 1989: 33, 38) and the nation.

Whatever uncertainties may exist about the conclusions drawn so far about the term 'Canaan' as a territorial designation, several of the 12 references to the term among the 382, fourteenth-century BCE Amarna tablets (Moran 1992) clarify them. In tablet 8, the Babylonian king complains to the Egyptian pharaoh about the fate of his merchants.

Now, my merchants ... were detained in Canaan on business matters ... in Hinnatuna of Canaan [= Hannathon in the lower Galilee; see Joshua 19: 14]. Šum-Adda ... killed my merchants and took away their money ... Canaan is your [the pharaoh's] country, and its kings are your servants. In your country I have been despoiled. Bring them to account and make compensation for the money that they took away.

In tablet 9, the same king writes to the pharaoh that

In the time of Kurigalzu, my ancestor, all the Canaanites wrote here [to Babylon] to him, saying, 'Come to the border of the country [of Canaan] so we can revolt [against Egypt] and be allied with you'. My ancestor sent them this reply, saying, 'Forget about being allied with me. If you become enemies of the king of Egypt ... will I not then come and plunder you?'

From these two tablets, written to the pharaoh, it appears that the territory of Canaan was understood to be under the control of Egypt.

This conclusion is further supported by two tablets sent from the pharaoh to his vassals. Tablet 162 contains Akhenaten's threat to Aziru, ruler of Amurru (at this time, confined to the Lebanese Beqa'), that Amurru, evidently still considered to be within the land of Canaan but increasingly under Hittite influence, should remain loyal to Egypt.

What happened to you among them that you are not on the side of the king, your lord ... If for any reason whatsoever you prefer to do evil, and if you plot evil, treacherous things, then you, together with your entire family, shall die by the axe of the king. So perform your service for the king, your lord, and you will live. You yourself know that the king does not fail when he rages against all of Canaan [or, as an alternative reading of the obscure language in this last phrase, 'And you know that the king does not want to go to the entire land of Canaan when he is angry'].

The second tablet, 367, written to Endaruta, ruler of Akšapa (= Achshaph, Joshua 12: 20, south of modern Haifa), describes one Hanni who was sent by the pharaoh to Endaruta.

You are to guard the place of the king where you are. The king herewith sends to you Hanni, the son of Maireya, overseer of the king's stables in Canaan. And what he tells you heed very carefully and carry out very carefully.

The position of the 'overseer of the king's stables in Canaan' suggests organised Egyptian administration of Canaan. This likelihood would be further strengthened if Rainey (1996: 7–8) is correct to read the disputed *pi-ha-ti ša ki-na-'i*, 'the province of Canaan', in tablet 36, which recounts an exchange of copper from Alashia (Cyprus) for grain from Canaan.

These inscriptions indicate that the term 'Canaan' represented a demarcated territory during the late Bronze Age. There is, thus, a historical reality behind its portrayal in the Hebrew Bible.

Several factors are likely to account for the persistence of this mid-second-millennium BCE image of Canaan into around the eleventh century BCE and subsequently through the composition of the Torah centuries later, long after Egypt had lost control of the area that was to become Israel: (1) the facts of Egyptian administration of the territory – Gaza as Egypt's primary base for operation in Canaan, where Ramses III (*c.* 1150 BCE) built a temple to Amon;[8] and Egyptian military fortresses at places such as Beth-shean, south of the Sea of Galilee on the eastern border of Canaan/Israel; (2) the battle of Qadash (*c.* 1275 BCE) that determined the northern limit of Egyptian influence (hence, Canaan). Interestingly, the boundaries of the Assyrian provinces (eighth century BCE; see Talmon 1994), separating southern Syria (Damascus) from the area to its north, correspond to this division following the battle of Qadash. It seems most unrealistic to assume that these factors would not have been expressed in the traditions of the commoners who lived in this area.

Where there are not natural boundaries to facilitate the persistence of territorial distinctions, political factors – above all war, such as the battle of Qadash, structures like China's Great Wall and Hadrian's Wall, and treaties, for example, the division of Charlemagne's Empire after his death – have facilitated the existence of territorially bounded conceptions. In some of these examples, we observe only a rough correspondence between the territory of an earlier society and that of its successor, for example, modern France and Germany as the successors of the territories of, respectively, Charles the Bald and Louis after the Treaties of Verdun (843 CE) and Meersen (870 CE), with the territory of Lothair's kingdom, between that of Charles and that of Louis, in dispute (and remaining so, up to the twentieth century: Alsace-Lorraine!). And the border between Scotland and England does not correspond precisely to Hadrian's Wall. However, to focus entirely on the vagueness of such territorial correspondence is to ignore the centuries-long, developing traditions of territorial demarcation. After all, the linguistic division between what was to become France and what was to become Germany long predates the emergence of modern means of communication and educational reform.

Nonetheless, the case for the category of the successor territory will be strengthened if there is a fairly precise correspondence of boundaries. Our question thus becomes: is there a relation between the boundaries of the Egyptian province of Canaan and those of the land of Israel in the historically later description of Numbers 34: 2–12?

It must be admitted that the fourteenth-century BCE Amarna letters provide no detailed information about the boundaries of Canaan, even though the reference to one border in tablet 9 is suggestive. However, we are able to obtain a better idea of the boundaries of the Egyptian province from the later records of Seti I and Ramses II (thirteenth century BCE). The Egyptian fortress of Sile marked the northeast border of Egypt (*ANET*: 254–5), separating the Nile delta from the Sinai desert, thereby distinguishing Egypt from (as formulated in the late thirteenth-century BCE Papyrus Anastasi I) 'the end of the land of Canaan' (*ANET*: 478). Here we have a border fortress that corresponds to a natural boundary. Papyrus Anastasi I makes clear that religious significance was accorded to this territorial boundary, referring to Sile as the fortress of 'The Ways of Horus'. (Let us note in passing that religion is often a bearer of territorial traditions and their boundaries, and obviously so when temples are situated at borders.) Canaan's northwest border was designated by the fortress of 'Ramses Meri-Amon, the town which is in the Valley of the Cedar' (= Lebanon, *ANET*: 255–6). This Egyptian fortress was also known as Sumur (= 'Simyra' of Ramses II in Papyrus Anastasi I, *ANET* 477) in the Amarna tablets (109, 131).

Evidently, according to the Papyrus Anastasi I, the eastern border of Canaan was also a natural boundary, the Jordan River, the eastern border of biblical Israel

(Joshua 22: 10–11; Numbers 34: 12). Once again, the correspondence of borders between those of an earlier society and those of its territorial successor would be abetted when those borders are natural boundaries.

These and other Egyptian records describe these boundaries of the territory of Canaan: (a) in the west, from southwest Sile, continuing north along the Mediterranean coast, to northwest Sumur; (b) in the north, from northwest Sumur, continuing east southeast through Beqa', south of Lebo-Hamath but north of Damascus, to the northern Jordan Valley; (c) in the east, from the northern Jordan Valley, continuing south through Beth-shean (presumably the *Bitsanu* in Amarna tablet 289), along the Jordan River to the Dead Sea. There is, thus, a remarkable similarity between these late Bronze Age borders of Canaan and the description of Canaan as the promised land of Israel in Numbers 34: 2–12. Did the image of the territorial extent of Canaan persist in Israelite memory, thereby influencing, centuries later, the Israelite understanding of its territory? Beyond the similarity in borders, the likelihood of this possibility would be further supported by: (1) the otherwise enigmatic description, in Joshua, of Israelite settlements east of the Jordan River as being outside the land of Israel; and (2) the also enigmatic conception of 'the land that remains' (to be conquered, Joshua 13: 2, Judges 3: 3) as referring to areas of southern Lebanon that were part of Canaan but never part of Israel.

Clearly, the Israelites considered themselves to be the legitimate heir of Canaan. But why should the biblical authors have described Israel as being the successor territory of Canaan, even to the point of insisting on a correspondence of boundaries? The reason is, no doubt, to justify their boundaries; for no society can over time tolerate boundaries that might otherwise be understood to be capricious. The assertion of legitimacy of the bounded promised land of Israel took two forms in the Hebrew Bible: (1) as sanctioned by God, thereby justifying their existence in the order of the universe; and (2) as successor to the, in effect, immemorial territory of Canaan. However, the second form was only possible if the image of Canaan had been firmly entrenched within Israelite collective self-consciousness. What deserves both our attention and to be emphasised is the historical tenacity of the territorial image (Kallai 1998: 14).

Utterly unremarkable are observations – much the fashion today – that historians, in this case the biblical authors and editors, operate with narrative stereotypes, such as the above use of 'Canaan', in the service of promoting a programmatic ideal.[9] All histories convey, in varying degrees, the concerns of the time in which they were written: either thematically, through the choice of subjects, or historiographically, by the use of selected categories (Grosby 2003). This 'subjectivity' is unavoidable; and it accounts for the adage that each generation must write its own history. There, thus, should be no doubt that the biblical narrative's exploitation of the territorial designation 'Canaan' is dominated by the Israelite loss of sovereignty over the land at various times throughout its history. For example, the description of the boundaries of the land at Ezekiel 47: 13–23 obviously represents a goal to be achieved in the aftermath of the Babylonian subjugation of Judah (ideally, Israel) at the beginning of the sixth century BCE. These boundaries are evidently patterned after those of Numbers 34: 2–12, which, in turn, were understood by the ancient Israelites to have been based upon the territory of Canaan. What is remarkable, especially in antiquity, is the undeniable fact of the persistence, over numerous generations, of the territorial designation 'Canaan' in Israelite self-consciousness.

As one territory may be recognised to be the successor of another, so, too, the inhabitants of the later territory are recognised to be the descendants of the former, resulting in the territorially circumscribed, trans-generational continuum so characteristic of nationality. This continuum is evident in the Hebrew Bible, for example, Calebites, Jebusites and Gibeonites were recognised as ancestors of the Israelites; although, of course, a continuum disrupted (and transformed) by religio-political developments ('Yahwism' or 'Yahweh alone'), manifested during the reigns of Hezekiah and especially Josiah, that resulted in some of those territorial ancestors being classified as the religiously oppositional 'Canaanites'.

The exploitation of the reference to Canaan in the Hebrew Bible operates at two levels. First, the term is used as a symbolic vehicle for political and religious polemic in the eighth through sixth centuries BCE. The second level is the use of the term as bearer of the territory of the centuries-long Egyptian province. This latter use should not be lost within the first.

LANDSCAPE

Territorial boundaries were not only entrenched in Israelite historical consciousness; they were also embedded within it as landscape. To appreciate this embeddedness, one must return to an earlier sense of landscape. Yi-Fu Tuan (1974: 133) observed that this earlier sense, before the end of the sixteenth century CE when it had come to designate pictorial representation of scenery, referred to topographical experience of the real world. We get a good idea of this earlier experience of landscape from the description of what is ostensibly and often wrongly viewed as primarily the familial relation between Jacob and his twin, elder brother Esau in Genesis 25.

About the elder brother, we are told he 'emerged red, like a hairy mantle all over; so they named him Esau'. Of the two attributes of Esau, red and hairy, the latter attribution of being hairy (Hebrew, *sa'ir*) is introduced here as a clumsy word play to provide an etymology for his name (*sa'ir* → Esau). The first attribute, being red, is awkwardly repeated later – awkwardly because it is no longer a condition of birth but, now, of diet. 'And Esau said to Jacob, "Give me some of that red (Hebrew, *adom*) stuff to gulp down, for I am famished, which is why he (Esau) was named *Edom*"'. Thus, the physical description of Esau as being red, either at birth or subsequently through diet, is in the service of another etymological word play (*adom* → *Edom*) that is, in fact, being dictated by territorial considerations, namely that red (*adom*) Esau was *Edom*, the territory that bordered Israel; and, as such, portrayed in personal terms as the brother of Jacob (= Israel).[10] Moreover, there is also a topographical experience of landscape being related here, because, as many have observed, the mountains of Edom, when viewed from Israel, have a red tinge to them.

Much less obvious but equally dictated by territorial tradition is the description of Esau at birth as being 'hairy'. This attribute is repeated in Genesis 27 in the description of the contrast between Esau and Jacob, 'Jacob answered his mother Rebekah, "but my brother Esau is a hairy [*sa'ir*] man and I am smooth-skinned [Hebrew, *halak*)]"'. As is well known, this physical contrast serves the trickster Jacob in carrying out his mother's plan to deceive the blind father, Isaac, by obtaining the blessing intended by Isaac for the first-born Esau. However, as Zecharia Kallai (1998: 217) observed, the contrast between smooth-skinned (*halak*) Jacob and hairy (*sa'ir*) Esau is actually a play on words, the clear intention of which is territorial: to describe the southeast boundary of Israel (Jacob) that separates it from Edom (Esau). That boundary is conveyed by the territorial formula in Joshua 11: 17 (and 12: 7) as 'from Mount *Halak* which rises toward *Seir*' (Edom), with the more convincing word play of *sa'ir* → *Seir*. It thus appears that this territorial formula dictated the composition of the physical distinction between Jacob and Esau.

The natural boundary of Mt Seir distinguished not only the southeast border of Israel from Edom, but also seemingly designated the historically earlier border of Egyptian Canaan, so one concludes from both the description of the military campaign of Ramses III (early twelfth century BCE, *ANET* 262) and probably Armana tablet 288 (where 'the land of Šeru = Seir). As in the Hebrew Bible, in these Egyptian records, Mt Seir served as a toponym for Edom.

CONCLUSION

Obviously, the Islamic, Arab conquests of societies such as Egypt and Syria disrupted, indeed shattered, much of the cultural continuum of those societies. Gone forever was, for example, the ancient worship of *Dea Syria* (note well the religio-territorial designation!). Nevertheless, just as obvious is the persistence of territorial designations such as Egypt and Syria: the phenomenon of the successor territory!

To recognise this persistence is not to indulge in a geographical determinism, thereby denying the unpredictability and processual fluidity of historical factors; for example, the conversion of Idumea to Judaism during the period of the Second Temple (Josephus, *Antiquities*, chapter 9, book 13). It is, however, to recognise the persistence of those territorial distinctions that, while subject, as symbols, to a transformation of their referential content, are not thoroughly shattered. It is to recognise not the constancy of 'material factors' or 'laws', but of significations, even if necessarily subject to modification of their varied content (Cassirer 2000: 75).

When territorial designations become stable, having been firmly embedded in the collective self-consciousness of a society through religious, historiographical, and legal traditions, then there may exist a nation. The analytical significance of Anthony Smith's (2004: 18) long and worthy efforts to distinguish nation from ethnic community exists precisely in his attempt to clarify those factors that contribute to this *relative* conceptual stability of the collective self-consciousness – the (necessarily uneven) shared self-understanding – constitutive of a nation: (1) self-definition, including a proper name; (2) shared myths and memories of origins; (3) a distinctive, common public culture; (4) possession of a historic homeland; and (5) common rights and duties for all members. When there is a nation, then common to all of these factors is a bounded, territorial focus that distinguishes the collective self-consciousness of a nation from that of other social relations.

It is this relative stability of the nation that seemingly distinguishes it from the sociologically more amorphous ethnic community, for example, the ancient Israelites, English, or French in contrast to, respectively, the Aramaeans, Jutes or Salians – seemingly because the apparent categorial contrast may at times be a result of our lack of evidence. However, the lack of evidence may itself be analytically significant: the absence of the symbolic representation of a territory conveyed through and stabilised by a historiographical tradition – broadly understood here to include fancy as well as fact, as one finds, for example, in ancient Israel (the literary complex of Genesis through 2 Kings; Josephus' *Antiquities*), sixth-century Sri Lanka (the *Mahavamsa*), eighth-century Japan (the *Nihon Shoki*), medieval France (Gregory's sixth-century *History of the Franks* and the eleventh-century *Song of Roland*), and England (Bede's eighth-century *Ecclesiastical History of the English People* and Geoffrey's fanciful twelfth-century *History of the Kings of Britain*) – likely indicates a stunted development, hence instability, of the objective articulation of the self of a collective self-consciousness.

The sociological problem in the constitution of the nation is that both of its referents – people and land – must achieve a degree of conceptual stability. Their legitimacy must be established and maintained such that there is a significant degree of cultural uniformity, that is, a territorial kinship. This is accomplished through traditions that assert the stability of the image of the territory itself, through recognition of (1) its relation to the perceived order of the universe, and/or its immemorial character, that is, its temporal depth as a successor territory.

NOTES

1 The definitive defences of the relations, see Na'aman 1994; Rainey 1996. The relation has been unconvincingly challenged by Lemche 1991.
2 I leave aside here philosophical-anthropological speculation as to why this persistence should occur.
3 Perhaps Joel 3: 12 captures this transition of meaning borne by the topographical significance of the burning depths of the valley, where *ge-hinnom* is the 'Valley of Jehoshaphat', that is, the valley of [God's] judgement.
4 On the territorial tie in African societies, see Schapera 1956. See also Lowie 1927, where the historical contrast between consanguinity and territoriality is rightly rejected.
5 The word 'Canaan' may be derived from the Hurrian (Nuzi) *kinaḫḫu* = purple. In support of this possibility is the Greek φοῖνιξ = purple as the etymology of 'Phoenicia', hence, the land of purple because of the colour of the dye from shells along the coast. However, objections have been raised to this derivation for 'Canaan'; see Zobel 1970. Long ago, Eduard Meyer (1907: 1.2.419) observed that the original meaning of the word was hidden. Still, Meyer (1907: 2.1.88) rightly acknowledged that the term had, by the middle of the second millennium BCE, become a designation for a territory and its population, 'Kana'an ist der einheimische Landesname'.
6 Much of the documentation for this section relies upon Na'aman 1994 and Rainey 1996. See also Aharoni 1979: 66–77.
7 Exodus 12: 19; 12: 48; 12: 49; Leviticus 16: 29; 17: 15; 18: 26; 19: 33–4; 23: 42; 24: 16; Numbers 9: 14; 15: 13–14; 15: 29; 15: 30; Joshua 8: 33; Ezekiel 47: 21–2, and perhaps Psalm 37: 35.
8 Papyrus Anastasi I, *ANET*, 478; Papyrus Harris I, *ANET*, 261, where 'the Canaan' = Gaza. During the XIXth and XXth Dynasties (c. 1300–1100 BCE), the city of Gaza, the Egyptian centre in Canaan, was referred to as 'the Canaan'.
9 So Lemche 1991: 101, 151.
10 The literary motif of describing territorial proximity, specifically a shared boundary, as gentilic kinship is also obvious in the portrayal of the relations of Moab, Ammon and Israel in Genesis 19: 30–8, where Lot, father of Moab and Ammon, is cousin of Jacob.

REFERENCES

Aharoni, Y. (1979), *The Land of the Bible*, 2nd edn, London: Burns and Oates.
Alt, A. (1953), *Kleine Schriften* I, Munich: C. H. Beck.
ANET Ancient Near Eastern Texts relating to the Old Testament, ed. J. B. Pritchard (2nd rev. edn), Princeton: Princeton University Press.
Cassirer, Ernst (2000), *The Logic of the Cultural Sciences*, tr. S. G. Lofts, New Haven: Yale University Press.
de Vaux, R. (1978), *The Early History of Israel*, Philadelphia: Westminster Press.
Grosby, Steven (1991), 'Religion and nationality in antiquity', *European Journal of Sociology*

32: 229–65, reprinted in *Biblical Ideas of Nationality: Ancient and Modern*, Winona Lake: Eisenbrauns, 2002.

Grosby, Steven (2003), 'A *Gôy* by any other name: The problem of nationality in antiquity', www.bibleinterp.com.

Grosby, Steven (2005), 'The nation as a problem for philosophy', *Hebraic Political Studies* 1: 5–21.

Hastings, Adrian (1997), *The Construction of Nationhood*, Cambridge: Cambridge University Press.

Kallai, Zecharia (1998), *Biblical Historiography and Historical Geography*, Frankfurt am Main: Peter Lang.

Lemche, N. P. (1991), *The Canaanites and Their Land*, Sheffield: JSOT Press.

Lowie, Robert (1927), *The Origin of the State*, New York: Harcourt, Brace and Co.

Maitland, Frederic William (1897), *Domesday Book and Beyond*, Cambridge: Cambridge University Press.

Malamat, A. (1989), *Mari and the Early Israelite Experience*, Oxford: Oxford University Press.

Mazar (Maisler), B. (1930), *Untersuchungen zur alten Geschichte und Ethnographie Syriens und Palästina*, Giessen: Alfred Töopelmann.

Mazar (Maisler), B. (1986), *The Early Biblical Period*, Jerusalem: Israel Exploration Society.

Meyer, E. (1907 [1953]), *Geschichte des Altertums*, 2nd edn, Darmstadt: Wissenschaftliche Buchgemeinschaft.

Moran, W. (1992), *The Amarna Letters*, Baltimore: The Johns Hopkins University Press.

Na'aman, N. (1994), 'The Canaanites and their land', *Ugarit-Forschungen* 26: 397–418.

Rainey, A. F. (1996), 'Who is a Canaanite? A review of the textual evidence', *Bulletin of the American Schools of Oriental Research* 304: 1–15.

Schapera, I. (1956), *Government and Politics in Tribal Societies*, London: C. A. Watts and Co.

Schniedewind, William (2004), *How the Bible Became a Book*, Cambridge: Cambridge University Press.

Smith, Anthony D. (2004), *The Antiquity of Nations*, Cambridge: Polity Press.

Sutcliffe, Adam (2003), *Judaism and the Enlightenment*, Cambridge: Cambridge University Press.

Tadmor, Hayim (1994), *The Inscriptions of Tiglath-Pileser III, King of Assyria*, Jerusalem: The Israel Academy of Sciences and Humanities.

Tuan, Yi-Fu (1974), *Topophilia*, Englewood Cliffs, NJ: Prentice-Hall.

Zobel, H.-J. (1970), '*Kn'n*', *Theologisches Worterbuches zum Alten Testament* IV: 224–43, Stuttgart: W. Kohlhammer.

Chapter 8

ETHNOSYMBOLISM IN THE ANCIENT MEDITERRANEAN WORLD

Sebastian Garman

It is no accident that concepts central to the tradition of sociology, such as family, community and nation, are so difficult to define. The 'weness' of things has always presented difficulties for social sciences, unlike etic categories such as household, institution or state. One problem, of course, is that *Gesellschaft* can suddenly be transformed into *Gemeinschaft* by crisis or threat and the difference between interaction and communion is always difficult for the outsider to identify. To overcome some of these problems ethnosymbolists attempt to make sense of the bonding and mobilisation of political communities, 'identity communities' (Armstrong 2004: 11) or 'cultural communities' (Smith 1986: 13) by examining their myths, symbols, sentiments and memories over time periods long enough to note transitions, changes and continuities of expression. In this respect the seminal works are that of Armstrong (1982) with his myth-symbol complex and *mythomoteur* and Anthony D. Smith (1986) with his focus on the idea, first popularised in France, of ethnie.

The concept of ethnie has not been universally well received because of the difficulties in distinguishing it from that of nation (see, for example, Greenfeld 1992) or, with qualified approval, because of the dangers of reification it presents (Malkin 2001; Eriksen 2004). In his first sustained analysis Smith rejects the idea of 'people' because of the variety of meanings that expression evokes. He cites Schermerhorn with approval (Smith 1986, note 4: 230) whose tripartite definition of ethnic communities (a sense of shared ancestry, shared history and shared symbols that define their peoplehood) he elaborated into the six dimensions of shared name, myth, history, culture, associated territory, and solidarity. Whereas Schermerhorn was restricting his idea to ethnic minorities, Smith is searching for a category of identity community with universal and historical application that can be a minority, a majority or even the only residents in a particular domain. It is interesting in this regard that Armstrong suggested that Smith was in danger of walling himself in with his ideal-typical definition of nation but with his 'vigorous defence of the ethnie as a usual preparatory stage overcame this restriction' (Armstrong 2004: 11). Nevertheless, the phrase 'usual preparatory stage' draws attention to a further restriction with which Smith is associating both himself and ethnosymbolism. Of the eight themes he identifies as deriving from the claims of ethnosymbolism (Smith 1999), five frame the discourse within an explicit discussion of national origins and continuities. The ancient Mediterranean world reveals varieties of political community, including ethnie, that are overlapping and subject to relative changes in significance over time. In what follows I see no reason why ethnies should not be studied in their own right and in relation to other political communities, without assumptions about the predating of nations. At times, communities of the ancient world cohere into political forms that we might call nations, but that is not the primary reason for focusing upon them.

Myths, symbols, sentiments and memories are mediated, iterated and defended by institutional means. Serious talk needs serious modes and means of expression. Perhaps because of the enormous influence of Benedict Anderson (1983) on the way political anthropology and sociology discuss political communities there has been much work on what is imagined at the expense of the institutional modes of imagining, and perhaps more importantly the means by which groups keep serious messages alive in the popular imagination, or as a resource to be drawn on in times of need. If political communities are imagined they are also enacted (Garman 2001). It is to counteract such bias that Smith acknowledges the influence of George L. Mosse on the commemorative monuments and festivals to the war dead in his recent work (Smith 2003: ix). In scholarship of the ancient Mediterranean world, the influence of Jane Harrison's distinction between the thing said and the thing done in rites has been significant. The pioneering sociology was that of Fustel de Coulanges who had such an influence on Durkheim, who in turn influenced the seminal study by Robert Will (1925–9). As Berger (1973: 49) points out, 'both religious acts and religious legitimations, ritual and mythology, *dromena* and *legoumena*, together serve to 'recall' the traditional meanings embodied in culture and its major institutions' for they reiterate 'the continuity between the present moment and the societal tradition ... it has been rightly said that society, in its essence, is a memory'.[1]

When we turn to Greek and Roman literature from the fifth century BC onwards we find in some ways a pleasing similarity of preoccupation, problematising and debate to those that concern us here. Herodotus (c. 484–c. 420 BC), for example, was fascinated by the customs, histories and connections between peoples, including those of ethnicity, in the context of an Athenian imperialism, whilst Pausanias (second century AD) was preoccupied with Greek identity and the festivals, myths and rites that united political communities, at a time of

Roman hegemony. For scholars of our own era, Herodotus is the starting point for discussions of ethnicity with his famous account of what defines Greek identity (8.144.2–3) where he lists the four elements of commonality: kinship (assumptions about common blood or *homaimon*), language, cults and customs. Konstan (2001: 32–3) translates the relevant passage as 'but there is also the fact that the Greek people [*to Hellēnikon*] are of the same blood and the same tongue, that we have in common the edifices of our gods and our sacrifices, and that our traditional ways are all alike'. These words Herodotus places in the mouths of the Athenians confronting ambassadors from Sparta and Persia after the battle of Salamis but before the decisive battle of Plataea. Written after the event, it seems generally agreed that this is a propagandist expression of 'an ideal of Panhellenic solidarity, self consciously cast in terms of ethnic identity' (Konstan 2001: 33). The stress on culture and cult as much as kinship might have been seen as an innovation by Athenians (Hall 1997: 44) with perhaps a message of irony and warning for his audience (Thomas 2001: 215), since by now Athens had established an empire with hegemony over some 300 city states (Konstan 2001: 34) and was reinforcing boundaries against all other Greeks with a new stress on its autochthonous foundation myth and the proposed legal change by Pericles in 451 that only the offspring of Athenian parents on both sides could be Athenian citizens.

In fact the primary emphasis in Herodotus' account of the Athenian speeches both to the Persian envoy and to the Spartans is not Panhellenic ethnic identity. The Athenians indignantly reject the suggestion that they should join the Persians as allies, pointing out that the Persians had destroyed the statues of their gods and their temples, an observation that they elaborate in their speech to the Spartans before any appeal to Panhellenism is made. This is a useful illustration of the point that ethnicities and shared political identities were defined by cult activities throughout the Mediterranean world in the archaic period. The matrix of gods, heroes and cults, and cult sites are seen to be sacred representations of peoples to be guarded from the desecrations of strangers and enemies even in classical times and shaped the means of hegemonic assertion by Rome. It is to this issue we now will turn.

The peoples who came to be identified as descended from Hellen imagined themselves as sea borne with homes upon the isthmuses and islands in opposition to the strangers of the hinterland. The Epirotes, for example, were seen as barbarian not primarily because of their non-polis political institutions, but because of their hinterland location in opposition to the coastal colonies of the seventh century BC (Malkin 2001) even though they, themselves, traced their origins by genealogy from the Greeks. The colonies of Sicily appeared to define themselves in part through their colonial identity in opposition to the native populations of the interior as well as invaders, notably those of Carthage (Antonaccio 2001). Nevertheless the emic identity by which communities were forged and maintained focused on the cult within the polis.

Perhaps as a reaction to the overlarge claims of the myth and ritual school, there has been a longstanding suspicion of the connections made between myth and ritual in Greek and Roman thought (Rose 1958; Kirk 1970). Whilst it is widely acknowledged that Greeks were free with their myths and could rework them for cultural purposes, it is generally agreed, following Nilsson (1951: 16), that 'myth was of fundamental importance for their practical and political life. Their right of possessing a country may be at stake'. This is particularly true of hero cults since heroes had cults as well as myths and more heroes had cults than myths; these being important for Greek politics where state and religion were one. Greek religion was archetypically Durkheimian in that religion, society and politics are inextricably linked. As groups came to be recognised, their members shaped representations, personifications and cultic iteration at all levels of society. Hence the insistence of Malkin (2001: 6) that Herodotus 'is often misrepresented as saying that 'religion' defines who is Greek but ... Herodotus speaks not of gods but of cults'.[2]

For Nilsson (1951: 18–21) the sociology involved is revealed by examining the institution of synoecism, the fusing of two or more political communities into one state. Pausanias (VIII, 26), for example, gives us a description of the founding of the Great City, Megalopolis, when the Spartan supremacy on the Peloponnese broke down after the battle of Leuctra in 371 BC. The founders moved many settlements with their cults and gods from western Arcadia into the new city. However, when the cult proved to be too firmly rooted in its territory to be moved, as with that of Zeus Lykaios on Mount Lykaion, then either a branch of it was established in the city or a procession was established between one community and the other. The expansion of the Athenian state demonstrates the same logic. When the possession of the island of Salamis became politically strategic to the Athenians at the end of the seventh century BC, cults were transferred from Salamis to Attica as well as people. There is a degree of reciprocation in this to encourage a synthesis so that when the Salaminians were moved 'they were connected with the Athenian state also through the entrusting Attic cults to them' (Nilsson 1951: 33).

In a recent examination of the myth-symbol complex of the polis, Sourvinou-Inwood (2000: 22) concludes that the Greek polis both articulated religion and was articulated by it because religion became the polis' central ideology, 'structuring and giving meaning to all the elements that made up the identity of the polis, its past, its physical landscape, the relationship between its constituent parts'. She emphasises the importance of rites and stories for the maintenance of group solidarity and the perpetuation of civic and cultural as well as religious identity both in the archaic and the classical polis, especially in times of crisis. As she points out, it was the popular perception that to maintain the relationship with its gods was the way in which the polis guaranteed its existence.

Particularly interesting for a sociologist is Sourvinou-Inwood's analysis of the categories of polis cult based on the status category of the worshipping group. Perhaps the most important for our argument here are the 'central polis cults', which encompass the whole polis. These are cults of civic divinities that protect the polis and are symbolically, geographically and politically located in the Shilsian centre. One set of cults of this group tended to be focused on the Agora, the civic and social centre of the state, whilst in many poleis, the common hearth of the city, the altar-hearth to Hestia, was located in the administrative centre, the prytaneion, or city hall. Centrally located, also, were those of deities presiding over central polis institutions.

The hero cults were the other important civic guardians with associated festivals and rites focused on the imagined graves of mythical figures and heroised founders of cities in a manner analogous to the patron saints of the cities of Medieval Europe, and tended to be centrally located. Moving out from the symbolic centre, each significant social grouping was defined and identified by the cults in which they could and could not participate. Political identity was therefore articulated by the degree of joining and cults were defined according to whether they were restricted to polis members only, whether they admitted strangers, or whether they existed to express the interaction with other polis groupings.[3]

FOUNDATION MYTHS AND POLITICAL REPRESENTATION

We have identified the architectural and sociological setting in which meanings were carried within the community. As Malkin (1987) observes, the closer to the centre of Greek cities we approach, the more cults are focused around guardians of the cities' security, continuity and identity. Established and maintained through cults, the symbolically charged messages were solemnised, interpreted and iterated in archaic and classical eras by way of festivals, games, funerary orations and epinician poetry. By the time of the rhetor Isocrates (436–338 BC) and his pupils, speechwriters, orators, pamphleteers and historiographers as well as dramatists had shaped the myth-symbol complex in Athens into a widely recognised ideology, as did the literati for other city-states.

In his review of the evidence, Nilsson concludes that although myths were not used as ritual texts by Greek peoples, they 'were the chief content of the hymns and choral odes sung at the festivals of the Gods' (1951: 11). Myths played a fundamentally important political role as well as acting as strategic social signifiers. Within states they had to be used with caution by elites since they were charged with local, regional, class and status meanings. They helped define and negotiate power relations between status groups. As heroes represented city-states, so peoples, gentes, families, craft groups and other social subdivisions maintained their own special patrons among the gods. However, myths were widely and creatively used to mediate and realise political relations with other peoples and states, both within Greek-speaking communities and with those they came into contact with beyond.

This combination of cityscape, architecture, cult, religion and politics became enhanced in the classical polis where the state gained authority in and control over all cults (Sourvinou-Inwood 2000: 24). With the new Athenian self-definition of humanism, democracy and the protector of those in need carried by the figure of Theseus in contrast to the older and more rooted cult figure of Heracles (Nilsson 1951: 53), cults and mythological representations were developed through the Acropolis, the Panathenaia and the burial of the war dead (Nilsson 1951; Loraux 1986).

Greeks interpreted hero mythology as their ancient history. Because foundation heroes were tied to particular peoples in particular territories as distinct from the gods who tended to serve as a shared symbolic currency, heroes were of particular importance to politics, history and ethnicity. Heroic myths tended to have an important charter function; poleis founded claims to territory on myth. By the fourth century BC, historians, politicians and rhetors were aware of the unbelievable nature of the stories and tried to rationalise them, yet the political messages carried remained as important as ever.

Since the issue of whether Greeks and Romans believed their own myths has caused such debate, especially in the wake of modernist challenges to the truth or otherwise of national traditions and their invention, it is perhaps worth illustrating the point with an example, that of the most famous speech of the greatest Athenian propagandists, the rhetor and speech writer Isocrates. His *Panegyricus* was written to be read to the Greeks assembled at the Olympic games in 386 BC. Isocrates was well aware of the difficulties myths presented for credibility and in a later speech, the *Panathenaicus*, he explicitly dissociates himself from the lies of mythical and miraculous tales (Nilsson 1951: 90). Yet, the *Panegryricus* is contrived to reinforce strategically important mythological truths for the Athenian people. We will draw attention to only two. He begins his speech by iterating a well-rehearsed set of mythological claims at the heart of Athenian self-definition: 'the Athenians as autochthons, that they have not driven out others, and that they are not a people mixed of many' (Nilsson 1951: 90). As Nilsson demonstrates, this mindset of the Athenians is so well established that public figures feel called on to reinforce it on public occasions to such an extent that it can be regarded as a political paradigm.

Isocrates reminds his Panhellenic audience that the Athenians had saved the children of Heracles, the Heraclidae, and protected them in their hour of need so that later they could go on to conquer the Peloponnese and found Sparta. In this he is reinforcing a series of interlinked Athenian mythologically rooted claims, of which he reminds his audience: that Athenians were the first to institute laws and society and having done so had been able to open their city to protect people in need from wrong. This is a pointed reproach against the Spartans who, having been protected and helped in their foundation days by the Athenians, should have now had the ingratitude to make war on Athens.

Foundation myths were keystones of the political ideologies of city-state of the ancient Mediterranean world from archaic times to the late Roman Empire. As Plutarch notes in a much-quoted sentence, 'the beginning is the greatest thing in everything, but especially in the establishment and founding of a city' (Plutarch, 8.321). The story of foundation linked the people by charter to the land they occupied, explained the context of the social order that was familiar to them and provided exemplars and precedents for conduct, especially in times of crisis. To adapt Mary Douglas, myths are good to think with (Douglas 1966).

In this, the issue of autochthony was of strategic interest. By the classical period it had come to mean 'indigenous' rather than 'earthborn', in contrast to *epelus* meaning immigrant or foreigner.[4] To the Athenians of the fifth and fourth centuries BC the autochthonous myth helped sustain the ideology of 'exclusivity of the native population, contempt for foreigners, and the elimination of the role of women in the reproduction of the race' (Konstan 2001: 40). Nilsson agrees that the opposition of autochthony and conquest was central to assumptions about claims to territory for Greek peoples since few had inhabited their territories for long periods and only the Athenians and Arcadians made claims to primordial attachments. In contrast, the Dorians of the Peloponnese were sensitive to the issue of how they acquired their territory and justified it through myth for 'they never appealed to mere force, but the war whose result was conquest must needs be a *justum bellum* ... the conquest once made, the right of possession was inherited by the descendants to the latest age'.[5] For most Greek peoples, colonisation and settlement were, if not within historical memory, at least evoked by the oral traditions of their communities through the cult of the *oikist*, the founder hero, celebrated annually with sacrifices and athletic games. Indeed, it has been suggested that anxieties and guilt surrounded the whole process of colonisation (Dougherty 1993), conquest and amalgamation with native populations, both through the separation of the settler community from its mother city and the violence that ensued. In any event the process was rationalised and explained by later generations, typically by the device of a ruptured genealogy or by a founder hero who was either married or whose child married an eponymous native.[6]

THE ROMAN FOUNDATION MYTH

The Roman city-state emerged into historical and literary consciousness in the Hellenic period some 400 years after its own postulated foundation, and as it became an increasingly powerful force in Mediterranean politics its elites relied on Greek artists, philosophers, teachers and rhetors to help shape their representations of power and authority (Gruen 1993). From the time of the second Punic War to the reshaping of the city under Augustus, Rome grew as an ideal, a personification, and a memory: a cityscape formed through art, architecture, cult and story until eventually, and consciously, linked with the cult of the Emperor.[7]

In this, the civic cults were key. As Woolf (1994: 120) reminds us, 'Roman identity was based to an unusual degree on membership of a political and religious community'. Roman religion was essentially practical and civic, with public cults and attendant festivals, games, processions and theatrical displays and managed by public officials rather than professional priests (for a useful introduction, see Rives 2000: 247–57). As Rome grew in importance its sacred centre, focused on the Capitoline hill with the Capitoline triad (an essentially Roman combination of cults to Jupiter Optimus Maximus, Juno and Minerva), gained symbolic resonance by the appropriation and adaptation of cults of peoples it conquered or came into contact with by synoecism (Nilsson 1951: 23–4) or absorption since 'the Romans showed proper deference to the deity of an enemy state but carried off her image anyway, consecrating it afresh and providing a new sanctuary' (Gruen 1993: 87).

How the foundation myths were linked to the cultic centres is still uncertain. Through festivals, games, funeral orations and processions, stories were adapted and iterated for political purposes. However, the role of theatrical displays, votive games, drama and praise poetry seems to have been of central importance (Gruen 1993: 195–220; Wiseman 1998; Champion 2003; Galinsky 2003) until the first permanent theatre built by Pompey was established.

It is entirely possible that representations of the strands of foundation myth of Rome, the Romulus and Remus stories, the legends of the seven kings, and the Aeneas journey, are all derived from Greek models, as well as the minor stories such as those of Odysseus and Evander. As in Athens, however, the use of heroes for domestic purposes had to be cautiously managed because of the charged class and status connotations (see, for example, Wiseman 1995). As late as Augustus, for example, great families avoided linking their household foundations with Romulus and Remus and when finally Augustus contemplated such a move, it was through Quirinius, the deified representation of Romulus, that it was achieved. Not so the Aeneas stories. By adopting a Trojan identity and weaving stories and genealogical links, the Roman elites gained status and self-esteem in the Hellenic world until they, too, came to believe themselves dominant both culturally and politically (Gruen 1993: 21–51).

CONCLUSION

It has been recently said of Anderson's idea of the nation as an imagined community that critics, by focusing on the adjective rather than the noun, have failed to note sufficiently the Romantic connotations of Anderson's use of the word community. By imagining communities in terms of cooperation, belonging, cohesion and consensus rather than recognising other constructions, such as communities constituted through conflict, we are failing to explore how 'different conceptualisations of community shape the nationalisms modelled on them' (Creed 2004: 58). Creed suggests that this Romantic inheritance of European nationalism and its communal model is perhaps one reason why there has been such bloodshed. He calls for a focus on the 'foundation notion of community' of political groups, in particular their rituals and symbolic expression, as a means to understanding how violence is contained and managed in some communities and not in others (2004: 56).

In the case of the Athenian polis in the fourth century BC, the myths and images of Theseus, founder of synoecism and symbol of Athenian democracy and Athena, the latter linked in reliefs to decrees of alliance or proxima, became increasingly evident, replacing the anarchic and violent Heracles (Nilsson 1951; Loraux 1986: 282–3). According to Loraux, this Athenian 'imaginary' was most evident in the institution of the funeral oration where the community was represented, not only as one living corporate body but also in union with ancestors and those that died on its behalf. For Loraux this is an ideology in the proper Marxian use of the word. By shaping and reiterating abstractions representing unity, cooperation and willing submission, elites helped to mobilise power whilst disguising the reality of domination, division and exploitation. Since the regular iteration of this matrix of myths and symbols sustained the polity and enabled it to create an identity beyond that which could be imposed by force or bought by peace and prosperity, it can be seen to have been an effective *mythomoteur*. It was shaped in an era of ethnic revival of Greek peoples, and was given impetus and sharpened articulation by the wars with Persia. Central to it was the notion of autochthony.

This Athenian *mythomoteur* was likely to have had interesting material consequences. It has been suggested here that the peoples of the Mediterranean littoral shaped and reshaped themselves through cults. Put another way, they were also used to mobility and migration, for 'being brought from elsewhere (*epaktos*)' or in 'the state of being derived from another place (*eisagogimos*)' was normal

(Purcell 1990: 29). Yet the period between the sixth to the fourth centuries of ethnic revival among Greek peoples led to xenophobia and boundaries, with potentially damaging consequences for the survival and success of the Athenian state (Purcell 1990: 57–8).

Not so for Rome. Constituted by synoecism and conquest of other ethnies, its foundation stories are imbued with conflict, rule-breaking and violence to such an extent that they continued to embarrass those who recorded them. With a foundation myth that was neither linked to language nor common descent, but was grounded in membership of political and religious communities, the stories all stressed the progressive incorporation of outsiders and continued to do so.

In a sociological discussion of the reasons for the failure of the polis to adapt, Runciman identifies three institutional advantages for Rome: the strength of the ties between patrons and clients; the successful extension of citizenship within other Italian territories; and the frequent manumission of slaves (Runciman 1990: 357). Underpinning these institutional forms was a creative and flexible adaptability of group cohesion denied by the expectations of autochthony of the Athenian polis, with its concomitant democracy (Runciman 1990: 364–6). Purcell concurs with this conclusion. As he points out, 'the case for the system which rested on the mythos of autochthony seems strong' but in the end the involution and exclusiveness was its nemesis (Purcell 1990: 58).

From an ethnosymbolist point of view, this short review of the ancient Mediterranean world further shows: first, that ethnies have universal geographical and historical significance; and second, that myth-symbol complexes once shaped and absorbed into popular memory can resonate over considerable time periods with large political and social consequences. These arguments have generated much scholarly interest in both the social sciences and the humanities. As the editor of a recent book devoted to the theme of ethnicity in the ancient Mediterranean, quoting Smith, points out, ethnie are both mutable and durable. He continues, 'my view, happily shared by most of the contributors ... [is that we] should acknowledge primordiality as a historical force that derives its essence from long-term existence as a belief widely shared and functions in moulding attitudes and influencing actions (Malkin 2001: 16–17).

Gellner once observed that the substrate of human societies generates many surface possibilities of which nationalism is one rare manifestation (Gellner 1983: 34–5). It is Smith's ethnosymbolic contribution to an exploration of this substrate that makes ethnosymbolism one of the most significant approaches to nationalism in our time.

NOTES

1 See Burkert (1979) for one such discussion. Berger refers us to Halbwachs (1952) for the 'sharpest formulation' of this point in sociology. Not all find this emphasis on the polarity between formula and cult helpful in scholarship of the ancient world, leading to a call by Calame for its replacement with a general category of 'énonciations de la pensée symbolique' (Buxton 1994: 152). For more general discussions of society and memory, see Connerton (1989) and Fentress and Wickham (1992). For the Greek context, see Shrimpton (1997).

2 Malkin quotes Parker (1998) to the effect that where, when, and with whom you worship iterates and defines political identity among Greek peoples: 'the connection in Greek society between who you are and who you worship is absolutely pervasive'. As Malkin notes, this has implications for what Greeks actually meant by 'shared blood'.

3 As Sourvinou-Inwood (2000: 29) points out, the Greek cities were tribally articulated in much of what they did and so the cults of civic and hero deities were strategic because tribes 'and other polis subdivisions participated in the cults symbolising the unity of the polis because they reinforced the unity and defined the subdivisions as part of a symbolically potent whole.'

4 See Rosivach (1987) for Athenian autochthony. For a discussion of the significance of autochthony for Greek foundation myths in general, see Konstan (2001: 37–40).

5 Nilsson (1951: 14). The Dorian leaders were mythologised as the Heracleidae, the sons of Heracles. The Dorian incursion into Greece in the distant past was justified in several ways including the use of the mythic theme of the '*Return* of the Heracleidae'. The most famous, of course, of the Dorian groups were the Spartans. For an examination of Spartan use of myth to claims to their lands, see Malkin (1994).

6 Genealogies, kinglists and eponyms are strategic devices for foundation myths in traditional communities everywhere (Garman 2001) and since much space would be needed to do them justice the decision has been made to leave them out of this account. In the Greek context Thomas (1989) is a useful introduction. See also Malkin (1994: 6–17) for a challenging discussion of their sociological function, in particular his point that genealogy mediated between a people and precedents of past action.

7 On the growing symbolism of cityscape, see Purcell (1992) and Edwards (1996). For the Augustan appropriation, see Zanker (1988).

REFERENCES

Anderson, B. (1983), *Imagined Communities: Reflections on the Origin and Spread of Nationalism*, New York: Verso.

Antonaccio, C. (2001), 'Ethnicity and colonization', in I. Malkin (ed.), *Ancient Perceptions of Greek Ethnicity*, Cambridge, MA: Harvard University Press, 113–57.

Armstrong, J. A. (1982), *Nations before Nationalism*, Chapel Hill: University of North Carolina Press.

Armstrong, J. A. (2004), 'Definitions, periodisation and prospects for the *longue durée*', in M. Guibernau and J. Hutchinson (eds), *History and National Destiny: Ethnosymbolism and its Critics*, Oxford: Blackwell, 9–18.

Berger, P. (1973), *The Social Reality of Religion*, Harmondsworth: Penguin.

Burkert, W. (1979), *Structure and History in Greek Mythology and Ritual*, Berkeley: Berkeley University Press.

Buxton, R. (1994), *Imagining Greece: The Contexts of Mythology*, Cambridge: Cambridge University Press.

Champion, E. (2003), 'Agamemnon at Rome: Roman dynasts and Greek heroes', in D. Braund, D. and C. Gill (eds), *Myth, History and Culture in Republican Rome*, Exeter: University of Exeter Press.

Connerton, P. (1989), *How Societies Remember*, Cambridge: Cambridge University Press.

Creed, G. W. (2004), 'Constituted through conflict: Images of community (and nation) in Bulgarian rural ritual', *American Anthropologist*, 106, 1: 56–70.

Dougherty, C. (1993), *The Poetics of Colonization. From City to Text in Archaic Greece*, Cambridge: Cambridge University Press.

Douglas, M. (1966), *Purity and Danger*, London: Routledge.

Edwards, C. (1996), *Writing Rome: Textual Approaches to the City*, Cambridge: Cambridge University Press.

Eriksen, T. H. (2004), 'Place, kinship and the case for non-ethnic nations', in M. Guibernau, M. and J. Hutchinson (eds), *History and National Destiny: Ethnosymbolism and its Critics*, Oxford: Blackwell, 49–62.

Fentress, J. and Wickham, C. (1992), *Social Memory*, Oxford: Blackwell.

Galinsky, K. (2003), 'Greek and Roman Drama and the Aeneid', in D. Braund and C. Gill (eds), *Myth, History and Culture in Republican Rome*, Exeter: University of Exeter Press.

Garman, S. P. (2001), 'Foundation Myths', in A. S. Leoussi (ed.), *Encyclopaedia of Nationalism*, New Brunswick, NJ: Transaction Publishers, 97–101.

Gellner, E. (1983), *Nations and Nationalism*, Oxford: Blackwell.

Greenfeld, L. (1992), *Nationalism: Five Roads to Modernity*, Cambridge, MA: Harvard University Press.

Gruen, E. S. (1993), *Culture and Identity in Republican Rome*, London: Duckworth.

Halbwachs, M. (1952), *Les cadres sociaux de la mémoire*, Paris: Presses Universitaires de France.

Hall, J. (1997), *Ethnic Identity in Greek Antiquity*, Cambridge: Cambridge University Press.

Herodotus (1998), *The Histories*, tr. Robin Waterfield, Oxford: Oxford University Press.

Kirk, G. S. (1970), *Myth: Its Meaning and Functions in Ancient and Other Cultures*, Cambridge: Cambridge University Press.

Konstan, D. (2001), 'To Hellēnikon ethnos: ethnicity and the construction of Ancient Greek Identity', in I. Malkin (ed.), *Ancient Perceptions of Greek Ethnicity*, Cambridge, MA: Harvard University Press.

Loraux, N. (1986), *The Invention of Athens: The Funeral Oration in the Classical City*, Cambridge, MA and London: Harvard University Press.

Malkin, I. (1987), *Religion and Colonization in Ancient Greece*, Leiden.

Malkin, I. (1994), *Myth and Territory in the Spartan Mediterranean*, Cambridge: Cambridge University Press.

Malkin, I. (ed.) (2001), *Ancient Perceptions of Greek Ethnicity*, Cambridge, MA: Harvard University Press.

Nilsson, M. P. (1951), *Cults, Myths, Oracles, and Politics in Ancient Greece*, Lund: Gleerup.

Parker, R. (1998), *Cleomenes on the Acropolis: An Inaugural Lecture Delivered Before the University of Oxford on 12 May 1997*, Oxford: Clarendon Press.

Pausanias (1935), *Description of Greece*, Books VI–VIII, Cambridge, MA: Loeb Classical Library.

Plutarch (1970), *The Rise and Fall of Athens*, tr. Ian Scott-Kilvert, Harmondsworth: Penguin.

Purcell, N. (1990), 'Mobility and the polis', in O. Murray and S. Price (eds), *The Greek City: From Homer to Alexander*, Oxford: Clarendon Press, 29–58.

Purcell, N. (1992), 'The city of Rome', in R. Jenkyns (ed.), *The Legacy of Rome: A New Appraisal*, Oxford: Oxford University Press.

Rives, J. (2000), 'Religion in the Roman world', in J. Huskinson (ed.), *Experiencing Rome: Culture, Identity and Power in the Roman Empire*, London: Routledge, 245–75.

Rose, H. J. (1958), *Handbook of Greek Mythology*, 6th edn, London: Routledge.

Rosivach, V. J. (1987), 'Autochthony and the Athenians', *Classical Quarterly*, 37: 294–306.

Runciman, W. G. (1990), 'Doomed to extinction: The polis as an evolutionary dead-end', in O. Murray and S. Price (eds), *The Greek City: From Homer to Alexander*, Oxford: Clarendon Press, 347–67.

Shrimpton, G. S. (1997), *History and Memory in Ancient Greece*, Montreal: McGill-Queen's University Press.

Smith, Anthony D. (1986), *The Ethnic Origins of Nations*, Oxford: Blackwell.

Smith, Anthony D. (1999), *Myths and Memories of the Nation*, Oxford: Oxford University Press.

Smith, Anthony D. (2003), *Chosen Peoples: Sacred Sources of National Identity*, Oxford: Oxford University Press.

Sourvinou-Inwood, C. (2000), 'What is polis religion?', in R. Buxton (ed.), *Oxford Readings in Greek Religion*, Oxford: Oxford University Press, 13–37.

Thomas, R. (1989), *Oral Tradition and Written Record in Classical Athens,* Cambridge: Cambridge University Press.

Thomas, R. (2001), 'Ethnicity, genealogy, and Hellenism in Herodotus', in I. Malkin (ed.), *Ancient Perceptions of Greek Ethnicity*, Cambridge, MA: Harvard University Press, 213–33.

Will, R. (1925–9), *Le culte*, Paris: Félix Alcan.

Wiseman, T. P. (1995), *Remus: A Roman Myth*, Cambridge: Cambridge University Press.

Wiseman, T. P. (1998), *Roman Drama and Roman History*, Exeter: University of Exeter Press.

Woolf, G. (1994), 'Becoming Roman, staying Greek: culture, identity and the civilising process in the Roman east', *Proceedings of the Cambridge Philological Society*, 116–43.

Zanker, R. (1988), *The Power of Images in the Age of Augustus*, tr. A. Shapiro, Ann Arbor: University of Michigan Press.

Part IV

ETHNOSYMBOLISM IN
EASTERN EUROPE AND RUSSIA

Chapter 9

THE JEWS AND THE FORMATION OF MODERN NATIONAL IDENTITY IN POLAND

Joanna B. Michlic

———◁▷———

Although the problem of antagonism toward others has been a subject of empirical and theoretical studies for almost one hundred years (Sumner: 1906), theories of nationalism generally take for granted the other in the formation of national identity and nationalism. Still, some scholars from various fields including history, sociology and political psychology have in the last decade turned their attention to the other evaluated as a rival, adversary or enemy in the formation of modern national identity (Wingfield 2003: 1–18; Triandafyllidou 1997: 15–25). They contend that the external or internal other perceived as the enemy constitutes an important part of the process of formation and re-evaluation of national identity (Triandafyllidou 1997: 20–3; Kecmanovic 1996) and that in some cases an imagined threatening other can be as important in influencing the self-conception of the nation as an actual threatening other (Aho 1994: 3–15; Hertz 1988: 158–9).

This chapter is a brief overview of the dynamics of the internal other perceived as the threat to a modern nation based predominantly on the matrix of exclusivist ethnic nationalism. It focuses on the perception of the Jewish minority as the most harmful or threatening other in modern Poland since the rise of modern Polish exclusivist ethno-nationalism in the 1880s.[1] In order to systematically examine the nature, continuity and change of the concept of the internal other and assess its impact on national communities over a long span, it is vital to apply the ethnosymbolic approach to the study of nations and nationalism advocated by Anthony D. Smith (Smith 1986, 1991). Smith's two seminal articles on the relationship between culture and politics (1996: 445–58) and ethnic nationalism and the plight of minorities (1994: 186–98) provide a useful conceptual framework for the study of the role of the other in the formation and re-evaluation of modern national identity. In fact, Smith's argument about the use of ethnic symbols, myths and memories by ethno-nationalists in the project of purification of both culture and people that leads to cultural and social exclusion (Smith

1994: 191–6) is vital in the empirical examination of any internal others perceived as an enemy.

One difficulty in studying the other lies in the fact that it manifests itself in multifarious forms and intensities, fluctuating from one national community to another (Doob 1964: 256–7; Herle 1994: 30). Thus the other proves to be intractable like the subjective symbolic aspects of national identity: symbols, myths and memories that occupy a central place in the ethnosymbolic approach to national identity and nationalism. Yet, without the careful examination of the role of the internal other in these symbolic aspects of national identity, there is little chance of understanding why the other has been so central to and persistent in some national communities and so irrelevant to others. Furthermore, without looking closely into the relationship between the concept of the other and national symbols, myths and traditions, there is little chance of understanding the presence of the other in national discourse over a *longue durée*.

The concept of the threatening other appears more persistent and pronounced in nations in which ethno-nationalism had played a key role in the formation of modern national identity and had continued to dominate political culture over a *longue durée*. In such nations, the ethno-nationalist elites create a version of national mythology in which the internal other is closely interwoven with national symbols, myths and memories. In fact, in these nations the other constitutes a salient element of major national myths of decline, revival and rebirth: the other is defined as the culprit responsible for the political, cultural and economic decline of the nation in both past and present. It is also classified as the actual and potential obstacle in the process of revival of the nation in both the present and the future.

The internal other presented in this form is applied for a variety of social, political and cultural ends such as raising national cohesion, social and political mobilisation, delegitimisation of political opponents (Kecmanovic 1996: 31–7) and also the rationalisation and justification of anti-minority violence (Michlic 2000: 60–1). Thus without the study of the role of the other in the national myths and memories, there is little chance of understanding the inner world of ethnic conflicts and the phenomena referred to as 'paranoid' or 'pathological' forms of ethno-nationalism (Crowley 1995: 155) in which the persistence of negative prejudicial views held against minorities continues even when these minorities represent an insignificant percentage of the population.

The dominant beliefs towards the Jewish minority in communist Poland between 1945 and 1989 that were cultivated by segments of non-elites and communist political elites in which ethno-nationalism was strongly fused with communism are a good illustration of this phenomenon of 'pathological' ethnonationalism. The outburst of anti-Jewish sentiments during the first years of the political transformation that began in Poland in 1989 is another good example of the same phenomenon. This phenomenon could only be explained by looking back at the role of the perception of the Jew as the enemy in the formation of modern Polish national identity that began in the 1880s.

In the 1880s the core ethno-nationalist Polish movement National Democracy introduced anti-Jewish images and stereotypes into the national discourse. These anti-Jewish images and stereotypes were not new, but arose in the post-1864 period among Conservative, traditionalist, and Roman Catholic circles that also recycled older anti-Jewish prejudices (Toruńczyk 1983: 1–15). However, in the case of the National Democracy, anti-Jewish concepts came to constitute one of the core aspects of its ideology (Walicki 2002: 22–41). Its key arguments were that Jews were not suited for integration into the Polish nation because they were culturally and ethnically alien and that furthermore they were an older and more powerful people than the Poles. Secondly, the National Democrats argued that alone among the ethno-cultural groups inhabiting the Polish territories, the Jews constituted a unique case, one that had in the past and could yet have in the future a disastrous impact on the Polish state and Polish national 'well-being'. The National Democrats thought that: (1) Jews were permanently engaged in the process of the Judaisation *(zażydzenie)* of the Polish universe, including its territory, economy, language, customs and traditions; (2) Jews were also traitors to the Polish national cause as they frequently represented foreign interests, especially those of the chief external Polish enemies, the Germans and Russians; (3) Jews were carriers of anti-Polish doctrines, values and norms such as freethinking, Socialism and Communism; and (4) Poland was an innocent and suffering victim of the Jewish invasion.

In the National Democrats' version of national mythology, these anti-Jewish tropes came to represent a powerful emotive tool of nation building. It contributed to a vision of Poland that lacked in tolerance of cultural and religious diversity in the face not only of the Jewish, but also of other minorities living in Poland.

However, in contrast to the image of other minorities, in the National Democracy's worldview the Jew signified the archetype of everything defined as 'not-Polish' or 'anti-Polish': the Jew was always characterised as the perpetrator vis-à-vis the Pole as the victim, and as a threat to all aspects of national life. Thus, polarisation between Poles (defined as an ethnic Catholic community) and Jews came to represent the key aspect of the modern collective self-definition of Poles (Steinlauf 1997: 14).

In his first major and most popular work, the so-called 'Bible of modern Polish nationalism' *Myśli nowoczesnego Polaka* (*Thoughts of A Modern Pole*), first published in 1902, Roman Dmowski, the founder of National Democracy, developed the theme of the Jew as the cause of all past and present misfortunes and weaknesses of the Polish nation, including the lack of a strong ethnic Polish bourgeoisie. The latter position was first crystallised in political and social thought in the writings of the eighteenth-century bourgeois thinker Stanisław Staszic, who had a significant influence on Dmowski. Dmowski used Staszic's social ideas for the purpose of awakening the modern Polish nation:

> Thanks to the Jews Poland remained a nation of nobles down to the middle of the nineteenth century and even longer as it is such in certain degree today. If they had not existed, a part of the Polish people would have organised itself to perform the social functions which they fulfilled and would have emerged as a rival force to the nobility as a third estate which has played such an important role in the development of European societies and has become the principal force in modern social life. (Dmowski 1904: 40)

Dmowski also introduced the theme of the Jew as the threat to the present and future Polish national existence and provided a carefully constructed explanation as to why the Jews could not be considered a part of the Polish nation-to-be. In this explanation a sense of fear of the other, intertwined with a sense of both inferiority and superiority, is transparent:

> We have to come alive and expand our existence [as a nation] in all aspects. Our aim should be to become a strong nation, one, which cannot be defeated. Where we can we should civilise foreign elements and expand our potential by absorbing these elements into our nation. Not only do we have a right to do so but this is also our duty ... Our national organism should absorb only those [foreign elements] that are capable of an assimilation that should serve to expand our growth and collective potential – a category Jews do not fall into. Their distinctive individuality that developed over hundreds of years does not allow us to assimilate their majority into our nation – our nation is too young and our national character has not yet fully been formed. In fact it is the Jews who are in a better position to assimilate our majority into their culture and even to assimilate a part of us in a physical sense. [The other reason we cannot assimilate them] lies in the character of their race, which has never lived in the way in which a society of our type has lived. [The Jews] have far too many characteristics that are alien to our moral code and that would play a destructive role in our lives. Mingling with the majority of them would lead to our destruction: the young and creative elements on which the foundation of our future existence depends would be dissolved by the Jewish elements. (Dmowski 1904: 214–15)

Dmowski also believed that an expulsion of the Jews from Polish territories would put an end to all social, economic and political troubles experienced in the late pre-independence period. In his project of purification of Jews from Poland, he was inspired by the medieval Spanish policy of the expulsion of the Jews; 'All Poland's troubles are the result of centuries of Jewish invasion. If we want to be a great independent nation, we must get rid of the Jews as the Spaniards did in the fifteenth century'.[2]

In *Kwestia żydowska, cześć I: Separatyzm Żydów i jego źródła* (*The Jewish Question Part I: Separatism in the Case of the Jews and Its Source*), Dmowski divided the Jewish community into two sections – the first and larger section comprised of Jews who were either religious or secular, both Socialist and Zionist, and the second smaller group comprised culturally assimilated Jews. Dmowski evaluated the entire first group as a hostile community that had consciously 'embarked on a battle' with the Polish nation, while the second group of culturally assimilated Jews he criticised for failing to transform themselves into 'proper, rightful Poles.' Their Polishness, according to Dmowski, was shabby, weak and untrustworthy. In contrast their Jewishness was overwhelming and transparent. Through their cultural activities and their works they were engaged in forcing Jewish ideas and values upon Polish Christian society.

> With the fast growing numbers of Jewish intelligentsia, the number of assimilated Jews has been expanding but has been losing its quality. This great production of assimilated Jews has shown signs characteristic of mass production, namely the superficial and shallow aspects. The numbers of Poles of Jewish origin have increased enormously but they have been shabby second-rate Poles …This intelligentsia has created its own Jewish sphere with a separate soul and separate attitude. Moreover, it has felt its power growing and therefore it has come to desire to force its own values and aspirations upon Polish society. (Dmowski 1909: 29)

In *Upadek Myśli Konserwatywnej w Polsce* (*The Fall of Conservative Thought in Poland*), Dmowski re-stated his previous position on assimilated Jews. For him the culturally assimilated Jew was a representative of characteristics totally incompatible with the Polish Catholic traditions and values. Thus, the culturally assimilated Jew, like the Orthodox Jew, was also identified as a force directed against the Polish nation, its traditions and its values. According to Dmowski, antagonism and incompatibility in a cultural, ethnic and racial sense were the key tenets of the relationship between Poles and Jews. Thus, the Jews as a collectivity were the enemy of both Polish society and Christian religion.

> The Jew cannot represent traditional aspects of European society, even when he insists on adopting such traditions. The entire tradition of European society

is alien to the Jew. Furthermore, it stands in opposition to all the values with which the Jewish soul converged during long centuries. The Jew despises the entire history of European people. He hates their religion and looks at their social hierarchy as a system that he can destroy and next take over. His instinct leads him towards the action aiming at the destruction of European respect for tradition and of European attachment to religion. (Dmowski 1914: 118–19)

Dmowski insisted that his outlook on Jews was not shaped by prejudice, but was based on objective grounds and by concerns over the fate of Poland – the revival of the nation and its polity. Thus the self-defence against the 'Jewish threat' was primarily codified as a necessity and could not be evaluated as morally and socially wrong. 'In spite of everything, I can honestly say that I do not feel hatred towards the Jews. And in general I am not guided in politics by hatred. I only care about Poland and its well-being, and regard it as my duty not to allow anyone to cause my country any harm'.[3]

Thus, at the end of 'the long nineteenth century', when the 'dream' of Poland regaining its independence was coming closer to realisation, the social belief in the Jew as the chief internal enemy emerged as a provider of answers to all the significant questions about the troubling aspects of social, political and economic life past and present. These perceptions of Jews gained in popularity among other political movements such as the modern peasant movement (Struve 2003: 103–26; Walicki 2002: 23–5) and among cultural elites and non-elites in the first decade of the twentieth century.

The concept of the Jew as the chief threat continued to exert a powerful influence during the post-independence period, 1918 to 1939. In fact, the inter-war period represented a turning point in terms of further development of this social construction and in terms of its impact on political culture, on Polish society at large, on the Jewish minority and on Polish–Jewish relations. By the end of the Second Republic, both non-elites and a significant section of the Polish political elites and the Roman Catholic Church perceived Polish Jews as the chief internal enemy of the Polish nation, harmful to all aspects of its development: political, economic, social and cultural. The post-independence era (1918–39) was also the first historical period in which Polish Jews experienced the full force of the most radical form of Polish exclusivist ethno-nationalism in action (Hagen 1996: 351–81). In the 1930s, the Polish government that was, in principle, against using violence as means of solving the so-called 'Jewish Question', had difficulty containing anti-Jewish hostilities organised and exercised by the radical offshoots of the National Democracy. The hostilities resulted in the deterioration of inter-ethnic relations between Poles and Jews, on local, national and also international levels, and in increasing the emigration of Jews from Poland to the Yishuv in

Palestine and to the West (Melzer 1997: 53–80, 131–53).

The representation of the Jew as the harmful alien to Poland and its nation did not undergo re-evaluation during and after the Nazi destruction of 90 per cent of Polish Jewry during the Second World War when Poland was occupied by the two totalitarian regimes of the Third Reich (1939–45) and Soviet Union (1939–41). Instead, it persisted in the underground ethno-nationalist political camp having an impact on ways in which a significant segment of the underground political and military elites related to Polish Jews throughout the war. As in the inter-war period, National Democracy and its offshoot radical organisations used the concept of the Jew as the threatening other most frequently and in the most elaborate form. The pre-1939 theme of Judeo-Bolshevism and Judeo-communism was further elaborated and adapted to the socio-political conditions of the Second World War.

With the exception of the left-wing clandestine anti-communist political parties such as Polish Socialist Party, the Democratic Party, and other smaller left-wing groups and members of the liberal intelligentsia, a significant segment of the clandestine political parties and organisations used the negative image of the Jew as a main reference in their discourse on Jews and the future Polish nation-state. They advocated the ethnically homogenous model of the post-war Polish nation-state as most desirable. They still continued to view the Jew as the chief impediment to the social and economic development of the ethnic Polish population. The prevalence of this ethno-nationalist perspective, which contradicted the official stance of the Polish government-in-exile based in London, was conducive to the process of excluding Polish Jews from the structure of the underground state, and from the fabric of society in the Nazi-occupied part of Poland, despite moments of unity between Poles and Jews that took place during the defence of Warsaw in September 1939.

The exclusivist ethno-nationalist perspective also had a noticeable impact on the ways a significant segment of underground political and military elites related to Jews as victims of Nazi extermination. As a result, these elites perceived Jews as a group of suffering human beings, but as being outside of the 'universe of national obligations', and in many cases as deeply inimical to Polish values, interests and existence. At the same time the majority of the Polish underground political elites disapproved of the Nazi extermination of Jews and condemned it as a 'barbaric and anti-Christian practice'. However, this position did not prevent instances of individual and group killings of Jews by extreme right-wing military units and also by civilians. The most severe case of anti-Jewish violence conducted by members of Christian Polish civilian population was the anti-Jewish violence of early July 1941 in the Łomża province in the North Eastern part of Poland (Gross 2002).

On the level of daily interaction between Poles and Jews, the image of the Jew as the harmful alien contributed to a range of indifferent attitudes towards Jews. This image was one of the main factors of low societal approval among the Christian Poles for the rescue activities of Jews (Steinlauf 1997; Gross 1988) – creating an atmosphere in which both Polish rescuers and rescued Jews lived in fear of not only the German occupiers, but also one's neighbors and acquaintances. In some cases, it was also conducive to an approval of the outcome of the Nazi genocide of Jews (not their methods), and to hostile actions towards fugitives.

The concept of the Jew as the chief threatening other continued to influence Polish political culture, attitudes and behaviour towards Polish Jews during the post-war Communist period (1945–89). This was already manifested in the immediate post-war period characterised by the stormy political situation (Paczkowski 1993; Kersten 1990, 1993) that resulted in the Communist takeover of power. In this period the myth of the Jew as the threatening other was reinforced by the political situation and prevalent rumours of Jewish collaboration *en masse* (Judeo-communism) with the hated Communist party and the Soviet Regime.

The concept of the Jew as the enemy was expressed most strongly in the revival of the ethno-national myth of Poland's 'decline'. The dissemination of the image of Judeo-Polonia was one of the key factors that led to the outbreaks of anti-Jewish violence between 1945 and 1947 (Szaynok 1992; Engel 1998: 43–86; Cichopek 2000) and was also applied in the rationalisation and justification of this violence by the clandestine anti-communist elites and the key representatives of the Polish Roman Catholic Church (Michlic-Coren 2000: 50–9).

Later, in the 1960s, the concept of the Jew as the threatening other constituted a part of the language and imagery of the anti-Zionist campaign of 1968–99 (Stola 2000) that resulted in a forced exile of the majority of the remaining Polish Jewry in the post-war Poland. The core ethno-nationalist Communist elite led by Mieczyslaw Moczar interwove the themes of Judeo-Stalinism and Judeo-anti-Communism into their version of national myths of decline. They used the concept of Judeo-Stalinism as a means of cleansing the Polish communist party, the Polish United Workers' Party (PZPR), of the heritage of the Stalinist dark, infamous years 1949–53 by attributing its errors to solely the communist Jews. They also created the concept of Judeo-anti-Communism in order to show that the communist Jews were solely responsible for the inadequacies of the Communist system from 1945 to 1968. In this latter concept the Jew turns into the ideological enemy of Polish communism. Thus, the Jew becomes 'the anti-Polish Communist' who prevented the development of the 'correct' version of Polish communism that would have brought about the economic and social rebirth of the nation in the post-war period. The concept of the 'Jew as the anti-Polish communist' was the only original aspect of the ethno-nationalist Communist version of the representation of the Jew as the threatening other. Apart from it and the socialist lexicon in which the myth was expressed, the themes of the ethno-nationalist Communist version of the Jew as the threatening other did not differ much from the major themes advocated earlier by anti-Communist right-wing political elites.

In the 1970s and 1980s, the Communist regime employed the concept of the Jew as the threatening other against political opposition: the Committee for the Defence of the Workers (KOR) and the first Solidarity movement *Solidarność*. Finally, the same image of the Jew re-emerged openly in the anti-Communist camp, particularly in the right-wing sections of the Solidarity movement and in the circles of the so-called Closed Catholic Church (Michlic 2004: 461–76) during the political and economic transformation of Poland in 1989 and 1990, which led to Poland's regaining full sovereignty.

Various themes of the Jew as the threatening other were once again interwoven with national myths, memories and symbols and in such a form appeared in the press and public discourse of the time. The disseminators of the national myths of past and present decline blamed the Jews for the decline of Poland during the Communist period and for hindering the political and economic transformation of 1989–90. Another version of this myth claimed that the Jews might prevent the future development of a great Polish nation. As in the past, the disseminators of the myth referred to the Jew as the pernicious enemy of Poland and its people, as the exponent of international finance, and also as the carrier of cosmopolitan and spiritually debased Western values.

Anti-Jewish sentiments reached their peak during the first free presidential election of the late 1990s (Kula 1991: 21–54). In the presidential race, right-wing anti-Communist political circles labeled Mazowiecki, the leading member of the progressive Catholic intelligentsia and the chief opponent of Lech Wałęsa, as a Jew. One high-ranking Roman Catholic clergyman subjected Mazowiecki to a thorough investigation into his family genealogical tree. He accused Mazowiecki of having Jewish ancestry and thus of being a 'hidden Jew' (Gebert 1991: 723–55).

Various surveys conducted during the 1990 presidential election also indicated that anti-Jewish sentiments enjoyed a significant public acceptance. For example, according to one survey, 50 per cent of Lech Wałęsa's electorate and 25 per cent of Tadeusz Mazowiecki's electorate were convinced that 'Jews had too much power in Poland' (Gebert 1991: 727). Some schoolchildren, living in the capital, who were unlikely to have had any interaction with members of a Jewish community in their lives, also shared the opinion that 'the Jews wanted to govern Poland and wished to have power over the Poles'. Their negative attitudes towards Jews were rooted in the ethno-national mythology. According to one poll conducted in three Warsaw high schools, 25 per cent of the interviewed children expressed such views (Tuszyńska 1990: 3–26). This indicates that these children absorbed these views through their families, schools and the mass media.

The sudden, intense and widespread outburst of anti-Jewish mood in the newly free, sovereign post-Communist Poland shocked many members of the Polish liberal, left-wing and progressive Catholic intelligentsia, as well as members of the minute Jewish community in Poland that constitutes less that 1 per cent of the population. An inquiry about the nature of Polish anti-Semitism and about the concepts of Polish national identity followed this first reaction of astonishment and shock. In the sea of conflicting views about anti-Semitism and its scope in Polish society, claiming it either as a salient or as an irrelevant social issue, some scholars began to point to the historical connection between the contemporary anti-Jewish sentiments and the pre-1939 historical period (Kula 1991: 45–9). They began to attribute the recurrence of anti-Jewish sentiment in the 1980s and early 1990s to the heritage of the inter-war period and concluded that 'what has once entered the cultural subconscious cannot easily be removed' (Ambrosiewicz-Jacobs and Orla-Bukowska 1998: 267).

Still, in the new post-Communist Poland important groups of public intellectuals, politicians, and Roman Catholic laymen and clergymen representing the Open Catholic Church have critically discussed, deconstructed and removed the perception of the Jew as the threatening other from contemporary national myths, symbols and memories. Members of non-elites, particularly youth engaged in activities such as 'Colorful Tolerance' and affiliated with organisations such as the Wroclaw-based scholarly circle of students called *Hatikva-Nadzieja,* have also rejected the anti-Jewish ideas in the national discourse.[4]

This process of challenging and deconstructing the perception of the Jew as Poland's threatening other constitutes part and parcel of the most salient post-1989 development that is called the rebuilding of Poland on the model of civic nationalism that does not define Polishness in a narrow ethno-national sense and that treats with respect the variety of cultures and faiths of minorities that had dwelled and still dwell on the Polish territories, and their memories. Good illustrations of this development can be found in the declarations of the first non-communist prime minister Tadeusz Mazowiecki (1927–). In one of his parliamentary speeches in 1989, Mazowiecki, a politician and writer representing the liberal Catholic intelligentsia in the first Solidarity movement, insisted that:

> The Polish state cannot be an ideological or religious state. It has to be a state in which no citizen would experience discrimination or would be treated in a privileged way because of his ideological convictions ... The government wishes to cooperate with the Roman Catholic Church and all other denominations in Poland ... Poland is a homeland of not only Poles. We live on this

land together with representatives of other 'national groups'. The government wishes that they would see themselves as a part of Poland and would cultivate their languages and their cultures, and thus enrich our common society.[5]

Another good illustration of the connection between the deconstruction of the concept of the Jew as the threatening other and the process of rebuilding Poland on the model of civic nationalism is the new language used in references toward Jews, past and present, by leading politicians such as Aleksander Kwaśniewski, former President of Poland (1995–2005), representatives of state institutions and representatives of important social and religious institutions (Polonsky and Michlic 2004: 40–2, 130–2, 155–65). Their description of the Jews as 'Polish Jews,' 'our co-citizens' and 'co-stewards of this land' reflects the inclusion of the Jews into the realm of Polishness (Michlic 2002: 29–32) and their firm rejection of ethno-nationalist myths and memories of Poland in which there is only room for a single culture and a single faith, ethnic Polish and Roman Catholic. Champions of civic and pluralistic Poland in the post-communist era often refer to the cultural traditions of the pre-modern, multi-ethnic and multi-religious Jagiellonian Poland (1386–1572) as a historical heritage (Świeżawski 2000: 145–146) on which the new post-1989 civic and pluralistic Polish society could be built and which would constitute an alternative to the ethno-nationalistic model of society rooted in the late nineteenth century.

The post-1989 developments reveal that the question of 'what Polishness do Poles need?' is an essential issue for contemporary Polish society and that it is still open to contestation. The deconstruction of the representation of the Jew as the threatening other and its removal from national myths, memories and symbols constitutes one of the key features of the project of building the forward-looking optimistic civic and pluralistic Poland. In this new project the components of national myths, symbols and traditions are reselected, recombined and re-codified, new cultural elements are added and thus new understanding of collective traditions and myths are encouraged.

In the post-1995 period, the civic model of Poland has reached a level of confidence and influence that it has never had before. This development indicates that vital changes have been taking place in the realm of Polish national identity, its national symbols, myths and memories: the Jew as the threatening other has begun to be deconstructed and thus disposed of from national memories, myths and symbols by the champions of civic and pluralistic Poland. The present study of the evolution of Polish national memories, myths and symbols has shown the usefulness of the ethno-symbolic approach for understanding national identity in Poland, and for assessing the scope of recent changes in Polish national identification and their parameters.

NOTES

1 This chapter includes arguments put forward in J. B. Michlic J. B. (2006), *Poland's Threatening Other: The Image of the Jew from 1880 to the Present*, Lincoln: Nebraska University Press.

2 Quotation of Roman Dmowski's statement from *Gazeta Warszawska*, 19 April 1935, cited in Rabinowicz 1965: 184.

3 Roman Dmowski, Speech of 1 October 1912, cited in Nowaczyński 1921: 238.

4 *Kolorowa Tolerancja* is a social initiative of high-school youth that began in Łódź in 1999. One of its main actions is to clean anti-Semitic and racist graffiti in Łódź and other cities. *Hatikva* is a Hebrew name for hope and *nadzieja* is a Polish name for hope. The organisation Hatikva-Nadzieja was established in 2000 as an educational circle at the University of Wrocław. I thank Joanna Czernek, a member of Hatikva, for discussing with me the aims of the organisation.

5 Speech of Tadeusz Mazowiecki made in the Polish parliament in August 1989, cited in Rev. Czajkowski, M., 'Chrześcijanin na trudne czasy', *Tygodnik Powszechny*, 28 August 2003, 1.

REFERENCES

Aho, J. (1994), *The Thing of Darkness. A Sociology of the Enemy*, Seattle: University of Washington Press.

Ambrosiewicz-Jacobs, J. and A. M. Orla-Bukowska (1998), 'After the fall: Attitudes towards Jews in post-1989 Poland', *Nationalities Papers*, 2, 256–72.

Cichopek, A. (2000), *Pogrom Żydów w Krakowie 11 sierpnia 1945 r.*, Warsaw: Żydowski Instytut Historyczny.

Crowley, J. (1995), 'Minorities and majoritarian democracy: The nation-state and beyond', in K. Benda-Beckman and M. Verkuyten (eds), *Nationalism, Ethnicity and Cultural Identity in Europe*, Utrecht, Netherlands: European Research Centre on Migration, 145–62.

Dmowski, R. (1904), *Myśli nowoczesnego Polaka*, Warsaw: Warszawska Spolka Wydawnicza.

Dmowski, R. (1909), *Kwestia żydowska. Separatyzm Żydów i jego źródła*, Warsaw: Gazeta Warszawska.

Dmowski, R. (1914), *Upadek Myśli Konserwatywnej w Polsce*, Warsaw: Warszawska Spółka Wydawnicza.

Doob, L. W. (1964), *Patriotism and Nationalism: Their Psychological Foundations*, New Haven: Yale University Press.

Engel, D. (1998), 'Patterns of anti-Jewish violence in Poland, 1944–1946', *Yad Vashem Studies*, 26, 43–86.

Gebert, K. (1991), 'Anti-Semitism in the 1990 Polish presidential election', *Social Research*, 58, 723–55.

Gross J. T. (1988), *Upiorna dekada: trzy eseje o stereotypach na temat Żydów, Polaków, Niemców i komunistów*, Crakow: TAiWPN Universitas.

Gross J. T. (2002), *Neighbors. The Destruction of the Jewish Community in Jedwabne, Poland*, New York: Penguin.

Hagen, W. (1996), 'Before the 'Final Solution': Toward a comparative analysis of political anti-semitism in Inter-War Germany and Poland', *The Journal of Modern History*, 68, 351–81.

Herle, V. (1994), 'On the concepts of the "Other" and the "Enemy"', *History of European Ideas*, 19: 1–3, 27–34.

Hertz, Aleksander (1988), *The Jews in Polish Culture*, Evanston, IL: Northwestern University Press.

Kecmanovic, D. (1996), *The Mass Psychology of Ethno-nationalism*, New York and London: Plenum Press.

Kersten, K. (1990), *Narodziny systemu władzy. Polska 1943–1948*, Poznań: SAWW.

Kersten, K. (1993), *Między wyzwoleniem a zniewoleniem Polska 1944–1956*, Londyn: Aneks.

Kula, M. (1991), 'Problem postkomunistyczny czy historycznie ukształtowany problem polski?', *Biuletyn Żydowskiego Instytutu Historycznego w Polsce*, 4, 21–54.

Melzer, E. (1997), *No Way Out. The Politics of Polish Jewry 1935–1939*, Cincinnati: Hebrew Union College Press.

Michlic-Coren, J. (2000), 'Anti-Jewish violence in Poland, 1918–1939 and 1945–1947', *Polin*, 13, 34–61.

Michlic, J. (2002), 'Coming to terms with the "Dark Past": The Polish debate about the Jedwabne Massacre', *Acta. Analysis of Current Trends in Anti-Semitism*, 21, 1–47.

Michlic, J. (2004), 'The 'Open Church' the 'Closed Church', and the discourse on Jews in Poland, 1989–2000', *Communist and Post-Communist Studies*, 37, 461–76.

Nowaczynski, A. (1921), *Mocarstwo anonimowe: ankieta w sprawie żydowskiej*, Warsaw: Perzynski Niklewicz.

Paczkowski, A. (1993), *Zdobycie władzy 1945–1947*, Warsaw: Wydawnictwo Szkolne i Pedagogiczne.

Polonsky, A. and J. B. Michlic (eds), (2004), *The Neighbors Respond. The Controversy over the Jedwabne Massacre in Poland*, Princeton and Oxford: Princeton University Press.

Rabinowicz, H. M. (1965), *The Legacy of Polish Jewry*, New York: Y. Yoseloff.

Smith, Anthony D. (1986), *Ethnic Origins of Nations*, Oxford: Blackwell.

Smith, Anthony D. (1991), *National Identity*, Harmondsworth: Penguin.

Smith, Anthony D. (1994), 'Ethnic nationalism and the plight of minorities', *Journal of Refugee Studies*, 7: 2/3, 186–98.

Smith, Anthony D. (1996), 'Culture, community and territory: the politics of ethnicity and nationalism', *International Affairs*, 72: 3, 445–58.

Steinlauf, M. C. (1997), *Bondage to the Dead. Poland and the Memory of the Holocaust*, New York: Syracuse University Press.

Stola, D. (2000), *Kampania antysyjonistyczna w Polsce 1967–1968*, Warsaw: Instytut Studiow Politycznych Polskiej Akademii Nauk.

Struve, K. (2003), 'Gentry, Jews and peasants: Jews as Others in the formation of the modern Polish nation in rural Galicia during the second half of the nineteenth century', in N. Wingfield (ed.), *Creating the Other. Ethnic Conflict and Nationalism in Habsburg Central Europe*, New York, Oxford: Berghahn Books, 103–26.

Sumner, W. G. (1906), *Folkways: A Study of the Sociological Importance of Usages, Customs, Mores and Morals*, Boston, MA: Ginn.

Świeżawski, Stefan (2000), *Lampa wiary. Rozważania na przełomie wieków*, Kraków: Znak, 145–6.

Szaynok, B. (1992), *Pogrom w Kielcach 4 Lipca 1946*, Wrocław: Bellona.

Toruńczyk, B. (1983), *Antalogia myśli politycznej 'Przeglądu Wszechpolskiego (1895–1905)'*, London: Aneks.

Triandafyllidou, A. (1997), 'Nationalism and the threatening Other: The case of Greece', *The ASEN Bulletin*, 13, 15 – 25.

Tuszyńska, A. (1990), 'Nie jestem rasistką', *Kultura*, 513, 3–26.

Walicki A. (2002), 'Naród i terytorium. Obszar narodowy w myśli politycznej Dmowskiego', *Dzis*, 7, 22–41.

Wingfield, N. (ed.) (2003), *Creating the Other. Ethnic Conflict and Nationalism in Habsburg Central Europe*, New York and Oxford: Berghahn Books.

Chapter 10

LEV GUMILEV AND RUSSIAN NATIONAL IDENTITY DURING AND AFTER THE SOVIET ERA

Mark Bassin

———◁▷———

The importance of geographical space to the constitution of nationhood is universally recognised. All nations associate themselves with a portion of territory that they identify as their own national 'homeland' – the region where the group came into existence, underwent its formative historical experience, and over which it believes it is naturally entitled to patrimonial rights. Among other things, this homeland vision has profound ideological resonances, the significance of which is insightfully discussed in Anthony D. Smith's work on ethnosymbolism. Smith emphasises the critical function of 'nationalised' territory in providing a locus of identity for the group, and shows how 'homeland memories' work to bind the group together psychologically. The shared belief in a land of common origin, he suggests, is one of the most effective means of primordialising and indeed naturalising a vision of nationhood. (Smith 1999, 2001, 2002)

However, the territory-nation nexus, together with the associated notion of homeland, are not merely characteristic features of ethno-national identification. Beyond this, they can be and are deployed as important operational parts of the nationalist ideology itself. Considered from this standpoint, geographical space is not a material entity, a real-existing parcel of soil and water through which the group refracts and manipulates its self-image, but rather a discursive *subject* of the national imagination. As such, it is open to the same internal contestation, manipulation and debate as all other aspects of the identity structure. Thus, while all members of a given national community may believe they possess a homeland in common, they commonly identify it in different ways, using very different boundaries. And while all can agree that their nationhood involves some sort of emplacement in and connection to geographical space, the specific nature and meaning of these roots can be understood in very different ways.

This essay seeks to explore these latter points through a consideration of the ideological conflation of territory, landscape and ethnicity in the writings of Lev Nikolaevich Gumilev (1914–94). The scholar son of two of twentieth-century Russia's greatest poets, Anna Akhmatova and Nikolay Gumilev, who spent some thirteen years in Stalinist labour camps, Gumilev was an important intellectual figure. Throughout the 1960s and 1970s, Soviet anthropological science was intensively debating the nature of ethnicity and the dynamics of ethnic interaction. Although Gumilev's professional training was in history and archeology, he actively joined in this debate, formulating his own highly idiosyncratic theory of *etnos* and ethnogenesis. His ideas found no official acceptance; to the contrary, they were shunned and denounced in the strongest terms by the guardians of ethnographical canon (Kozlov 1978; Kozlov and Pokshishevskii 1973; Bromlei 1983: 213–14; 'Publikatsiia ...' 1995), and Gumilev himself remained professionally marginalised. His theories however were popular among some circles of the educated Soviet public. Since 1991, moreover, the celebrity and influence of his work have grown immeasurably, in Russia and across the former Soviet Union (Naarden 1996; Lavrov 2000; Laruelle 2000; Karel'skaia 2005). In this sense, the ideas examined in this essay remain very much alive and active today.

The first part of this essay considers the particular way in which Gumilev developed a 'scientific' theory of *etnos* as a landscape feature based on natural-ecological principles. It will then examine how he deployed these to draw focused political conclusions about inter-ethnic relations in the Soviet Union of his day.

ETHNICITY, GEOGRAPHY AND LANDSCAPE

In spite of the bitter excoriation visited upon Gumilev by the Soviet ethnographic establishment, their perspectives shared a common point of departure. Since the 1950s, Soviet ethnography had actively sought new ways of defining and representing its subject matter. Among other things, this involved a revision of traditional Soviet terminology, which invoked the key concepts of 'nation' and 'nationality' through an unwieldy and confusing plethora of designations: *narod, natsiia, narodnost', natsional'nost'* and so on. The key marker of the new approach was the introduction of the term *etnos* or ethnos, which on a conceptual level was intended to replace all others (Bromlei 1973, 1983; Skalnik 1986; Pimenov 2003). Thus it was from official ethnographic discourse that Gumilev took up the term, and in the same spirit he was concerned above all with identifying those qualities that made it a distinctive and unique form of human organisation.

Gumilev's perspectives on these issues, however, set him decisively apart from official perspectives, for his vision was founded on a profound and uncompromising essentialism. Ethnicity, he insisted, was a natural and not social phenomenon. Accordingly, it was to be explained solely in terms of the processes and laws of the natural world, and remained quite unaffected by the dynamics of social organisation (Gumilev 1994: 271). As sorts of natural organism, *etnosy* were entirely self-contained entities, which moved through a common lifecycle of youth, maturity, and eventual decline. He called this lifecycle *etnogenez*, or ethnogenesis (Gumilev 1989: 250–89). The essential ethnic marker was a 'behavioural stereotype', created when the ethnic group came into existence and then passed on from generation to generation. Each behavioural stereotype was unique to a single group. The ethnic identity that it bestowed, moreover, was immutable. The stereotype itself did not change in any significant sense over the course of the ethnic lifecycle, and it could not be willfully modified. Gumilev argued that the behavioural stereotype was not biologically inherited but rather was learned in the course of infancy and early childhood. Once absorbed, however, it served as the existential parameter of the individual's ethnic persona. No one was able to surrender or renounce their personal ethnic stamp, nor could they become a genuine part of any other ethnic group (Gumilev and Ermolaev 1993: 178).

What exactly did Gumilev mean by characterising the *etnos* as a natural-organic entity? Although he frequently described the practice of endogamy, or marriage within the ethnic unit, as an important strategy for preserving ethnic cohesion, he believed as just noted that the all-important behavioural stereotype was not transmitted genetically but rather learned. He affirmed repeatedly that ethnicity could not be understood in strict racial-biological terms. Rather, he framed the relationship of the *etnos* to the natural world differently, in terms of an ecology of ethnicity. He developed this notion in two directions, which differed substantially in their argumentation and implications. On the one hand was his famous assertion – proclaimed in the title of his magnum opus *Ethnogenesis and the Earth's Biosphere* – that *etnos* was a component element of the biosphere (Gumilev 1989). Elaborating a grandiose vision of galactic dimensions, Gumilev claimed that the ethnic life of humankind was part of the biosphere's 'living matter' (*zhivoe veshchestvo*) and as such was driven ultimately by periodic *izlucheniia* or radiations of cosmic energy that penetrate from outer space down to the earth's surface. Alternatively, Gumilev identified the naturalism of the *etnos* more prosaically, in terms of its organic interrelationship with the 'geographical landscape' (*geograficheskii landshaft*). It is this second, as it were 'terrestrial' dimension of Gumilev's naturalist perspective that is of interest for our purposes.

Gumilev's ideas about the ecology of ethnicity drew heavily on the grand tradition of landscape science in Russia, which developed as an important branch of the earth sciences. In the late nineteenth century, the soil scientist V. V. Dokuchaev proposed a typology of discrete geographical macro-regions, in each of which the combined phenomena of the organic and inorganic realms – for example, geology, physiography, climate, flora and fauna – interconnected into a single network to create a cohesive and distinctive totality (Dokuchaev 1949 [1898–9]; Vucinich 1988: 154–5). Dokuchaev himself referred to these organically cohesive geographical regions as 'natural zones', but they eventually came to be designated using the German term *Landschaften*, or in Russian *landshafty*. These landscapes were identified as holistic parts of the ecological zones of tundra, taiga, mixed forest, steppe or prairie grasslands, and desert. The landscape concept was further developed in the twentieth century by the bio-geographer and evolutionary theorist L. S. Berg (Berg 1930), who stressed the dependency of organic life on the material conditions of the geographical environment as a critical factor shaping the course of evolution itself. To the extent that all organisms must adapt to their respective landscapes, Berg argued, they are fundamentally shaped by them.

> The geographical landscape affects organisms in *an imperative* (*prinuditel'no*) *manner*, compelling all the individuals, so far as the organisation of the species permits, to vary in a determined manner. There is no place here for chance: consequences follow with the same fatal constancy as chemical reactions or physical phenomena. If geographical conditions [in different regions] are identical or similar, then identical or similar results are bound to follow ... Tundra, forest, steppe, desert, mountains, aquatic environments, island life, life in lakes and seas: each of these natural environments stamps its mark on the organisms [that inhabit them]. Species that are unable to adapt [to their geographical environment] are obliged to emigrate into other geographical landscapes or to perish. (Berg 1969: 265 [original emphasis]).

This sort of holistic thinking about the intrinsic interconnection between organic life and geographical environment received new public attention in the 1960s, as part of a new interest in ecological problems in the Soviet Union (Weiner 1999: 312–73). This was the time that Gumilev was developing his ideas, and his thinking about ethnicity was shaped by these ecological precepts. All *etnosy*, he claimed, displayed a 'close interconnection with their respective geographical landscape', in the sense that each represented a 'necessary component part' of this landscape, 'interacting with its fauna and flora' (Gumilev 1994: 258, 268). Indeed, the natural-geographical landscape acted as a sort of vital platform for ethnic development, which 'shelters and nourishes' the *etnos*, thereby defining its most important life-parameters (Gumilev 2000: 182–3; 1991: 133). Critically, Gumilev conceived of this ecological interaction in terms of the same determinism expounded by Berg, and judged that an *etnos* was existentially dependent on the conditions and dynamics of an external geographical milieu (1976: 120). Indeed, Gumilev deferred explicitly and repeatedly to Berg's authority. He not only endorsed Berg's thesis regarding the dependency of organic life on its geographical environment, but also adopted it for his own purposes with the argument that those 'individuals' Berg spoke of as subject to environmental determination included entire *etnosy* as well. 'The geographical landscape influences ethnic processes in an compulsory manner' (Gumilev 1989: 173; 1993: 270). It was this existential dependence of ethnic groups on the conditions of the natural-geographical environment, Gumilev argued, that distinguished them from all forms of social organisation, for the latter were not subject to such dependency. Very much to the contrary, social development is driven by the forces of production and proceeded according to its own laws and dynamics, subject 'neither to geographical nor to biological influences' (Gumilev 1989: 37; 1976: 120).

Over the entirety of their life-histories, Gumilev maintained, ethno-organisms remained dependent on their respective geographical environments. Landscape conditioned the *etnos* in its most formative stage, in the sense that the process of ethnogenesis itself could only commence in regions that possessed significant landscape variability. This meant that certain geographical regions offered more favourable conditions for it, a point Gumilev illustrated through complex maps and tables correlating landscape zones to specific incidences of ethnogenesis in history. At the same time, this demonstrated his deeper point about the natural-geographical character of the entire process (Gumilev 1970a: 52–4; 2000: 292). From the moment of their formation, *etnosy* were compelled to adapt to the geographical conditions they encountered. The most important evidence for this was the respective behavioural stereotype itself, which was critically shaped by external environmental influences and which Gumilev identified as the 'highest form of adaptation (*adaptatsiia*)': 'The habits of everyday life, modes of thought, the perception of art objects, treatment of elder generations and relations between the sexes – all of these are conditional reflexes which enable the optimal adaptation (*prisposoblenie*) to the [geographical] environment ...' (Gumilev 1970: 50, 51; 2000: 29). Indeed, the geographical environment 'even shapes (*formirovat'*) aesthetic and moral values' (1994: 254). Ultimately, the diversity between ethnic groups is to be explained by their ecological dependency on landscape. There is after all great variation in the natural character of landscapes across the globe, and this ecological diversity will engender correspondingly diverse patterns of ethnic adaptation (Gumilev 1971: 82).

HOMELAND AS AN ECOLOGICAL NICHE

Building on this final point, Gumilev developed the notion of an 'ecological niche' to refer to the geographical region of origin for a given ethnic group. The latter's organic embeddedness in this particular region was the most fundamental condition of its existence. It was only here, fully and naturally integrated into a local ecological network or 'biocenosis', that an *etnos* could secure its survival in a normal and healthy manner. Its behavioural stereotype, its material culture, economy, *genre de vie*, and spiritual life were all inextricably tied to the specific natural-environmental conditions of its ecological niche. The natural-ecological emplacement of an *etnos* was moreover reinforced on the level of group psychology, which recognised and valorised its respective ecological niche as its native *rodina* or homeland. 'All *etnosy* have their homelands. The ethnic homeland is that mixed landscape region where it first took shape as a new system.' All *etnosy* 'have their own regions of origin, each defined by a unique combination of landscape elements. As such, this "homeland" represents one of the component parts of that system we call *etnos*' (Gumilev 1989: 180). The *etnos* was thus tied, ecologically and spiritually, to its respective home region, and its survival outside of this region for any protracted period of time was 'unthinkable' (Gumilev and Ivanov 1992: 54–5). Importantly, Gumilev argued that under normal conditions any given landscape zone could provide a niche for only a single *etnos*. Each *etnos* is attached to a 'different environing landscape' and therefore has undergone 'a different historical experience' (Gumilev 1995: 36).

Should the geographical conditions of its native landscape zone change, then the *etnos* is confronted with three choices: re-adapt, perish, or emigrate. Emigrant *etnosy* tend naturally to seek out landscapes resembling those they have left behind, but are almost always unsuccessful. In this case, once again three alternatives are possible. Commonly, the *etnos* simply perishes. Alternatively, under the formative influence of the natural conditions of a new landscape, it may be transformed into a new *etnos*, a process which often involves the amalgamation of several immigrant ethnic groups (Gumilev and Ivanov 1992: 54; Gumilev 1989: 132, 167). Gumilev presented a vivid example of this process in the case of Italy:

> All of the peoples who settled in Italy – Eutruscans, Latins, Gauls, Greeks, Syrians, Langobards, Arabs, Normans, Schwabians, and French – lost their former character (*oblik*) gradually, over two or three generations and combined to form an Italian mass, a distinctive and mosaic *etnos* with specific character traits, behavior, and structure ...' (1989: 173)

The third possibility was that the original *etnos* would survive the rupture with its ecological niche intact but at the cost of the fundamental deformation of its ethnic character. We will return to this latter process further on in this chapter.

On the basis of these ethno-ecological principles, Gumilev outlined a model of inter-ethnic contact and coexistence. In view of the essential individuality and mutual incompatibility of different ethnic groups, he maintained that they should avoid intermixing at all costs. 'Above all we must recognise the traditional boundaries – temporal as well as spatial – of our ethnic commonality, and clearly understand the boundary that divides members of our own group from everyone else (*gde svoi, a gde chuzhie*)' (1991: 141). He argued in this spirit that an *etnos* must remain within the boundaries of its native ecological niche. Doing so would make it possible for different groups to coexist 'physically separated (*rozno*) but in peace' (1995: 49–50). Respect for these boundaries and the inviolability of the behavioural stereotypes of all groups would assure that poly-ethnic agglomerations are able to maintain the diversity (*pestrota*) and 'mosaic quality' (*mozaichnost*) that is necessary to sustain the ecological integrity of each constituent member (Gumilev 1971: 82; 1991: 256; 1989: 479; 1994: 267; Gumilev and Ermolaev 1993: 130–1). Safely ensconced in their individuated ecological niches, adjacent *etnosy* may however develop mutual interrelations if they are drawn together naturally by shared inherent affinities and a native 'complementarity' (*komplementarnost*). Gumilev called the relationship that developed on the basis of genuine complementarity, a 'symbiosis'. Such an arrangement was the 'optimal form' of inter-ethnic contact, for it provided the basis for peaceful interaction, 'good neighbourliness' (*dobrososedstvo*) and genuine friendship (Gumilev 1994: 267; Gumilev and Ivanov 1992: 54). In the final analysis, only '*etnosy* that live on their own territorial homelands and remain faithful to their own tradition of their Fatherland' (*otechestvo*) could genuinely coexist with their neighboring *etnosy* (Gumilev 1995: 49).

As long as this ethno-ecological arrangement was maintained, Gumilev argued, the dynamics of symbiosis meant that ethnic diversity worked dialectically to bring the respective groups closer together. 'The more complex and diversified the collectivity of ethnic groups, the stronger it was, and more resistant to fracture.' Indeed, the affective affinities of symbiotic complimentarity could be strong enough to bond a poly-ethnic assemblage into a cohesive unit akin in certain respects to an *etnos* itself (Gumilev 1989: 133–4, 479). Gumilev termed this assemblage a *superetnos*. He believed that the historical experience of Russian-Eurasian civilisation provided a model of precisely that poly-ethnic harmony that comes from careful observation of the ethno-ecological principles he outlined. 'Already in ancient times,' he explained, 'the forms of ethnic symbiosis were very clearly manifested in the central part of the Eurasian continent. Different *etnosy* occupied different landscape regions that corresponded to their [different] cultural and economic skills.' These groups did not interfere with, but rather helped, each other, always careful to respect the others' ethnic integrity and the sanctity of its ecological niche. Thus, he maintained, the Great Russians settled in 'the azonal floodplains and meadow landscapes of the rivers of the boreal forest, where a unique symbiosis developed with the cow, which was used above all as a source of the organic fertiliser necessary for the infertile podzol soils of the forest' (Gumilev and Ivanov 1992: 55). They left the vast spaces of the steppe to the Turks – Kazakhs and Kalmyks – and Mongols, and the forests to the Ukrainians and Finno-Ugric peoples. In Siberia, the Yakuts settled in the broad floodplains of the Lena river, while the Evenks lodged in the expansive watersheds of the taiga, and Paleo-Asiatic peoples occupied the tundra (Gumilev 1989: 133–4; 2000: 292; Gumilev and Ivanov 1992: 55). Gumilev's scheme of ethno-geographical settlement may be over-generalised and in places plainly inaccurate, but the point he is trying to make is clear enough. Each ethnic group retained its organic connection with its respective ecological niche, and this pattern of natural emplacement conditioned the harmony that was characteristic – so Gumilev claimed – for inter-ethnic relations across Eurasia.

'ONE GIANT COMMUNAL APARTMENT'

Gumilev's speculations about the ecological foundations of ethnicity took on a specific political resonance in the context of shifts in the official nationality policy of his day. From the 1930s to the mid-1950s, the Stalinist policy of *druzhba narodov* or 'Friendship of the Peoples' had supported a sort of crypto-primoridialist vision of ethnicity, which resonated in significant ways with Gumilev's own perspective. National groups were idealised as homogenous entities possessing timeless and immutable ethnic essences, and based in primordial ethno-national homelands (Tillett 1969; Slezkine 1996; Martin 2001; Suny and Martin 2001). These premises began to be significantly realigned as part of the de-Stalinisation campaign begun in the late 1950s by Stalin's successor Nikita Krushchev. Khrushchev was convinced that the persistence of ethno-national identification within the Soviet population, and its encouragement through official policies such as *druzhba narodov*, represented a major obstacle to the political and economic modernisation and integration of the country. Instead, he insisted that the mutual assimilation (*sblizhenie*) and even amalgamation or fusion (*sliianie*) of the various Soviet nationalities should become an immediate goal of Soviet nationality policy. He advocated the elimination of ethno-national criteria in Soviet public life and the eventual dissolution of all ethnic groups through the creation of a single meta-national entity – an all-subsuming *sovetskii narod* or 'Soviet nation'. Indeed, at one point Krushchev took measures that directly contravened the ethno-territorial principle upon which Soviet federalism was based, by transferring jurisdiction over the Crimean peninsula from the RSFSR to the Ukrainian republics in the interest of 'rationalising' economic development (Hodnett 1967: 2–3; Rutland 1984: 158–9; Thompson 1989: 71; Simon 1991: 225, 254–5). Khrushchev's radicalism on these issues was modulated by his successors, all of whom spoke with greater discretion about inter-ethnic relations, made calculated concessions to ethno-national sensibilities, and were careful to use the provocative term *sliianie* with much greater caution. Despite this, however, the assimilationist impulse that he championed was not abandoned (Thompson 1989: 76–7). To the contrary, the vision of the *sovetskii narod* gained an ever more prominent place in public political discourses throughout the 1970s and 1980s (Veingol'd 1973; Kim 1975; Kaltakhchian 1976; *Sovetskii Narod* 1987).

For important sections of the Soviet Union's many nationalities, however, *druzhba narodov* had provided an important basis for political accommodation with the Soviet system, by offering a means of integrating into Soviet society while preserving – at least in principle – some measure of ethno-national individuality. For them, the new official discourse of assimilation and fusion were powerfully unsettling, and it served to excite and mobilise ethno-national sentiments across the board in the USSR in the 1960s and 1970s (Shanin 1989: 420; Simon 1991: 279–90ff.; Tolz 2001: 204; Pimenov 2003: 15). The sharpest edge of this ethno-nationalism developed among the non-Russian nationalities, who saw the homogenising *sliianie* project and the summons to blend into a putatively supra-national *sovetskii narod* as a thinly veiled resurrection of the Russifying chauvinism that the revolution of 1917 had been intended to overcome in the first place. As such, it represented a palpable threat to their ethnic survival. They were now joined, however, by ethnic Russians themselves. Across the decades of *druzhba narodov*, ethnic Russians as well had begun to become sensitised to the challenges to their own status as a discrete ethnic entity, effectively one of many who like everyone else in the USSR had to articulate their national identity and defend their national interests on an explicitly ethno-centric basis.

Against this background, the direct political thrust of Gumilev's scholarly and highly historicised ruminations about the ecological nature of *etnos* comes readily into focus. He shared the burgeoning concern with the assimiliationist overtones of official nationalities policy, and was obviously seeking to demonstrate the danger that this portended. As we have seen, he insisted on the absolute individuality of each ethnic unit, which necessarily meant that different *etnosy* were uncombinable. It was not that they were unable to coexist or interact in a harmonious manner – his notion of 'symbiosis' allowed precisely for this – but rather that they could not be 'fused' into a single unit without destroying their structural integrity. This point was obvious already in his first publications on the question of ethnicity (for example, 1971), but at this early date he was not able to formulate it in an explicit fashion. In his later work, however, from the *perestroika* period and thereafter, Gumilev was able to name his subject, and he seized the opportunity to deliver a withering attack on the *sliianie* project of the Soviet government. 'There are no good reasons for advocating a policy of assimilation and fusion ...Why should we try to squeeze the behavior of an Abkhazian and a Chukchii, a Lithuanian and a Moldavian into a single model?' Why indeed seek to create on planet Earth 'a single *etnos*' and a 'giant communal apartment?' (Gumilev 1994: 257, 293; 1995: 49–50).

'More than anything else,' Gumilev wrote in his final years, 'we must acknowledge the traditional boundaries – temporal and spatial – of our commonality with
our own particular ethnic community (*obshchnost'*), and clearly understand the
lines that separate us from all others' (Gumilev 1991: 141). Salvation could come
only from respecting and supporting the *mozaichnost'* or diversity that was naturally characteristic for ethnicity everywhere and represented the 'optimal form
for human existence' (Gumilev 1995: 36). In the final analysis, it was precisely this
diversity which throughout history has provided the 'plasticity enabling Homo
Sapiens to survive as a species on the planet Earth' (Gumilev 1971: 82; 1994: 256;
1995: 49–50).

Gumilev referred back to the scientific principles of his ethno-ecology to
reaffirm his argument against ethnic merging or *sliianie*. Given the absolute
dependency of *etnosy* on the geographical environment, he explained, it stood
to reason that the former can only be merged into a single entity if the physical
characteristics of the latter were uniform as well. 'The salvation of humankind lies
in [preserving] ethnic diversity,' he affirmed, for only this can allow each *etnos* 'to
establish relations with the natural world that are optimal for both sides. After
all, [natural-geographical] landscapes are diverse and the biocenoses in each of
them are unique: consequently the forms of [ethnic] adaptation to them must be
different in each case' (1971: 82). 'How can a single *etnos* be created for the entire
planet? This would require, at a minimum, the destruction of natural-climatic
zonality, the cyclical movement of the atmosphere, and the differences between
forest and steppe and – of course – those between mountains and valleys' (1989:
305; 1994: 293). Gumilev used this argument to reject the creation of a meta-*etnos*
in the Soviet Union. 'For the most part,' he observed, each of the *etnosy* of the
USSR 'occupies its own special ecological niche or ethno-landscape (*etno-land-
shaftniy* zone and has its own unique historical destiny, that is to say an original
behavioural stereotype and a particular tradition of interactions' with its neighboring *etnosy*. 'The merging (*sliianie*) of these groups,' he concluded, 'would be
possible only with the complete leveling of the various physical landscapes of the
country, which it must be acknowledged will not be achieved, even in a long-term
perspective' (Gumilev and Ivanov 1992: 54).

KHIMERA: ETNOS AS AN ECOLOGICAL PARASITE

Gumilev's rejection of meta-ethnic assimiliation and homogenisation spoke to
concerns shared by all Soviet nationalities in the post-Stalin period. At the same
time, however, he developed his ethno-ecological principles in a rather different
direction, in regard to an issue that was relevant more specifically to the Russian
nationalist revival of the 1960s and 1970s (Yanov 1978; Brudny 1998). Here

Gumilev mobilised his ecological vision of *etnos* and landscape in order to present an elaborate and highly tendentious perspective on an issue that had traditionally been one of the defining preoccupations for Russian nationalist ideology. This was the nature of the Jewish *etnos* and the significance of its relationship with the Russians in the past, present and future. The Jewish question was of immediate importance to Russian nationalism in the late Soviet period (Forster and Epstein 1974; Nudel'man 1979; Friedgut 1984; Woll 1989), and Gumilev's attention to it insured that his work would receive careful attention.

We have already noted how in Gumilev's scheme the rupture with a native landscape caused by the forced emigration of an *etnos* out of its home region leads either to the demise of the group or to its amalgamation with other groups under the influence of new natural-geographical conditions. There was however a third option, by means of which a migrant *etnos* is able to survive intact despite its deracination. It does so by means of a new strategy for self-preservation, which involves the calculated invasion and occupation of a landscape already serving as the ecological niche of a different *etnos*. Unable to establish itself as a natural part of the organic network of the new region and to draw sustenance from it, the invader *etnos* resorts to the manipulation and exploitation of indigenous ethno-ecological systems. Gumilev famously termed this situation a *khimera* or chimera (Gumilev 1989: 480). He borrowed the designation from the biological sciences, where it was used to describe a relationship he claimed was structurally identical:

> In zoology, chimeric relationships refer for example to those that form when tapeworms are present in the organs of an animal. The animal is able to exist without the parasite, while the parasite will perish without its host. When the latter lives in the body of the former, however, it takes part in its lifecycle. By necessitating an increased inflow of nutrition and introducing its hormones into the blood or bile of its host organism, the parasite alters the latter's biochemistry. (1989: 302)

In the realm of the ethnosphere, Gumilev characterised a *khimera* as an 'ethno-parasite' (*etnos-parazit*) which 'exploits the indigenous population of the country along with its flora, fauna, and precious minerals' (Gumilev 1989: 304). And just like a biological parasite, an ethno-parasite disrupted the life processes of its host and critically undermined its welfare. Because the *khimera* stands outside of the normal ethnic life cycle, its presence has the effect of deforming the natural ethnogenetic processes of those *etnosy* with which it cohabits. This produces what Gumilev called 'zig-zags' in the natural course of organic development that can be detected throughout the course of ethnic history (2004a: 123).

Invariably, the coexistence of the two groups in a single ecological niche engenders a maleficent and destructive relationship. Deprived of an organic anchor in its primordial landscape, the character of the invader *etnos* becomes irredeemably degraded. This degradation does not, however, necessarily mean weakness. Very much to the contrary, deracinated *etnosy* survive precisely by developing traits which, however pernicious and unnatural, give them critical advantages over their more normal co-habitants. Indeed, even rootlessness itself is turned to advantage, in the sense that this independence from the natural world enables the invader *etnos* – like a resilient weed – to penetrate and prosper virtually anywhere (Shnirelman 2002: 49). The natural energies of the indigenous *etnos* are sapped and dissipated, and as long as the invader is not overcome its unfortunate host is reduced to a condition of debilitating dependency. A *khimera* leads inevitably to the 'overloading' of the respective natural-geographical region and the transformation of a healthy ethno-ecological system into a dysfunctional 'anti-system'. All of the aboriginal organic life of the geographical region – its flora and fauna no less than the *etnos* itself – is seriously disrupted and threatened ultimately with destruction (Gumilev 1980: 35).

Although Gumilev refered to the various chimeric relationships that have darkened ethnic history across the ages, he was preoccupied with one example above all: the Jewish *etnos* (Gumilev and Ivanov 1992: 50). In Gumilev's analysis, the Jews emerge as a prototypical *khimera*, providing the best example of the disruption and devastation that chimeric contacts are certain to entail. In the case of the Jews, the rupture of the primordial nexus with the natural environment occurred at an early moment in their ethnogenetic cycle, and they were subsequently constrained to lead the greatest part of their historical life in diasporic conditions. Wherever they settled, the Jews acted as a chimera in regard to indigenous populations, bringing with them the full range of problems associated with this condition.

In regard to the Jews, Gumilev makes one highly significant qualification of his ethno-ecological laws. He allows that in a strict sense they *were* able to re-establish an ecological connection of sorts to a landscape, a 'natural' re-emplacement which then became part of their ethnic character and helped shape their ethnic identity. The ecological niche in question, however, was not a normal landscape but rather the 'anthropogenic environment', in other words urban settlements and trading routes created and sustained through human design rather than natural-geographical processes. In this manner, Gumilev argued, the Jews became an 'organic' part of landscapes that were quintessentially non-organic and unhealthy, an association which served to underscore the fundamentally anti-ecological and unnatural character of the Jewish *etnos* overall (Gumilev and Ivanov 1992: 54, 56; Gumilev 2004a: 123). Like all landscape environments, these urban landscapes then worked to shape the ethos of the ethnic group, fostering the cosmopolitanism characteristic for the Jews and their proclivity for commerce and merchantry (Shnirelman 2002: 56).

For Gumilev, the Jews were a parasite *etnos* par excellence. Their entire ethnic character exemplified the sort of utter degradation and depravity that came as a consequence of the rupture with the natural world. Wherever they penetrated and settled, they sought to establish themselves and take advantage by underhanded and deceitful means (Gumilev 2004a: 91–2). Everywhere they deliberately fostered 'skepticism and indifference' and 'putrefaction (*razlozhenie*) and stagnation', in order to erode the spiritual and moral resistance of their hosts, thereby more easily extending their control over them (Gumilev 1980: 35; 2004a: 260). A particularly effective strategy toward this end, Gumilev somewhat improbably argued, was the practice of exogamy, that is, marriage outside the ethnic unit. While normal *etnosy* naturally practised endogamy as a strategy for ethnic reproduction and survival, the Jews developed the practice of deliberately marrying their women into foreign indigenous elites, in order to produce generations of 'métis' or 'bastard' offspring (Gumilev's terms) that could eventually seize power in the name of the intruder (Rogachevskii 2001: 363). Jewish barbarity was further demonstrated by their extensive slave-trading activities, which they pursued relentlessly and which everywhere brought them enormous profit and power at the cost of untold human misery (Gumilev 1989: 303–4; 2004a: 114–15).

Gumilev's consideration of Russia's exposure to the Jewish *khimera* focused largely on the historical contacts between ancient Rus' and the nomadic civilisation of the Khazars. The Khazars were an ancient people who inhabited the steppe zones along the northeast coasts of the Black Sea. Since the nineteenth century, they had been a subject of special interest for Russian scholarship. This was partly because their exotic and powerful civilisation had vanished without a trace, and partly because they were commonly believed to have converted to Judaism, thus setting them quite apart from all of ancient Russia's other neighbours on the southeastern steppe. Gumilev shared this interest in the Khazars. Throughout his career, he devoted much scholarly energy to the archeological, ethnographic and historical-geographical study of Khazar civilisation (for example, Gumilev 1966, 2004a; also see Aleksin and Gumilev 1962, Gumilev 1964, 1974). He argued against the commonly accepted view, however, by insisting the conversion of the ethnic Khazar masses to Judaism never actually took place. Rather, the Khazars began as a secluded and self-contained *etnos*, whose primordial natural economies of fishing and viticulture reflected an organic and harmonious adaptation to the conditions of their ecological niche (Gumilev 2004a: 129). In the eighth century, however, Khazaria began to be penetrated by renegade Jews from Byzantium and the Caucasus. Manifesting all of their evil traits, the Jews gradually began to establish a predominant position for themselves in Khazar society. 'Jewish beauties' intermarried with the Khazar elite, to devastating effect (Gumilev 2004a: 118–19, 125). Ruthlessly applying all of their merchant skills in commerce and usury, the Jews quickly came to control the profits of the various caravan routes that criss-crossed Khazar territory. They were able to augment these profits considerably by introducing contraband items, in particular slaves taken among other places from the local Khazar population itself (Gumilev 2004a: 130–1).

The dominating Jewish elite developed their native 'anthropogenic landscape' by constructing a mighty commercial centre at the oasis of Itil, which developed into a sort of prototypical example of ethno-parasitism. Gumilev characterised the Khazar *khimera* as a sort of 'merchant octopus' (*kupechieskii sprut*): an aggressively powerful and expansionist state, based on the ruthless repression and exploitation of the indigenous ethnic population and determined at all costs to invade and crush all neighbouring entities (Gumilev 2004a: 146). This latter crusade brought ancient Kievan Rus' into contact with Khazaria (Gumilev 2004a: 282). Finally, in the tenth century, the Russians succeeded in prevailing over their *khimera*-challenger, and with its military and commercial power broken, Khazar civilisation dissipated into the sands of the southern steppes.

Although there is no lack of testimony to Gumilev's personal anti-semitism (for example, Tiurin 1992; D'iakonov 1992; Gershtein 1993, no. 11: 174, no. 12: 141; Chernykh 1995: 145–7; Savchenko 1996: 250; Rogachevskii 2001), in his scholarly analysis he remained focused on the ancient past, and never explicitly discussed the Jewish *khimera* as a threat to contemporary Russia. Under the circumstances, however, this was hardly necessary. In Russia, as elsewhere, historiographical discourses provided one of the most important media for the elaboration and dissemination of anti-semitism. Thus for Russian nationalism of the late Soviet period – heavily coloured in any event by anti-semitic sentiment – the saga of ancient Khazaria provided an optimal thematic trope for discussion of the Jewish question, which offered conclusions of obvious, if unstated relevance to the present day. It was for this reason a subject of considerable popularity, which extended well beyond Gumilev's own contribution (Shnirelman 2002; Rossman 2002: 43ff.).

As part of this, however, Gumilev's work occupied a category of its own, and was of immense significance (Rossman 2002: 34). Its weight came on the one hand from his unquestioned scholarly expertise in the subject, founded on extensive field work and numerous publications. On the other hand it came from his 'scientific' rendition of the issue which both cast the problem in terms of specific natural-ecological aberrations on the part of the Jewish *etnos* and placed it in the context of a larger argument about the relationship of ethnicity to the natural world and the geographical landscape. With this, he offered Russian nationalism an apparently balanced, objective and neutral account of the sources of Jewish ethno-parasitism. The full appreciation of this particular dimension of Gumilev's work can be seen in the fact that his historical study of Khazaria and its relations to Russia began as a commission in the mid-1970s by a leading organ of conservative Russian nationalism, the journal *Molodaia Gvardiia* (Gumilev 2004b: 6–7).

CONCLUSION

This consideration of Lev Gumilev's 'ecology of ethnicity' has argued that the entities of territory and landscape can have a relevance to ethno-national discourses other than their straightforward function as terrestrial spaces where the affective attachments of the group are concentrated. Beyond this, these factors can be conceptualised as active natural agents that are critical for the constitution of ethnic life itself, and as such incorporated into explanatory perspectives on the nature of ethnicity. Gumilev's deployment of ethno-ecology remained profoundly connected with the wider ethno-national challenges, prejudices and political concerns of the late Soviet period.

ACKNOWLEDGEMENTS

I would like to thank Dr Denis Shaw for sharing with me his extensive knowledge of ecological science in Russia, and the editors for their many helpful suggestions and corrections.

REFERENCES

Aleksin, A. A. and L. N. Gumilev (1962), 'Khazarskaia Atlantida', *Aziia i Afrika segodnia* 2: 52–3.

Berg, L. S. (1922), *Nomogenez, ili evoliutsiia na osnove zakonomernostei*, Petrograd.

Berg, L. S. (1930), *Landshaftno-geograficheskie zony SSSR*, Leningrad: Institut Ratestenievodstva.

Berg, L. S. (1969), *Nomogenesis, or Evolution Determined by Law*, tr. J. M. Rostovtsov, Cambridge, MA: MIT Press.

Bromlei, I. V. (1973), *Etnos i etnografiia*, Moscow: Nauka.

Bromlei, I. V. (1983), *Ocherki teorii etnosa*, Moscow: Nauka.

Brudny, Y. M. (1998), *Reinventing Russia: Russian Nationalism and the Soviet State 1953–1991*, Cambridge, MA: Harvard University Press.

Chernykh, E. N. (1995), 'Postscript: Russian archaeology after the collapse of the USSR', in P. L. Kohl and C. Fawcett (eds), *Nationalism, Politics, and the Practice of Archeology*, Cambridge: Cambridge University Press, 139–48.

D'iakonov, I. (1992), '"Ognennyi D'iavol"', *Neva*, 4: 225–8.

Dokuchaev, V. V. (1949 [1898–9]), K izucheniiu o zonakh prirody, *Izbrannye Sochineniia*, 3: vol 3, 47–55.

Forster, A. and B. R. Epstein (1974), *The New Anti-Semitism*, New York: McGraw-Hill.

Friedgut, T. H. (1984), *Soviet Anti-Zionism and Anti-Semitism*, Jerusalem: Soviet and East European Research Center.

Gershtein, E. (1993), 'Lishniaia liubov'. Stseny iz moskovskoi zhizni', *Novyi Mir* 11, 12: 151–85, 139–74.

Gumilev, L. N. (1964), 'Gde ona, strana Khazariia', *Nedelia* 24, 7–13 June.

Gumilev, L. N. (1966), *Otkrytie Khazarii. Istoriko-etnograficheskii etiud*, Moscow: Nauka.

Gumilev, L. N. (1970), 'Etnogenez i etnosfera', *Priroda* 1: 46–55.

Gumilev, L. N. (1971), 'Etnogenez: prirodnyi protsess', *Priroda* 2: 80–2.

Gumilev, L. N. (1974), ' 'Skazanie o khazarskoi dani' (opyt kriticheskogo kommentarii letopisnogo siuzheta)', *Russkaia Literatura* 3: 164–74.

Gumilev, L. N. (1976), 'G. E. Grumm-Grzhimailo i rozhdenie nauki ob etnogeneze', *Priroda* 5: 112–21.

Gumilev, L. N. (1980), 'God rozhdeniia 1380', *Dekorativnoe Iskusstvo*, 12: 34–7.

Gumilev, L. N. (1989), *Etnogenez i biosfera zemli*, Leningrad: Iz-vo Len, Universiteta.

Gumilev, L. N. (1991), ' 'Menia nazyvaiut evraziitsem ...' ', *Nash Sovremennik* 1: 132–41.

Gumilev, L. N. (1993), 'Etno-landshaftnye regiony evrazii za istoricheskii period, *Ritmy Evrazii: epokhi i tsivilizatsii*, Moscow: Ekopros, 252–70.

Gumilev, L. N. (1994), 'Ia, russkii chelovek, vsiu zhizn' zashchishchaiu tatar ot klevety', *Chernaia Legenda: Druz'ia i nedrugi Velikoi stepi*, Moscow: Ekopros, 247–323.

Gumilev, L. N. (1995), 'Istoriko-filosofskie trudy kniazia N. S. Trubetskogo (zametki poslednego evraziitsa)', in N. S. Trubetskoi, *Istoriia. Kul'tura. Iazyk*, Moscow: Progress-Univers, 31–54.

Gumilev, L. N. (2000), *Konets i vnov' nachalo. Populiarnye lektsii po narodovedeniiu*. Moscow: Rol'f.

Gumilev, L. N. (2004a), *Dreveniaia Rus' i velikaia step'*, Moscow: Airis.

Gumilev, L. N. (2004b), *Etnosfera. Istoriia liudei i istoriia prirody*, Moscow: AST.

Gumilev, L. N. and V. I. Ermolaev (1993), 'Gore ot illiuzii', *Ritmy Evrazii*, Moscow: Ekopros, 174–87.

Gumilev, L. N. and K. P. Ivanov (1992), 'Etnicheskie protsessy: dva podkhoda k izucheniiu', *Sotsiologicheskie Issledovaniia*, 1: 50–7.

Hodnett, G. (1967), 'What's in a nation?', *Problems of Communism*, 16, 5: 2–15.

Kaltakhchian, S. T. (1976), 'Sovetskii narod', *Bol'shaia Sovetskaia Entsiklopediia*, Moscow: Sovetskaia Entsliklopediia, 24: 25.

Karel'skaia, L. P. (2005), *L. N. Gumilev*, Moscow: MarT.

Kim, M. P. (1975), *Sovetskii narod: novaia istoricheskaia obshchnost' liudei*, Moscow: Nauka.

Kozlov, V. I. (1978), 'Etnicheskaia obshchnost' (etnos)', *Bol'shaia Sovetskaia Entsiklopediia*, Moscow, Sovetskaia Entsliklopediia, 30: 298.

Kozlov, V. I. and V. V. Pokshishevskii (1973), 'Etnografiia i geografiia', *Sovetskaia Etnografiia* 1: 3–13.

Laruelle, M. (2000), 'Lev Nikolaevic Gumilev (1912–1992): biologisme et eurasisme dans la penseé russe', *Revue des études slaves*, 72, 1–2: 163–89.

Lavrov, S. B. (2000), *Lev Gumilev: Sud'ba i idei*, Moscow: Svarog i K.

Martin, T. (2001), *The Affirmative Action Empire: Nations and Nationalism in the Soviet Union, 1923–1939*, Ithaca, NY: Cornell University Press.

Naarden, B. (1996), "'I am a genius, but no more than that': Lev Gumilev (1912–1992), ethnogenesis, the Russian past, and world history', *Jahrbücher für Geschichte Osteuropas* 44: 54–82.

Nudel'man, R. (1979), 'Sovremennyi sovetskii antisemitizm: formy i soderzhanie', *Antisemitizm v Sovetskom Soiuze. Ego korni i posledstviia*, Jerusalem: Biblioteka Aliya, 24–52.

Pimenov, V. V. (2003), 'Poniatie "etnos" v teoreticheskoi kontseptsii Iu.V. Bromleia', *Akademik Iu.V. Bromlei i otechestvennaia etnologiia, 1960–1990e gody*, Moscow: Nauka, 12–17.

"'Publikatsiia moikh rabot blokiruiutsia'. Kto i pochemu otvergal L. N. Gumilevu' (1995), *Istochnik* 5: 84–9.

Rogachevskii, A. (2001), 'Lev Gumilev i evreiskii vopros (po lichnym vospominaniiam)', *Solnechnoe spletenie*, 18/19: 358–68.

Rossman, V. (2002), 'Lev Gumilev, Eurasianism and Khazaria', *East European Jewish Affairs* 32, 1: 30–51.

Rutland, P. (1984), 'The Nationality Problem and the Soviet State', in N. Harding (ed.), *The State In Socialist Society*, Albany: State University of New York Press, 150–78.

Savchenko, A. (1996), 'Sem' let riadom so L'vom Gumilevym', *Novyi Mir* 2: 240–50.

Shanin, T. (1989), 'Ethnicity in the Soviet Union: Analytical perceptions and political strategies', *Comparative Studies in Society and History*, 31, 3: 409–24.

Shnirelman, V. A. (2002), *The Myth of the Khazars and Intellectual Antisemitism in Russia, 1970s-1990s*, Jerusalem: Vidal Sassoon International Center for the Study of Antisemitism, Hebrew University.

Simon, G. (1991), *Nationalism and Policy toward the Nationalities in the Soviet Union: From Totalitarian Dictatorship to Post-Stalinist Society*, Boulder, CO: Westview Press.

Skalnik, P. (1986), 'Towards an Understanding of Soviet *Etnos* theory', *South African Journal of Ethnology* 9, 4: 157–66.

Slezkine, Y. (1996), 'The USSR as a communal apartment, or how a socialist state promoted ethnic particurlarism', in G. Eley and R. G. Suny (eds), *Becoming National: A Reader*, New York: Oxford University Press, 203–38.

Smith, Anthony D. (1999), *Myths and Memories of the Nation*, Oxford: Oxford University Press.

Smith, Anthony D. (2001), 'Ethno-Symbolism', in A. S. Leoussi (ed.), *Encyclopaedia of Nationalism*, New Brunswick, NJ: Transaction Publishers, 84–7.

Smith, Anthony D. (2002), 'When is a Nation?', *Geopolitics* 7, 2: 5–32.

Sovetskii Narod: novaia internatsional'naia obshchnost' liudei (1987), Kishinev: Shtiintsa.

Suny, R. G. and T. Martin (eds) (2001), *A State of Nations: Empire and Nation-Making in the Age of Lenin and Stalin*, Oxford: Oxford University Press.

Thompson, T. L. (1989), *Ideology and Policy: The Political Uses of Doctrine in the Soviet Union*, Boulder, CO: Westview Press.

Tillett, L. (1969), *The Great Friendship: Soviet Historians on the Non-Russian Nationalities*, Chapel Hill: University of North Carolina Press.

Tiurin, A. (1992), 'Pis'mo v redaktsiiu', *Neva* 4: 223–5.

Tolz, V. (2001), *Russia: Inventing the Nation*, London: Arnold.

Veingol'd, I. I. (1973), *Sovetskii narod: novaia internatsional'naia obshchnost' liudei.Sotsiologicheskii ocherk*, Frunze: Kyrgystan.

Vucinich, A. (1988), *Darwin in Russian Thought*, Berkeley: University of California Press.

Weiner, D. R. (1999), *A Little Corner of Freedom: Russian Nature Protection from Stalin to Gorbachev*, Berkeley: University of California Press.

Woll, J. (1989), 'Russians and Russophobes: Antisemitism on the Russian literary scene', *Soviet Jewish Affairs*, 19, 3: 3–21.

Yanov, A. (1978), *The Russian New Right: Right-Wing Ideologies in the Contemporary USSR*, Berkeley: Institute of International Studies, University of California.

Chapter 11

NATIONAL SYMBOLS: ETHNICITY AND HISTORICAL CONTINUITY IN POST-COMMUNIST 'NEW EUROPE'

Athena S. Leoussi

This chapter offers a brief survey of the ethno-cultural orientations of the constitutions of seven post-communist states which had been part of the Soviet bloc,
as either 'satellites' of the USSR or integral components of the USSR, and which,
in May 2004, joined the European Union: the East European states of Poland,
Hungary, Czech Republic and Slovakia; and the three Baltic states which refused
to join the Commonwealth of Independent States founded in 1991: Estonia,
Latvia and Lithuania (Crampton 1994: 407; Hosking 1992).[1] By joining the EU,
these seven states joined the West European world of national states – a world
of deep historical consciousness, democratic institutions and free economy. At
the same time, they rejected communist internationalist and class conceptions
of human solidarity, identity and destiny, and Russian assimilationist ideology
and cultural policies (Connor 1984). Indeed, the parliament of Latvia, upon its
joining the EU, specifically condemned 'the totalitarian communist occupation
regime implemented in Latvia by the Union of Soviet Socialist Republics' and
appealed to the EU to comprehend 'the bitter experience of Latvia and to be
fully aware of Latvia's history as an integral part of the history of the entire united
Europe'.[2]

The concept of 'dominant ethnie' or 'dominant nation' is most useful for
analysing the cultural nature of the new, post-communist states. It describes
the desire of an ethno-cultural community or nation for cultural self-expression through and within 'its own' national state (Brubaker 1996: 415). First used
by Anthony D. Smith, in 1991, the idea of an 'ethnic core' or 'dominant ethnie'
describes a situation in which social identities and solidarities, in both pre-modern
and modern states, are built around a 'dominant ethnie, which attracted other
ethnies or ethnic fragments into the state to which it gave a name and cultural
charter' (Kaufmann 2001: 51–3; Smith 1986, 1991; Grosby 1995). Given that
ethnies are associated with a given territory, the boundaries of the state are also
determined by 'the myths and memories of the dominant ethnie, which include

the foundation charter, the myth of the golden age and the associated territorial claims or ethnic title-deeds' (Smith 1991: 39).

The more general, theoretical implication of this chapter is its contribution to the exploration of Anthony D. Smith's claim that ethnic origins, historical experiences and memories, and ethno-cultural traditions and symbols play a central role in the formation, renewal and re-birth of modern nations and national states (Smith 1989; Hutchinson 2005). The constitutions of new, post-communist states – as foundational charters of societies which claim to be democratic, that is to say, if not shaped, at least ratified from 'below', by *people*'s choices – offer important material for testing this ethno-symbolic thesis at the dawning of the twenty-first century, as against the alternative, 'modernist' position of state formation on the basis of civic-territorial principles, a modern, scientific culture, and the individualistic pursuit of wealth through a market economy, typified by Ernest Gellner (Gellner 1983).

The chapter focuses on constitutional preambles and the constitutionally-established state symbols of the seven post-communist states of the EU. It considers them as distinct bodies of evidence regarding the ethno-cultural particularism of these states vis-à-vis the formal articles of constitutions. The latter tend to be more formulaic and universalistic, conforming with UN and other international conventions. Whereas the former are freer from such restrictions, and can thus be more subjective and particularistic. State symbols, like all symbols, have the additional advantage of suggestion.

I will examine the extent to which the seven post-communist states are ethnic states rather than multi-cultural and civic, by examining their constitutional preambles and state symbols according to the following three criteria: first, their invocation of the principle of national self-determination as the foundational principle of the new state, and, more generally, their presentation of the state as the home of a particular nation; second, their references to the past: the extent to which they present the new state as either a revival of an 'old', ethno-historic state or the final achievement of statehood by a particular ethno-cultural community; and third their references to non-ethno-cultural issues and especially to economic and political reforms along market, democratic and civic lines as central orientations of the state.

EAST EUROPEAN STATES

Czech Republic

We, the citizens of the Czech Republic in Bohemia, Moravia and Silesia,
at the time of the restoration of an independent Czech State,
loyal to all good traditions of the ancient statehood of the Lands of the Czech
    Crown and the Czechoslovak statehood,
resolved to build, protect and develop the Czech Republic in
the spirit of the inviolable values of human dignity and freedom,
as the home of equal and free citizens who are conscious of their
duties in respect of others and their responsibility in respect of the whole,
as a free and democratic State based on the respect for human rights
and the principles of civic society,
as part of the family of European and world democracies,
resolved to jointly protect and develop the inherited natural and cultural,
    material and spiritual wealth,
resolved to abide by all well-established principles of the rule of law,
through our freely elected representatives, adopt this Constitution of the Czech
    Republic.

Nation and state

The first post-communist constitution of the Czech Republic entered into force on 1 January 1993, immediately after the dissolution of Czechoslovakia on 31 December 1992. The preamble to this constitution, published in 1997, makes no reference to the association of the Czech state with any specific ethnic group: 'We, the citizens of the Czech Republic in Bohemia, Moravia and Silesia ... adopt this constitution of the Czech Republic'.[3] This may be explained by the fact that in the Czech Republic, in contrast to the strongly heterogenous Czechoslovakia, ethnic Czechs are demographically dominant, constituting, in the 2001 census, 94 per cent of the population. The minorities consist mostly of Slovaks, Poles,

Germans, Hungarians, Ukrainians and Roma (Zwilling 2004). In any case, the preamble presents the Czech Republic as the home of all Czech citizens – 'the home of equal and free citizens ...'

History and symbols of the state

The preamble presents the Czech Republic as an old, pre-modern, 'ancient' state now revived. In fact, it dates the origins of modern Czech statehood to the eleventh-century medieval Kingdom of Bohemia whose territory came to overlap significantly with that of the present-day Czech Republic. It also establishes the historical continuity of the Czech Republic with modern Czechoslovakia, itself founded in 1918. Finally, it describes the political culture of the independent Czech Republic as combining all the 'good traditions' of the earlier states, with the new principles of free and democratic states: 'respect for human rights and the principles of civic society'.

Article 14 of the constitution establishes two coats-of-arms for the Czech Republic: 'the large and the small'. Both have medieval historic roots. The large coat-of-arms consists of a shield divided into four parts. In its first and fourth parts there is a silver two-tailed lion captured mid-jump with a golden crown, and in the second and third parts, a crowned female eagle appears, with some variations in her colours and attributes. The female eagle was originally the official symbol of Bohemia (Bideleux and Jeffries 1998: 213). It was the emblem of Wenceslaus I, the Premyslid Duke of Bohemia (921–929/935) who spread Catholic Christianity throughout his territories, was assassinated by his jealous and pagan younger brother, and was canonised by the Catholic Church, becoming the patron saint of the Bohemian state, St Wenceslas, of the Christmas carol. Gradually, however, during the Middle Ages, a silver lion, the symbol of the Premyslid dynasty since 1213, replaced the female eagle. It remained the symbol of the Czech lands until 1918 when, with the creation of Czechoslovakia, new state symbols were devised. These combined both Czech and Slovak symbols, and signified 'not only a change in the state rights but also a continuum of the historical evolution of the Czech lands with a newly formed state.'[4] The small coat-of-arms of the new Czech Republic consists of a shield bearing the silver two-tailed lion.[5] Under communism, Czechoslovak symbols, albeit somewhat modified, were preserved.

Culture of the state

No specific reference is made, in either the preamble or articles in the constitution, to the ethnic or other nature of Czech culture. However, there is concern for an unspecified inherited cultural wealth: 'We, the citizens of the Czech Republic ... resolved to jointly protect and develop the inherited natural and cultural, material and spiritual wealth ...' In fact, the Czech preamble is culturally both particularistic (for example, the appeal to Czech history) and universalistic or civic, that is, culturally inclusive. Indeed, it claims to express the will of all the *citizens* of the Czech Republic to build a state according to universalistic and humanist values – 'the inviolable values of human dignity and freedom'. In addition, there is no mention of an official language in the 1992/3 constitution, although the Czech language is implicitly the state language (Zwilling 2004: 3; Branchadell 2004). Given this, national minority rights, as human rights, are guaranteed in article 10 of the 1992/3 constitution which gives human-rights treaties precedence over domestic law (Zwilling 2004: 2).

Republic of Hungary

Until the ratification of the new Constitution of our country, in order to promote the peaceful political transition toward a constitutional state implementing multi party-system, parliamentary democracy and social market economy, Parliament established the text of the Constitution of Hungary as follows ...

Nation and state

The first post-communist constitution of Hungary, of 23 October 1989, which proclaimed it a parliamentary republic, was essentially a revision, albeit a radical one, of the 1949 constitution. The preamble to the 1989 constitution, ratified in 1990, does not make any ethnic, cultural or historical references. Its main concern is the establishment of democratic and market institutions: 'to promote the peaceful political transition toward a constitutional state implementing multi party-system, parliamentary democracy and social market economy'. We may thus describe the Hungarian preamble as 'civic'.

Nevertheless, there are ethno-historical references – to the Hungarian nation (the Magyars), the pre-modern, medieval origins of the Hungarian state and its Christian cultural heritage – elsewhere in the constitution. These we find in a series of amendments to the 1989 constitution. Their core vehicles here, as in most constitutions, are the state or national symbols.

History and symbols of the state
In 1990, a new act established that:

> The Coat of Arms of the Republic of Hungary is a vertically impaled shield coming to a point in the middle of the rounded base. Four red and four silver horizontal stripes alternate on the dexter. A triple green crest rises from the sinister base, its middle mound bearing a gold coronet transfixed by a silver patriarchal cross against the red field. Atop the shield rests the Holy Crown of St Stephen.'[6]

This is considered 'the chief emblem' of Hungary, 'symbolising its history'.[7]

The Hungarian state emblem affirms the ethnic, medieval and Christian foundations of the post-communist state. The crucial motif here is the 'Holy Crown of St Stephen'. This invokes the foundation of the Hungarian Kingdom by St Stephen. The son of the Árpád ruler Geza (970–7), Stephen or István converted his family to Western, Catholic Christianity. And when he was crowned King of Hungary in 1000 AD the crown was provided by the Pope, known henceforth as the 'Holy Crown of St Stephen' (Bideleux and Jeffries 1998: 191). Stephen supported with great zeal the creation of Catholic institutions in his territories, making lavish land grants to monasteries and bishoprics, and pursued the Catholic Christianisation of the pagan Magyars often with a great deal of violence. István died in 1038 and was canonised, becoming St Stephen, patron saint of Hungary (Makkai 1990: 17).

The year 1000 AD is confirmed by law, Act I of 2000, which commemorated 1000 AD as the year of foundation of the Hungarian state by St Stephen, while the 'Holy Crown', as 'the historical symbol of the Hungarian Kingdom', was placed in the Hungarian Parliament on 1 January 2001.[8]

Culture of the state
The official provisions examined above associate the post-communist Hungarian state with a Christian, Catholic ethnic culture, and thus with the course of West European civilisation. However, the constitution does not establish Catholicism as the state religion: '... the Church functions in separation from the State' (article 60 [1]); and guarantees 'freedom of thought, conscience and religion' (article 60

[3]). Regarding language, although Hungarian is the official language, the state protects the languages of its national and ethnic minorities.

From a demographic point of view, ethnic Hungarians constitute the dominant nation in Hungary, 'the Hungarian majority', constituting 96.6 per cent of the population, while there are 13 officially recognised and registered minorities all represented in Parliament and specifically protected by Act LXXVII of 1993 on the Rights of National and Ethnic Minorities.[9] This Act defines a 'national or ethnic minority ... [as] any ethnic group with a history of at least one century of living in the Republic of Hungary ... the members of which are Hungarian citizens, and are distinguished from the rest of the citizens by their own language, culture and traditions, and at the same time demonstrate a sense of belonging together, which is aimed at the preservation of all these ...'

Republic of Poland

Having regard for the existence and future of our Homeland,
Which recovered, in 1989, the possibility of a sovereign and democratic deter-
mination of its fate,
We, the Polish nation – all citizens of the Republic,
Both those who believe in God as the source of truth, justice, good and beauty,
As well as those not sharing such faith but respecting those universal values as
arising from other sources,
Equal in rights and obligations towards the common good – Poland,
Beholden to our ancestors for their labours, their struggle for independence
achieved at great sacrifice, for our culture rooted in the Christian heritage of
the Nation and in universal human values,
Recalling the best traditions of the First and the Second Republic,
Obliged to bequeath to future generations all that is valuable from our over one
thousand years' heritage,

Bound in community with our compatriots dispersed throughout the world,
Aware of the need for cooperation with all countries for the good of the Human
    Family,
Mindful of the bitter experiences of the times when fundamental freedoms and
    human rights were violated in our Homeland,
Desiring to guarantee the rights of the citizens for all time, and to ensure
    diligence and efficiency in the work of public bodies,
Recognizing our responsibility before God and our own consciences,
Hereby establish this Constitution of the Republic of Poland as the basic law
    for the State, based on respect for freedom and justice, cooperation between
    the public powers, social dialogue as well as on the principle of subsidiarity
    in the strengthening [of] the powers of citizens and their communities.
We call upon all those who will apply this Constitution for the good of the Third
    Republic to do so paying respect to the inherent dignity of the person, his or
    her right to freedom, the obligation of solidarity with others, and respect for
    these principles as the unshakeable foundation of the Republic of Poland.

Nation and state

On 29 December 1989, the new post-communist parliament of Poland, elected
in June of that year, renamed the 'People's Republic of Poland', 'The Republic
of Poland'.[10] On 2 April 1997 a new post-communist constitution that replaced
the provisional constitutional act of 1992, declared that this Third Republic was
the state of the 'Polish Nation'. According to the preamble, all the citizens of
the Republic constitute the Polish nation: 'We, the Polish Nation – all citizens
of the Republic'. Nevertheless, Polish nationality is not conceived only in civic
terms, but also ethno-cultural. This is evident in a number of crucial passages in
the preamble, such as the inclusion in the national community of Poles living
outside Polish territory – 'Bound in community with our compatriots dispersed
throughout the world' – and the undertaking by the Republic in article 6 to
'provide assistance to Poles living abroad to maintain their links with the national
cultural heritage.' This statement refers to the diaspora of about 17 million Poles,
mainly in the USA.[11]

History and symbols of the state

The preamble establishes the ethnic and historical continuity of the new Republic
of Poland with 'one thousand years' of Polish statehood and culture. It thus presents the new Republic as a revived, 'old' state. It recognises the interrupted character of Polish statehood and stresses the importance for the survival and revival
of the state of successive periods of struggle for independence. This it does, first,
by establishing 1989 as a date of revival and restoration of Polish statehood: '... our

Homeland, Which recovered, in 1989, the possibility of a sovereign and demo-cratic determination of its fate'; and second, by describing the 'Polish Nation' as 'Beholden to our ancestors for their labours, their struggle for independence achieved at great sacrifice'. The moral debt of the nation to those who fought for its independence is translated, in article 19, into the Republic's commitment to 'take special care of veterans of the struggle for independence, particularly war invalids'.

In the preamble we also find an explicit appeal to the Polish nation to remember their long cultural heritage and political experiences of both freedom and oppression. First, the Polish nation is called upon to remember, keep and transmit to future generations the best of their cultural heritage. This goes back to the adoption of Christianity in 966 following the baptism of the Piast Prince Mieszko, ruler of the Polanian tribe. This date is also regarded as the beginning of the Polish state.[12] This, so-called 'First Republic', ended with the third partition of Poland in 1795: 'Recalling the best traditions of the First and the Second Republic [1918–39], Obliged to bequeath to future generations all that is valuable from our over one thousand years' heritage'. And second, Poles are urged to remember, although without specifying them, the sufferings of Nazi and communist rule: 'Mindful of the bitter experiences of the times when fundamental freedoms and human rights were violated in our Homeland' and ensure these freedoms and rights in the Third Republic.

Like the preamble, the Polish coat-of-arms also invokes the deep historical roots of post-communist Poland. Article 28 of the 1997 constitution establishes that 'The image of a crowned white eagle upon a red field shall be the coat-of-arms of the Republic of Poland'. The white eagle is the oldest Polish national symbol. It has both legendary and historical origins. Historically, it is associated with the forma-tive period of Polish statehood. It was initially the emblem of the Piast dynasty. A first crude image of the white eagle is found on the silver denarius of Boleslaw Chrobry (Boeslaus the Brave), who, in 1025, became the first crowned King of Poland.[13] When, in 1295, the Piast Duke, Przemysl II, was crowned King of Poland, the white eagle assumed a crown and became a Polish national symbol. The use of the white eagle was forbidden when Poland lost its independence towards the end of the eighteenth century and was re-used upon Polish independence in 1919 as the official state symbol. Under communism the crown was removed, but the eagle was preserved. The crown was restored by the Third Republic.

Culture of the state

The preamble mentions Christianity as the first of two sources of the national culture, 'our culture', the second being 'universal human values'. At the same time, it equates universal values with Christian values. In fact, it defines the 'Polish

Nation' from the point of view of its beliefs or cultural orientations, rather than its language: 'We, the Polish Nation – all citizens of the Republic, Both those who believe in God as the source of truth, justice, good and beauty, As well as those not sharing such faith but respecting those universal values as arising from other sources'. Another characteristic of the preamble is its recognition of the historic and ethnic origins of the national culture: the national culture is an ancestral inheritance and a tradition handed down by earlier generations of Poles: 'Beholden to our ancestors ... for our culture rooted in the Christian heritage of the Nation and in universal human values'. Consequently, the preamble, despite its 'modern' secular and humanistic pronouncements, in effect establishes Christianity as the primary source of the national culture. Nevertheless, article 25 of the constitution separates Church and other religious unions from State, although not in the repressive and hostile manner of the Soviet communist regime, but rather, in the form of religious freedom, equality and co-operation between religious organisations and the state, as well as the impartiality of state authorities regarding the religious convictions of citizens. Meanwhile the relations between the Polish state and the Roman Catholic Church are exceptionally regulated by a Concordat with the Vatican: 'The relations between the Republic of Poland and the Roman Catholic Church shall be determined by international treaty concluded with the Holy See, and by statute'. Clause 2 of article 25 further guarantees the freedom of expression of religious or philosophical convictions 'within public life'. As Mazurkiewicz has observed, this clause has been of crucial importance for Polish religious sensibilities and historical experience of religious repression, enabling the 'placing of the crucifix in the Parliamentary hall' (2001).

The various ways in which the Roman Catholic Church has been linked to the post-communist Polish state are not surprising. This Church has played a leading role in the history of Poland not only as a spiritual institution, but also as an institution that supported Polish national expression, national unity, and national resistance and independence (Davies 1982). Indeed, its role is officially recognised as that of an institution 'which has always been associated with the concept of Polish statehood', the creation of formal structures of public administration being closely associated with the ecclesiastical structures which followed the adoption of Western Catholic Christianity from 966 onwards (Bideleux and Jeffries 1998: 117).[14] Its national role was crucial in the nineteenth century, in the Russian- and German-occupied zones of partitioned Poland where the Polish language had been suppressed, and again under Soviet occupation. Its resistance to totalitarian communism was further supported from 1978 onwards, by the Vatican, under the Polish Pope John Paul II.[15]

The special relationship, however nuanced, between Roman Catholicism and post-communist Poland can also be explained by the fact that the Third

Republic, with 98 per cent of ethnic Poles, is 'one of the most homogenous countries of Europe both in terms of nationality and religion.'[16] This homogeneity is relatively new and the result of World War II ethnic cleansing and extermination (Crampton 1994: 41; Brubaker 1996: 417; Mazurkiewicz 2001).

Slovak Republic

We, the Slovak People, Bearing in mind the political and cultural heritage of our predecessors, the experience gained through centuries of struggle for national existence, and statehood,

Mindful of the spiritual bequest of Cyril and Methodius, and the historical legacy of Great Moravia,

Recognizing the natural right of nations to self-determination,

Together with members of national minorities and ethnic groups living in the Slovak Republic,

In the interest of continuous peaceful cooperation with other democratic countries,

Endeavouring to implement democratic forms of government, guarantee a life of freedom, and promote spiritual, cultural and economic prosperity, we, the citizens of the Slovak Republic, have, herewith and by our representatives, adopted this Constitution ...

Nation and state

The preamble to the first post-communist constitution of the Slovak Republic, one of the two successor states to Czechoslovakia, adopted on 1 September 1992, links the new state primarily with ethnic Slovaks, 'the Slovak nation': 'We, the Slovak nation, bearing in mind the political and cultural heritage of our predecessors, the experience gained through centuries of struggle for national existence, and statehood, mindful of the ... historical legacy of Great Moravia, Recognizing the natural right of nations to self-determination, Together with members of national minorities and ethnic groups living in the Slovak Republic ... we, the citizens of the Slovak Republic, have, herewith and by our representatives, adopted this Constitution.'

History and symbols of the state

The preamble to the 1992 constitution of Slovakia legitimises the foundation of Slovakia with arguments of two types: first, historical and, second, 'natural rights' arguments. Thus, the historic desire and struggle of previous Slovak generations for statehood is invoked and also historical continuity with the first, pre-modern political organisation of Slavs, the Great Moravian state of the ninth century (833–906). Under the leadership of Mojmir, a Czech-Moravian tribal leader, this was a political union of various Slavic tribes that included both Czechs and Slovaks. It is interesting to note that the Czechs could associate their post-communist state-hood with a pre-modern 'Czech' state, the Bohemian Kingdom, formed after the dissolution of the Great Moravian state. Whereas the Slovaks, as an entirely new polity, sought the legitimacy of political pre-existence by invoking a multi-ethnic, albeit Slavic confederation. The 'right of nations to self-determination' is further invoked as a 'natural' legitimation of the new Slovak state. Finally, the preamble declares the democratic structure of the Slovak state and the endeavour of all its citizens to 'guarantee a life of freedom' for all citizens.

The Slovak state emblem is 'a red early Gothic shield featuring a silver double cross on the middle of three blue symbolic mountain peaks' (articles 8 and 9). According to the official website of the government of Slovakia, the 'main compo-nent' of the state symbol 'is the cross with two pairs of arms which is designated in Slavonic countries as the Cyrillo-Methodian cross'.[17] This cross, also called the patriarchal cross, which we also found in the Hungarian state emblem, and which will reappear, below, in the Lithuanian state emblem, originated in the ninth century in the Eastern Roman, Byzantine Empire where it became widely used. According to the official website of Slovakia, the Cyrillo-Methodian cross links Slovakia with 'the heritage of the three co-patrons of Europe – St. Benedict, St. Cyril and St. Methodius'.[18] It thus links Slovakia not only with religion, but, as importantly, in the context of Slovak incorporation into the EU, with a pan-European Christian heritage. Finally, the triple peak on which the cross stands symbolises mountainous Slovakia and provides a shorthand definition of the Slovak nation's territory or 'title-deeds'.[19]

Culture of the state

The Slovak preamble incorporates Slovak cultural identity into a broader, Slavic identity. This identity is also religious, and, most interestingly, rooted in

Orthodox Eastern Christianity – not Catholicism, despite this denomination's historical dominance in the region: 'We, the Slovak nation ... Mindful of the spiritual bequest of Cyril and Methodius ...' The preamble here refers to the ultimately failed attempt of Rostislav, Mojmir's successor, with the help of the two brothers, Cyril and Methodius, sent to Moravia by Byzantium, in 863, to convert the people of Great Moravia from paganism to Orthodox Eastern Christianity. Cyril and Methodius had to compete with the missionary activities of the German Catholic Church which, in the end, prevailed, and with them, German culture (Hupchick and Cox 1996: Map 9). Nevertheless, and as the preamble indicates, Cyril and Methodius, through their missionary work as well as their creation of a written alphabet for Slavic (Glagolitic), created a spiritual unity between the Slavs of Moravia and Byzantium. This spiritual unity was also invoked after the foundation of Czechoslovakia, by the pan-Slavist artist Alphonse Mucha, in his painting 'Holy Mount Athos, Sheltering the Oldest Orthodox Literary Treasures' (1926) which formed part of his great cycle, 'The Slav Epic' (Dvořák 2000: 153). Despite the religious references of the preamble and the state shield, article 1 of the constitution separates church from state: 'It [The Slovak Republic] is not linked to any ideology or religious belief'.[20]

As the preamble suggests, linguistically, too, the Slovak state is associated with the Slovak nation. Article 6 of the constitution establishes one official language throughout Slovakia: 'Slovak is the state language on the territory of the Slovak Republic'. Nevertheless, Slovakia, as indeed Hungary, has protective policies towards the cultures of its minorities, Hungarian, Romany, Czech and others, who, in 2003 constituted 14.2 per cent of the total population.[21]

THE BALTIC STATES

Republic of Estonia

With unwavering faith and a steadfast will to strengthen and develop the state, which is established on the inextinguishable right of the people of Estonia to national self-determination and which was proclaimed on 24 February 1918, which is founded on liberty, justice and law, which shall protect internal and external peace, and is a pledge to present and future generations for their social progress and welfare, which shall guarantee the preservation of the Estonian nation and culture through the ages, the people of Estonia, on the basis of [article]1 of the Constitution which entered into force in 1938, and by a referendum held on 28 June 1992, adopted the following Constitution.

Nation and state

The preamble to the first post-communist constitution of the Republic of Estonia, which came into force on 3 July 1992, connects the Estonian nation with the Estonian state. This it does in two ways: first, by legitimating Estonian independence, at first from Russian (1918) and later, in 1991, from Soviet rule, through the invocation of the principle of national self-determination: 'With unwavering faith and a steadfast will to strengthen and develop the state, which is established on the inextinguishable right of the people of Estonia to national self-determination and which was proclaimed on 24 February 1918 ...'; and second, by including, among the purposes of the Estonian state, the preservation of the Estonian nation and culture: '[the state] which shall guarantee the preservation of the Estonian nation and culture through the ages'.

History and symbols of the state

The preamble presents the 1992 Estonian Republic, a state 'founded on liberty, justice and law', as a revived state, tracing the first Estonian state back to 1918. After World War I, Estonia, previously a province of the Russian Empire, proclaimed its independence which it preserved until 1944 when it was occupied and annexed by the Soviet Union (1944–91). As a twentieth-century state, Estonia can be described as a 'new' state, one without pre-modern antecedents. Nevertheless, the state symbols of the 1992 Republic affirm a pre-modern political continuity with the medieval city of Tallinn and a national consciousness that goes back to the nineteenth century.[22]

The Estonian coat-of-arms consists of a golden shield with three emblazoned lions, *passant gardant* and is framed by two gilded branches of oak crossing at its base. This design originates in the thirteenth-century coat-of-arms which the Danish King Valdemar II presented to the city of Tallinn (meaning 'Danish Fortress') which he founded in 1219, when he ruled northern Estonia (Lieven 1994: 10). It is similar to the Danish national coat-of-arms which also originates in the reign of the Valdemars. In 1788, and under Catherine II, Empress of Russia, the emblem of Tallinn became the coat-of-arms of the Province of Estonia. In 1925 it was adopted as the coat-of-arms of the independent Republic of Estonia.[23] All these historical ethno-national and civic symbols were suppressed following Soviet occupation in 1940.

Culture of the state

The preamble does not specify what Estonian culture is. However, article 6 of the constitution establishes that 'The official language of Estonia is Estonian'. No reference to a national religion is made in the preamble while article 40 allows 'freedom of conscience, religion and thought' and declares that 'There is no state church'. While articles 49 and 50 provide national minorities with cultural autonomy, reviving an Estonian attitude to minorities which went back to 1925 (Taagepera 1993: 225). This is important given the large Russian minority of Estonia, settled there after annexation to the USSR. Thus, while in 1934, 88.2 per cent of the Estonian population were Estonians, the others being mostly Germans and Swedes, in 1989, Estonians constituted 61.5 per cent of the population and Russians 30.3 per cent . Since then, and after independence, the Russian population has decreased to 25.6 per cent in 2002, and the Estonian increased to 67.9 per cent .[24] According to Taagepera, the official-language policy and the demographic trends since 1989 could thus result in an extensive re-Estonianisation of Estonia (Taagepera 1993: 225).

Republic of Latvia

The people of Latvia, in freely elected Constitutional Assembly, have adopted the following State Constitution ...

Nation and state

The preamble to the post-communist constitution of Latvia, which followed its independence from the USSR in 1991, is short. It simply declares the free and democratic adoption of the constitution by the 'people of Latvia' and can thus be characterised as 'civic'.

History and symbols of the state

The first Latvian post-communist constitution, a democratic constitution, was ratified in 1992 and amended in 1998. Its origins lay in the constitution of 1922 which accompanied the foundation of the first Latvian state in 1918. The application of the 1922 constitution was interrupted in 1940 following invasion and occupation of Latvia by the USSR.

If the preamble makes no ethno-cultural or historico-political references, nevertheless such references can be found in various articles of the constitution and in the design of state symbols. The website of the Latvian Institute usefully details the history, form and meaning of all Latvian state symbols.[25] The Latvian coat-of-arms is a modern creation, dating from the time of first Latvian statehood, in 1918. However, it includes some old symbols which connect modern Latvia with historic Latvian regions: 'The national coat of arms combines symbols of Latvian national statehood', which is modern, with 'symbols of ancient historical districts'. Thus, the sun symbolises modern Latvian ethno-national statehood. It was first used to distinguish the Latvian riflemen of the Russian Imperial Army during the First World War. It has seventeen rays, symbolising the '17 Latvian-inhabited districts'. The historical regions are symbolised by their traditional symbols: Kurzeme-Zemgale (Western Latvia) is symbolised by a red lion; Vidzeme and

Latgale (Eastern Latvia) by a griffin. The two heraldic animals support a shield with the sun on the upper part and three stars above it, symbolising the three historical districts which constitute modern, independent and united Latvia. Branches of oak, the national tree of Latvia, surround the base of the shield.

Culture of the state

The ethnic character of the Republic of Latvia is evident: first, and as in all other cases, in the ethnic name of the Republic, and second in its official language which, as article 4 mentioned above also specifies, is the language of the Latvians – 'The Latvian language'. The state assumes no obligation to protect minority languages. However, article 114 guarantees to 'Persons belonging to ethnic minorities' the right to 'preserve and develop their language ...' Linguistic freedom has been particularly important for the large but now declining minority of the Russians of Latvia, as indeed for those of Estonia. In 2002 Russians amounted to 29.2 per cent of the population and ethnic Latvians to 58.2 per cent (Crystal 1997: 275).[26] Religious and national minority issues are addressed in a standard manner in Chapter VIII of the constitution which incorporates UN guidelines on 'Fundamental Human Rights' into the constitution of Latvia. Thus, 'the church shall be separate from the State' and religious freedom is guaranteed.

Republic of Lithuania

The Lithuanian nation having established the State of Lithuania many centuries ago,
– having based its legal foundations on the Lithuanian Statutes and the Constitutions of the Republic of Lithuania,
– having for centuries defended its freedom and independence,
– having preserved its spirit, native language, writing, and customs,
– embodying the inborn right of each person and the People to live and create

freely in the land of their fathers and forefathers – in the independent State
of Lithuania,
– fostering national concord in the land of Lithuania,
– striving for an open, just, and harmonious civil society and law-governed
State, by the will of the citizens of the reborn State of Lithuania, approves
and declares this Constitution.

Nation and state

The preamble links the Lithuanian state with the Lithuanian nation as the
primary bearer of sovereignty. It is the Lithuanian nation which founded the first
state of Lithuania 'many centuries ago', defended its freedom and preserved its
spirit, language and customs. It also presents the territory of the Lithuanian state
as an ethnic territory and thus an ethnic homeland: 'the land of their [the Lithuanians'] fathers and forefathers'. At the same time, it indicates the democratic,
inclusive and pluralist intentions of the Lithuanian nation striving for an 'open,
just and harmonious civil society'.

History and symbols of the state

The first post-communist constitution of Lithuania was approved in the referendum of 25 October 1992. The historic status of Lithuania as an old state and
nation is stressed both in the preamble and various articles in the constitution.
In the preamble, we find references to the centuries-old state of Lithuania and to
the right of the Lithuanian nation, who founded and defended the independence
of its state, and preserved its culture, to 'live and create freely in the land of their
fathers and forefathers'.

The political history of Lithuania goes back to the thirteenth-century Kingdom
of Lithuania. Following the marriage, in 1386, of the Prince of Lithuania, Wladi-
slaw V Jagiello to the Polish Princess Jadwiga, fifteenth-century Poland-Lithu-
ania became, under the rule of Jagiello, the single largest European state, one
that stretched from the Baltic to the Black Sea, and one rivalling the Austrian
Habsburgs (Hupchick and Cox 1996: Map 3). In 1795, the Lithuanian-Polish
state disappeared from the map of Europe and Lithuania was annexed by Russia
until 1918. Article 17 also invokes the past by naming Vilnius as the capital of the
reborn Lithuanian state: 'the long standing historical capital of Lithuania'.

Lithuanian state symbols echo the preamble. The state emblem is 'a white
Vytis on a red background' (article 15). The white Vytis is the figure of a white
knight charging on a white horse, holding a sword in one hand and with a blue
shield hanging from his left shoulder. The shield has a double gold (yellow) cross
on it. The white Vytis was first used as the state emblem in 1366 on the seal of the
Grand Duke of Lithuania, Algirdas. Despite its early crusading connotations, the

white Vytis with the cross obscures the fact that Lithuanian kings and people long resisted Christianisation which was being forced on them by the crusading Teutonic Knights under Papal command. In the end, Lithuanian monarchs began converting to Christianity in 1251, but also defeated the Knights in 1410 at the battle of Tannenberg (Lieven 1994: 43–4).

At first, the charging knight was interpreted as the figure of the ruler of the country; later, however, and especially at the time of the Lithuanian national revival in the nineteenth and twentieth centuries, and the eventual establishment of an independent Lithuania in 1918, it was interpreted as a riding knight chasing an intruder out of his native country.[27] It is also worth noting here the religious significance of the knight, signalled by the cross on his shield. Through the double cross which we find on the Vytis and on other official symbols, Lithuanians affirm, or, as we should say, re-affirm and publicly revive religious values and the religious content of the Lithuanian cultural heritage. These values are not compulsory, as constitutional separation of church from state makes clear, but may act as public ethical guidance in post-communist Lithuania (Lieven 1994: 367). The white Vytis, along with all other pre-communist state symbols, was suppressed during the communist era.

Culture of the state
According to the preamble, the 'Lithuanian nation' had 'preserved its spirit, native language, writing, and customs' for centuries. The reborn state would enable Lithuanian culture to be free again, this time from communist repression. Although rather vague about the nature of the Lithuanian 'spirit' and 'customs', the preamble is particularly emphatic about the importance of the Lithuanian language and writing as distinctive characteristics of the Lithuanian nation. It also shows national pride in the preservation of these cultural characteristics over centuries. The Lithuanian language, an Indo-European language, is, indeed, one of the oldest languages in Europe and the 'most successful in preserving its ancient system of phonetics and most of its morphological features'.[28] The constitutional implication of the above is article 14 which establishes Lithuanian as the only official, 'State language'.

Nevertheless, the constitution guarantees to citizens who 'belong to ethnic communities' the right to 'foster their language, culture, and customs' (article 37). Such ethnic communities in Lithuania are the Russians (6.3 per cent) and Poles (6.7 per cent), Lithuanians constituting, at the 2001 census, 83.5 per cent of the population.[29] The same pluralism applies to religious communities. In Lithuania, as in Poland, the Roman Catholic church, the traditional Lithuanian church, was suppressed under communism, becoming during the fifty years of Soviet occupation a fortress 'in defence of church and nation' and thus a symbol of national opposition (Lieven 1994: 366). After independence, there has been a 'tremendous increase in religious 'rites of passage' – baptisms, marriages and funerals' (Lieven 1994: 367). The constitutional framework of this pattern has been, first, the liberation of religious life: 'Freedom of thought, conscience and religion shall not be restricted' in Lithuania (article 26). This freedom includes the freedom to manifest, 'in public or in private', one's 'religion or faith in worship, observance, practice or teaching'; and second, the separation of State from Church: 'There shall not be a State religion in Lithuania' (article 43).

ETHNICITY AND HISTORICAL CONTINUITY IN POST-COMMUNIST 'NEW EUROPE'

This brief survey of the constitutional preambles and state symbols of the post-communist member states of the EU confirms the ethno-symbolic thesis, namely, the continuing importance and, indeed, revival of ethno-historic motifs in the constitution and cultural orientations of states at the end of the twentieth century and the beginning of the twenty-first.

It also shows that state symbols embrace and establish the dominance of particular ethnies more fully and deeply than the text of constitutional preambles and articles. It thus shows the independent importance of symbols as vehicles of ethno-cultural, collective identity. State symbols tend to articulate symbolically, and thus indirectly, a particularism that the more discursive parts of constitutions do not (Marsland 2001; Smith 2002:15).

Nation and state

All post-communist states examined here are nation-states, in the sense of ethno-national states or ethnic homelands. They are associated with a single and thus 'dominant' ethnie by deriving their name, history, territorial legitimacy, claims to sovereignty and, in practice, their central cultural values, and not just their language, from the name, history, territorial attachment, political aspirations and culture of a single ethno-cultural community. These 'dominant ethnies' are, in all cases, majority communities. We also find explicit claims on the state as the independent and national home of a core ethnie in the preambles to the Polish, Slovak, Estonian and Lithuanian constitutions. These linkings between dominant ethnie and state nowhere involve the repression of national minorities or their exclusion from public life.

History and symbols of the state

In addition to the principle of national self-determination to which most post-communist states under consideration appeal (Poland, Slovakia, Estonia,

Table 11.1 Dates of origin of the post-communist states of the 'new Europe' according to their constitutional preambles and state symbols.

State	Pre-modern foundation date	Modern (20th-century) foundation date	Historical-political motifs in state symbols
Czech Republic	Preamble claims state origins in 11th century CE, mediaeval Kingdom of Bohemia		Arms of the three historical (medieval) regions of the Czech Crown Lands: Bohemia, Moravia, Silesia
Hungary	Act of 2000 establishes 1000 CE as foundation date of Hungarian state by St Stephen (State symbol, the crown of St Stephen, reinforces symbolically this foundational narrative)		The oldest component of the Hungarian state emblem is the Holy Crown of St Stephen, although the present crown is different from the one St Stephen actually received from Pope Sylvester II in 1000 CE
Poland	Preamble claims state origins in 966 CE, 'First Republic', year of adoption of Christianity following baptism of Piast ruler Mieszko		Crowned white eagle: emblem of the Piast dynasty and of the Kingdom of Poland founded in 1025
Slovakia	Preamble claims state origins in the first, pre-modern political organisation of Slavs, the Great Moravian state of the 9th century CE (833–906)	First Slovak state: 1992	No specifically political motifs
Estonia	Symbolic association, through revival of the 13th-century coat of arms which the Danish King Valdemar II presented to the city of Tallinn, with medieval Tallinn	First Estonian state: 1918 (also mentioned in the preamble as state foundation date)	13th-century emblem of the city of Tallinn: three blue lions and golden oak branches
Latvia	Symbolic claims to historical-political continuity with early modern Latvian-inhabited districts	First Latvian state: 1918	'New' symbol, incorporating symbols of historic, ethno-culturally Latvian districts going back to the 16th-century: red lion for Western Latvia; griffin for Eastern Latvia
Lithuania	Preamble claims state origins in 13th-century Kingdom of Lithuania		The white Vytis (charging knight), first used as state emblem in 1366

Lithuania), there is a second basis of political legitimacy to which *all* these states appeal: the past. These post-communist societies appeal either to memories and experiences of earlier, pre-communist, as well as pre-modern, and mostly medieval, national statehood or/and to age-old national struggles for achieving, maintaining or regaining statehood. They thus present themselves as originating in and as being held together by a common, national past. Even the Slovaks, Estonians and Latvians who did not have a state until the twentieth century affirm medieval and early modern political roots.

At the same time, the revived past must be combined with modern political (for example, democratic and international human rights norms), scientific, educational and economic principles (Smith 2002). This pattern confirms Anthony D. Smith's ethnosymbolic proposition regarding the dependence on core ethnic communities and identities of modern nations and states. This desire for a synthesis of the old with the new is the desire, first observed by Edward Shils and amplified by Clifford Geertz and Irving Louis Horowitz, for both identity and for the benefits of the modern economy and democracy (Geertz 1963; Horowitz 2001: 74).

The past must also be modified and adapted to modern demands (Hutchinson 2005). Thus, in the case of revived state symbols such as the crown (for example, on the Polish eagle, or St Wenceslas' and St Stephen's crowns in the Czech and Hungarian state symbols), its revival now signifies not monarchy, but national sovereignty.

Soviet communism had put its stamp, the 'hammer and sickle', on most state symbols within its zone. All post-communist states considered here revert, in their symbols, to their national-Romantic, pre-hammer-and-sickle period of collective identification and historical consciousness (Gleason 1992: 24; Lieven 1994: xxxvi).

Culture of the state

All the constitutions under consideration are instruments of nation-building and cultural homogenisation, primarily through establishing the language of the ethno-cultural community after whom the state has been named as the only official language of the state. However, minority languages and cultures, in accordance with EU laws, are either guaranteed freedom or, as in the cases of Hungary and Slovakia, are actively and by law protected by the state (Branchadell 2004). The religious orientations of the post-communist states of the EU are more complex. Two preambles, the Polish and Slovak, refer explicitly to national Christian traditions. No constitution establishes an official, state church. However, some state symbols incorporate Christian motifs in their design. State symbols may thus be divided into religious and secular.

Table 11.2 Language policies and religious symbolism in the post-communist states of the 'new Europe'

State	per cent of national majority in the population	Official language	Active state protection of minority languages	Religious motifs in state symbol
Czech Republic	94 (2001)	Czech*		None
Hungary	96.6 (2004)	Hungarian	Yes	The Cyrillo-Methodian cross
Poland	98 (2004)	Polish		None
Slovakia	85.8 (2003)	Slovak	Yes	The Cyrillo-Methodian cross
Estonia	67.9 (2002)	Estonian		None
Latvia	58.2 (2002)	Latvian		None
Lithuania	83.5 (2001)	Lithuanian		The Cyrillo-Methodian cross on the shield of the Vytis

* Not formally established in constitution.

The symbols of Hungary, Slovakia and Lithuania are religious. The most common Christian motif is the Cyrillo-Methodian cross, associated with the evangelising activities, among the Slavs as well as the Hungarians, of Eastern, Byzantine Christianity. Ironically, Eastern Christianity never became dominant in these parts of East-Central Europe, which were eventually pulled into the orbit of Western, Roman Catholicism and the Reformation. The state symbols of the Czech Republic and Poland are secular, as are the symbols of the two tradition-ally Lutheran states, Estonia and Latvia. Religious denomination does not seem to explain the religious references of state symbols.

NOTES

1 The text of the constitutions is taken from national official websites and national embassies.
2 www.saeima.lv
3 www.europa.eu.int
4 Official site of the Czech Republic: www.czech.cz
5 www.web.uhk.cz
6 Hungarian constitution, article 76, 30 November 1998, Embassy of Hungary.
7 www.hungemb.hr/eng
8 www.ekormanyzat.hu/english?kateg=english:1272, Government Portal, 28 April 2003.
9 www.europa.eu.int/comm/enlargement/hungary, archived 1 May 2004.
10 www.sejm.gov.pol/english/konstytucja/konse.htm
11 www.poland.gov.pl/?document=318

12 www.poland.gov.pl/?document=324
13 www.info-poland.buffalo.edu/classroom/eagle.html, website of the Polish Information
    Center, University of Buffalo, 2000; see also Bideleux and Jeffries (1998: ch.5), and www.
    poland.gov.pl/?document=326
14 www.poland.gov.pl/?document=397
15 www.poland.gov.pl/?document=397, see also Mazurkiewicz (2001).
16 www.europa.eu.int/comm/enlargement/poland/index.htm, data from 1 May 2004.
17 www.culture.gov.sk
18 www.culture.gov.sk
19 www.culture.gov.sk
20 www.culture.gov.sk
21 See articles 33 and 34 of the constitution and www.government.gov.sk
22 www.president.ee/eng/ametitegevus/riiklikud_symbolid.html
23 www.president.ee/en/estonia/symbols.php
24 www.europa.eu.int/comm/enlargement/Estonia
25 www.latinst.lv
26 www.europa.eu.int/comm./enlargement/latvia
27 www.neris.mii.lt/homepage/vytis.html
28 www.europa.eu.int/comm/enlargement/lithuania. See also Lieven (1994: 117–18).
29 www.europa.eu.int/comm/enlargement/lithuania

REFERENCES

Bideleux, R. and I. Jeffries (1998), *A History of Eastern Europe: Crisis and Change*, London:
    Routledge.
Branchadell, Albert (2004), 'The new member states of the European Union:
Linguistic Demography and Language Policies', *Noves SL*, spring-summer 2004, www6.
    gencat.net/llengcat/noves/hm04primavera-estiu/branchadell1_3.htm.
Brubaker, Rogers (1996), 'Nationalising states in the old 'New Europe' – and the new', *Ethnic
    and Racial Studies*, 19: 2, 411–37.
Connor, Walker (1984), *The National Question in Marxist-Leninist Theory and Strategy*,
    Princeton: Princeton University Press.
Crampton, R. J. (1994), *Eastern Europe in the Twentieth Century*, London: Routledge.
Crystal, David (ed.) (1997), *The Cambridge Factfinder*, Cambridge: Cambridge University
    Press.
Davies, N. (1982), *God's Playground: A History of Poland*, vol. 2, *1795 to the Present*, Oxford:
    Clarendon Press.
Dvořák, Anna (2002), 'The Slav Epic', in Sarah Mucha (ed.), *Alphonse Mucha*, Prague: Mucha
    Ltd and Malcolm Saunders.
Geertz, C. (1963), 'The Integrative Revolution', in C. Geertz (ed.), *Old Societies and New
    States*, Glencoe: Free Press.
Gellner, E. (1983), *Nations and Nationalism*, Oxford: Blackwell.
Gleason, G. (1992), 'The 'national factor' and the logic of Sovietology', in Alexander J. Motyl,
    The Post-Soviet Nations: Perspectives on the Demise of the USSR, New York: Columbia
    University Press.

Grosby, Steven (1995), 'Territoriality: the transcendental, primordial feature of modern societies', *Nations and Nationalism* 1: 2, 143–62.

Horowitz, I. L. (2001), 'Ethnicity and foreign policy in multi-ethnic states: the American model', in Athena S. Leoussi (ed.), *Encyclopaedia of Nationalism*, New Brunswick, NJ: Transaction Publishers, 73–80.

Hosking, G. (1992), *The First Socialist Society*, Cambridge, MA: Harvard University Press.

Hupchick, Dennis and Harold Cox (1996), *A Concise Historical Atlas of Eastern Europe*, London: Macmillan.

Hutchinson, J. (2005), *Nations as Zones of Conflict*, London: Sage.

Kaufmann, E. (2001), 'Dominant ethnie', in A. S. Leoussi (ed.), *Encyclopaedia of Nationalism*, New Brunswick, NJ: Transaction Publishers, 51–3.

Lieven, A. (1994), *The Baltic Revolution: Estonia, Latvia, Lithuania and the Path to Independence*, New Haven: Yale University Press.

Makkai, László (1990), 'The Foundation of the Hungarian Christian State', 950–1196', in Peter F. Sugar (ed.), *A History of Hungary*, London: I. B. Tauris, 15–22.

Marsland, D. (2001), 'National symbols', in A. S. Leoussi (ed.), *Encyclopaedia of Nationalism*, New Brunswick, NJ: Transaction Publishers, 220–2.

Mazurkiewicz, Piotr (2001), 'Autonomy of the Church and freedom of religion in Poland', in G. Robbers (ed.), *Church Autonomy: A Comparative Survey*, Frankfurt-am-Main: Peter Lang, 359–380.

Smith, Anthony D. (1989 [1986]), *The Ethnic Origins of Nations*, Oxford: Blackwell.

Smith, Anthony D. (1991), *National Identity*, Harmondsworth: Penguin.

Smith, Anthony D. (2002), 'When is a nation?', *Geopolitics*, 7, 2: 5–32.

Taagepera, R. (1993), *Estonia: Return to Independence*, Boulder, CO: Westview Press.

Zwilling, Caroline (2004), 'Minority protection and language policy in the Czech Republic', *Noves*, autumn 2004, www6.gencat.net/llengcat/noves.

Part v

ETHNOSYMBOLISM
IN THE MIDDLE EAST

Chapter 12

DILEMMAS OF MIDDLE EAST POLITICS

John A. Armstrong

The significance of Islamic faith for the emergence of nations in the Middle East is widely recognised, but often distorted. This brief chapter cannot fully examine the nature of the Islamic religion, but is meant to distinguish its impact. Other creeds, notably Christianity, have created civilisations that have helped produce nations bordering on the historical space adjoining Islam. Initial conquests by Arabs during the seventh and eighth centuries of the 'Christian Era' transformed the world by terminating the Persian Empire, as it had been known in earlier times, and truncating the Byzantine Empire as it had persisted following Rome's collapse in its western regions. In their places polities arose in the Fertile Crescent of South-western Asia and large parts of northern Africa and the Arabian peninsula, as well as the Iberian peninsula that had not belonged to these empires. The stage appeared set for the Islamic crescent to become fully rounded. Muhammedan's prediction that 'they [Muslims] will take Kustantiniye' (Byzantium, Constantinople) had to wait until 1453. During much of this time, that sacred target preserved Christianity in Asia Minor, the Balkan peninsula and, through their powerful triremes, most of the Mediterranean waters and islands. Intermittent action by powers like the Frankish kingdom kept Islam from northwestern and northern Europe.

Nevertheless, the centuries from 800 to 1050, and in many respects the three or four following, were what Maurice Lombard termed 'Islam in its first grandeur' (Lombard 1971: 20). Its economy thrived despite lack of control in the Mediterranean; there remained the uncontested Indian Ocean and the caravan trade almost monopolised by Muslims. Consequently, not only material treasures, but vistas of human wisdom and discovery opened, especially in those conquered lands, like Egypt and Syria, steeped in the rediscovered Greek culture. By comparison to Western polities of the early Middle Ages, Muslims were also ahead in most branches of intellectual activity. Like the Western European polities, Muslims were advanced in architecture and construction. Representational arts were held back by strictures against depictions of human forms, and occasionally even

Figure 12.1 Courtyard mosaic of date palm showing Arab nostalgia for the nomadic symbol of fruitfulness.

animals of a totemic character. But plant life was freely and effectively presented, as represented in the Great Mosque of Damascus.

The flowing waters, nomadic symbol of fruitfulness, skillfully channelled to central Damascus, were mirrored in the Mosque courtyard mosaics by blue waters and lush green shade trees. Much of the mosaic decorations were produced by Byzantine craftsmen, but supported by Muslim architectural planners who had made the huge Mosque a wonder of the Islamic medieval world. Functionally, it was, of course, a centre of theology antedating the medressa and spread to the large section of Spain conquered by Arabs familiar with the 'Malikite' law school of Sunni Islam. The greatest mosque was Al Azhar (972) in eastern Cairo, still probably the most renowned teaching institution for devout Sunnis throughout the world. At sunset the very large complex presents a striking but soberly decorated exterior, while the wide doors reveal both rich carpets and wall hangings framing a bustling internal activity. Altogether, Muslim culture around the millennium was far ahead of the West, and thus appeared to Muslims, who had little concern for Europe or for Byzantine efforts to regain footholds in Syria, except perhaps in 946–67, when appeals to Muslims in Iraq and Hejaz had some response (Sivan 1968: 14, 16, 19). Not until the West European Crusades did expressions of bitter resentment appear, like a Syrian Muslim's poem, 'The Crusaders do not spare anyone, and proceed zealously to acts of violence!' causing panic among

Figure 12.2 Al Azhar.

women and other Syrians, because the Muslim inhabitants neglect counter-attacks as jihad. Increasingly the 'Franc' Crusade was perceived, in contrast to the Byzantine counter-attacks, as a war of religions (Sivan 1968: 24–5). But it required a half century before an effective champion, Saladin, appeared among the Syrian Muslims. Clearly fundamental causes for the incapacity of the Muslim drive for victory in the eleventh century must be considered. At the forefront was Islam's inability to maintain an active, united front against the new Christian assailants. During the first centuries of Muslim conquest, a succession of rulers, first the Omayyad dynasty, then the Abbasid, had been recognised as 'caliphs', that is, titular commanders and unifiers of the Muslim forces. However, as Emmanuel Sivan points out (1968: 24) no recognised caliph was available to call firmly for unity.

Indeed, the disputed Fatimid Shi'te caliph in Cairo, did little. After 1125, sultans could be found to fill the gap of leadership, although it would be seven centuries before an Ottoman sultan received wide recognition for his assumed title of caliph. In this long interval, the absence of a supreme ruler, even for a major portion of the Dar-ul-Islam, was a severe handicap for governance. To be sure, Koranic lawyers counselled that a *de facto* sultan must be obeyed, even 'If he was an Abyssinian slave'. More generally, as often in Christendom, obedience to a ruler was expected in Islam. But the experience with Crusaders, and two centuries later the frightful encounter with Asian pagan hordes under Genghis Khan, produced an urgent need for unity against the new assailants.

As a result, not only did usually successful contenders for Middle Eastern Muslim thrones attract endorsements from the religious establishment, but also the latter was eager to see the forcible ascent of men who could serve Islam by ousting previous sultans – or even caliphs – who were manifestly incompetent. The title of Defender of the Faith (subsequently conferred on occasion by Popes on Christian monarchs) became one important credential for Muslim rulers who had carried out successful jihads. However, there was no equivalent of the Pope in Islam, nor (in spite of the strong significance of genealogy for group identity) was the sacral awe attached to individual rulers in Europe common in Islam; hence some form of regicide was an acceptable method for change, even if destabilising. Concomitantly, while family dynasties were common, they were sometimes displaced, or even more frequently individual claimants to a dynastic accession were passed over.

If regular provisions could have been relied on, such personnel instability might not have endangered the overall Islamic cause. But neither the Sunni Sharia nor its Shi'ite counterparts were reliable in matters of state. Lengthy training in the medressas built during the early Middle Ages had strong influence for uniformity of judicial officials, backed both by *esprit de corps* and public opinion, that on rare occasion produced outcries in the street, the market place, or even the Friday mosque service. Strong sultans had powerful means for prevailing. Most took drastic measures for assuring personal loyalty from officials.

Considerable infusion of non-Muslims, especially when Christians constituted a minority diaspora, were preferred because the Sharia permitted drastic measures with them. Sometimes such steps were demanded publicly even against Christians installed in office by legitimate Muslim rulers. Sivan (1968: 55) relates how an Armenian (Gregorian Christian) vizir, who had brought thousands of Armenians into Egypt, even permitted Christian churches for their use. In 1137, a Muslim crowd demanded his ouster; one instigator arranged for Muslim soldiers to protest against him by attaching Korans to their lances, a customary symbol for rejecting an 'infidel' commander.

An alternative to enlisting Christians (or occasionally Jews and Hindus) as subordinates for Muslim rulers was for the latter to buy young infidel slaves. Formally Muslims could not be enslaved, although over the centuries some Muslim families used subterfuges to have promising sons admitted to the 'slave corps'. In any case, after thorough indoctrination, most were 'converted' to Islam. The second most famous of these corps was the Mameluke ('possession') as it emerged in Egypt, after the model of experiments by the early caliphs during the ninth century. Subsequently, the Ottoman Janissaries became even more renowned. Mameluke slaves originated in Central Asia and the Caucasus. They were not allowed families until active military service had been completed during their middle years, and were segregated from Muslim as well as non-Muslim populations. By the thirteenth century as a military force these soldiers had defeated Mongol and other invaders, to the applause of Muslims through the Middle East.

Many ultimately rose to the high rank of amir, frequently used as governors. On the other hand, medressa law graduates occupied major civilian posts, particularly as cadis (judges), up to chief justice in Cairo and corresponding posts in major Syrian cities, then under Egyptian rule. Generally these successful officials cooperated readily in spite of their diverse training. High civilian officials, usually from the Sharia ulema, often included controller of the army; directors of roads and ports; hospital controllers; and provisioners for troops and staff. Each official of such rank had access to great wealth but it could be confiscated if the sultan chose to exercise the 'sword arm' of the Sharia against charges of embezzlement, real or trumped up. In contrast to the worst period of Ottoman high officialdom, Mameluke top officials were often reinstated after a time, whereas it was a saying in Constantinople that every candidate for high office passed by the donkey bearing the beheaded corpse of his predecessor in the post. Nevertheless aspirants were never wanting for the perilous but potentially lucrative assignment.

Clearly such drastic overriding (in the case of Muslims) of the Sharia right of asylum would be considered by any modern bureaucracy as creating an insufferable atmosphere that would stifle any official enterprise, much less efficiency. Nevertheless, certain features of the late Medieval or early modern officialdom were admirable. In terms of military and administrative practice, if one discounts the terrible restrictions young men faced, their preparation was probably as good as early modern education in several major West European systems. In their capacity to integrate different kinds of experience, Egypt in particular, and many of its contemporaries in Asia, seem remarkable.

As the 'sword arm' mention brings to mind, Muslim officials were often divided into 'men of the sword', mainly Turkic, at least in linguistic preference; 'men of the pen', mostly accountants and technical experts (including many Copts, by then fully acculturated to commercial Arabic); and 'men of the law', customarily versed in classic Arabic through employing the Sharia and other classic texts. Despite such linguistic variety, that would disrupt many European offices and most Americans, most non-military officers were fluent in Persian as well. One civil official of Coptic origin in Cairo was diligently acquiring Turkic to appear at royal Court.

The last paragraphs dwelling on the instruments of rule are important for perceiving 'realpolitik' in almost every Muslim polity. At the same time religious influence remains. Early caliphs hoped to preserve a semi-universal polity with religious objectives rather than polities that, as all have for many centuries admitted, are a species of the nation-state. By far the most convincing evidence, dominantly contemporary but representing faithfully data going as far back as the fifteenth century, is presented by the French geographer Xavier de Planhol, who explicitly entitles his massive work, 'the prophet's nations' (Planhol 1993). For the historical record of these centuries, the final volume of the late American historian Marshall Hodgson (1973, entitled 'The Gunpowder Empires') is at least equally authoritative. Like embryonic nations of early modern Europe, Muslim multinational polities with a range of ethnic cores appear. As a common Christianity became fragmented by Orthodox, Protestant, and Roman Catholic cores, Islam has been fragmented by Sunni and Shi'ite denominations and less obvious subdivisions, often leading to war and mutual deadly persecutions, perhaps increasingly as centuries elapsed in striving for religious unity. For the most part non-Muslims are not to be persecuted for not conforming in faith, but only if they remain docile in a deliberately ordained 'state of humiliation' including sumptuary laws restricting riding to donkeys, wearing distinctive headgear, and avoiding intercourse with Muslim women, who as apostates would be killed – yet Muslim men might marry non-Muslim women. All rulers were enjoined not only to wage war against infidels, but also to refuse adamantly to surrender any city where a mosque had been established. Such an injunction was a barrier to any peace negotiations, especially when sacred books, according to some Zionists and their Christian supporters, assert that the Bible demands that specific territories may never be subject to negotiation.

Other barriers to the success of Islamic polities, even during the last period of their predominance, arise from popular beliefs not necessarily derived from religion. It is true that Islam and the nomadic history with its intense concern for genealogy were endorsed by Muhammed's disciples ('know your genealogies–do not be like the Nabateans who reply they come from such and such a village'), but rulers and most observers denounced the unruliness of nomadic ways, whether among Arabs or Mongols. The city, not the tent, was the real goal of a religious life, where regular communal prayer, sanctity of the household (harem), and provision of alms, perhaps earned by merchants in caravan trade, rather than pastoral or agricultural labour, were feasible for the devout. Equality of Muslims was furthered by Sharia commands that any who migrated to a city were to be permitted full rights there. However, this precept militated against the proud but useful attachment of burghers to the towns they had become attached to by nostalgia and familiarity, a kind of territorial loyalty that became, in the eighteenth-century West, a vital part of republican inculcation of citizenship. Similarly, while not rejecting agriculture, Islam rejected any preference for the kind of peasant attachment to the land, long familiar in Europe, east and west. Islamic practice also rejected as impious, or at least worthless, all festivals and glorification of the rural calender. The shifting date of Ramadan, at times highly onerous in disregard of the seasons (much more so than Easter Lenten observation) is a striking instance. Nevertheless, it is noticeable that the large peasant populations converted to Islam in key regions like Persia, continued to observe rural calendars that in some instances were unavoidable for successful cultivation. There, Islam was only partially successful in eliminating the landlord aristocracy that had burdened the peasantry.

Certain more material difficulties for emerging polities were unavoidable results of the geographic locations of Muslim conquests. Their vast expanse hindered communications in large polities, as did the scarcity of navigable rivers. Able seamen were usually available, though fewer in proportion to population than in northern Europe. In North Africa and the Middle East, timber suitable for large, sea-going ships was almost exhausted and hard to import. Nevertheless, certain commercial activity like that of the lower Egyptian spice merchants could find adequate merchant vessels. However, the special needs of warships to protect that trade during hostilities or to make long maritime expeditions to Europe and the Far East were often impossible. As a result the striking advantage of the central position of the principal Muslim polities was often negated by lack of sea power.

Earlier reference to Byzantine triremes hinted that a declining empire, reduced itself to a city-state by northern European Crusaders, was able to hold out for a long time with some assistance – and considerable hindrance – at sea by Western Mediterranean city states. Even during the final siege of 1453, the innumerable but very light blockading vessels mobilised by the Ottomans were quite incapable of maintaining a tight blockade against the heavier European vessels (Eickhoff 1966; Ahrweiler 1966).

The geopolitical analysis of late Medieval polities confirms Islamic cultural pre-eminence. Its internal governance and its far-reaching economic success were in the long run less sustainable, due to Islam's religious requirements, and its diminishing geographic and strategic advantages. The successes of the Mameluke and Ottoman regimes during the sixteenth century, however, bolstered self-assurance in the core Islamic world. Outside observers occasionally note the tendency of Islamic thinkers to assume that the best civilisation had already been attained, but such complacency is not unknown among Christian commentators. Before considering the potential impact of such thinking, it is desirable to contrast the impact of peripheral European polities at the sharp edge of contacts with Islamic powers during the early modern period.

In the first volume of his magisterial work *The Mediterranean*, Fernand Braudel notes the immense significance of Astrakhan to the caravan Black Sea route between Turkey and Central Asia (Braudel: I, 13). ' Ivan the Terrible took Astrakhan in 1556. This time the door was shut and bolted, in spite of the Turkish attempt of 1569–70, the great unknown event of history'. Thus threads of Russian history connected with those of Iberian history, as I see them interwoven with the two peripheral experiences of Islam and Christianity. Muslim Constantinople's failure to link up with Sunni Turkestan, through bypassing Shi'te Persia, meant that Turkey's effort to attain a new Sunni caliph presiding over Islam would be delayed for centuries.

During those centuries Russia progressed under successors of Ivan toward becoming a great Eurasian power, with inevitable but unforseeable results for neighbouring Islamic countries. In the meantime the Iberian states were taking a different route. The first was Portugal, directly assaulting with its stronger warships the fragile Indian Ocean trade that Turkey was absorbing (after reducing to a second-rate force the Mamelukes who had controlled the Afro-European end of the great spice route). For the sixteenth century, the Portuguese successes appeared more significant than Spanish advances against Islam. In fact the central polity of the waning Iberian Middle Ages, Castile, a pastoral society by economic criteria, had from the eleventh century used a semi-nomadic tactic against the Muslim Arab and Berber dynasties who controlled most of the peninsula. By exceptional mobility Castilian guerrillas defeated Muslim forces in the arid north-central portion of the peninsula, then relied on a line of strong castles to anchor

a new frontier bordered by a devastated strip, discouraging attempts to restore
the previous frontier. By repeating such tactics, the Castilian forces attained the
Tagus River and the old Visigothic capital of Toledo in the early twelfth century.
After that both flanks were supported, the western by Portuguese forces aided
by French crusaders along the Tagus and the Atlantic coast, while on the right
the new kingdom of Aragon, incorporating Barcelona on the Mediterranean,
advanced far across the Ebro. Outnumbered Islamic forces retreated slowly. Total
numbers of Arabs moving into Spain over the centuries were counted in tens
of thousands, and much more numerous clannish Berbers were rarely available.
Christians remained numerous in the reconquered area around Toledo, but south
of Valencia Muslim families, giving up urban life, stubbornly resisted in the well-
watered but mountainous Mediterranean hinterland. Here, in the first centuries,
considerable leeway for a Muslim lifestyle was allowed. Castilians, though, who
had once been ousted from their land, were determined to regain it entirely. A
striking example was the Great Mosque of Cordoba, which at the reconquest was
first taken over as a cathedral with all its intricate Moorish arches and columns,
but during the early sixteenth century was reserved exclusively for Catholic
worship. Then a smaller, though still extensive, Gothic chapel was installed in the
midst of rows of columns, destroying their symmetry. On viewing the site, King

Figure 12.3 Cordoba mosque with intruded Gothic chapel.

Figure 12.4 Hanafi mosque in Tunis.

Charles, subsequently Holy Roman Emperor and no ally of Muslim architecture, exclaimed, 'You built another chapel, of which we have many, but destroyed a unique monument!'

Charles' predecessor, Isabella the Catholic, presided in 1492 over the occupation of Granada, the last Muslim kingdom in Iberia. The elaborate Moorish palace was retained, but Muslim inhabitants banished. Charles then had a ponderous new palace erected nearby for himself. He and his successors also provided a symbolic force of Spanish soldiers for the Habsburg frontier fortresses along Austria's southern border, facing Ottoman forces aimed at encroaching on the Slavic Christians.

By then, most Muslims and Jews had been forcibly deported, the latter to the Maghreb, but more often to the Ottoman empire. Muslims, on the other hand, usually preferred the more familiar Maghreb. Algeria and Tunis became protectorates of the Ottomans, ultimately with governors (Beys) of an autonomous nature. These Turks, usually conforming to the Hanafi law school, had mosques with minarets of many sides symbolising that law school, whereas Maghreb natives preferred the square Malikite minarets.

The most populous area, Morocco, kept its independence and its Malikite minarets and adherence. But it, too, profited from a large influx of Andalusian clerics, trained in the law schools there, usually as Malikites (Laroui 1975; II, chap. 12). But Morocco had been much more important with its Kutabiya mosque as a religious training centre.

More significant for international affairs were the measures Maghreb officials took to allow 'Barbary' corsairs to operate from their sea ports, including a few in Morocco. Turkey turned a blind eye to their depredations in the Mediterranean, and sometimes far into the Atlantic. By the seventeenth century Ottoman naval power lagged far behind the Iberian fleets, often reinforced by the Knights of Malta. The Constantinople authorities were probably glad to see the religious enemies harassed by a kind of maritime guerrilla that also supplied the metropolitan slave market (often for ransom), and that was replenished by coastal raids as well as captured ships. But such attacks on Christian civilians widened the gap between Islam and its neighbours up to the nineteenth and early twentieth centuries, when France forcibly assumed power over all three Maghreb polities (Laroui 1975: II).

As early as the sixteenth century, as Braudel demonstrates, Russia's strategic land power was already at least as important as the foremost Muslim power, as were the combined Iberian powers. Boris Nolde, who began his massive analysis of Tsarist archives before the Bolshevik Revolution, emphasises (Nolde 1952: I, 2–5) that in the sixteenth century Russia was still a small power, even compared to Sweden. But, given its location, its potential was enormous. As late as 1481 Ivan III had directed his high officials to continue large payments of tribute to

Mongol-Tatar Islamic khans in Kazan and other principalities, although one had become a Muscovite satellite (Nolde 1952: 14–15). By 1489, however, Kazan had become a Muscovite ally against the principal Mongol ruler, greeted Ivan's advice on its own khan's approaching marriage, and in practice had become Ivan's client. Up to that time Muscovy had often deferred to nearby khans, but because of their descent from Genghis rather than their Muslim connections, whereas would-be Genghisids like Tamerlane were scorned by pious Muslims as 'fruit of the tree of unbelief'. By the mid-seventeenth century, after a brief war conquered Kazan, however, its rulers were compelled to allow Orthodox monasteries on their territory, while their authority over Christian peasants was limited (Nolde 1952: I, 98–102). Subsequent Russian expansion during the seventeenth and early eighteenth centuries was enormous in the northeastern regions of Eurasia, but these subarctic regions were of little concern to Islam, just as the great Iberian expansion in the Americas had little effect during earlier centuries among Muslims.

Conversely, Russian advance toward the Black Sea under Peter the Great, Empress Anne, and Catherine II not only subjugated Muslim outposts along the Volga but directly threatened Turkish domination of the Black Sea and somewhat later Iranian influence on the Caspian. In both seas, outside naval power was ineffective before the nineteenth century. By then overland expansion by Russia in the Caucasus and Central Asia was sharply limiting Muslim rule, including important Islamic centres of learning like Bukhara. In some ways Russian military campaigns there resembled, in reliance on local recruits and guerrilla tactics, the Iberian advance centuries earlier. Indeed, the Cossacks had found a way to beat the semi-nomads composing most early Muslim forces at their own game.

It must be admitted, too, that Russian and early Castilian advances, like those of their thoroughly Islamic opponents in regions like the Crimea and North Caucasus, depended on support from royal sponsors for more advanced arms and techniques. The latter increasingly demanded rights that they refused to the Ottomans. For example (Nolde 1953: II, 20 ff.), a few years later the Russians demanded to be allowed to rebuild a fortress at Azov to control both wandering Tatars and Cossacks, but objected to such constructions by the Turks and Crimean Tatar clients. Step by step, Russia moved toward incorporation of the key Black Sea position, the Crimean peninsula. In 1774 Catherine withdrew troops that had penetrated there and declared the Crimean Khanate independent, apart from a purely religious authority by the Ottoman sultan by then claiming the right of caliph. After complicated bargaining, Catherine's representatives arranged a little ethnic cleansing, deporting Christians (Greeks and Armenians) who had remained in Crimean territory to south Russian land, leaving a Crimea almost entirely Muslim. In 1784 Catherine had the Crimea renamed Taurid Region as an integral part of her empire, while leaving some Muslim judges in local authority

(Nolde 1953: II, 179). Nevertheless, as in Valencia after the Aragon regime had become irrevocable, a 'massive' emigration (in this instance mainly to Turkey) occurred. Similar migrations to officially Islamic areas took place throughout the nineteenth century, mainly from Russian annexations in the Caucasus (half a million) and the Balkans (in millions of Muslims), mostly via indirect pressures following the 1878 Russo-Turkish wars, and later by more direct cleansing by local Christian nationalists. (Karpat 1985: 70–7).

Thus a series of harsh migrations of large populations occurred. Generations later, confronted by the drastically altered world situation arising from the development of industrial predominance in the West, Edward Said, instead of seeking Western countries' motives for economic development, sought to discover another, a phenomenon some termed 'Orientalism'. This consisted of a Western sense of confrontation when 'dealing with the East in fields of learning', augmented by travellers' experience (Said 1978: 201–4). For Said, the Western conception of Orientalism consisted of 'the sensuality, the tendency to despotism, the aberrant mentality, the habits of inaccuracy' of 'Orientals'. It is hardly surprising that a man of Arab origin, brought up in Palestine and Egypt was offended, especially when he observed the streams of travellers from Western Europe (French and British, but joined by numerous Americans after World War II) purveying such stereotypes without adequate media for rebuttal or balancing 'the whole adversarial knowledge ... a frozen, reified set of opposed essences ... that had stimulated generations of hostility, war, and imperial control' (Said l978: 350–2).

Said emphasised that the stereotype combination he described had assumed a strongly political coloration. This is brought out in a familiar way as a sharp critique of Zionists and Israel. He cites the late Israeli intelligence general, Yehoshafat Harkabi (Said 1978: 307), whom I knew rather well through two visits and correspondence, and found his information accurate though his overall assessment expectedly favoured the Israeli case. I wonder if Said, fluent in French, ever came across the proverb, cutting several ways, *'La bête est très méchante, si on l'attaque, elle se défend!'* ('The beast is very wicked; if one attacks it, it defends itself').

In this book, at least, Said's remarks on Israel's military superiority are not frequent. In general he recognises the great weakness of Muslims as compared to Westerners, but he does not dwell on military capacity. To do so, as David Ralston does in his recent book (Ralston 1990: 13–106), would distract from Said's interesting sociological analysis of intellectual and scholarly communities' influences. Quite possibly, too, Said did not feel thoroughly comfortable analysing military subjects, any more than he did with the technological and economic factors mentioned earlier. Given his remarkable skill in analysing literature and its influence on specialists, Said's choice may well have given us a penetrating book rather than a smattering of subjects. My contact with Middle Easterners at home and abroad suggests, however, that they have been fascinated by such 'practical subjects'. This is especially true of Arabs. One (a Christian Lebanese) was almost in tears over an Arab defeat at Israeli hands about thirty years ago, saying 'can't they ever win?' But the pride of the Arabs goes back to the great conquests, and the practical recognition that victory was required to banish stereotypes, secure respect, and make more material gains.

In many respects, the new Egyptian army, developed by the Ottoman governor Mehemet Ali after the Mameluke army, discussed above, had been thoroughly defeated by Napoleon's trained French invaders. Gradually Mehemet shook off the Ottoman overlords and became virtually independent. With an Egyptian army largely officered by purged Mamelukes he conquered Syria from the Ottomans. He wished to expand his Egyptian enterprise to industrial development to support independence and a costly conscripted military force. Such an enterprise required a modernised administration, but Mehemet was a thorough dictator, appointing officials for their personal loyalty rather than on the French model of a state bureaucracy, slowly being trained from new schools to appreciate loyalty (rare anywhere in Muslim governance) to Egypt as territorial entity. After his death this structure suffered the fate usual to dictatorships.

A successor was conciliated by Turkey with the title of Khedive, but Mehemet's descendants were unable to manage a complicated position. Enterprises like the Suez Canal, supported by France, later by the British, succeeded at the cost of heavy debts to the Western powers, entailing what amounted to a protectorate. Far into the contemporary period, new dictators like Gamal Nasser sought freedom of action by harsh police measures against organisations like the Muslim Brotherhood, but brought on intervention by France, Britain, and Israel, effectively terminated by the US President Dwight Eisenhower, at considerable diplomatic cost.

Elsewhere in the Muslim world, dictatorial leaders were strongly inclined to follow the Mehemet Ali example – pushing military, technological, administrative modernisation with little concern for popular or even general elite participation. For centuries Iran, formally always independent and Shi'ite, had not copied many Arab or Turkish trends. Shortly after World War I, a military coup by 'Iranian cossacks' drove out the Qazar dynasty, bringing Reza Shah to power for twenty years, but at the mercy of British and Russian occupying forces. In 1941, faced with the possibility of a German coup, his son acceded to the throne as Shah Mohammad Reza Pahlevi with the endorsement of the two major foreign powers (Zonis 1971: 18–22; Ibragimbeili 1977: 34, 212–24). The new Shah strengthened his rule by using some dynasty funds for internal development like health, education and agriculture, and distributed Crown land to peasants (long at the mercy of landlords). But the Shah, like Mehemet Ali, kept real power in his own hands, aided by appointees, mainly from the military, including the director of the SAVAK secret police.

The opposition consisted of clerics (mullahs) of Shi'ite Islam, supported by teachers and other intellectuals as well as the bazaar merchants. Despite considerable clandestine US assistance (by then replacing Britain's) in 1979, the Shah was driven into exile. However, the intellectual supporters and many others among the opposition soon learned that his real successors were high clerics (Ayatollahs) headed by Khomeini, who sought to establish an intensely Koranic state (in the Shi'te interpretation), strictly reducing the rights of women and all students. In the next sixteen years some modifications occurred, but US influence was almost eliminated.

Like many other Muslim countries, mostly Arab, the Iranian response to the overwhelming Western military superiority was recourse to isolation, undiplomatic treatment, and sometimes support of violent organisations. Iran's predicament prior to 1990 was its situation between the West (increasingly headed by the United States) and the Soviet Union. It was the only Middle Eastern country to have been invaded by Soviet forces, that sought to detach its Turkish-speaking province, Azerbaijan, by setting up a socialist puppet state while occupying the

Figure 12.5 Children in a kolkhoz nursery near Odessa, 1956.

Figure 12.6   Mother and child weeding in a kolkhoz field, 1958.

province in 1945–6. Such tactics had been used for decades to enforce rule by
Moscow in Soviet Azerbaijan, originally annexed by Tsarist Russia, and gradually
spread to all the Muslim-heritage 'republics' of the USSR.

The largest in population, the Uzbek Republic, retained the most Sunni Islamic
attachment, and a high birth rate, evidence of attachment to traditional values
made feasible by family ability to raise very young children while continuing to
work at assigned tasks adjacent to home. In a Ukrainian kolkhoz, on the contrary,
parents were assigned to distant field tasks, with nurses in a communal building
containing apparently unsanitary conditions for infants.

During the late Soviet period, legitimisation for the Communist system tended
to come from the victory in World War II, the 'Great Patriotic War'. Symbolically,
patriotic brides were exhorted to drop their bouquets on the Moscow Red Square
Tomb of the Unknown Soldier. Conversely, predominantly Azeri brides were
expected in Baku to drop their bouquets on the monument to the 'Twenty-Six
Commissars' alleged to have been executed there when captured by forces directed
during the Revolution by 'British imperialists'. The monument, in a public park,
is alleged to depict a mulinational group of Bolsheviks, but the historic group
was in majority Armenian in the midst of a predominantly Azerbaijani Muslim
city. In this manner, not only were the 'international' symbols deceptively thrust

Figure 12.6 Moscow, 'Tomb of the Unknown Soldier'.

on the Muslims, but also their own symbolic emblems were denied a place. In the upshot antagonism between Muslim Azeris and Armenians was extremely heightened when the latter sought nearby Azerbaijani territory containing an Armenian majority. In a little known but bloody war, Armenians greatly exceeded their original claims, while constantly recalling the 1990 pogroms that had driven urban Armenian minorities out of Baku. The touted Soviet formula for 'brotherhood' was exploded as soon as Moscow's overbearing hand was withdrawn, with two emerging nations completely alienated from one another. This tragic fiasco has, in many respects, joined other ambitious formulas for peace among nations. The efforts of the Western powers have so far not succeeded, nor has the late Edward Said's call for the West to understand the 'Oriental' Islamic nations, except for profoundly learned observers like Marshall Hodgson and Xavier de Planhol. A striking new approach has recently been advanced by Samuel Huntington, rejecting the notion of a 'universal civilisation', seeking some more realistic approach to world division (Huntington 1997: 68–77). Drawing on Arnold Toynbee, Huntington starts with the religious foundation of civilisations ultimately providing the fundamental basis for understanding.

One could raise several objections to this theme, but I shall confine mine to the question of Muslims and Western peoples. All of us will, I think, agree that cleavages between some nations within Western civilisation remain so acute that true understanding is rare. At intervals Huntington does not see that a similar situa-

Figure 12.8 Baku, Monument for the 'Twenty-Six Commissars'.

tion has existed among Muslims. Conflicts between Sunni and Shi'ite that once led to massacres recur on smaller scales today. Huntington sticks by his earlier statement that 'Islam has bloody borders' (Huntington 1997: 258) although he is sceptical about borders in general. Certainly Islam has been more warlike than some other societies. I do not draw the comparison here between civilisations because one can surely in each find some movement, if not a whole nation, that is sufficiently 'bloody'.

The real distinction that requires much historical examination is whether belligerence is more characteristic of Islam than other civilisations, and whether that belligerence is directed in the long run against non-Muslims much more than Muslims. Here, the big practical issue is whether Muslims of non-Arabic heritage will stick together. Today Kemal's Turkey is, I think, the real touchstone. Its adherence to the United States alliance was matched by Turkey's determined effort during the early twenty-first century to gain admission to the European Union. Undemocratic political and legal provisions were to be repealed, and adoption of European standards set, at least at the minimal level, by recent admittees in East Europe. A free election was conducted at the risk of opening the way for religious fanatics that Kemal's legacy was determined to exclude. In fact the new premier, while a determined Muslim, rejected legal adoption of Koranic principles. Attaining the European level economically was harder. In foreign policy Ankara broke with the Arab states and Iran by military cooperation with Israel, including flights of war planes training over Turkish air space.

Planhol regards Turkey as the only Middle East power to attain stable nationhood. A somewhat more recent guess is that several such entities are emerging. Though by no means a democracy, by rejecting Russian garrisons, yet cooperating with NATO forces in Afghanistan, Uzbekistan has rejected a Muslim alliance, as have many other dictators brought up under Soviet atheism to fear religious interference. In Southeastern Asia, non-Arab polities reject an Islamic front, such as Huntington seems to consider likely. Consequently, while far from certain I consider probable the emergence of two camps, with Arabs endeavouring to obtain a united front against Israel and the West; the other derived from Islamic civilisation accepting only strictly religious alignments but adhering to political alliances with non-Islamic powers in the Far East, North America, and Europe. In fact, arrangements of expediency have characterised most civilisations for centuries, without requiring their nations to be copies of outside cultural units. Untidy, perhaps, but eminently practical.

NOTE

All photographs in this chapter © John A. Armstrong.

REFERENCES

Ahrweiler, Helene (1966), *Byzance et la Mer: La Marine de Mer, La Politique, et les Institutions Maritimes de Byzance au VIIe–XVe Siècles,* Paris: Presses Universitaires.

Armstrong, John A. (1982), *Nations before Nationalism*, Chapel Hill: University of North Carolina Press.

Braudel, Fernand (1972), *The Mediterranean and the Mediterranean World in the Age of Philip II*, vol. 2, English translation, New York: Harper and Row.

Chaunu, P. (1973), *L'Espagne de Charles Quint*, Tomes 1 and 2, Paris: Société d'Édition d'Enseignement Supérieur.

Eickhoff, Ekkehard (1966), *Seekrieg und Seepolitik zwischen Islam und Abendland*, Berlin: De Gruyter.

Grunebaum, Gustav E. (1953), *Medieval Islam*, 2nd edn, Chicago: University of Chicago Press.

Guichard, Pierre (1977), *Structures Sociales 'Orientales' et 'Occidentales' dans l'Espagne Musulmane*, Paris: Mouton & École des Hautes Études en Sciences Sociales.

Hodgson, Marshall G. S. (1974), *The Venture of Islam*, 3 vols, Chicago: University of Chicago Press.

Huntington, Samuel P. (1997), *The Clash of Civilizations and the Remaking of World Order*, New York: Simon and Schuster Touchstone Books.

Ibragimbeili, Khadzhi Murat (1977), *Krakh 'Edel'vaisa i Blizhnyi Vostok* [The Collapse of 'Edelweiss' and the Middle East], Glavania Redaktsiia Vostochnoi Literatury.

Karpat, Kemal (1985), *Ottoman Population, 1830–1914: Demographic and Social Characteristics*, Madison: University of Wisconsin Press.

Kortepeter, Carl Max (1972), *Ottoman Imperialism during the Reformation: Europe and the Caucasus*, New York: New York University Press.

Laroui, Abdullah (1975), *L'Histoire du Maghreb*, vols 1 and 2, Paris: François Maspero.

Lombard, Maurice (1971), *L' Islam dans sa Première Grandeur VIIIe-XIe Siècle*, Paris: Flammarion.

Mandami, Mahmood (2005), 'Whither political Islam?', *Foreign Affairs*, LXXXIV, no. 1, January–February 2005: 148–55.

Nolde, Boris (1952–3), *La Formation de l'Empire Russe: Études, Notes et Documents*, vols 1 and 2, Paris: Institut des Études Slaves.

Petry, Carl F. (1981), *The Civilian Elite of Cairo in the Later Middle Ages*, Princeton:Princeton University Press.

Planhol, Xavier de (1993), *Les Nations du Prophète: Manuel Géographique de Politique Musulmane*, Paris: Fayard.

Ralston, David B. (1990), *Importing the European Army: The Introduction of European Military Techniques and Institutions into the Extra-European World, 1600–1914*, Chicago: University of Chicago Press.

Said, Edward W. (1994 [1978]), *Orientalism*, Vintage.

Sivan, Emmanuel (1968), *L'Islam et la Croisade: Idéologie et Propagande dans les Réactions Musulmanes aux Croisades*, Paris: Maisonneuve, Libraire d'Amérique et d'Orient.

Zonis, Marvin (1971), *The Political Elite of Iran*, Princeton: Princeton University Press.

Chapter 13

THE MUSLIM *UMMA* AND THE FORMATION OF MIDDLE EASTERN NATIONALISMS

Haim Gerber

An interesting argument that sometimes figures in the literature on nationalism is the claim that Islam and nationalism are incompatible, if not diametrically opposed. This chapter will claim that this argument is empirically unfounded, and that Islam has always been tolerant of ethnic differences within the *umma* and to a certain extent even encouraged them. While this is pretty obvious as far as the Arabs are concerned, in this chapter I will show that it applied as well to the Turks, who are the main focus of this study. An additional point that this chapter claims is that the fact that Islam allowed cultural diversity was the key to the development of a written Turkish high culture that at the end of the day contributed significantly to the emergence of a fully fledged Turkish nationalism, even though for hundreds of years the Turks (or, more correctly, the Ottoman elite) described themselves as Muslims or, more readily, as 'Ottomans', starting to see themselves proudly as Turks only in the later decades of the nineteenth century. This argument is not primordialist. It is closer to the stand of the ethnosymbolists, who claim that though nationalism as such is modern, it is usually based on deeper historical roots, and does not appear as a *deus ex machina* (Smith 1996).

The argument I am trying to develop here is based, curiously enough, to a large extent on Gellner's theory, though it is a Gellner modified by Brendan O'Leary (Gellner 1983; O'Leary 1998). Gellner, as is well known, saw the development of nationalism as closely connected to the development of a written, secularised and universal high culture within a society, which he thought was crucially necessary to the development of modern industry and related areas of the economy. Once a universal immersion in such written high culture took place, individuals became wrenched from their pre-industrial moorings. Culture replaced social structure, in Gellner's words, and the appropriate ideology was nationalism. O'Leary seized this analysis and used it to criticise Gellner's additional claim that it was entirely fortuitous which group would develop nationalism and which would remain without one. In his suggestion, it was exactly those societies possessing written high culture that are more likely to develop nationalism when the time becomes ripe (O'Leary 1998: 59). Anthony Smith suggested another important comment on Gellner's theory (Smith 1996: 378–82). Gellner suggested that in the process of modernisation the pre-modern languages were isolated and doomed, to be replaced by the modern high culture. Smith suggested that in most actual societies the case was rather that the old languages became modernised, academy-backed versions, rather than new languages. This analysis will be exemplified here by the Turkish historical trajectory. But we begin with the *umma* and its supposed stifling of any development in the direction of ethnic nationalism within Islam.

The argument depicting the Muslim *umma* as working against nationalism is a central one in Armstrong's famous study (Armstrong 1982), and an important one in Hasting's *Construction of Nationhood* (1997: ch. 9). In both books it is claimed that Christianity fostered nationalism, since there did not develop any resistance to conveying God's message in different languages. As against this, Islam is said to have developed such objection to fanatical proportions, particularly through its objection to the translation of the Qur'an from Arabic, the sacred language of Islam. Hastings even claims that on account of the sacredness of Arabic there was a strong tendency to develop an assimilationist approach towards all those joining Islam (Hastings 1997: 200ff.). Armstrong constructs the logic of this argument around the assertion that while Christianity was a territorially based religion, Islam was established by nomads and was based for ever on the ethos of nomadism, which fostered nostalgia rather than territorial attachment. This is said to have happened twice in Islam – in its original rise in Arabia and again in the rise of the Ottoman empire (Armstrong 1982: 85ff. and *passim*). All these assertions are debatable, and are in any case no more than minimally correct. But the main point for our purposes is portraying the *umma* as blocking the way for the development and prosperity of non-Arabic cultures. This assertion is groundless.

The unity of the Muslim *umma* is indeed one of the basic tenets of original Islam (Rosenthal 1968: 21ff.). Since this community came into being on a small scale and under the leadership of a charismatic prophet, it was naturally close-knit and politically united. The divine message was one, and to fissure the body politic was tantamount to committing heresy as well. Closely connected with this perception was the sacred nature of the constituent text of Islam, the Qur'an. The Qur'an refers to itself as text that was given in Arabic for a purpose, and this only enhanced the basic approach of Islam to Arabic as its sacred language. Under these circumstances, it was only logical (although of course by no means necessary or unavoidable) that Islam would be keen to create and preserve for Arabic a strict political and cultural superiority and even exclusivity within the world of Islam. Surprisingly, this was not to be the case. A study of some major Arabic texts from the classical period shows that the thesis about the hostility of Islam to ethnicity and otherness may have been a myth right from the very beginning of this civilisation.

NASSAR'S THEORY

The study in question is Nasif Nassar's study of the Qur'an and a number of classical Arabic intellectuals of the first order (Nassar 1978). In the Introduction Nassar says it is a common fallacy to think that the term *umma* in the middle ages had the singularly uniform meaning of the religious community of Islam. In reality, he notes, Islam absorbed into its ranks whole ethnic groups which it was unable to Arabise, if it made any effort in this direction at all. Some Muslim philosophers at that time were sensitive enough to recognise this fact and adapt their use of the language accordingly. They gave the term *umma* a secular meaning of ethnic group and reserved the term *milla* to the purely religious group, Islamic but also sometime non-Islamic. He then goes on to survey some of the most important Muslim thinkers and show their exact variations on this common theme, the concept of *umma* (1978: 8ff.). In fact, Nassar shows that the pluralistic usage of the term starts already in the Qur'an, which reflects an earlier layer of the language than that of the time of the absorption of the Persians and the Turks. There is no complete agreement in this constituent text between *umma* and the Muslim community, though that meaning is extant in that book as well. But in addition, *umma* in the Qur'an can also mean human groups in general, as well as various types of religious groups (Nassar 1978: 15ff.).

One later example cited by Nassar is the historian Mas'udi (d. 956), variously considered the greatest Arab historian, who did not apply the term *umma* to Muslims or the Muslim community at all. The Muslim community was called *milla*, but so were other religious groups (Nassar 1978: 87). Ibn Khaldun (d. 1502) was less consistent than Mas'udi, and employed the term sometimes to non-religious communities, like the proto-nations of the ancient world and classical Islam – the Israelites, the Greeks, the Romans, the Arabs, the Persians (Ajam), the Turks, and so forth. Sometimes he referred by *umma* to a tribe or tribal confederacy. Sometimes the concept does refer to the Muslim community (Nassar 1978: 114 ff.).

It is interesting to go beyond these general theoretical comments and look at how Muslim perceptions moulded actual ethnic diversity in Islamic history. This ethnic diversity found expression mainly (though not exclusively) in the cases of the Persians and the Turks. In this chapter I shall limit myself mainly to the case of the Turks. Their case is a better one for our purposes, since the Persians entered Islam already possessing an ancient and glorious high culture, while the Turks accepted Islam at the time they were just shedding tribalism and nomadism. They entered Islam hardly possessing a trace of written high culture to speak of. It stands to reason that they could have been submerged within Arab culture and disappear. In fact, there were clear signs of such a process taking place at the beginning of their contact with Islam. And yet, it was not to be. I will argue that the explanation is to be sought in the fact, noted by Nassar above, that Islam developed a sense of cultural exclusivity only concerning the Qur'an. In other words, though Arabic was indeed the sacred language of Islam, this only meant that the Qur'an was not to be translated to other languages. This did not spill over to other areas of cultural, even religious production, and thus room was left for the eventual appearance of authentic Turkish high culture, in the sense of legal and literary language.

THE TURKS IN HISTORY

Basically, the history of the Turks and their relations with Islam must be divided into two chapters. Their origins are in central Asia, in the area north of China. They first entered the world of Islam in the tenth century, when a number of them were brought as elite soldiers by the Caliph al-Mu'tasim. Thereafter they trickled into the Middle East in small numbers for an extensive period of time. They served as soldiers of fortune for all kinds of local lords, and in due course started to rise to political power themselves. They were particularly prominent in the era of the crusades, when most local rulers in the area were of Turkish origin. But this phase was characterised by their being an island in a sea of Arab population. Most of these dynasties were short-lived and soon disappeared without leaving a trace. Somewhat different was the fate of the Mamluks, ruling dynasty of Egypt from 1250 to 1517. This dynasty was also composed of soldiers of fortune of Turkish origin. They survived longer, but the pattern remained: all these dynasties had one basic feature in common, namely, that they lacked a social base of peasant and city population. Lacking such a base, these dynasties neither created nor participated in any cultural production of their own. What is known about them is known through Arab writers. They themselves left no cultural trace.

The second chapter in Turkish history under Islam started with the Battle of Manzikert in 1071, in which the Seljuk empire defeated the Byzantine army in eastern Asia Minor, thereby opening the way for a large-scale penetration of tribal Turks from Iraq to this area. The weakness of the Byzantine empire in the ensuing centuries practically created here a political vacuum, and this was quickly filled by a rash of tribal Turks, probably fleeing pressure put on them by stronger elements in central Asia. The upshot was a gradual Turkification and Islamisation of Asia Minor in the two centuries after 1071. Converted Greeks and newly settled tribal Turks soon started to create principalities based on peasantry, urbanites and ruling elites. It was only a matter of time before such newly formed societies would start to form states and cultures of their own. The strongest and most enduring of these states was of course the Ottoman state, that came into being as a tiny principality in north-east Anatolia at about 1290.

There is a fierce discussion raging in the literature as to the early nature of the Ottoman state, specifically relating to its Islamic nature as a state enforcing the holy war. There are strong indications that at least for a century and a half it was not a regularly orthodox Islamic polity, but an eclectic fringe principality trying to survive as best as it could, using Muslim and Christian elements without discrimination. It certainly had nothing to do with nomadism. It possessed a bureaucracy resembling that of the Ilkhanids, or Seljuks of Iran, using manu-mitted slaves as high bureaucrats, and using Persian in phrasing state documents (Lowry 2003: 74ff.). But from the middle of the fifteenth century onwards it increasingly developed a bureaucracy and a world view wholly in keeping with other Islamic states in the Middle East, before or contemporary. It is the relations between Arabic and Turkish in the ensuing cultural development that we wish now briefly to explore. And no doubt the most important issue here is first of all the issue of religious literature.

THE SIJILL (QADI PROTOCOLS)

Every Muslim society was based on a legal system in which the *qadi* (Muslim judge) played a leading role. This was at least the theory as to how Muslims arranged their world. In reality, though, it is open to question whether the *qadi* in classical Islam was indeed the sole judge, enforcing the *shari'a* in all areas of life. This is bound to remain a theoretical question, since we possess no specimen of *qadi* protocols stretching back to that early period. In fact, the first of them that are extant today go back to the middle of the fifteenth century, the period of the consolidation of the Ottoman bureaucracy. Could it be that the two facts are somehow related? While this point is not easily proven, in my estimation it is more than possible. For some inexplicable reason the Ottoman empire based itself on salaried bureau-cracy and archival documentation and went further in this than any other Islamic empire in the past. It was also more serious in preserving these documents for posterity, which results in the fact that we have today a central Ottoman archive with tens of millions of documents, and an estimated nine thousand volumes of *qadi* protocols from Turkish and Arab cities that came under Ottoman control (Akgündüz 1988). Here I will talk on the *qadi* records, reserving discussion of the archive to the next section.

While some of the *qadi* records in the Turkish-speaking areas in the fifteenth century were in Arabic (Inalcik 1981), more and more they came to be written exclusively in Turkish (Ongan 1974). There is no sign of any legalistic-Islamic objection to the fact that the *sijill* would be written in a language other than Arabic. While the study of this source as a mine of information is now going on for some fifty years (for example, Gerber 1988), assessing the social meaning of this source on the society by which it was created has hardly begun. Some things, though, are obvious. In towns, the *qadi* was a key legal and administrative figure. While the Ottoman *qadi* on the whole preserved his process of professional education, source of legitimisation and mode of action from classical Islam, there is no doubt that the Ottomans also used this officeholder as part of their bureaucratic machine, by assigning to him many administrative tasks. The surviving protocols show that the *qadi* enforced mainly the *shari'a*, the formal law of Islam, with minor additions and omissions. In addition, it is quite clear that contrary to classical Islam, under the Ottomans there were no other legal bodies that competed with the *qadi* court, besides aberrant interventions by provincial governors, which were considered illegal and even sinful.

The high profile of the *qadi*'s court in terms of Islamic morality, legitimacy and distinct bureaucratic nature of the Ottoman state created a situation whereby the *qadi* records, *sijill* in Arabic and Turkish, constituted a uniquely important cultural artefact. There is little doubt, in fact, that the *qadi*'s court was the central institution in the Ottoman town, and its work must have affected the lives of everybody living in it. In the first place, it dealt with the law proper: from criminal matters to family matters, from divorce to child maintenance to division of post-mortem estates. But it went much further than this. The court also served as a public notary, that is, validated all sorts of contracts and affidavits. Every such recourse to the court meant the handing out of a document to one or both parties, and this massive documentation permeated the entire public and commercial life of the city. The lower classes were involved in this no less than the elite, probably even more so (Gerber 1988, 1994). Thus, the *qadi* court, by issuing enormous quantities of religiously highly appreciated documentation, contributed in no small degree to the creation of a written high culture, to use Gellner's term. While this certainly did not mean that all those whose lives were affected by this documentation could actually read, it does mean that many more could do so than we care to realise, and that many who could not read and write were nevertheless sociologically part of this culture. Scribes were a crucial social layer, and a whole literary genre, called *sakk* collections, dealt with the art of composing such court documents (for example, Dabbağzade 1832–3).

The upshot of all this is that the need to provide religious-legal services to a non-Arabic-speaking population for some reason was not seen by the jurists as a problem, despite the fact that the material in question was of religious, and hence sacred, nature. The outcome was that since the beginning of their settled life in Anatolia the Turks started to develop a religious written culture of their own.

FATWA (RESPONSA LITERATURE)

This development went further than just *qadi* protocols, since Muslims as of old developed areas of legal expertise that were part and parcel of the *shari'a*. One such layer of thought and practice was the *fatwa* literature. A *fatwa* is a legal question (*responsa*) posed to a legal expert, either privately or as part of a formal legal process. The *fatwa* layer of Islamic law stood between the practice-oriented work of the court and the purely theoretical nature of the law manuals. It dealt with real-life situations and with real people, hence it had to be in the language of those using the service. So the voluminous *fatwa* literature that was developed by the Turks is written in Turkish, not in Arabic, though necessarily every mufti must have known Arabic (see, for example, Abdallah Efendi 1849; Ali Effendi 1862) Again, no jurist is known to have ever objected to this situation.

It is interesting, on the one hand, that the layer above that of the *fatwa*, that is the law manuals, was more or less a monopolised province of Arabic: the few Turkish scholars who wrote influential law manuals did this in Arabic, as the manual of Molla Husrev (d. 1480) indicates (Husrev 1882–3). On the other hand, the law manual considered the most authoritative in the Ottoman legal system, Ibrahim al-Halabi's *Multaqa al-Abhur*, was written in Arabic by a Syrian jurist (Halabi 1891–2). But this may well have been fortuitous rather than due to religious-cum-cultural sensitivity. And in any case there is an important exception to this rule, namely, that the Turks never ventured into the purely theoretical province of the sacred law. This exception has to do with the career of the Ottoman Grand Mufti Ebu Suud el-Imadi (d. 1574) (Repp 1986). While Ebu Suud is not known to have composed a legal manual, he did compose a document of somewhat similar nature. This was the so-called *maruzat*, a Turkish-language collection bearing the form of *fatwa* collection, which in effect was something fundamentally different, more akin to a manual (Horster 1935; Gerber 1994: 88ff.). In it, the mufti dealt with a series of issues that remained controversial in Islamic law and that Ebu Suud felt should be resolved more definitely. The most salient among them was the statute of limitation, which lacks a consensus in Islamic law hence in effect did not exist. Ebu Suud decided on a statute of limitation and marshalled the authority of the Sultan to pass such a law as an Ottoman state law. But he put this also in a *fatwa* bearing his signature and responsibility as a Muslim scholar. Ebu Suud here clearly showed a rare audacity to intervene in the *shari'a* process and innovate. In traditional Islamic law such decisions are left to the consensus of the jurists. But more interestingly, numerous documents from the subsequent centuries show that his innovation was accepted unproblematically, both for his own personal authority and because it was backed by that of the Sultan. Ebu Suud, and other, later, heads of the Ottoman learned hierarchy, those who left

fatwa collections for posterity, were accepted by Arab jurists as important authorities, though without any apparent deference to their formal position. Ebu Suud
was often cited as supporting a solution that was rejected by the writer in question. Islamic law always was a jurist law and so it remained under the Ottomans
(Gerber 1999: 60ff.). But the statute of limitation was always cited positively and
enforced. Clearly, Turks, even when writing in Turkish, were a legitimate wing of
the body of interpreters of the holy law, and nobody suggested that there was any
problem with the fact that they did this in a language other than Arabic.

THE ARCHIVES

Unquestionably one major aspect of the cultural life of the Turks under the
Ottoman empire is the activity around the central Ottoman archive itself. It
is undoubtedly one of the most impressive archives ever created by a historic
state. It contains tens of millions of documents, by no means all devoted to tax
collection, although it is true that like all imperial archives it too was probably
originally established mainly to facilitate taxation. Thus, the highly impressive
land and populations surveys conducted in the sixteenth century were certainly
intended for tax purposes. But this archive grew to encompass many other aspects
of life, not purely limited to the gaze from above. Particularly important was, for
example, the 250-volume *muhimme defterleri*, that contained copies of 'important' decrees issued by the central government to the provinces (Heyd 1960).
Such decrees usually started their life after some sort of a complaint launched
by someone in the province, and on arrival it was inscribed into the protocol of
the *qadi*, and read aloud by a crier in the market place. Oftentimes these decrees
reveal details on minute issues of life in the provinces. So too was the nature of the
books of complaints, a huge series of volumes that contained citizens' complaints
addressed to the Sultan from every corner of the empire (Gerber 1994: 154ff.).
That such a tremendous body of documentation was preserved and has come
down to us is a remarkable administrative achievement, and goes to show that the
Ottoman state is in many ways underestimated. It would be difficult to fathom
fully the daily effect of this archive on the life of citizens in the Ottoman state.
But it may be illuminating in this respect to consider just one institution, that
of the *waqf*, or charitable endowments. The central Ottoman archive probably
treasures millions of documents on just that institution, admittedly one of the
main social institutions, in a state where they alone took care of providing all
social services, including hospitals, mosques, schools, bath houses, food for the
poor (provided in public kitchens), and rations of food allotted to service people
and men of religion. The number of such recipients of services was very large
indeed, and they all had their patents of authorisation bearing the elaborate seal

of the Sultan. Turkish-language documentation was a crucial part of the life of the recipients and most of them must have been literate in this language. All these endowments had to register minutely their revenues and expenses, and large number of these accounts are preserved in the archives as well (Gerber 1988). This is just one example, showing that Turkish language documentation permeated many aspects of the life of the Turks under the Ottoman empire.

HISTORIOGRAPHY

The Ottoman state started at about 1290 as a tiny frontier principality, devoid of any importance. It naturally attracted no historiographical attention at the time. But a century later it began to impress with its worldly success and a budding historiography came into being (Ménage 1962). Given that *qadi* court records, dealing with sacred materials, were unproblematically written in Turkish, there is little surprise that the new historiography was written in Turkish too. And this historiography grew apace with the growth of the empire. From private enterprises and slim volumes in the early period, in the early seventeenth century the state started to nominate an official historiographer to record its glorious annals, and historians such as Mustafa Naima fulfilled this task with multi-volume histories that were faithful records of wars and important nominations (Woodhead 1993). Ahmed Jevdet in the nineteenth century was a harbinger of modernity among other things in the sense of adding much materials on European history, including chapters entirely unrelated to Ottoman history, and all that in a neutral and impassionate tone (Bowen 1986). All in all, there grew up an impressive body of Turkish-language historiography, which constituted a central part of a Turkish written high culture. All these books were only published in the nineteenth century, and it is a pertinent question just how many people in Istanbul and beyond were affected by them in the preceding centuries. The answer is of course not many, but it is relevant to add here that cities like Istanbul in Ottoman times possessed a substantial number of public libraries, holding large treasures of Arabic and Turkish collections of manuscripts, libraries built and maintained by large-scale endowments, usually created by men of state. Few pre-modern societies possessed such treasure-houses of knowledge entirely open to the public. The number of readers must have been bigger than we realise today. Here, particularly, the advantage of possessing an empire was the crucial point in helping develop a written Turkish high culture.

THE NINETEENTH CENTURY

In the nineteenth century the Ottoman empire undertook a major project of transforming the state according to Western lines, known as the *Tanzimat* (Lewis 1961). Beginning in 1839, it was largely inspired by the heavy military losses sustained in the later eighteenth century, particularly to Russia. It was realised that without overhauling the military structure, the empire's days were numbered. It was also in turn realised that an effective army meant much more than just so many soldiers deployed in the field. It meant proper technical training and Western schooling in general, and even Western-inspired laws. Importation of Western experts and teachers, with their modern knowledge and techniques, in newly built technical schools had started already in the eighteenth century, but it was all accelerated many times over in the nineteenth. And no other field in the reform movement had undergone changes as impressive as education. It is true that in terms of mass education the achievement was modest. Schools rarely reached the village level, where most of the populace still lived. But even as it is, it was a daunting task for such a poor and enormous state, and as far as the urban middle class was concerned the schooling system available in the last generation of the empire was probably up to the best Western standards. That Ottoman intentions themselves were more than sincere is best proven by the fact that a French-speaking high school was opened in Istanbul in 1868, and an English-speaking college was tolerated since the last quarter of the nineteenth century. It is noteworthy that both institutions were in no way isolated foreign enclaves, but became quite popular with the bourgeoisie of the capital. For a traditional polity like the Ottoman empire, locked as it was for so long in total war with the West, it was a major change.

An important chapter in the nineteenth century was also the emergence of printed high culture, after the publication of books started slowly in 1727. After the middle of the nineteenth century the trickle became a flood, and the main gateway for the introduction of a major European influences. All this was unprecedented, but in a way it was a continuation of things whose bud had already existed before the nineteenth century. And just a small proof of this is the fact that a major component of the new sea of publications was all the classic Ottoman-Turkish books mentioned before – *fatwa* collections, histories and the like, many of them running into second and third editions. The world of Turkish high culture was not conceived by contemporaries as newly formed, but as a continuation – and it started to be a matter of mass consumption.

It is well known that fully fledged Turkish nationalism came into being only at the beginning of the twentieth century. But if O'Leary and Anthony D. Smith are to be believed that the standardisation in writing of a high culture and the spread of this high culture in a society are the key developments in preparing pre-modern societies to nationhood, then it seems that the Turks could have taken the nationalist path in the previous century, when so many other nationalisms erupted, having developed such a high and common culture between the sixteenth and eighteenth centuries. That they did not do so at the time was probably due to their control of the empire, to which they were obliged to feel committed more than others.

Thus, the ruling Ottoman class did not speak a language different from that of the common people. When a Turkish-speaking peasant applied to the Sultan in complaint, it was in his own language, though somebody must have helped him write the document. And it was even more so in the nineteenth. At least among large sections of the elite and the urban population Turkish high culture became a key component of their identity. This is probably to be considered a natural consequence when a group is nurtured on the basis of a high culture: it creates emotional attachment, a community. Using the 'filter' mechanism that O'Leary employed to adapt Gellner (O'Leary 1998: 52–3, 73) to the developing world, it was natural for these urban elites to propagate and universalise the veneration of this traditional and well-established high culture within their Turkish-speaking social environment.

REFERENCES

Abdallah Efendi (1849), *Behjet el-Fetava,* Istanbul: Matbaa-i Amire.
Ahmed Akgündüz (1988), Şer'iye Sicilleri, vol. 1, Istanbul: Türk Dünyası Araştırmaları Vakfı.
Ali Efendi (1862), *Fetava-i Ali Efendi,* Istanbul: Matbaa-i Amire.
Armstrong, John, A. (1982), *Nations before Nationalism,* Chapel Hill: The University of North Carolina Press.
Bowen, Harold (1986), 'Ahmad Djevdet', *Encyclopedia of Islam,* 2nd edn, vol. 1, Leiden: Brill.
Dabbağzade Numan (1832–3), *Tuhfat al-Sukuk,* Istanbul: Matbaa-i Amire.
Ebu Suud el-Imadi (1972), *Şeyhülislam Ebssuud Efendi Fetvaları,* Istanbul: Enderun Kitabevi.
Gellner, Ernest (1983), *Nations and Nationalism,* Oxford: Blackwell.
Gerber, Haim (1988), *Economy and Society in an Ottoman City: Bursa, 1600–1700,* Jerusalem: Hebrew University.
Gerber, Haim (1994), *State, Society and Law in Islam: Ottoman Law in Comparative Perspective,* Albany: State University of New York Press.
Gerber, Haim (1999), *Islamic Law and Culture, 1600–1840,* Leiden: Brill.
Gerber, Haim (2004), 'The limits of constructedness: Memory and nationalism in the Arab Middle East', *Nations and Nationalism,* 10: 251–68.
Halabi, Ibrahim (1891–2), *Multaqa al-Abhur,* Istanbul: Matbaa-i Uthmaniyye.
Hastings, Adrian (1997), *The Construction of Nationhood,* Cambridge: Cambridge University Press.
Heyd, Uriel (1960), *Ottoman Documents on Palestine,* Oxford: Oxford University Press.

Horster, Paul (1935), *Zur Anwendung des Islamischen Rechts im 16. Jahrhundert,* Stuttgart: W. Kohlhammer.

Husrev, Molla (1882–3), *Durar al-Hukkam fi Sharh Ghurar al-Ahkam,* Istanbul: Matbaat Muhammad Esad.

Inalcik, Halil (1981), 'Osmanlı Idare, Sosyal ve Ekonomik Tarihiyle Ilgili Belgeler: Bursa Kadı Sicillerinden Seçmeler', *Belgeler,* 10: 1–91.

Lewis, Bernard (1961), *The Emergence of Modern Turkey,* Oxford: Oxford University Press.

Lowry, Heath (2003), *The Nature of the Early Ottoman State,* Albany: State University of New York Press.

Ménage, Victor L. (1962), 'The beginnings of Ottoman historiography', in Bernard Lewis and Peter M. Holt (eds), *Historians of the Middle East,* Oxford: Oxford University Press, 168–79.

Nassar, Nasif (1978), *Mafhum al-Umma Bayna al-Din wa al-Ta'rikh,* Beirut: Dar al-Talia.

O'Leary, Brendan (1998), 'Ernest Gellner's diagnoses of nationalism, or, What is living and what is dead in Ernest Gellner's philosophy of nationalism', in John A. Hall (ed.), *The State of the Nation,* Cambridge: Cambridge University Press, 40–88.

Ongan, Halit (1974), *Ankara'nın Iki Numaralı Şer'iye Sicili,* Ankara: Turk Tarih Kurumu.

Repp, Richard (1986), *The Mufti of Istanbul,* Oxford: Oxford University Press.

Rosenthal, E. I. J. (1968), *Political Thought in Medieval Islam,* Cambridge: Cambridge University Press.

Smith, Anthony D. (1996), 'Memory and modernity: Reflections on Ernest Gellner's theory of modernity', *Nations and Nationalism* 2: 371–88.

Woodhead, Christine (1993), 'Naima', *Encyclopedia of Islam,* 2nd edn, vol. 7, Leiden: Brill.

Chapter 14

HISTORICAL ETHNO-SYMBOLS IN THE EMERGENCE OF THE STATE OF ISRAEL

Allon Gal

European, especially East-European political Zionism, often proclaimed itself to be revolutionary in the course of Jewish history;[1] and similarly, the culture of the new Jewish community in Eretz-Israel frequently professed to be a radically new 'Hebrew culture'. Yet, recent sensitive and scrupulous studies (Almog et al. 1998 [1994]: pts 1, 5; Smith 1999 [1995]: 203–24; 2003: chs 4, 6)[2] reveal important elements of religious continuity with the Jewish past: inside the Zionist movement, within the Yishuv (the pre-Israel Jewish community in Eretz-Israel), and in the State of Israel.[3] I shall here focus on Zionism, from the time of the constituent Zionist settlement in the Land of Israel in the early 1880s up to the early 1960s, and its associations with Jewish history and religion, as reflected in some of its core symbols.

To claim a religious association for Zionism may seem paradoxical when we remember that historically Zionism developed as a dynamic anti-status-quo force, negating passively awaiting Messianic times and the miraculous ingathering of Jews back into Zion; and that it generally negated Jewish life in the *Golah* (Exile, Diaspora) where the rabbinic tradition was still influential. Moreover, to overcome social-conservative forces (often labelled as 'under the wings of the Jewish plutocracy') that stood in the movement's way, Zionism evolved as a mass-mobilising, intensely democratic, and socially progressive movement. Also, the Zionist settlers in Eretz-Israel confronted a country partly populated by Arabs, largely desolated – and this dictated that the Zionist movement organise itself along even more voluntary and egalitarian-pioneering lines for a long period. Consequently, it is no coincidence that Zionism allied itself at crucial crossroads chiefly with democratic-pluralistic (English-speaking) countries (Mosse 1993: 121–45; Gal 2004a).

The 'historical riddle' then is: how did this modern, social nationalist movement relate itself to the Jewish past? In order to solve this riddle it must be recognised that for the Eretz-Israeli Zionists, secular and religious alike, the Bible was the major medium of their relatedness with past nationhood and heritage. This orientation was deep and at least *two*-dimensional. The Bible's primary significance for them was as nationalists – the book adeptly unfolded a history of a wholesome and vigorous Jewish independent life in the historic homeland; and this happened 'without a Diaspora'. Thus, the pioneers enthusiastically adopted the language of the Bible and, hence, became even more intimately related to the First Temple period. In numerous ways, the Bible was indeed the bedrock of the new Hebrew culture in Eretz-Israel (Aberbach 2005: 235–42; Shavit 1998; Shapira 1998 [1994]).

At the same time, mainstream Zionists, who were chiefly social liberals and democratic, humanist socialists, responded to the social and moral contents of the Bible. With its prophetic vision of a world of justice, righteousness and the brotherhood of man, the Bible had an immense potential for them toward democratic patterns and social reform.[4] The Bible's concrete nature of thought, its concern with the deed, its practical application of lofty ideals, all had tremendous meaning for their social-moral pursuit (Shapira 1998 [1994]).

Therefore, two main interpretations of the Bible's relevance to Zionism developed in the Yishuv and Israel. One emphasised an independent, wholesome national life, its heroes being the valiant judges and the great kings; and the other approach emphasised spiritual and ethical values, deriving its historical, ethnic symbols largely from the Torah's moral-social legislation and the prophets' lives and legacy. In general, these two attitudes did not exclude each another and were often interwoven. Indeed, most core ethno-symbols, as we shall see, reflected *both dimensions* of the Zionist cause – the urge for a full-blooded independent national life and the aspiration for a special society in the light of Jewish ethics and universal ideals (Shapira 1997: 155–74; Aberbach 2005: 223–32, 235–40).

David Ben-Gurion, the foremost leader of the Zionist movement since the early 1940s and the first Prime Minister of Israel, who was known for his immense interest in the Bible, exemplifies that synthesis. One of his favorite Biblical figures was Joshua, the conqueror of the Promised Land; yet, Ben-Gurion admired Joshua not particularly in his role as a warrior, but rather (as in the Alt-Noth school of biblical analysis) as a leader who paved the way for a gradual settlement that showed bravery and stamina. Moreover, Ben-Gurion accepted Joshua as a prophet, a disciple of Moses and a resolute advocate of Monotheism amidst his own people and confronting the heathen. Furthermore, Ben-Gurion admired the Hebrew prophets (naming his son 'Amos') and persistently praised their spiritual, social and ethical legacy. The ethno-symbols associated with his life and work reflected both the pursuit of a vigorous nationalist restoration and the urge for an ethical-spiritual renewal for and by Jews. (Uffenheimer 1989; Dinur 1973: 7–9; Shapira 1997: 217–47).

Two fundamental ethno-symbols ingrained in Zionism are intimately associated with two counter-Exilic historic endeavours: the exodus from Egypt and the return from the Babylonian exile. The Exodus *is* indeed a major ethno-symbol for both secularist and religious Zionists; Passover has been meaningfully celebrated by Zionists of all shades. Importantly, the story about the pilgrimage from an enslaving empire to the Promised Land is not merely nationalist as it is consistently loaded with social-ethical values of universal significance. Egypt is not only an empire that oppresses other peoples, but is itself a *'beit avadim'* (a house of slavery). The liberated Hebrew nation thus needed to reshape itself on new foundations, antithetical to the Pharaoh's Egyptian ones – free farmers and artisans obeying only God. The kings in the new Jewish state should also humbly obey God's commandments. The envisaged freed nation's leading ideal was: 'every man under his vine and under his fig tree' (1 Kings 5: 5, Micah 4: 4; Walzer 1985; Feliks 1972; Schweid 2004: ch. 2). Now the modern national trend of return to the Land of Israel persistently explicated and elevated the Exodus story to a noble, major ethno-symbol. In contradistinction to the Egyptian *'beit avadim'*, now presumably akin to an exploitative kind of capitalism, the ideal was of the urban and rural workers and labourers living decently in liberty. Thus, for the entire democratic Zionist settlement, especially in the cooperatives and in the kibbutzim, the Biblical story and the related ethno-symbols were deeply meaningful (Schweid 2004: 229–40).

Beyond the Passover's traditional *Haggadah*, many variations were creatively elaborated and used by rural and urban pioneers alike. Among the secular ones, though, the miraculous aspects of the narration were marginalised, while emphasis was laid on the national and social elements, all with a strong flavour of a blossoming Spring (Liebman and Don-Yehiya 1983: 49–50; Tzur and Danieli 2004: 10–42; Ariel 1962: 227–82).[5]

The Zionists painfully felt that the Jewish people had become detached from Nature during their long Exile; thus, coming back to the historic homeland, and intertwined with the Zionist ethos of tilling the land, was the urge to return to authenticity and to come close to Nature. Yet, this urge rarely crystallised into a *Blut-und-Boden* pattern; there was no nature-like hero in the whole range of Zionist ethno-symbolism. Perhaps the closest to this image was the Biblical Samson – associated with a vitalistic power cult – about whom the leader of the rightist-conservative Revisionist movement (that bolted from the World Zionist Organisation in 1935), Ze'ev Jabotinsky, wrote an appreciative novel. However, this superhuman hero has never gained a major place among the ethno-symbols or ancient figures adopted by Zionism (Avineri 1981: 166–75).

Historically, the 'back-to-the-soil' urge in the firm liberal/labour majority of the Zionist endeavour took a rather qualified and spiritualised course. The great prophets' legacy was always present; and the running phrase among Zionists in Eretz-Israel was 'Zion shall be redeemed with judgment and those who return to her with righteousness' (Isaiah 1: 27). Indeed, the prominent figures here were prophets such as Elijah, the spirited defender of Navot's farm against the corrupting and dispossessing foreign influences, and Amos, Micah and Isaiah, eminent pursuers of justice and ethics (Schweid 2004: 229–40; Uffenheimer 1973: chs 2–6; Urbach 1985: 175–279). Obviously, the quest for national restoration encompassed past judges and kings such as David, as symbols of national heroism and sovereignty. But the biblical kings were often conceived as restrained by some degree of public awareness, humbled at times by prophets' criticism and having soft-spots (Goldberg 1972).

Of the agricultural biblical holidays adopted and adapted by the Zionists, one is Shavu'ot (Pentecost) which, in ancient times, celebrated the first fruits and the harvest. After the destruction of the Second Temple, in rabbinic times, the ancient agricultural festival gradually became an anniversary of the giving of the Torah at Mount Sinai. While religious Zionists did not neglect this tradition, mainstream Zionism emphasised the agricultural festival to which they gave nationalist and social meanings. The nationalist aspect of the holiday is obvious: Jewish labour in the homeland has yielded successful results. The celebrations also reflect democratic and social values: at the heart of the ceremony are mass rallies offering first fruits to the democratic authorities of the nationalised land – the Jewish National Fund (Keren Kayemet le-Israel). The social and nationalist aspects originate from the well-known Zionist interpretation of the biblical injunction: 'The land shall not be sold forever for the land is Mine' (Leviticus 15: 23) as does the institution of the Jubilee Year, which stipulates that all landholdings which have changed hands revert to their original owners in the fiftieth year (Liebman and Don-Yehiya 1983: 50–1, 156–7; Shelem 1972; Ariel 1962: 303–26).

Another agricultural holiday adopted and adapted by the Zionists is the Tu bi-Shevat. The main ceremony which was creatively taken from this rather minor festival, that went back to the Second Temple era, is the planting of trees. In its Zionist version the ceremony came to celebrate the Zionist vow to redeem the largely desolated land and to prepare the ground for a wholesome national development. Zionist publications have widely disseminated the now famous saying of the Sages: 'If the Messiah comes when you are planting a tree, first finish planting and only then go out to receive him' (Avot d'Rabi Natan 31). Similarly to Shavu'ot, this holiday reflected social values, for example, the achievement of a national goal by hard work (menial labour included) and by constructive means. Indeed, 'the greening of Eretz-Israel' was, from the start, a deeply ingrained element in the Zionist endeavor. Typically, many *sabras* (native-born Israelis) bear the names of trees and flowers. This holiday has also become the official anniversary of the

Knesset, the Israeli Parliament, adding a further socio-political significance to that date (Ariel 1962: 167–85).

The '*Shivat Tzion*' endeavour (from 520 BC up to the conclusion of the rebuilding of Jerusalem's walls in 433 BC), like the Exodus, provided the Zionists with some of the most fundamental ethno-symbols. The building up of Jewish Jerusalem by the returnees and the hostility they experienced from local ethnic groups became powerful elements in the Zionist collective memory. Thus, the labour Zionist movement in Eretz-Israel, which often refers to Ezra and Nehemiah, is ever-inspired by the latter's phrase: 'With one of his hands each laboured in the work, and with the other hand he held a weapon' (Nehemiah 4: 11; Ben-Gurion 1997).

Similarly, the Maccabean revolt against the rule of the Hellenistic Seleucids (168–164 BC) was commemorated in the Zionist mind as double-faceted – first, as a national revolt against a despotic-imperialist power, and secondly, as the building-up of a militia-like, genuine people's army that enabled the astonishing success of the small nation. Hanukkah, the holiday celebrating the Maccabees' victory, was, like Passover, adopted and adapted by the Zionists, secular and religious alike. Among the secular Zionists, the religious aspect, namely the miracle of the Temple *menorah* (the candelabrum of the Temple that burnt for eight days on a scanty amount of oil), was played down, while the national and the social-popular factors became prominent (Liebman and Don-Yehiya 1983: 51–3; Ariel 1962: 127–66).

The Zionist movement also drew on the many Jewish uprisings against Roman domination. Thus, it embraced the fall of Masada, the last fortress in the Great Revolt against Rome (66–73 CE). Jewish religious tradition had hardly acknowledged these revolts, focusing instead on the destruction of the Temple. In the Yishuv and later in the State of Israel, a civil religion developed which was partly composed of historical ethno-symbols, including, following the Zionist example, the fall of Masada. Jewish youth movements and Israel Defense Force units climbed Masada to hold various ceremonies of honour. The popular Zionist cry – 'Masada shall not fall again!' – became the national symbol for the persistence of the national will to survive against all odds. This nationalist zeal was interwoven with a vehement rejection of Rome's 'oppressive and cruel social value system' which was also integrated into the Zionist ethos (Neusner 1987; Herr 1972; Liebman and Don-Yehiya 1983: 40–4, 148–51; Yadin 1966: Introduction, chs 1, 2, 15).[6]

One uprising which has been etched deeply into the nation's memory, is the revolt led by Shimon Bar-Kokhba and Rabbi Akiva (132–5 CE). The traditional, annual day that tenuously commemorates this calamitous revolt is Lag ba-Omer. The holiday, upgraded in the Zionist movement and later in the Israeli educational system as well, symbolised – in the Zionist mainstream reinterpretation, as in the case of Masada – both the nation's unyielding spirit of freedom, and an abhorrence of 'Roman values' characterised by inhuman slavery, brutal warfare and the emperor worship. The main Zionist custom of Lag ba-Omer adapted by the Zionists, was the public lighting of bonfires. It came to symbolise both of these basic ideas (Abramsky 1961: 3–45; Herr 1972; Ariel 1962: 283–302).[7]

Zionism and the State of Israel also embraced traditional Jewish symbolic objects, most notably the *menorah* and the Shield of David. The *menorah* (the seven-branched candelabrum), described in the Bible as a prominent feature of the Tabernacle erected by the People of Israel in the wilderness, as well as in the Jerusalem Temple, had for centuries served as a Jewish symbol in synagogues, and had been historically used as an emblem by a variety of Zionist organisations and associations. Eventually, it was adopted as the symbol of the State of Israel. Significantly, the design of the *menorah*, now flanked by two olive branches symbolising both peace and prosperity, is based on the representation on the Arch-of-Titus; this adoption expresses the idea of Judaea Resurrecta – the restoration of Jewish sovereignty, about 2000 years after the last Hasmonean prince used the same symbol on his coins (Strauss 1972). At the same time, the *menorah* is also the symbol of light, a motif conspicuous in some major Zionist and Israeli historical ethno-symbols. And light was itself a compound ethnic symbol, much used in modern Hebrew literature. Thus, according to Liebman and Don-Yehiya: 'Light was a widely used symbol in modern Hebrew literature, which was known, not coincidentally, as the literature of the enlightenment. Light symbolises good and beauty, wisdom and honesty, faith and hope for freedom. Fire is also a symbol of redemption – testimony to the victory of light over darkness ... [and to] eternal rebirth' (1983: 114).

The Shield of David (*Magen David*), at the centre of the Israeli flag, is a Jewish symbol several hundred years old. The early pre-Herzlian Hibbat Zion societies used it as a national emblem. Theodore Herzl, the founder of political Zionism, who was not aware of the emblems used by that movement, made the following entry in his diary in the middle of the year 1895: 'The flag that I am thinking of – perhaps a white flag with seven gold stars. The white background stands for our new and pure life; the seven stars are the seven working hours; we shall enter the Promised Land in the sign of work.' Eventually, the Zionist flag got a white background with the Shield of David in its midst and two blue horizontal strips inspired by the *tallit* (prayer shawl). Israel adopted the Zionist flag, in which two ethno-symbols stand for continuity and self-reliance – the *tallit* and the blue Shield of David; while the white background stands, however elusively, for Herzl's social-ethical vision of decency (Simon 1972).

In conclusion, a major characteristic of Zionism's symbols is their Jewish historical, ethnic and religious inspiration. Many of these symbols draw, first, on past periods of Jewish experience of sovereignty in their historic homeland; second, on the many Jewish uprisings against foreign domination which have marked Jewish historical experience; and third, on the historic endeavours of Jewish communities to reject the condition of exile.

Another basic characteristic of Zionism's ethno-symbolism is its strong bent towards moral and social renewal. Typically, the nationalist renaissance was conceived also in ethical-universalistic terms. Significantly, the same historical memories and myths that nurtured the nationalist urge – rich, complex and multi-layered as they were – also served to nourish the moral quest.

These twin qualities of the historical ethno-symbols that I discussed above combined to produce, eventually, a modern, democratic and enlightened national state which at the same time based itself on Jewish history and traditions millennia old.

Since the late 1960s, some changes have occurred, due partly to globalisation processes and the protracted conflict with the Arabs: the 'thinning-out' of the secular camp's historical culture; the 'normalisation' and capitalisation of the Israeli economy; and the rise of fundamentalism among religious Zionists. However, in my judgment, the Judaic, social, and democratic tradition in Israel – as it was shaped and sustained by the historical ethno-symbols outlined above – is vibrant and still developing (Gal 2004b).

NOTES

1 For a comparative discussion of American/European Zionisms' ethno-symbols see Gal 1999: 362–6. This article discusses chiefly 'classic' European Zionism.
2 For a discussion of the founders of Israel's vision of a 'moral state' see Liebman and Don-Yehiya 1983: 86–7, 214–7 and *passim*; Zionism as 'moral renewal' is analysed in Smith 2003: 52–65, 85–94; for 'moral awakening' and 'moral innovators' in cultural nationalism see Hutchinson 1987: 30–40 and Hutchinson 2005: ch. 2. The article has benefited from the above-mentioned works; of Almog et al. (editors) 1998 [1994], I owe much in particular to the articles by Shlomo Avineri, Shmuel Almog, Anita Shapira and Chaim Schatzker. Interestingly, Liebman and Don-Yehiya conclude that roughly until the establishment of Israel, 'The settlers who constituted the adherents of Zionist-socialism were too intimately associated with the religious tradition, too familiar with its broad outlines, yet also too estranged from its basic values to either ignore it or unconsciously transform it' (1983: 58). They also conclude, though, that 'the new civil religion', emerged in the 1960s, was more closely linked to tradition (1983: 166)
3 This short article does not allow for historiographic justice. However, it seems that the English-speaking world encouraged scholarly inquiry into the religious dimension of Zionism. This is true of pioneering works such as Hertzberg's book of 1959 (80–100), Smith's article of 1973, and perhaps even Luz's book of 1988 [1985] which has its roots at Brandeis University in Waltham, Massachusetts.

4 Sociologically, there was a long Jewish political tradition for progressive Zionists to draw
   upon (see Eisenstadt 1992: chs 1, 2, 9; Elazar 1993: 1–127; Sokol 2002; the ongoing four-
   volume project, Walzer et al. 2000, 2003; and Schweid 1984 for a systematic interpretation
   of the whole gamut of Jewish holidays as carrying a progressive-modern potential). However, most social Zionists in the period discussed in this article were tuned to absorb inspiration and guidelines chiefly from the legacy of periods of sovereignty.
5 Ariel 1962 is used in this and subsequent discussions as a historical *source* typical of the
   labour/liberal approach to holidays and history in the period discussed here. See also
   Baruch and Levinsky 1956; Eyali 1953. For a historical survey of the First and Second Temples see Ben-Sasson 1976, vol. 1.
6 Cf. Zerubavel 1995: chs 5, 8, 11; as in this and in other cases, this study ignores the social-
   moral renewal aspect altogether.
7 Cf. Zerubavel 1995: chs 4, 7, 10; and see note 6 above.

REFERENCES

Aberbach, D. (2005), 'Nationalism and the Hebrew Bible', *Nations and Nationalism*, 11, 2:
    223–42.
Abramsky, S. (1961), *Bar-Kokhba: President of Israel*, Tel Aviv: Massadah Publishers, in
    Hebrew.
Almog, S., J. Reinharz and A. Shapira (eds) (1998 [1994]), *Zionism and Religion*, Hanover,
    NH: Brandeis University Press/University Press of New England.
Ariel, Z. (ed.) (1962), *The Book of Holidays and Celebrations*, Tel Aviv: Am Oved Publishing
    House, in Hebrew.
Avineri, S. (1981), *The Making of Modern Zionism: The Intellectual Origins of the Jewish State*,
    New York: Basic Books.
Baruch, Y. and Y. Levinsky (eds) (1956), *The Book of Holidays*, Tel Aviv: Dvir, in Hebrew.
Ben-Gurion, D. (1997), *Like Stars and Dust: Essays from Israel's Government Year Book*, Sede
    Boqer Campus: Ben-Gurion Research Center and Ben-Gurion Heritage Institute.
Ben-Sasson, H. (ed.) (1976), *A History of the Jewish People*, 1. Cambridge, MA: Harvard
    University Press.
Dinur, B. (1973), 'Preface' in B. Dinur (ed.), *Types of Leadership in the Biblical Period*, Jeru-
    salem: Israel Academy of Sciences and Humanities, in Hebrew.
Eisenstadt, S. N. (1992), *Jewish Civilization: The Jewish Historical Experience in a Comparative
    Perspective*, Albany: State University of New York Press.
Elazar, D. J. (ed.) (1993), 'Communal Democracy and Liberal Democracy in the Jewish Polit-
    ical Tradition', *Jewish Political Studies Review*, spring 5, 1– 2: 1–127.
Eyali, M. (ed.) (1953), *Holidays and Celebrations*, Tel Aviv: Gazit, in Hebrew.
Feliks, J. (1972), 'Agriculture in the land of Israel', *Encyclopaedia Judaica*, Jerusalem: Keter
    Publishing, vol. 2, 382–98.
Gal, A. (1999), 'Jewish return to history in American Zionist thought 1897–1967', in S. N.
    Eisenstadt and M. Lissak (eds), *Zionism and the Return to History, A Reappraisal*, Jerusalem:
    Yad Ben-Zvi Press, in Hebrew, 361–88.
Gal, A. (2004a), 'David Ben-Gurion's Zionist foreign policy, 1938–48: The democratic factor',
    in E. Karsh (ed.), *Israel: The First Hundred Years*, vol. 4, London: Frank Cass, 13–28.

Gal, A. (2004b.), 'On Israel, the diaspora and Zionist democracy', *Studies in Zionism, the Yishuv and the State of Israel*, in Hebrew, 14: 509–36.

Goldberg, A. (1972), 'David in modern Hebrew literature', *Encyclopaedia Judaica*, Jerusalem: Keter Publishing House, vol. 5, 1333–4.

Herr, M. D. (1972), 'Rome in Talmudic Literature', *Encyclopaedia Judaica*, Jerusalem: Keter Publishing House, vol. 14, 242–4.

Hertzberg, A. (ed.) (1959), *The Zionist Idea*, Philadelphia: The Jewish Publication Society of America.

Hutchinson, J. (1987), *The Dynamics of Cultural Nationalism*, London: Allen and Unwin.

Hutchinson, J. (2005), *Nations as Zones of Conflict*, London: Sage.

Liebman, C. S. and E. Don-Yehiya (1983), *Civil Religion in Israel: Traditional Judaism and Political Culture in the Jewish State*, Berkeley: University of California Press.

Luz, E. (1988 [1985]), *Parallels Meet: Religion and Nationalism in the Early Zionist Movement (1882–1904)*, Philadelphia: The Jewish Publication Society.

Mosse, George L. (1993), *Confronting the Nation: Jewish and Western Nationalism*, Hanover, NH and London: Brandeis University Press/University Press of New England.

Neusner, J. (1987), *Vanquished Nation, Broken Hearts: The Virtues of the Heart in Formative Judaism*, Cambridge: Cambridge University Press.

Schweid, E. (1984), *The Cycle of Appointed Times: The Meaning of Jewish Holidays*, Tel Aviv: Am Oved Publishers, in Hebrew.

Schweid, E. (2004), *The Philosophy of the Bible as a Cultural Foundation in Israel*, Tel Aviv: Lamiskal Publishing House, in Hebrew.

Shapira, A. (1998 [1994]), 'The religious motifs of the Labor movement', in S. Almog et al. (eds), *Zionism and Religion*, Hanover, NH: Brandeis University Press/University Press of New England, 251–72.

Shapira, A. (1997), *New Jews Old Jews*, Tel Aviv: Am Oved Publishers, in Hebrew.

Shavit, Y. (1998), 'The status of culture in the process of creating a national society in Eretz-Israel', in Z. Shavit (ed.), *The Construction of Hebrew Culture in Eretz-Israel*, Jerusalem: Israel Academy for Sciences and Humanities and Bialik Institute, in Hebrew, 9–29.

Shelem, M. (1972), 'Kibbutz festivals', *Encyclopaedia Judaica*, Jerusalem: Keter Publishers, vol. 10, 959–63.

Simon, M. (1972), 'Flag', *Encyclopaedia Judaica*, Jerusalem: Keter Publishers, vol. 6, 1334–8.

Smith, Anthony D. (1973), 'Nationalism and religion: The role of religious reform in the genesis of Arab and Jewish nationalism', *Archives de Science des Religions*, 35: 23–43.

Smith, Anthony D. (1999 [1995]), *Myths and Memoirs of the Nation*, Oxford: Oxford University Press.

Smith, Anthony D. (2003), *Chosen Peoples*, Oxford: Oxford University Press.

Sokol, M. (ed.) (2002), *Tolerance, Dissent, and Democracy: philosophical, historical, and halakhic perspectives*, Northvale, NJ: Jason Aronson.

Strauss, H. (1972), 'Menorah on the Arch of Titus' and 'The Menorah in art', *Encyclopaedia Judaica*, vol. 11, 1363–70.

Tzur, M. and Y. Danieli (eds) (2004), *The Kibbutz Haggada: Israeli Pesach in the Kibbutz*, Jerusalem: Yad Yitzhak Ben-Zvi, in Hebrew.

Uffenheimer, B. (1973), *Ancient Prophecy in Israel*, Jerusalem: Magnes Press, in Hebrew.

Uffenheimer, B. (1989), 'Ben-Gurion and the Bible', in M. Cogan (ed.), *Ben-Gurion and the*

Bible: The People and Its Land, Beer Sheva: Ben-Gurion University Press, in Hebrew, 54–69.

Urbach, E. E. (1985), *On Zionism and Judaism: Essays*, Jerusalem: The Zionist Library, in Hebrew.

Walzer, M. (1985), *Exodus and Revolution*, New York: Basic Books.

Walzer, M., M. Lorberbaum and N. Zohar (eds) (2000, 2003), *The Jewish Political Tradition*, New Haven: Yale University Press, 2 vols.

Yadin, Y. (1966), *Masada: In Those and These Days*, Haifa: Shikmona Publishers, in Hebrew.

Zerubavel, Y. (1995), *Recovered Roots: Collective Memory and the Making of Israeli National Tradition*, Chicago: University of Chicago Press.

Part VI

ETHNOSYMBOLISM
IN THE FAR EAST AND INDIA

Chapter 15

ETHNOSYMBOLISM IN CHINA AND TAIWAN
Peter Ferdinand

INTRODUCTION

If one of the defining characteristics of the ethnosymbolist approach to nationalism is a concern with the *longue durée*, then it is particularly appropriate to apply it to China. With records of Chinese history going back between three and five thousand years, few states have a *durée* that is longer. Chinese nationalism is not just a product of twentieth-century modernisation. Key elements of Chinese identity go back not just centuries but millennia. We shall see that some fundamental symbols of Chinese ethnic or national identity recur in different guises as dynasties and regimes change, another key tenet of the ethnosymbolic interpretation of nationalism. But the significance of nationalism in China is not merely intellectual. One of the PRC's most fundamental and emotional external disputes is with Taiwan. Essentially this is a dispute over sovereignty and national territory. Nationalism is inextricably involved. If the conflict turned military, the resulting devastation would affect far more than just these two states.

On the other hand, if modernisation is, as some have argued, a crucial (possibly *the* crucial) facilitator of nationalism, then Taiwan ought to be a very good test case. According to the OECD, by 1999 Taiwan had achieved a per capita GDP of US $15,720 in constant 1990 figures, which puts Taiwan among the industrialised states of the world – the equivalent figure for the UK in 1998 was $18,714. Since its per capita income in 1950 was $936, this represents an enormous achievement – the comparable figure for the UK in 1950 was $6,907 (Maddison 2001: 304, 277). Has this development stimulated nationalism, particularly as there are no internal disagreements over the boundaries of the state, it being an island?

This chapter will firstly discuss the complexities of Chinese identity and highlight the dominant orthodoxy of unity that pervades the writing of its history. It will show how some of the key symbols of Chinese identity have recurred to underpin it, whether as positive or negative examples. After that it will discuss the problems of establishing a distinctive Taiwanese identity, particularly one focused on a cosmopolitan, civic nationalism, and emphasise the importance of the lack of a prior ethnic identity to underpin it. This suggests that, at least in the case of Taiwan, modernisation has not been a sufficient condition for the emergence of nationalism. Finally it will suggest that a distinctive Taiwanese identity is made more problematic by the increasing cosmopolitanism on the mainland.

CHINESE IDENTITY

Not surprisingly for a country the size of China, the people are heterogeneous. Partly this means that there are many minorities – fifty-five are officially recognised by the People's Republic, but ethnographers put the figure much higher. In addition ethnic Chinese are also divided on the basis of spoken language. There are eight major dialects of spoken Chinese with differences so great that some have argued that they are greater than, say, between English, German, Swedish and Danish (Zhuang 1996b: 30). Regional variations in each dialect further complicate the picture and hinder or prevent comprehension in oral communications.

The dominant ethnic group are Han Chinese, who supposedly are descended from the mythical Yellow Emperor who supposedly reigned along the Yellow River between 2697 and 2598 BC, though neolithic settlements there can be traced back to around 12,000 years ago. Though their descendants spread throughout what is now China and beyond, the term Han originally signified people from northern China, in particular designating the dynasty that established the basic shape of China between roughly 206 BC and 200 AD (Olson 1998).

How was the state formed and how has it cohered for so long, despite periodic internal disputes and wars? What part does 'nationalism' play in this? Hutchinson suggested a general distinction between political and cultural nationalism (Hutchinson and Smith 1994). We shall see that this does not really hold for China.

Fundamentally there are two overlapping characterisations derived from the ambiguous understanding of 'China' by the Chinese. Pye (1996: 109) has expressed it graphically: 'China is really a civilisation pretending to be a nation-state'. The first characterisation is that of China as the centre of civilisation and enlightenment. Traditionally this was the role that it ascribed to itself vis-à-vis neighbouring peoples. Thus being 'Chinese' meant being 'civilised'. It meant following Han customs, but did not imply any ethnic or racial identity (Cheng 1980: 17). Though it depended in part upon alterity, defining oneself in contradistinction to other(s), it also encouraged civilising assimilation.

The second meaning of 'China' is more political, designating territory and people ruled from the national capital by the Emperor, President or Chairman. Here too the people were distinguished from others, but in this respect barriers were intended to repel. Fairbank (1988: 15) emphasised the lasting effect of fear of Central Asian invaders upon traditional institutions of Chinese rule – a fear that inspired one of the most potent symbols of the Chinese state, the Great Wall. To the south and west the natural borders of China were always more fluid and porous. Where territory was not under the direct control of the Emperor, neighbouring states were expected to pay tribute, in return for which they were to be blessed with the benefits of Chinese civilisation. It was only in the nineteenth century that Western imperialism imposed a more rigid Westphalian doctrine and practice of state sovereignty that required China to delimit its frontiers and treat all other states (at least in theory) as equals.

This changed the focus of Chinese rulers' concern from the centre to the periphery. Originally the main modern character for 'state', *kuo*, signified city, and principally *capital* city, in the Yellow River valley. This spotlighted the centre of power in the state, but left the outward perimeter of authority more vague. Emperors in general were more preoccupied with affairs, the closer the latter were to the capital. Distant regions were neglected – unless and until they became sources of resistance and rebellion. We shall see later that this affected the traditional relationship between the emperor and Taiwan. But since the challenge of Western imperialists in the nineteenth century and the principles of systemic order that they brought, Chinese governments have always been extremely preoccupied with defending the prerogatives of their sovereign territory and rights, whether or not they could enforce them. The justice of territorial boundaries has become an obsession for modern China, hence the heated emotions aroused in China from the 1980s by the fate of the Diaoyutai/Senkaku outcrops of rock 250 miles east of Okinawa, claimed by both China and Japan. Though the significance of the dispute partly stems from related issues over naval activity in international waters and control of possible maritime resources, the issue would have seemed absurd to Chinese rulers in earlier centuries. Yet in recent years, boatloads of Chinese and Japanese have kept going there to stake their national claims, risking naval confrontation from either side.

But whether 'China' was state or civilisation, there was one common supposition that ran through the writing of Chinese history by Chinese, namely that of fundamental unity. All 'civilised' people and/or all 'Chinese' should live together under the same system. This was the orthodoxy (*zhengtong*) that assured the continuity and legitimacy of the imperial system, and vice versa. It was a national policy that grew out of the dominant narrative that China's rulers commissioned of themselves. As Schwarcz (1991: 76–7) expressed it:

> In traditional China, history took the place of religion. To be more precise, historical mindedness – a scrupulous, textually anchored attachment to the communal past – became a sacred commitment over time. References to history were, and continue to be, a fertile source of moral value, literary allusion, and guidelines for self-cultivation.

Jenner (1992: 4–5) concurred:

> Chinese governments have, for at least 2000 years, taken history much too
> seriously to allow the future to make its own unguided judgements about them
> ... Nowhere has the homogenising effect been more successful than in creating
> the impression that the Han Chinese are a single ethnic group ... Historical
> myth-making has so far been remarkably effective not just in inventing a single
> Han Chinese ethnicity but also – and this is a far bigger triumph – in winning
> acceptance of it ... The religion of the Chinese ruling classes is the Chinese state,
> and it is through history that the object of devotion is to be understood.

This did not exclude regional identifications and loyalties within China. In
some eras and for some people these were defended fiercely (Levenson 1967).
Nevertheless traditional values were hierarchical, and they subordinated local
concerns to central ones. Here Confucianism played a crucial role in fusing
China-as-civilisation with China-as-state, at least until the twentieth century.
This made the roles of emperor and patriarchal father analogous. Each expected
and was entitled to respect, loyalty and deference. If unity and harmony prevailed
in families, the same would be true of the state, and vice versa.

Of course, there have been times of disunity, weakness and dissension. In the
1920s and 1930s China was bedevilled by warlordism. A few of these warlords
and some intellectuals advocated the establishment of a federal China. Even Mao
Zedong was sympathetic to this idea in the 1920s. Yet the federalist movement
was an exception that proves the rule of Chinese history. It was pushed aside
in the struggle to expel foreign imperialists and re-establish Chinese territorial
integrity. Local attachments were potentially too debilitating for national unity
(Duara 1993). Mao himself abandoned federalism and consciously modelled
himself on the great centraliser, Qin Shi Huangdi, the first Qin emperor who
unified the first China in the third century BC (Li 1994: 122–3).

NATIONALIST SYMBOLS
Symbols of identity

The first 'official' historian of China, Sima Qian (145–c. 90 BC), set the tone for
subsequent writers, certainly official chroniclers. He 'imagined', or at any rate
articulated, a 'founding myth' of the Yellow Emperor 2,000 years previously, who
had ruled the middle and upper reaches of the Yellow River in northern China
and from whom all Chinese were supposedly descended. Yet whilst this could
imply Chinese ethnic homogeneity, it was more ambiguous. Many Confucian
writers later propounded the doctrine that 'All men are brothers within the Four
Seas'. This encompassed all civilisation. Some went so far as to claim that all men

were descended from the Yellow Emperor, not just all Han (Cheng 1980: 103).

On the other hand, foreign invasions of China reminded the Han of the differences between them and outsiders, even though some of the new dynasties, for example, Mongol and Manchu, adopted Chinese customs of rule to legitimise their authority. Yet throughout the imperial era, popular attitudes towards 'legitimate' Chinese rule fluctuated. For instance, though the last dynasty, the Manchu Qing, presided at its height over a greater prosperity than China had ever known and lasted for over 250 years, there always remained among the Han a lingering undercurrent of resentment over alien rule.

In part this sentiment also reflected a change in popular and official attitudes that resulted from the increasing clashes with the West, though Dikötter (1992: 34) reminds us that racial stereotyping of roles was already beginning under the Qing dynasty in the eighteenth century. As Chinese officials and then Chinese scholars were forced into more intense interaction with Western counterparts, they came to absorb some of their ways of thinking. Since Social Darwinism enjoyed widespread acceptance at that time, especially among colonial representatives, this rubbed off on Chinese thinking. Chinese writers played up the racial basis of and justification for policies. The symbolic role of the Yellow Emperor reverted to that of the progenitor of all Chinese, not of all civilised people.

The communists, especially during the Cultural Revolution (1966–9), officially stigmatised ancient beliefs and ways of thinking. The 'four olds' (old customs, culture, habits and ideas) were all to be eradicated. Yet the Taiwanese song-writer Hou Dejian, who defected to the PRC in the early 1980s, wrote a song entitled *Heirs of the Dragon* which showed the continuing contemporaneity of the Dragon Emperor. It became almost an anthem for many Chinese on both Taiwan and the mainland and it contained the lines:

> In the ancient East there is a dragon;
> China is its name.
> In the ancient East there lives a people,
> The dragon's heirs every one.
> Under the claws of this mighty dragon I grew up
> And its heir I have become
> Like it or not –
> Once and forever, an heir of the dragon. (Schoppa 2005: 391–2)

The students were singing this song when the tanks rolled on to Tiananmen Square on 4 June 1989. Nowadays in China the Yellow River is still regarded as the original cradle of Chinese civilisation, even though more recent archaeological research has revealed evidence of early civilisations across China. It thus still provides the basis for a belief in national unity. In 1994, for instance, the Governor of Hunan province held a ceremony to commemorate the completion of a memorial arch to the Yellow Emperor, where President Jiang Zemin raised a memorial stone (Zhuang 1996b: 33).

Symbols of civilisational achievement

Chinese have also taken pride in the civilisational achievements of their ancestors. These were and are regarded as contributions to world civilisation, from which all people have benefited. These include the inventions of gunpowder and the Chinese script. The philosophy of Confucianism as a doctrine of social order was a social equivalent, which Chinese rulers believed conferred stability on all who accepted it, whether or not they were Chinese. In earlier ages these symbolised China's superiority over other peoples in Asia. More recently, since the arrival of Westerners in the nineteenth century, they symbolised an enduring right to equal respect for Chinese from the world community.

The Maoist era saw some modern equivalents. Although the doctrine of communism came from the West, via the Soviet Union, the Sino-Soviet split from 1961 left China more isolated and dependent upon its own devices. At the same time this presented the CCP with opportunities to come up with indigenous symbols of heroic achievements that could inspire the masses. This was especially the case for Chinese discoveries or inventions that were made in the face of Soviet opposition or discouragement. Examples were the Chinese testing of nuclear weapons in 1964, after the Soviet withdrawal of all assistance, the Chinese discovery of oil in Daqing in 1959 after Soviet oil experts had derided the possibility, and the building of the railway bridge across the river in Nanjing, when Soviet engineers had rejected its feasibility. These were propagandised by the PRC to show that the Chinese were just as capable of technological innovation as their ancestors. Even if none of these achievements were world 'firsts' or showed that China was leading the world, they at least demonstrated that China and the Chinese were as worthy of international respect in the modern age.

These achievements were carried out behind more or less closed doors. From 1949 China began to cut itself off from international contacts. This isolation accelerated after the Sino-Soviet dispute. During the Cultural Revolution China became quite xenophobic. This meant that the appropriate symbols for a modern, socialist China had largely to be imagined from within. The difference was that new ways of thinking were supposed to come from peasants and workers, primarily peasants. Thus many traditional symbols of Chinese identity were now turned from positive to negative. Intellectuals and artists were sent to live in the countryside to absorb appropriate ways of living from the wisdom of the peasants. The campaigns against the 'Four Olds' stigmatised old ways of thinking. Old forms of art were rejected because of their associations with the old imperial order. Peking Operas were banned because they glorified emperors and their system, to be replaced by a very limited number of 'revolutionary operas' produced by Mao's wife, Jiang Qing, and committees of her associates. The symbols of national identity became struggle: fighting the Nationalists and the Japanese in World War II.

Similarly religious monuments and edifices were torn down. This especially hit ethnic minorities such as Tibetans whose whole way of life had been based upon religious beliefs and practices. Out of a total of 2,700 temples in Tibet, 2,690 were destroyed during the Cultural Revolution. But the campaign struck at all sections of the Chinese population, as it was directed against superstitious beliefs in general.

Many traditional buildings were torn down to make way for 'modern' apartment blocks and wide boulevards, though there were virtually no cars to take advantage of them. A national symbol of the new way of life was the Great Hall of the People built on the edge of Tiananmen Square, an enormous edifice with suites of official rooms for each of China's twenty-nine provinces, lacking any discernible architectural merit. For the state the significance of the symbol lay in the fact that the whole edifice was built by armies of workers working day and night for only ten months in 1959.

The Cultural Revolution represented a recurring tendency in Chinese history for assaults on traditional beliefs and ways of life by iconoclasts who want to transform the country. This had happened after the downfall of the empire in 1911 with the May 4th Movement. Mao explicitly modelled himself on the founder of the Qin dynasty, Qin Shi Huangdi, who burnt most of the books that the Chinese had accumulated up till then and executed 260 Confucian scholars.

Yet the persistence of national sensitivities and nationalist traditions can be seen in the intemperate official response to a series of TV documentaries that were screened in China in 1988 entitled *River Elegy* (*Heshang*). The basic message underlying them was radical: all the backwardness and weaknesses of China should be attributed to the inland traditions associated with the Yellow River. If China wanted to modernise, it needed to turn towards the blue of the ocean and the outside world. Yellow was the colour of the past. Blue was the colour of the future. It repeatedly focused on the images of the Great Wall, Dragon and Yellow River to symbolise ancient and obscurantist traditions. However, the series created a furore and was only shown twice. After the Tiananmen Square events its makers were persecuted – according to Vice-President Wang Zhen: 'You vilify the Chinese nation and Chinese civilisation' (Su 1991: 296).

Symbols of Chinese identity and nationalism have recurred over the centuries. At times some of them have been praised and at others excoriated. Either way, they have sustained Chinese identity. For example, Waldron has shown the enormous change in the symbolism of the Great Wall. Traditionally it was seen only as a symbol of inhuman treatment by emperors, with thousands upon thousands of workers and slaves losing their lives in its construction. Yet from the time of the Enlightenment Western visitors to China commented favourably on it, and gradually this more positive assessment seeped back into China (Waldron 1993). More recently, even the communist regime appreciated it in its isolation. When after 1969 word spread that it was the one man-made object that could be seen from the moon, this made it into a source of Chinese pride, even though the story itself turns out to be apocryphal.

NATIONALISM ON TAIWAN

The first settlements on Taiwan go back thousands of years, but the original inhabitants seem to have come from island and maritime communities in the Pacific and Southeast Asia. Taiwan was first incorporated into China in the early Qing dynasty, after it became a haven for the last Ming opponents of the Qing. Troops came from the mainland to suppress the rebellion and this was followed by a large influx of Han male settlers. Once pacified, however, the imperial rulers largely lost interest in Taiwan. According to Roy (2003: 29–30), the Qing only asserted control again in the 1880s after complaints from foreign states over massacres of their shipwrecked sailors by local people. Then, in 1895, the island was ceded to Japan following the Sino-Japanese War. Since then, it has only formally been part of China for four years, between 1945 and 1949.

Thus all the people alive on Taiwan have had separate experiences and traditions from those on the mainland. Has this fused with modernisation into nationalism?

There are two other contextual factors that could make Taiwanese nationalism more likely. The first is the hostility from the mainland since 1949. Whatever the background of the various communities living on Taiwan, they share this experience of protracted military threat that in the past has occasionally spilled over into confrontation – the most recent being the mainland's 'test-firing' of missiles that overflew Taiwan at the time of the presidential elections in 1995.

The second external factor is the lack of recognition by other states. For individual Taiwanese, this was not so important until increasing numbers of them could travel abroad. As more of them did so from the 1980s onwards, the restrictions or conditions placed upon them by foreign states that they visited became irksome. Often they were classified as being 'stateless', with all the implications of being potential Third-World economic refugees that accompanied it. Or, as in Japan, they might be registered as coming from 'China', that is, the PRC. The citizens of a state that had made enormous economic progress and was being courted for investment even by developed countries resented the embarrassment. It regularly reminded them of the injustice of their unequal status and stimulated the drive for fairer treatment.

On the other hand there are significant obstacles to any kind of Taiwanese nationalism. The first and most obvious is the ethnic heterogeneity of the population. Admittedly this is not as great as on the mainland, but it is nevertheless significant. Writers tend to identify four main ethnic communities: the original Malayo-Polynesian tribes (nine in all); the Hoklo-speakers who came from Fujian province in waves over the last 1,000 years; the Hakkas, originally from north China but who were persecuted and driven further and further south, some of them coming to Taiwan in the thirteenth and nineteenth centuries; and the 'mainlanders' who came with the Republic of China (ROC) from all over China after 1945.

Nevertheless a second obstacle has been politics in Taiwan. Between 1945 and 1991 the official position of the government and the ruling Nationalist Party was that it was the government of the whole of China, not just Taiwan. Since the Guomindang (GMD) had come to Taiwan from the mainland and wished to return, it imposed an official doctrine that traced its continuity from the ancient Chinese state. In 1957, for instance, it established an annual ceremony to honour the Yellow Emperor, even though the heads of the GMD government have all been Christian (Zhuang 1996b: 32). Schoolchildren and students were required to study the history of China rather than Taiwan, and there was discrimination against students who spoke at school in local dialects rather than Mandarin.

Chinese who had come from the mainland after 1945 dominated the ROC regime on Taiwan. Already in February 1947 popular resentment at official corruption and discrimination had boiled over into a protest that provoked a violent crackdown in which anywhere between 3,000 and 10,000 lives were lost. During the 1950s there were possibly 90,000 victims of the official 'White Terror' with half of them executed. The regime depended on the activities of around 50,000 full-time and 500,000 part-time informers out of a population of under 10 million (Roy 2003: 73, 90–1). This division between mainlanders and Taiwanese was a political fault line that has underlain political relations up to the present. Opponents branded it a 'settler regime', like colonial states such as South Africa. This obviously complicated the possibility of any homogeneous sense of nationalism, whether Chinese or Taiwanese.

Since 1986, however, Taiwan has undergone gradual democratic transformation, symbolised by the establishment of the Democratic Progressive Party (DPP) which has been associated with the interests of the 'Taiwanese' as distinct from the 'mainlanders' and which won power in 2000. Some in the party have also called for Taiwanese independence. They have preached a Taiwanese nationalism that should serve as the basis of an independent, sovereign state.

SYMBOLS OF TAIWANESE NATIONALISM

There are certainly events and characteristics from Taiwan that can serve as symbols of such a nationalism. In their different ways they symbolise what makes Taiwan different from the mainland. One is the massacre of 28 February 1948. Until the era of democracy this was a taboo subject in Taiwan. But afterwards the regime was forced into admitting and then apologising for it. Once the new DPP won the presidential election in 2000, it created a memorial park in Taipei to symbolise the earlier repression and sufferings of the Taiwanese, not merely from the GMD but from the imposition of rule from the mainland (Edmondson 2002).

A second symbol, ironically, is colonial rule by the Japanese. In fact, when Taiwan was surrendered to the Japanese, the initial response on the island was to declare independence and resist handover. However, this was soon suppressed by the Japanese. Afterwards, although the Japanese behaved with some brutality towards the local population, they also developed the local economy. The main concern was to supply food and raw materials for the Japanese empire that led to economic development. Basic industries and infrastructure such as railways were built. And World War II largely passed Taiwan by, so that there was relatively little damage or loss of life, unlike on the mainland. All of this meant that Taiwanese with roots there that go back beyond 1945 tend to have quite a different, more positive attitude towards Japanese colonialism than that of Chinese on the mainland. A recent work on Taiwanese nationalism declares:

> After Taiwan came under Manchu rule, the island's active international trade was whittled down into trade only with China, causing Taiwan to lose its economic vitality and putting Taiwan on the periphery of China's economic sphere. Taiwan's reliance on the China market was the cause of the island's distress. Once Japanese colonial rule began and relations with China were severed, a modern infrastructure was introduced to the island, widening the gap between Taiwan and China. During the period in which Taiwan and China had no contact, Taiwan's international trade thrived and its economy boomed. (Hsueh 2005: 163–4)

Thirdly, there are symbolic differences between Taiwanese Chinese and Chinese from the mainland. In fact, these are relatively limited. Yet two features stand out. First, there are some different cultural traditions. For example, under

Manchu rule, the binding of women's feet was not practised by either the Hakkas or the aborigines on Taiwan. Now Taiwanese nationalists point to this as symbolic of differences from practices on the mainland (Brown 2004). Second, there are also linguistic differences. Although the official language on Taiwan under the GMD was Mandarin, the vernacular language was Minnan, which is much closer to the speech of southern China, especially Fujian province. In the democratic era 'Taiwanese' has established itself as an equal language to Mandarin in politics. And then too recent scientific discoveries have suggested that Taiwanese DNA is much closer to that of the southern Chinese rather than those of the north, that is, the homeland of the Yellow Emperor – differences that have widened since the large influx of male colonists in the seventeenth century because they usually married into the local matriarchal society. This too comes to serve as a symbol of difference from the mainland (Hsueh 2005: 84–5).

Fourthly, the presence of the aborigines, who came to the island before the Chinese, has also been turned into a symbol. Admittedly, over the centuries they have been forced to retreat into the inland, mountainous areas by repeated influxes of outsiders. But now, under democracy, they have acquired rights and a status roughly equal to that of the other inhabitants of the island. More importantly, for Taiwanese nationalists, they represent a non-Han Chinese ethnic dimension to Taiwanese society with a different way of life.

Democracy has created opportunities for these symbols to be popularised. The educational system on Taiwan is being recast so that it pays more attention to the language, customs and history of Taiwan than to those of the mainland – the reverse of practice up to the 1990s. And the DPP government is trying to 'brand' Taiwan through cultural promotion, designating a national colour (brick-red, the colour of local rice-cakes) so as to strengthen its separate identity and give it inter-national profile.

In fact, the diversity of the symbols bears out a fundamental characteristic of the new democratic state. It aims to be pluralist and cosmopolitan. Where the Chinese tradition celebrated hierarchy, orthodoxy and unity, the new Taiwan celebrates equality, diversity and pluralism. Though there are certainly tensions between ethnic communities on Taiwan (Kang 1996), and democratic politics there is nothing if not lively, the prevailing orientation is towards a kind of civic nationalism, based upon respect for civic values and ethnic equality (Zheng 1991: 49; Shi 2000: 53). At least for the moment, this is quite different from traditional nationalism on the mainland. Whether this aims at being an alternative China or an independent entity in its own right, it is a fundamental challenge to the mainland in either guise.

So do Taiwanese feel nationalism? There is certainly the basis for a common identity. The territory is distinct. Taiwan has been formally part of China for only four years in the last one hundred and ten. And even though large numbers of mainlanders came to the island between 1945 and 1949, few of their children have experienced life on the mainland, so the lived experiences are diverging. Former President Lee Teng-hui tried to create an inclusive nationalism by talking of 'New Taiwan People' in 1998, which covered everyone on the island. Mainland hostility has affected the attitudes of 'Mainlanders' and their children (Corcuff 2002). And the intellectual horizons of Taiwanese are much less parochial. Large numbers have travelled, lived or studied abroad and associate their success with world trends. Taiwan is a member of the WTO. Zhuang suggested that Taiwan's new culture should be cosmopolitan. It should seek to contribute to world culture, taking particular account of American and Japanese culture (Zhuang 1996a: 37). The social and intellectual conditions for a cohesive national identity are in place, especially since the external threat from the mainland, and the degrading treatment of Taiwanese visitors by the immigration services of some other states, provide a continuing challenge. There is no doubt about the growing sense of separate identity on the part of people living on Taiwan (Lu 1999) – and the desire that they should become the subject of their history rather than the object of it.

CONCLUSION

Nevertheless public-opinion surveys, which are regularly carried out on Taiwan, suggest that the Taiwanese remain hesitant and ambivalent on the subject of nationalism. This could be explained both by anxiety over the very real threats of military intervention from the PRC, and by the carrots of increasing opportunities for trade with the mainland for Taiwanese businesses. There are also the warnings from the US and other states against provoking the mainland by rash actions.

Another very important factor, however, is the continuing ambivalent identity of many Chinese Taiwanese. Are they one or the other? Most still regard themselves as a mixture of the two, although the proportion that put themselves down as either 'Taiwanese' or 'mainly Taiwanese' is gradually increasing. Partly this could be attributed to the lingering effects of an education system that for decades concentrated on Chinese-ness. Partly too there are the effects of family traditions which still associate people with their ancestral village or home town. For anyone of Han descent, there has to be a place of origin on the mainland to which they are ultimately tied.

But partly too, it represents the difficulty of creating a cosmopolitan, pluralist or civic nationalism without first creating an ethnic one. If one contrasts this process with, say, the emergence of a civic nationalism in the former Czechoslovakia or the Czech Republic, the sense of ethnic identity there preceded civic nationalism and provided a common mode of discourse that allowed it to emerge more easily (Ferdinand 1997). Though advocates of the new identity on Taiwan can highlight symbols from the ethnic communities that differentiate them from the mainland, it is more difficult to turn these into a common pluralist identity. It is still not easy for Han Chinese, for instance, to take pride in the ethnic symbolism of the aborigines and vice versa. Historically one group exploited the other. There is as yet no persuasive common ethno-symbolic narrative for all Taiwanese.

Perhaps in time this will emerge after the restructuring of the educational system to give it a Taiwanese focus. But it will take time. And the process will be complicated by changes on the mainland. This does not only refer to the economic development there, although that is crucial. It also refers to symbols of a new Chinese modernity that are appearing there. If identity and nationalism are defined in part by differences from others, then a cosmopolitan Taiwanese identity or nationalism has been made more difficult by an emerging cosmopolitanism on the mainland. The old orthodoxy is mutating.

Since the early 1990s the PRC has opened itself much more to the outside world. Formally the makers of the River Elegy documentaries lost the argument with the state. In practice, however, they won. China is becoming more cosmopolitan. Emblematic of this are Chinese membership of the WTO since 2002 and China's hosting of the Olympic Games in 2008. But an old symbol is being reburnished too: the Qing admiral Zheng He who led enormous trading fleets across the Indian Ocean as far as the east coast of Africa in the early fifteenth century. At that time there was no follow-up and its long-term effect was negligible. Now, however, his pioneering spirit is being celebrated with studies and exhibitions at home and abroad.

In addition at home, with rapid economic growth, Chinese cities are undergoing enormous expansion and construction. The cityscapes are changing from one year to the next. Increasingly they mimic – deliberately – modern cities elsewhere in the world, whether the US, Hong Kong or Japan. They symbolise the new China's drive to catch up with and emulate advanced civilisations. Where previously Chinese on the mainland could only take pride in the modernity of Hong Kong (even if under British colonial rule) because it showed what Chinese could do, but also because there was nowhere like it on the mainland, now they can see counterparts sprouting at home. Shanghai and Taipei now vie with Kuala Lumpur and Tokyo for the tallest buildings in Asia. Many of the new buildings are stylish, designed by world-class architects. So the dimension of Chinese nationalism that saw China as eminent civilisation re-emerges. It shows that China is still capable of at least emulating the most advanced in the world, even if not yet of surpassing them. This does not of course yet make for a pluralist state, but it does represent a further challenge to those on Taiwan who want to create a new, separate, modern alternative to orthodox Han Chinese nationalism. It is also a further reminder of the power of ethnosymbolism.

REFERENCES

Brown, Melissa (2004), *Is Taiwan Chinese?*, Berkeley: University of California Press.

Cheng, Te-k'un (1980), *The World of the Chinese: A Struggle for Human Unity*, Hong Kong: Chinese University of Hong Kong.

Corcuff, Stéphane (2002), 'Taiwan's 'Mainlanders', new Taiwanese?', in Stéphane Corcuff (ed.), *Memories of the Future: National Identity Issues and the Search for a New Taiwan*, Armonk: M. E. Sharpe, 163–95.

Dikötter, Frank (1992), *The Discourse of Race in Modern China*, London: Hurst.

Duara, Prasenjit (1993), 'Provincial narratives of the nation: Centralism and federalism in Republican China', in Harumi Befu (ed.), *Cultural Nationalism in East Asia: Representation and Identity*, Berkeley: Research Papers and Policy Studies, Institute of East Asian Studies, 9–35.

Edmondson, Robert (2002), 'The February 28 incident and national identity', in Stéphane Corcuff (ed.), *Memories of the Future: National Identity Issues and the Search for a New Taiwan*, Armonk: M. E. Sharpe, 25–46.

Fairbank, John K. (1988), *The Great Chinese Revolution, 1800–1985*, London: Picador.

Ferdinand, Peter (1997), 'Nationalism, community and democratic transition in Czechoslovakia and Yugoslavia', in David Potter, David Goldblatt, Margaret Kioh and Paul Lewis (eds), *Democratization*, Cambridge: Open University Press and Polity Press, 466–89.

Hsueh, Hua-yuan (2005), Pao-tsun Tai, Mei-li Chow, *Is Taiwan Chinese?*, Tamsui: Taiwan Advocates.

Hutchinson, John and Anthony D. Smith (eds) (1994), *Nationalim*, Oxford: Oxford University Press, 122–31.

Jenner, W. J. F. (1992), *The Tyranny of History: the Roots of China's Crisis*, Harmondsworth: Allen Lane.

Kang, Chao (1996), 'Xinde minzuzhuyi, haishi jiude?', *Taiwan Shehui Yanjiu Likan*, 21: 1–72.

Levenson, Joseph R. (1967), 'The Province, the Nation and the World: the Problem of Chinese Identity', in Albert Feuerwerker (ed.), *Approaches to Chinese History*, Berkeley: University of California Press, 268–88.

Li, Zhisui (1994), *The Private Life of Chairman Mao*, London: Chatto and Windus.

Lu, Jianrong (1999), *Fenliede guozu rentong 1975–97*, Taipei: Maitian.

Maddison, Angus (2001), *The World Economy: A Millennial Perspective*, Paris: OECD.

Olson, James S. (1998), *An Ethnohistorical Dictionary of China*, Westport, CT: Greenwood Press.

Pye, Lucian W. (1996), 'How China's nationalism was Shanghaied', in Jonathan Unger (ed.), *Chinese Nationalism*, Armonk: M. E. Sharpe, 86–112.

Roy, Denny (2003), *Taiwan: A Political History*, Ithaca, NY: Cornell University Press.

Schoppa, R. Keith (2005), *Revolution and Its Past: Identities and Change in Modern Chinese History*, 2nd edn, Upper Saddle River, NJ: Pearson Prentice Hall.

Schwarcz, Vera (1991), 'No respite from lethe: History, memory and cultural identity in twentieth-century China', in Wei-ming Tu (ed.), *The Living Tree: The Changing Meaning of Being Chinese*, Stanford: Stanford University Press, 64–87.

Shi, Zhengfeng (2000), *Taiwanrende minzu rentong*, Taipei: Qinwei Chubanshe.

Su, Xiaokang and Luxiang Wang (1991), *Deathsong of the River*, Ithaca, NY: East Asia Program, Cornell University.

Townsend, James (1996), 'Chinese nationalism', in Jonathan Unger (ed.), *Chinese Nationalism*, Armonk: M. E. Sharpe, 1–30.

Waldron, Arthur (1993), 'Representing China: The Great Wall and cultural nationalism in the twentieth century', in Harumi Befu (ed.), *Cultural Nationalism in East Asia: Representation and Identity*, Berkeley: Research Papers and Policy Studies, Institute of East Asia Studies, 36–60.

Zheng, Qinren (1991), *Lishi wenhua yishi dui woguo zhengce zhe yingxiang*, 3rd edn, Taipei: Guojia Zhengce Yanjiu Zhongxin.

Zhuang, Wanshou (1996a), *Taiwan Lun*, Taipei: Baoshanshi.

Zhuang, Wanshou (1996b), *Zhongguo Lun*, Taipei: Baoshanshi.

Chapter 16

THE MAKING OF A LANGUAGE OF PATRIOTISM IN MODERN BENGALI

Sudipta Kaviraj

To think of possible indignity to a land composed of mountains, forests and rivers, this chapter argues, is not a natural thing. Conceiving of nature as having a life similar to human beings, being objects of emotions, like human beings, is a historical fact, something that comes to be historically, when the modern emotion named nationalism appears in the history of societies. It is under very specific cultural circumstances that such emotions can be projected on to the natural world, or indeed, that the natural world itself is seen as a unitary, singular entity to which the entire apparatus of human emotions can be applied. The ideology called nationalism engendered unknown forms of affection – for historically unprecedented and entirely abstract things.

Although it goes strongly against our intuition, emotions are historical. This is especially true of *public* emotions, like patriotism. There is hardly anything natural about transferring a language of emotions used for natural communities like the family to the abstract modern association of the nation. People living in a space, in a territory and in nature, may universally admire the bounteousness of the world around them, but that does not amount to feeling the specific emotion called modern patriotism. Yet, the fact that it is *historical* does not make it, in Gellner's sense, fraudulent (Gellner 1983). Rather, this raises a question central to the work of Anthony D. Smith on the precise meaning of the *historicity* of nationalism.

Historicity, strictly speaking, is a two-sided, somewhat paradoxical notion: to suggest that something is historical, is to suggest that it draws on the past; yet, it also suggests that it is something that emerged at a particular, specifiable time, and did not exist before. The literature on nationalism has struggled with this conceptual problem. Is there a previously established ethnie which acquires, under the pressures of modern history, a new kind of self-valuing consciousness? Or does the response to a sense of political indignity bring forth a new sense of identity where none, strictly speaking, existed before? Is the identity old, but the sentiment new? Or is the identity itself forged by a new configuration of history, which does not leave us any other possibility except to treat the sentiment towards this new object also as unprecedented? There is no single, all-encompassing answer to this question. This chapter offers an answer that is parochially valid, correct for the Indian case.

Recognition of objects in the social world requires the prior existence of a language crafted to capture precisely those objects. A nation can begin to exist when both a descriptive and an evaluative language for it has been fashioned. It would be an inaccurate historical representation to say that authors created a language of veneration for a nation that already existed pre-linguistically. In fact, it is the forming of a language of emotion regarding the nation – in this case, the symbolic figure of the land-mother – that makes the figure of the nation historically visible. In this context, the chapter argues that the creation of a language appropriate for the expression of this new emotion, both linguistically and iconically, required a great deal of experimentation; and even when it consolidated in the period of high nationalism, there was always potential for instability. There were significant variations in what people saw as their country, the ways in which they imagined its form, and the exact kind of emotion they felt for it; and these variations were not merely formal, for each form had its own political implications.

The object of this chapter is straightforwardly Durkheimian. All societies, Durkheim argued, must have a language in which they value themselves, since one of the central devices for maintenance of societies is this mechanism for collective self-reverence. But social worlds change historically. Transformations of modernity must therefore create a crisis in this language of self-reverence, for a modern social world is populated by social and political objects of a different kind of construction from earlier ones. One of the central questions here is the paradox of sacredness: modern institutions always seek to use for their own purposes the established languages of sacredness, from the way in which ceremonies for the war dead imitate religious rituals, to the way palaces of modern power try to copy styles of ancient architecture. Modern institutions however are often secular, and their use of the language of the sacral is always plagued by awkwardness. The language of sacredness which these societies used successfully in their traditional past would not easily relate to those objects that modern people would like to value. And Durkheim was quite right in acknowledging that modernity has had persistent difficulty with fashioning a language of value entirely its own. This may have to do with the difficulty of retaining sacredness in isolated areas in a world which is gradually becoming desacralised. This chapter explores the alterations in this reverential language, and analyses the techniques by which this was brought about in the case of modern Bengali nationalism.

Essentially, I shall try to show here how writers moved the traditional language of piety and its associated iconography to apply it to the modern sacredness of the nation. I hope this will also reveal a central irony of modern nationalism: its undecidedness between the demands of rational calculation of self-interest, and an equally insistent need to constantly appeal to something not based on interest at all – an indivisible community. Furthermore, nationalism requires a language of identity of a particularly excessive kind, which not merely values the motherland (or fatherland), but values it above all others. This perception of the unique value of the motherland is matched by the excessive demands for exemplary action in her cause. This transition to action is usually prompted by the emotion of nationalist devotion, which is created in the quite literal sense, by literary operations on existing symbolic repertoires of a specific culture. From this point of view, the 'creation' of a language of nationalist affection can be seen, to use Ian Hacking's luminous phrase, as an enquiry into 'historical ontology' – of a new way of seeing things, and a new way of being of individuals (Hacking 2003). The argument I am suggesting in this chapter refers primarily to the emergence of a nationalist language in Bengali culture in the works of Bankimchandra Chattopadhyay.

THE MAKING OF A LANGUAGE: BANKIMCHANDRA AND *VANDE MATARAM*

A new emotion requires a new language to express it. And it is not an exaggeration to suggest that Bankimchandra Chattopadhyay devised the elementary aspects of this new language in an awkward song placed inside one of his last novels, which enjoyed an extraordinary career in the history of modern Indian culture (Chattopadhyay 1881 [1964]).[1] It is often said that Bankim's iconography in *Vande Mataram* is traditionalist and conservative but any serious attention to texts would show on the contrary that it is a highly innovative composition both in linguistic and iconic terms. It is a song sung by specific figures in the contingent narrative circumstances of that specific story. But the longer and larger history of that song must take account of the process by which it floats free of that narrative frame and context, and becomes a free-standing song of first Bengali and then Indian patriotism.

I wish to tell three stories regarding that song. First, the story of its writing, which is instructive, because it shows how innovative that undertaking was. Second, the story of the novel within which the song appears and is sung, the narrative preparation of that *bhava*. And finally the story of the song itself as a free-standing word icon, full of internal figural iconicities of its own, and its deeply ambiguous inheritance. The first point to note is the surprise that this song comes from Bankimchandra, one of the most resolutely unpoetic of Bengali writers. After some early misadventure into rhymed poetry, Bankim learnt his mistake and never left the more secure poetics of his literary prose, which could incorporate some stylistic attractions of poetry in a more controlled form within the capacious powers of this prose writing.[2] In stylistic form, he never strayed into poetry again, except on this utterly memorable occasion. But this breaking into poetry, in a literal sense, is highly significant. It showed a crisis in the narrative, a point where the new emotion of patriotism has reached an unbearable intensity, when its unrecognised and unsuspected cadences become too powerful for even Bankim's prose, and like emotion breaking into tears, this powerful, new, half-recognised, unknown emotion breaks for this first time in its own celebration into poetry.[3]

But this first ever occasion of breaking into poetry was not free of trouble. In formal terms, only the emotion is undeniable, and its irresistible expressive power is tangible; in terms of the crafting of a literary form for it, it was awkward and, in some fashion, flawed. Educated Bengalis, cultivated in the literary arts of three languages – Sanskrit, English and Bengali – were not slow to recognise its formal problems. A younger contemporary and admirer, Haraprasad Shastri, records a revealing incident in his autobiography (Shastri 1980). A small group of gifted young writers and admirers gathered for weekly hearings of the text when Bankim was composing *Anandamath*. When he read the narrative segment in which the song first appeared, there was stunned silence, not because the highly cultured audience thought the song was wonderful, but because they could not bring themselves to believe that Bankim, the greatest writer in the language, at the height of his imaginative powers, would produce something full of so many infelicities. Their alarm was not unjustified. The song begins with solemn Sanskrit:

Vande mataram
sujalam, suphalam, malayajashitalam, sashyashyamalam mataram.
[I revere the Mother! The Mother
Rich in waters, rich in fruit,
Cooled by the southern airs,
Verdant with the harvest fair]. (*Anandamath* [Lipner, 2005: 144–5])

Yet after a few stanzas it reaches a point of poetic climax and breaks ungrammatically into Bengali. To his startled audience this appeared not as an invention, but a slip. The more courageous among them, like Shastri, drew Bankim's attention to its formal and grammatical awkwardness, because they thought this might expose Bankim, despite his unassailable stature, to ridicule. Bankim, usually more forthcoming in discussion, Shastri tells us, simply said they could not convince him; of course what they said was true, but 'the song was right'. This is an extraordinary incident, if true, because Bankim was the most rationalistic of writers, never at a loss for providing entirely impeccable reasoned justification for his beliefs. But here he seemed to have no rational grounding for his conviction, only an inexplicable faith in the song's rightness in some inexplicable sense.

Obviously, there was a distinction here between what was grammatically and poetically correct. Beyond its poetic propriety, Bankim wished to say that it was *politically* right. But he needed a language of that politics, and Bankim's defence of himself remained inarticulate because he could not find that language, as he was himself half way towards making it form. I think the relation between the Sanskrit and vernacular in the *Vande Mataram* is similar to the discrepant tone of the last chapter in Machiavelli's *Prince*, a fault of form from the point of view of consistency of composition, but a triumph in finding a new linguistic register of an unprecedented emotion. As Federico Chabod asserts, without that last stylistically inconsistent chapter *The Prince* would not have been *The Prince* (Chabod 1958); without that stanza in Bengali the *Vande Mataram*, equally, would not have been the song it became.

We have now become so used to the image of the land-goddess that it is somehow inconceivable to think of a time when this was unknown. The tradition of devotion in Hindu religion has a great variety of goddesses, some of whom bear a maternal feminine form, but they are *not* the land. It is necessary therefore to see how this particular image is put together from an earlier iconic field. There are two parallel processes of image-making going on in the novel: in the song the image of the mother is being slowly built up in words; but in another scene of the novel, a directly iconic image is also built up directly through a play of images of Hindu gods. The *Mata* to whom that song is sung is not entirely an abstract literary metaphor. Mahendra, one of the main characters in the narrative, goes down into the underground temple of the *santan*s and is presented with a sculptural group of baffling complexity: it is a composite image, a statue of Vishnu, Bankim's preferred deity among the large Hindu pantheon, with Shakti[4] on his lap. Vishnu and Shakti are the presiding deities of two different, and in the Bengali context, contending strands of Hindu religion. In traditional terms, this composition is of course wholly ungrammatical, both Shaktas and Vaishnavas of Bengal would have found worshipping such a composite image doctrinally unacceptable. In the Bengali tradition of iconic composition, there were occasional instances of the combination of Kali and Krishna into an androgynous image, called *Krishnakali*, using the darkness and playing on the stark opposition of the two forms: one masculine, the other feminine. But such images were not very common, although there is evidence of imaginative variations played on the exact depiction of individual forms like Durga or Kali or Krishna. Thus, although both Vishnu and Kali came from the formal repertoire of image-making, his peculiar way of putting them together was highly untraditional. Besides, Bankim's construction of this image is not meant as an object for traditional prayer; it is meant specifically for a modern worship of a new object, the motherland, uneasily poised between a metonymy and a metaphor. This is a classic example of 'writing upon writing'.[5] Its *elements* are taken from earlier iconic forms and their language of use, but its actual figural form is not sanctioned by that pre-existing language: it defies its rules of iconic syntax. Yet there cannot be an entirely new language, the new expressions must mould the old language into a new one precisely by the repetitive and insistent use of such ungrammatic vision. To be intelligible, it must carry on with its pretences and semblances of continuity; hence the Sanskrit, hence the literary form of the *stotra*. But there is, surrounding all this, an unmistakable sense of displacement, a search for something that is really unprecedented, unthinkable and really ungrammatical, a secular sacredness.[6]

This expression of a nationalist emotion does not appear suddenly, in Bankim's work. There are some interesting preparations for these displacements in Bankim's earlier work. What Bankim uses for this invocation is the form of the *stotra* or *stava,* a classical format of worship that works through exaggeration of a deity's powers and beneficent capacities. Conventional religious *stotra*s were meant for a specific kind of religious act, for the quiet or noisy worship of the Hindu devotee to his deity, a process marked by an indelible selfishness. A devotee offered the prayer either in the privacy of his worship room, or the different form of privacy of the silence of a river at dawn, to his personal God. Occasionally, Hindus would worship together in a temple, where many devotees would chant a common prayer, but every single person was offering his own deeply individual application for mercy and compassion. So the community, to use Marx's contemptuous phrase, was a sack of devout potatoes, not a political community. Nor did it possess a conception of itself with any form of collective agency. Bankim wished to create a song that would be entirely different from this traditional *stava,* in its literary, formal point, a song in which the enunciation is not by discrete individuals, where the invisible lines of separation amongst the tiny circles of their single destinies are erased, and they are able to see themselves as a collective maker of a single enunciation. To accomplish this, the song must have such a character that its words would become futile if they were not spoken with this new, unknown, unfamiliar, exhilarating togetherness. In this sense, while the traditional *stotra* was essentially personal, the political anthem was equally essentially collective.

Bankim uses the stotra form in the *Vande Mataram*, a patriotic song, in *Anandamath*. Indeed, even the narrative framing of the song is indicative of its newness. It is sung by one of the rebel leaders, Bhavananda, to the astonished Mahendra, who gets more mystified as the lines unfold. After a couple of stanzas, Mahendra expressed his surprise, 'but this is not my mother, this is my land'; and implicit in this question is the astonishment of the traditional hearer of *stotra*s at the projected transfer of the sentiment of devotion to an unprecedented new object, a Land-Mother. Mahendra's aesthetic and sentimental perception initially objects to this unaccustomed connection, between the intense worshipping and protective love that the Mother deserves from her child, and the uninteresting givenness of the land, which is to be taken for granted, but now suddenly turned into a complex object of such reverential vision and sentimental devotion. It is not surprising that Mahendra is the great survivor in the novel. Others make their impact and go away into the mistiness of time, but Mahendra, the ordinary good man, survives, although transformed. The whole point of the novel, of its narrative jangle, of its cut and thrust, is the education of the common man in Mahendra; his political transformation by learning a new aesthetic of *deshbhakti* which means a worshipping devotion to one's country, a neologism that would quickly become a commonplace of nationalist discourse. He learns a new optics, a new vision of his land, and is given the gift of imagining it as formed as a mother. The untraditional nature of this aesthetic is therefore marked in the novel itself; Bankim provides an *internal* interpretation to what he was doing narratively, inside the narrative itself: within the novel the relation between Bhavananda and Mahendra represents the relation between the writer and the reader.

What is left behind and what is aesthetically new can be found by comparing the *aryastotra*,[7] the source, and *Vande Mataram*, the product. In my reading the *Vande Mataram* is the *aryastotra* transformed by the stress of living through the violent, desecrating chemistry of colonialism. The traditional song is to the Mother conceived as the mother, sustainer of the world. It is an imaginative and aesthetic conception of a premodern world which does not know of abstract space, populated by others, alien and different. It is an invocation of a Mother to all that exists in this world, and a hymn to her glory. It is wrong to call this a spirit of generosity. It simply does not have a conception of a world that is large enough, diverse enough, differentiated enough to hold other people and other gods, fundamentally, abstractly different from 'ourselves' – the worshippers.

Vande Mataram is a hymn to a Mother who is created in the image of her worshippers, whose characteristics are all related to their collective self. She is an emphatically Durkheimian goddess, not different from the human beings she sustains and protects; she is simply a resplendent re-description of themselves. She is the glorious form of the nature they inhabit, of the people they are. It is a glorification that bends back towards the self, which is the ultimate object of this devotion. Implicitly, the ontology of the social world has become wholly different. The song sees the world as abstract space, all parts of which are not equally hallowed. It is a world of maps and peoples, of frontiers, divisions, of selves and others. It is an emotion which presupposes the world created by modern geography books; in that conception India is not the world, but a part of the world, and presently an unjustly oppressed part. The emotion of devotion that this elicits is a fundamentally transformed emotion; from one of wonderment, satisfaction, supplication and thankfulness at being allowed residence in this wondrous scheme of things, it is now a tense emotion of grandeur, enthusiasm and only barely concealed animosity. In the case of the first Mother there were no references to power, because she symbolised all powers of the world; in the case of the second Mother, unjustly diminished and insulted, there is need to remind her children of the great, irresistible power that she can command:

abala kena ma eta bale? [8] ...
bahubaladharinim, namami tarinim, ripudalabarinim, mataram.
[Powerless? How so Mother?
To the Mother I bow low,
To her who wields so great a force.
To her who saves,
And drives away the hostile hordes!] (Lipner 2005: 145)

All the characteristics of the Mother are combative; her stance has been changed from a universal, sustaining repose, to an avenging power evoking conflict and victory.

SCULPTING OF A GODDESS OF SECULAR STRIFE

Clearly, what happens inside the song with words is similar to sculpting a figure out of marble. Linguistic newness is a strange thing: nothing that uses language for intelligibility can be entirely new. Yet, nationalism manages to create a new language which performs the impossible; it habituates people in using a language of sacrality while referring to entirely profane objects.

Closely observed, the song has two parts, describing two separate types of imagery. Usually, in Hindu religious iconography, the deity is worshipped in a state of peaceful repose, even though often he or she is the invincible last resort of vulnerable, terrified human beings. The god Rama for instance, despite his heroic exploits in the epic story of the *Ramayana*, where he overcomes challenges of evil, is always traditionally posed in calm reposeful state, devoid of traces of exertion and anger. The underlying idea is that although evil might be temporarily, contingently powerful, in a cosmically well-ordered world, the power of goodness incarnated in god's various forms is always ample to deal with such challenge. To describe the almighty in a state of agitation will be a kind of sacrilege, a shortage of confidence in his sufficiency of powers. Only in some particular traditions, like the text *Chandi*, much loved by Bengali devotees of the goddess Shakti, is the divine shown in an actively fighting state, where her wrath is depicted, and she is iconically shown as slaying the figures of evil. Bankim's song draws upon both these iconic systems equally. The first part of the song is placid, reposeful, continuing the usual conventions of depicting the calm, unagitated majesty of a deity, though her attributes are surprising: the waters, the fruits, the soft cool breezes, the abundant harvest. This too is an iconic invocation of power, but in a state of calm. In the second part, however, this power changes form into something that can be a force of a very different kind, a force of fighting against oppression – marked by the numbers of her willing soldiers, the raised weapons, the menacing roar of millions of voices raised in her defence. It is true that this awesome power is to be used only in just defence against subjection and dishonour; but this is a startling and surprising transformation of the aspect of a deity. The goddess has undergone in these few sentences a fateful transformation: she is now literally made up of human beings, and her purpose of incarnation is also an entirely mundane business of fight against injustice. She is a new goddess of strife in a disenchanted, political world, participating awkwardly in the fierce exchanges of mundane power in the modern world. She does not give sustenance and benefaction to all human beings; her divine invincibility is partial towards her own people.

In Bengali religious thought, there is a rich tradition of conceiving of the supreme being as a mother, a sustaining, protective, unconquerable force. But sustenance and protection are somewhat different ideas, at least, they give the same general idea somewhat different inflections. In the religious tradition of worshipping Shakti, the unconquerable force, there are two different iconic representations of these two differently inflected ideals. In purely iconic terms, the vaisnava tradition developed the image of the goddess Shri, who sustains the world, including her suppliant children, in an attitude of deep affection: and her iconic representation describes her as '*karunagravanatamukhi*', leaning forward a little in a gesture of pity, very similar to the Christian images of pietà. In the Shakta tradition of divine imagery, the emphasis is more on protection from evil, which takes the unconquerable feminine ideal into a more contestatory field of representation. Evil is given an embodied form; and the invincible mother takes on an appropriately warlike image as the triumphant Durga, who is warlike, but depicted at the moment of her triumph against demonic images of evil, the asura. As is well known, she can also take a more dark form, as Kali, who is dark, cognitively impenetrable, terrifying in her unpredictability, and pitiless like time (*kala*) which characterises even the most invincible power with mortality.

MEANINGS OF THE SONG

There has been an interminable controversy about the meaning of this song in the unending debates about Indian nationalism and its present significance. When the textual object is a song, and its reception is itself an occasion of public singing, often in political context, the taking of the song has, irreducibly, a large component of making by the singer; its interpretative mediation is crucial. It therefore becomes possible, precisely because of the abstractness of the song's locution to transpose a different context from the narrative one. A large section of its admirers, who sang the song regularly, would have been able to receive it as an anti-British patriotic text. At least, it is odd to suggest that Rabindranath Tagore, who is usually above suspicion in matters of communalism, set the song to its common tune[9] because it was a fluent vehicle of anti-Muslim communal rage. The complexity of *Vande Mataram*'s audience, its circle of reception, testifies to its complex historical meaning.

It is possible to suggest that for a large audience during the national movement, the *Vande Mataram* acquired a primarily nationalistic 'structure' of meaning. Within the song, as a free-standing text, there is no reference to Muslim rule, only a general and abstract reference to the Mother's capacity to stop her enemies (*ripudalavarinim*). It is also remarkable that the objection to the song from the Muslim and secularist intelligentsia is about its use of a Hindu iconic language: its composition in Sanskrit, its assimilation of the stotra form of adulation, its constant references to the Mother-goddess. Ironically, if the general deployment of a Sanskritic-Hindu semiotic is the basis of objection, there is hardly any nationalistic composition that can strictly pass such test. Tagore's famous patriotic songs,

> *he more citta punyatirthe jaga re dhire/*
> *ei bharater mahamanaber sagaratire*
> [O my heart, rise slowly in this holy place of pilgrimage
> On the shores of this sea of humanity that is India]

or, *janaganamanaadinayaka jaya he* (Hail to him who leads the mind of the entire people), would also fall by the same criteria. Eventually, the only song capable of passing such a secularist test would be the famous preamble or a selection of articles of the Indian constitution set to a fetching tune.

Yet, precisely because of its narrative context of hostility to Muslim rule, precisely because the authorial meaning is at least the first meaning of a text, *Vande Mataram* always attracts a different audience, a communal Hindu reception. Members of this audience respond powerfully to the song precisely because of the duality of the adversaries within its abstract meaning, precisely because the image of the Mother who is *ripudalavarini* (one who can repulse the enemy hordes) signifies a triumph over both the British and the Muslims. They like the song because within this broader modern patriotism it always folds a longer and more insidious enmity, and because this fine-crafted-text hatred not merely points to the British, but also makes the other hatred unforgettable; and the re-enactment of this, present, proximate contest always reminds of and connects to the other conflict in Indian history. This is the second 'structure' of meaning of *Vande Mataram*; and the destiny of the song has been a conflict over these two powerful structures of interpretation. When Nehru decided to call this the national song of India rather than its anthem, he subscribed to the first structure; but the BJP's[10] insistence of its chanting in all Indian schools seeks to incline its meaning towards the second. *Vande Mataram* wanted to create a battlefield with foreign rulers, when such a battle could happen only in a political dream; but it inadvertently started a cultural battle over its own meaning which is far from settled.

Even Tagore's later composition, which was eventually adopted as the national anthem, precisely because of the absence in its verbal body of such suggestions of offence, went through this tussle between the composition and reception meaning. The song was regarded as too long to be sung as an anthem, and only the first stanza, which helpfully enumerated major states of India's federal consti-tution, was taken as the official anthem of the state:

> Thou art the ruler of the minds of all people,
> dispenser of India's destiny.
> Thy name rouses the hearts of Punjab, Sind, Gujarat and Maratha,
> Of the Dravida and Orissa and Bengal;
> It echoes in the hills of the Vindhyas and Himalayas, mingles in the music of
>   Yamuna and Ganga
> and is chanted by the waves of the Indian Sea.
> They pray for thy blessings and sing thy praise.
> The saving of all people waits in thy hand,
> thou dispenser of India's destiny,
> Victory, victory, victory to thee.[11]

Still, what was poetical was not necessarily politically correct. Its mention of Sindhu – a reference to the region of Sind – remained an inconvenient oddity: if it was a reference to a region, this might be read as an irredentist desire for the province of Sindh lost at partition to Pakistan; if it meant Sindhi-speaking people, they were certainly part of India's immense mélange of languages. Political interventions into the verbal body of the songs always demonstrated the play of two meanings – the authorial and the receptional. While the author's meaning was foundational to the text, it was not, in the case of these compositions which became political with time, its only, or determinative meaning.

NATURE, SPACE AND RESIDENCE

Bankim's immense innovation lay in bringing together in miraculously effective combination three ideas that all existed in earlier Indian thinking, but entirely unconnected to each other. Traditional Indic culture did have highly elaborated images of the goddess Shakti, philosophical conceptions of nature, a very different tradition of aesthetic delectation of natural beauty, and an entirely prosaic understanding of space. The crucial point is that these were disparate, discrete, entirely unconnected. The goddess' images did not include nature. Aesthetic appreciation of natural scenes had nothing to do with the sacred; rather, in poets like Kalidasa,[12] it runs very close to a witty erotic vision of the world. Space is mundane, entirely bereft of emotional significance. Bankim creates a new language of nationalist worship by joining these unconnected strands into a convex symbolism. Neutral space of the country now comes to be marked by its natural features of striking beauty. That nature now merges with the figure of the divine mother, so that it becomes possible now for her inhabitants to transform into her children, thankful recipients of her natural and divine sustenance. For traditional thinking, these overlaps would have appeared ungrammatical, gratuitous conflations of discrete languages appropriate to disparate fields of reflection. For moderns, after the shock of the new is absorbed, this becomes the only language that can express a nationalist sentiment.

The new emotion is inextricably linked, in all nationalisms, to a theory of charged, significant, sacral residence. Space has to be given a new kind of sacredness. Traditional thinking in Hindu culture had a great richness of ideas about nature, or rather the nature of nature. Nature was thought of as *prakrti*,[13] also the name of woman – agitated, generative, fecund, creative, restless, irrepressible. She is therefore the image of a primal, unconquerable force. But again this was an enveloping conception of nature seen as a precondition of human existence and viewed as a source of general preservation and sustenance. It was not an image of a nature over which people could throw a *possessive* relation, a nature that was inextricably part of our self, or a selfness extended to nature and its neutrally existent features, like rivers, and mountains, paddy fields, and ponds. Undoubtedly the romantic poetic and artistic imagination had something to do with this new intensified idea of domicile; our living inside this world, making it special, just as living inside it made us sacred. Rain and sunshine, the cycle of seasons, the mundane business of sowing of seeds and harvesting grain, instead of being unsurprising, quotidian, grey processes, became aesthetic events, they became happenings, on the way to becoming sacred, their very occurrence a mark of peculiar speciality, precisely because these rains and sunshine, these hills and rivers, these grains and fields were those of the self. It is interesting to note how the new geography of abstract space, the space which is beyond my immediate apprehension, but which I know exists, plays an important part in this. It does not require much argument to show that things like rivers and mountains are not natural objects of love; and it requires a refiguring of the imagination to achieve affection of this intense and immediate nature for these inanimate objects. In earlier cultures, these may have been aesthetically admired, but not loved with this intense feeling of affection. Poetry accomplishes the astonishing function of what can be called the selfing of nature. In this mapped and diversified world, of neutral and natural space, one part, with its clear boundaries, now becomes precious, sacred, emotive and valuable, it becomes a moral home, the motherland. Residence in the physical world is made sacred, and poetry becomes the privileged expression of this feeling.

After Bankim, the image of the Mother is invested with an immense fullness, but the figural form of the country as mother, so insecurely and polemically established in Bankim's late fiction, once established, is never dislodged again. But this constant addition to her descriptive richness slowly makes for a change, at least a potential change in the axis of this image. This will be evident if we compare the constituents of the images of the Mother-Land in Bankim and some others. Even in the process of creation of value in nature, turning it into a home, the home land, there are clearly discernible stages. Bankim is still engaged in the basic process of iconic transfer, shifting the associations of the sacred image of the mother on to the unaccustomed features of the homeland, still trying to convince the puzzled audience of Mahendras, he is simply conferring characteristics of *shubha* (auspicious) or *su* (good) on apparently unexciting objects, convincing Mahendras of two things. That this natural world, always present and available to us, is nevertheless something that deserves thanksgiving; that it has to be regarded again through a complex aesthetic optics partly taken from the sensuousness of classical Sanskrit poetry, but transformed by lacing into it a new sense of the self's residence. What were the literary and iconic ingredients through whose transformed deployment Bankim founded this new language of political emotion? I think in conventional literature, it is possible to find an aesthetic appreciation of nature, a tradition of devoted worship of the mother goddess, and a mundane, prosaic conception of space. The new language brought these three entirely separate strands of thinking and writing in connection to produce the expressive idiom and iconic repertoire of modern Indian nationalism.

Classical Sanskrit poetry saw nature only as a thing to savour, enjoy, take pleasure from, as something that enhanced the human sense of sexual sensuousness, as a nature that adorned and went with the beauty of women. Using similar descriptive tropes, the new aesthetics of nature converts it into something valuable and anthropocentric in a new sense, connecting with a more urgent emotion of thankfulness for its bounty, and invoking, at the edge of that palette of feelings, more darkly *rudra* emotions like resentment at her humiliation, the spirit of sacrifice or an avenging anger. Compared to the earlier aesthetic of nature, the new aesthetic is sadly limiting, and it represents an appreciation of nature which is more intense, but more parochial. Earlier nature existed in two forms – a universal form in which it offered its beneficence to everyone, or a particular form when some of its particular features like specific scenes excited a highly specific sense of pleasure. The new emotion that envelops nature is different from both these traditional perceptions. Formerly, the beauty of nature, its sustenance, its mysteries, were supposed to be universal. They beautified the lives of all human beings, or in Kalidasa's aesthetics, of those who had the sensitivity to appreciate what it made so abundantly available. Now nature's beauty and bounty is felt more intensely, but not as a gift to all men, rather the special sacredness of a special part to a special group of its recipients. It is a mapped world, aesthetically and emotionally, intensely conscious of its boundaries, a world not joined by nature's universality, but a world broken by its parochial sacredness. It is already disenchanted, to use Weber's modernist phrase: from a world governed by god, it already appears like a world governed by the United Nations. This nature is also not particular in the sense in which romantic painting presented it, as a highly specific response of an artistic self to a particular landscape – a scene, a time of day, a strange play of light – which was intense but individual. The new visual and iconic celebration of nature is collectivistic, its beauties are visible to all its particularly favoured children.

I have argued elsewhere that this Mother is decisively created by the census, and commented on Bankim's great and surprising artistry in putting statistics at the heart of a poem (Kaviraj 1995: ch. 4). The Mother is not merely gifted with natural qualities, but also with the modern power of numbers: her children, who also make up her body, can roar with seven crore voices in her glory, just as much as they, somewhat unpractically, raise fourteen crores of hands bearing swords in her defence. The corporal image of her in Bankim's poem is very similar to the image of the Leviathan on the frontispiece of Hobbes's *Leviathan*, except that she was a woman, and there was a combination of the characteristics of the bountiful with the terrible. The carrying of two swords by each counted Bengali may be militarily inconvenient; but its point lies elsewhere, in the sense of invincibility and power that this counting produced. Bankim was wonderfully ingenious in turning the implement of colonial counting into a weapon of nationalist enthusiasm.

SUBSEQUENT ADVENTURES OF THE NATIONALIST ICON

It is interesting to see how, after Bankim's founding move, this image grows and changes at the same time. The only thing that stabilises after Bankim's inspired intervention is the impossibility of patriotism for Bengalis and later for Indians. Figurally, their patriotism always referred to a Mother, made out of these very diverse elements of tradition, from the theological and aesthetic imagination of the *rupa* (a term that denotes simultaneously *appearance* and *beauty*) of *shakti*, to the unrelated strands of aestheticising nature in erotic poems of the classical Sanskrit tradition. Bankim thus invents, not a new optics of nature, but a new *function*: he invents a *political* nature. He was after all the inventor of modern politics in Bengal, not in the form of debating societies, parliaments and legislatures, or movements, the visible theatres of politics. His greatest gift was to suspect and then show the subliminal presence of politics everywhere in colonial society. The response to colonial suppression of politics led to the invention of a politics that was ubiquitous. Even nature was political.

After this founding moment, this patriotic aesthetics grows in the subsequent history of Bengali literature, with a curious effect. Nearly all self-respecting poets compose songs to the glory of the motherland, who slowly acquires, through an intense exchange of iconic signification between literary and artistic representation, a highly typified figure of *Bharatmata* whose image dominates not merely fields of literary-poetic writing, but also painting, and eventually the popular Hindi film. As later poets add to the reasons and characteristics of the Mother-Land's incomparable splendour, these features become too full and diverse, and the image in a sense is ripped apart by this fullness of determinations. As a consequence, the single mother image gets distributed into several, even competing ones.

NOTES

This chapter was originally presented as a paper in seminars in post-colonial literature in the Insitute of Commonwealth Studies, University of London, and the seminar on commonwealth history, Oxford.

1   *Vande Mataram* was probably written sometime between 1872 and 1875, but it was first printed in 1881 as part of the novel *Anandamath* (Bhattacharya 2003: 68–70). Bhattacharya offers a detailed historical account of the composition of the song and political debates surrounding it. For an admirable English translation of the novel, with a critical edition of the text, see Julius Lipner (2005). This also contains an excellent, detailed introduction about the history of both the composition and reception of the song.

2   As one of the first writers in modern Bengali, Bankim had to be a most self-aware user of language. His relation to modern Bengali is a paradoxically dual one: it is true that he writes

in modern Bengali, but it is equally true that what we call modern Bengali is made to appear precisely through his writing. He does not have a pre-existing language called modern Bengali in which he writes his works. Rather, through his actual writing, he shows that something like this language is possible. He wrote an intriguing essay called 'Bangala Bhasa' (Bengali Language) which explores the various forms of Bengali idiom and techniques of their complex combined use in literary prose (see Chattopadhyay 1881 [1964], vol. 2).

3 For a more detailed analysis of the narrative framing of the song, see Kaviraj 1995, chapter 4. See also the detailed discussion of the relation between the song and the narrative in Lipner's edition of *Anandamath* (2005).

4 Shakti is the image of the primal feminine principle in Hindu theology, representing the generative forces of nature and creation: she is portrayed in several distinct forms: like the goddesses Durga or Kali.

5 I offer a more detailed argument about ingestion of external influences in intellectual history in Kaviraj 2006.

6 A phrase used by Hacking which he took from Foucault (Hacking 2003).

7 *Aryastotra* is a famous traditional *stotra* composition to the goddess Shakti, quoted by Bankim in his satirical sketch *Amar Durgotsav* (Chattopdhyay 1881 [1964], vol. 1).

8 This line, which translates literally as 'Why are you so powerless, Mother, despite such strength?' is also significantly one of the Bengali lines in the poem. But the song immediately after this slip resumes its more stately and imposing cadence in Sanskrit in the very next line.

9 The song was set to tune some time in the early years of the twentieth century, because it was reported widely sung during the Swadeshi agitations against the partition of Bengal in 1905.

10 Bharatiya Janata Party, the Hindu nationalist party which has played a major role in Indian politics since the eighties and had formed two successive coalition governments at the Centre. It lost to the Congress in the last general elections, but remains a major political force.

11 Tagore's own translation of the first stanza, which is sung as India's national anthem.

12 Kalidasa is regarded as the greatest Sanskrit poet of Indian antiquity.

13 *Prakrti* bears a complex set of connotations: it means nature, but it also refers to woman, and a philosophical conception of the feminine principle in Hindu thought.

REFERENCES

Bhattacharya, Sabyasachi (2003), *Vande Mataram: The Biography of a Song*, New Delhi: Penguin.

Chabod, Federico (1958), *Machiavelli and the Renaissance*, Cambridge, MA: Harvard University Press.

Chattopadhyay, Bankimchandra (1964), *Bankim Racanabali (BR)*, Sahitya Samsad: Kolkata, 2 vols (vol. 1, *Sahitya*, vol. 2, *Upanayas*).

Gellner, Ernest (1983), *Nations and Nationalism*, Oxford: Blackwell.

Hacking, Ian (2003), *Historical Ontology*, Cambridge, MA: Harvard University Press.

Kaviraj, Sudipta (1995), *The Unhappy Consciousness*, Oxford: Oxford University Press.

Kaviraj, Sudipta (2005), 'An Outline of a revisionist theory of modernity', *European Journal of Sociology* XLVI, 3, 2005.

Lipner, Julius (ed.) (2005), *Bankimchandra Chatterji: Anandamath or The Sacred Brotherhood*, New York: Oxford University Press.
Shastri, Haraprasad (1980), *Atmacharit*, Paschim Banga Pustak Parshad: Kolkata.
Smith, Anthony D. (1998), *Nationalism and Modernism*, London: Routledge.

Part VII

ETHNOSYMBOLISM IN AFRICA

Chapter 17

HOLY NIGERIAN NATIONALISMS
Obi Igwara

———◁▷———

The growing sense of political identity in Nigeria has become both national and religious. A journalist vividly portrayed the situation when he observed that Nigeria meant 'far less to the ordinary Nigerian than his Allah or God' (*New Nigerian* 6 December 1977, cited in Kukah 1991: 23). This emergent 'holy nationalism' has been conditioned by the rise of Islamic fundamentalism since the 1970s and, in response, Christian radicalism. The competition between the two groups is redrawing cultural boundaries and transforming identities and cultural power in Nigeria. Islam, which has historically united sections of the society, is increasingly losing its capacity to do so. It has become a diverse factor, particularly in northern Nigeria. In contrast, Christianity, not known for its unity, is increasingly becoming a unifying factor for large sections of society. [...]

RELIGIOUS DEVELOPMENTS IN NIGERIA

[...] Islam spread to Nigeria from across the Sahara. It was established first in Borno in the north-east of what is now Nigeria during the eleventh century and gradually spread into Hausaland where it coexisted with indigenous religions.[1] The Sokoto Jihad early in the nineteenth century brought about the imposition of Fulani Muslim hegemony over the Hausa states and led to the expansion of Islam to non-Hausa areas like Nupe and Ilorin. The Fulani empire comprised a loose confederation of linguistically differentiated peoples held together by a minority of Muslim Fulani overlords who acknowledged the suzerainty of a sultan based in Sokoto, making Sokoto in the north-west the heartland of Islam in Nigeria. Colonial rule reconstituted the imperial territory, first as the Protectorate of Northern Nigeria, and then as the Northern Region of the Nigerian federation. Although Islam spread beyond the original area of the Sokoto caliphate, the religion is most closely associated with the Hausa/Fulani groups. Borno itself had become a centralised Muslim state by the nineteenth century (Clarke 1984: 12). Islam was, prior to the eighteenth century, established in Oyo, the heart of the Yorubaland, but it was not until the end of the century that it became an important political factor due to the Jihad. Islam and Christianity played a major role in the late nineteenth century Yoruba internecine civil wars.

Christianity spread from the coast in the nineteenth century, establishing rapidly in the south and gradually in the north. European contact with the coastal region of Nigeria dates back to the fifteenth century, but that contact was primarily commercial except for the vain attempts by the Portuguese to Christianise the peoples of Benin and Warri. Christianity took root in both Yoruba and Igbo lands. In Yorubaland Christianity and Islam spread in a way that correlated closely to the savannah/forest, Oyo/non-Oyo divide, and in nearly all communities there were both Muslims and Christians (Peel 1989: 210). Among the Igbo, Christianity was the prevalent imported religion. Ellah observes that the traditional religious fervor of the Igbo has been adapted to the Christian faith, which attains maximum importance in Igboland, particularly in the urban areas (Ellah 1983: 128). The Protestants were the first to establish missions in Nigeria, followed by the Roman Catholics. Statistically, socially and politically, the Protestant missions became the most influential in Yorubaland. The situation in Igboland was different. The Catholics, although arriving late, spread at an astonishing rate after 1902 to control a larger following than the Protestant churches.[2] The origin of Yoruba-Igbo political rivalry and ethnic nationalism has been traced to Christian missionary activities in Nigeria (Ekoko and Amadi 1989: 113). [...]

In the north, Christian missions were not allowed to operate in Muslim areas because of the pledge made by colonial administrators to the Fulani rulers that they would not interfere with religious practice in the area (Parrinder 1953: 63–4, 83). However, in the 1930s the administration cautiously opened up the north to Western influence by allowing Christian missions to run leper colonies throughout the northern provinces and to proselytise in the middle belt areas. Colonial rule reconstituted the southern missionary territory, first as the Protectorate of Southern Nigeria, and then as the Western and Eastern Regions of the Nigerian federation. The close cooperation between colonial officials and missionaries in the south enabled Christianity to enjoy one of the fastest growth rates in its history (Ibrahim 1989: 74). Ironically, the Christian missions who heralded British rule in Nigeria also began the process of its termination: 'For the Church became the cradle of Nigerian nationalism, the only forum of nationalist expression until the beginnings of the Nigerian-owned press after 1879, and the main focus of nationalist energies until after 1914' (Ayandele 1966: 175). [...]

Religion became a political and conflictual issue in 1979, nineteen years after the declaration of Nigerian independence on 1 October 1960. The proposal to create a Federal Sharia Court of Appeal generated a bitter exchange at the Constituent Assembly. Christians protested that such a court compromised the secular nature of the state. For them such a move symbolised potential Muslim domination of Nigeria (Laitin 1986: 1). The debate resulted in religious riots. This was the first time that there had ever been serious rivalry, let alone widespread and violent conflict, between two religious groups in the history of the territory that now comprises Nigeria. According to Ekoko and Amadi (1989: 120), the enduring significance of the Sharia debate and the 'compromise solution proffered by the Presidential Constitution of 1979 was that for the first time in our [Nigeria's] corporate existence a religious question was openly forced to the forefront of national problems to the extent that it threatened the continued indivisible existence of the state'. Previous religious conflicts had been mainly between sects of the same religion. Thereafter, the cleavage between Islam and Christianity became increasingly confrontational and violent, with hundreds of Nigerians dying in religious riots.

The recent transition of religion into an overt conflictual political force is largely a consequence of government policy. A series of Muslim-led governments from 1979 contravened formally the secular basis of the state by implementing policies which were widely perceived as favourable to Islam and by extension to the dominant Muslim Hausa/Fulani group. Such contravention included massive government subsidies to pilgrims to Mecca, the granting of 10 million Naira to Muslims in 1982 to build a national mosque in Abuja, the new state capital, and the surreptitious way in which Nigeria became a member of the Organization of Islamic Conference (OIC) in 1986. These policies raised Muslim expectations and encouraged fundamentalist political activism in the northern states where Islamisation policies were rigorously pursued (Olupona 1988: 20). Islamic militants actively campaigned against secularism, seeking an Islamic state in Nigeria. Christians prepared to defend their religion. The result has been increasing political activity on both sides and violent clashes between members of the two groups, particularly in the north.

Christian and Muslim identities are now competing with the Nigerian political identity in importance. Institutions intended to foster nationalism, such as the universities, the National Youth Service Corps (NYSC), the federal government colleges, the armed forces, now foster religious solidarity (Igwara 1993: 226–9). Commentators have claimed that Nigeria has become polarised between 'Christian Nigerians and Muslim Nigerians' (Ekoko and Amadi 1989: 130), and asked whether the country was heading 'for a religious war that will destroy the basis of its existence as a nation-state?' (*Newswatch* 8 October 1990: 42). Such writers believe that religious cleavage is supplanting ethnicity as the basis of people's political identities and therefore obstructing the growth of national identity and cohesion. By this view, religion is a regressive force for nationalism. Yet, religion can be a proactive force for Nigerian nationalism in the sense that it is instrumental in the elaboration and development of national identity and cohesion. [...]

RELIGION AND THE LEGITIMATION OF NIGERIAN IDENTITY

The revitalisation of religion in Nigeria as fundamentalist, evangelical, spiritualist and other types may be seen as an increasingly important factor in Nigeria's quest for nationhood. The forms of 'nation-state' and of nationalist ideology that have developed in Nigeria are different from those of the European model adopted by classical nation-building theory. Classical nation-building theory holds that the political and national unit should be congruent (Gellner 1983: 1; Breuilly 1985: 3). The Nigerian nation is a weaker form of 'imagined community' than those found in Europe because it coexists with (and is often secondary to) more immediate forms of popular identity. It is the opposite of the ethnically and linguistic homogeneous entities which came to be seen as the standard form of nation-state in the West. It is more of a project, the achievement of which is in progress.

Nigeria is imagined as a homogeneous unit eliciting support from all peoples within its territory. The 1979 Constitution described Nigeria as one indivisible and indissoluble sovereign nation-state to be known by the name of the Federal Republic of Nigeria. Nigerian nationalism is, then, not unlike the classical European model that emphasises popular support and national unity. This similarity is underlined by Nigeria's colonial legacy. However, unlike the classical model, Nigerian nationalism accepts that a stable and free society can be a multinational state based on political accommodation and democracy. This is why the state pursues the project of nation-building, that is, planned policies that combine both a popular nationalist enthusiasm and the inculcation of nationalist ideology through the mass media, educational system and national institutions, and administrative regulations. Thus, nationalist ideology in Nigeria is more appropriately described as a blend of the European popular and the 'official nationalism' of the czars (Anderson 1983: 104). [...]

Religion is big business in Nigeria. There are approximately 1,500 new religious movements active in contemporary Nigeria (Hackett 1987: 2). They include neo-traditional movements, healing homes or prayer churches, Ethiopian or African churches, spiritual or Aladura churches, revivalist (Christian or Islamic) movements and spiritual science movements. Most people in Nigeria have had personal contact or involvement, either directly or indirectly through a friend or relative, with one of these movements.

Patronage of traditional religion has increased. This is evidenced by the increase in the growth of secret societies and cults, and of ritual sacrifice of people for wealth (*Quality* 14 July 1988: 8–10, 38).[3] The federal government in the 1970s proscribed membership of secret cults, making it a crime for all civil servants. The ban has not been effective. Benjamin Awolusi, the secretary general of a witches' cult, pointed out that: 'People will continue to kill for money. Unless government takes care of the needs of everybody and gives them food and clothing. But if every individual is to find his own money, some people will continue to kill' (ibid.: 9). The growth in religion is most conspicuous in the cities. Pastors and prophets are making money from the situation:

> There is hardly a street in Ajegunle [a poor suburb of Lagos] without a church of the spiritual kind. Along Okito Street alone at the Awodiora area of Ajegunle, there are about seven churches [*sic*]. Some of which are shops by day and prayer houses by the evenings. As one Ajegunle resident aptly [*sic*] put it 'most of the churches ... have a common purpose, that is to make money. They are everywhere with new ones springing up daily'. (*Thisweek* 3 October 1988: 22–3)

The proliferation of churches is regarded by some as a purely commercial venture, an articulation of the pecuniary interests of the church leaders.[4] What is not recognised by such commentators is that the industry exists largely because there is a demand for religion, and that such need is not a matter of false consciousness induced by an alienated social reality on the part of the increasing number of people who seek healing through religion.

Appeal to religion for healing is natural for many Nigerians. The traditional world of the African does not separate between sacred and secular. There is a general conviction rooted in traditional beliefs that God is immanent and active in peoples' lives and is both concerned and able to solve human problems. Faced with a problem – health, economic, legal, marital, sterility – most Nigerians turn to the *babalawo,* prophet, or mallam for help. Prayers are now offered daily for Nigeria with the belief that only God can save the country (Ikara 1989: 26). Nigerians are thus not just seeking individual healing but also national remedy through religion.

Recourse to religion as a corrective to a crisis of national identity is not unique to Nigeria. In Turkey and Malaysia, for example, alienated victims of maldevelopment turned to Islam (Ozay 1990: 3). In times of social, economic and political turbulence and uncertainty new strategies are devised by individuals and communities to cope and many of these involve religion. The religious emerges out of disorder and thus provides man's ultimate shield against the terror of anomie: 'To be in a 'right' relationship with the sacred cosmos is to be protected against the nightmare of chaos. To fall out of such a 'right' relationship is to be abandoned on the edge of the abyss of meaninglessness' (Berger 1969: 27). It is the sacred which ultimately enables individuals and communities to endure the hardship around them. The material expectations offered by secular ideologies often cause frustration because they cannot be fulfilled in one's own lifetime. The expectations of religious ideologies do not disappoint in the same way because they are not expected to be fulfilled in this world (Juergensmeyer 1993: 194). Religion thus provides both a sacred canopy against the threat of chaos and anomie, and raises new hopes for individuals and communities undergoing a period of economic and political uncertainty. Through the hope it raises, it offers salvation through the idea of the nation-state.

Many Nigerian analysts and commentators have tried to explain the revitalisation of religion in Nigeria from the perspective of elite manipulation of religion for individual, political and economic ends (Agi 1987: 91–2). Bala Usman identified three groups that are engaged in the manipulation of religion in the country: foreign powers, their stooges in Nigeria, and ruling elites (Usman 1987: 32–3). A group of academics from Ahmadu Bello University, Zaria, see the politicisation of religion as a conspiracy on the part of government. They accused the government of deliberately engineering the antagonism between the two faiths as a tactic to divert attention from the urgent political and economic problems that face Nigeria (*Newswatch* 24 February 1986: 17). The major limitation of this approach lies in its inability to distinguish between a genuine place for religion in any society and its so-called manipulation. Such an approach wrongly assumes that those manipulated have no minds of their own. The idea that ordinary Nigerians have been coerced by powerful elites into a false awareness that causes them to misunderstand their own best interests is ridiculous.

Others believe that the excessive resort to religion stems from fanaticism. For example, Bola Olowo points out that northern Nigeria is fertile ground for such fanaticism because of its floating population of Almajirais or Gardawa who obey the injunctions of their Mullahs, including killing and dying for the Islamic cause (*West Africa* 20 May 1991: 796). Certainly, the element of fanaticism cannot be discounted. However, most Almajirais depend on their Mullahs not only for spiritual guidance but also for material needs. It is thus difficult to say whether their so-called fanatical reaction is spiritually or materially induced. Lubeck has shown that the ideology which guided the Maitatsine *gardawa* 'to die for the cause of Islam' contained a clear class antagonism which cannot be reconciled with religious fanaticism (Lubeck 1985).

Yet others believe that the politicisation of religion is a response to poverty. For example, a journalist observed that Nigeria 'means far less to the ordinary Nigerian because, for years, it has not demonstrated its capacity to clothe him and house him' (*New Nigerian* 6 December 1977, cited in Kukah 1991: 23). Poverty is certainly a factor, but not a sufficient one to explain why the Nigerian identity is defined in religious terms, rather than in terms of region or class.

Some commentators have attempted to explain the phenomenon as the consequence of limited opportunities for political expression. The military banned political parties and activities in 1984 and, since then, they have banned other civil organisations which challenged governmental policies (Kukah 1991: 26). Such an explanation is inadequate. It sees religion as mere substitute for politics, implying that religious revival is just a passing phase. If this were the case, the reinstatement of secular parties in 1990 should have diminished the chances of politicising religion, but it did not. In 1991 the leader of the Islamic movement ordered his followers to kill Governor Madaki for blaspheming against the Prophet Mohammed. Large-scale religious riots have occurred in Katsina and Bauchi states in 1991 and in Kaduna state in May 1992 and in January 1993. These incidents suggest that more is seen to be at stake than mere political expression.

Another explanation that bears considering is the global reality of religion, particularly of the Islamic and Christian religions. Through the new satellite technology, rapid communication of religious developments in one part of the world is possible over almost unlimited space. By this perspective the demonstration effect of religious groups in other parts of the world influences religious groups and individuals in Nigeria. Thus Islamic fundamentalists are seen as being influenced by the Ayatollah Khomeini's revolution in Iran in 1979. Certainly the demonstration effect of religious activities in other parts of the world cannot be discounted. It certainly helped to encourage the Nigerian groups to use Islam to influence changes in their country. The global dimension of religion is also evident in the Nigerian Muslim show of solidarity with Muslims world-wide by their demonstration over the Salmon Rushdie affair, and in the growing American-style Christian evangelists in Nigeria. However, the globalisation process not only erodes inherited individual identities, but also encourages the revitalisation of particular identities as a way of gaining control over structured power. It is in the context of the latter feature that religion plays a significant role in the development, elaboration and problematisation of the national question. Globalisation, as it is itself a process of modernisation, both repels and attracts the rising intelligentsia, bringing about a confrontation between the 'scientific state' and traditional religion and belief systems (Smith 1983: 256). 'The crux of the matter was that the 'scientific state' demanded a heavy price for its benefits: it demanded ineluctably the 'privatisation' of religion' (ibid.: 240). The consequence is a 'crisis of faith among the intelligentsia and the clash between reason and revelation, science and tradition, sons and fathers, which so agitates them' (ibid.: 240). Moreover, the global argument would be relevant if the spatial visions of religious militants in Nigeria were based on a uniform Islamic or Christian worldwide space. To understand the critique and appropriation of secular Nigerian nationalism by religious militants we have to situate our analysis not just in the global context of Islam or Christianity but in the national and local contexts. Besides, the revitalisation of religion is not limited to global religions like Islam and Christianity, but also includes indigenous Nigerian forms of religious worship.

The problem of religious revivalism in Nigeria may therefore be described as that of the sacralisation of the Nigerian identity. By sacralisation I mean the process by which Nigerians come to perceive their society as the result of a revelation or supernatural principle, not just the result of human action. Through this process they symbolically reorder their lives, and their existence as Nigerians becomes more meaningful, more permanent as they come to perceive such existence as grace, a free gift from God.

HOLY NATIONALISM AND APOCALYPTIC VISIONS OF NIGERIA

The sacralisation of Nigeria and Nigerian identity may be seen as the goal of Islamic and Christian political activists. Their critique and appropriation of secular Nigerian nationalism does not mean that they are a regressive force for nationalism. They are very much concerned about the ideology underlying the Nigerian political structure. They are concerned about the rationale for having a state, the moral basis for politics, and the reasons why a state should elicit loyalty. They reject the idea that nationalism can be defined solely in secular terms or that the unifying and legitimating principle of a political order is a rational understanding that unites individuals and communities in a geographical region through common laws and political processes. They see no contradiction in affirming the state structure as long as it is legitimised not by the secular idea of a social contract but by traditional principles of religion (Juergensmeyer 1993: 7). Their ultimate goal is therefore the conversion of Nigerian nationalism to holy nationalism.

Nigerian nationalism as presently constituted is, for religious radicals, unacceptable and impure. Nigerian nationalism, as both a popular emotional force and an ideology for the elites to legitimate the exercise of, and the struggles for, state power, is despised as bereft of all morals. Elite-led secular nationalism is seen as oppressive, corrupt and illegitimate and characterised as the enemy of the people. The objective of religious radicals is a dual one: to purify elite secular nationalism of its evil, satanic tendencies, and to imbue it with holiness and godliness which it needs to be faithful to the people. The idea is to engender feelings of national loyalty which are transcendental, conditioned by moral and spiritual goals rather than the materialistic goals of secular nationalism. The appeal of such 'holy nationalism' is largely because it promises a national future that cannot easily disillusion: one's fate is tied to the fate of the nation and the nation's fate is tied to the will of God and God's benevolence is dependent on the right behaviour of individuals. Holy nationalism is then the ultimate stage in the progress of nationalism. It is the nationalism that inspires national reverence and makes national symbols – flag, pledge, constitution, anthem, awards – meaningful to individuals. In consequence, their flag becomes more than any other piece of cloth in their eyes, their constitution more venerable than any other document (O'Brien 1988: 40–1). At this stage the collective emotional force of nationalism merges with religion and both altogether become indistinguishable. God chose a particular people and promised them a particular land.

The idea of a holy Nigerian nation is contained in both radical Christian and Muslim beliefs and images. Muslims believe that the country's problems are due to immorality and the evil of secularism. Ibrahim Suleiman, a leading commentator on Islamic affairs, argues that:

> Historically and in practice, secularization is a development peculiar to Christian civilization. It is a child, albeit a bastard, of Christianity ... Secularization has become a sinister but convenient mechanism to blackmail Muslims and impede the progress of Islam and reduce it to the level of earthly concepts and ideologies. (*Sunday Triumph* 24 April 1986, cited in Ibrahim 1989: 77)

The perception of the state security forces 'as the contemporary expression of the devil' by the Maitatsine speaks for itself. Yakubu Yahaya, the leader of the Islamic movement in Katsina, described the federal, state and local governments as 'a group of cheats', running an ungodly government (*Tell* 6 May 1991: 19). Thus, for Muslim political activists, an Islamic state is a means of recapturing the national space from the secular world, thus decreasing the territory of the devil.

Evangelicals similarly believe that the country's problems are the work of the devil and his minions, that is, evil government officials (for evil government officials substitute Muslim rulers of the country). This view is illustrated by extracts from the *Prayer Bulletin*, an occasional newsletter of the Christian Students' Social Movement of Nigeria (CSSMN), one of the 'Born Again' organisations:

> Our economy is in shambles with the extent of damage not accurately known. ... Our economic situation makes it necessary for us to pray and ask the Lord to have mercy upon us. We also need to ask the Lord to deal with the men who compounded the problem – government officials. (CSSMN 1983b: 1, 3)[5]

> We must understand that quite a lot of the problems we face in this country today with relation to politics, agriculture, weather, etc. may be due in part to the fact that certain things have been programmed by the forces of darkness through interference in the heavenly bodies. (CSSMN 1983c: 3)[6]

Each group therefore believes that it is the embodiment of good and the other the embodiment of evil. For Muslims, secularity is Christian and, as such, evil while for Christians, Muslim rule is the evil.

The difference between Muslim and Christian activists over the issue of secularism is quite fundamental. Christians support the secular position of the state, even if they do not believe in the state as it is presently constituted, and try to force the state to make good on the promise of neutrality in religious matters as contained in Section 10 of the 1979 constitution. Although the Christian defence of the secular state may seem ambiguous, such a notion is set in relation to a meta-narrative in which secularisation is a materialisation of Christian values and, importantly, of civil rights in a state controlled by a section of the Muslim elite.

The two rival groups have strong conceptions of the national space. For them, the national space is a unified one, deeply material and non-divisible. The presence of any other group is seen as necessarily restrictive. For them, God created the Nigerian space and intends that space to be homomorphously filled with right-thinking Muslims or Christians, not both. Consequently, proselytisation is an important activity of both groups, the idea being to transform 'evil' Nigeria into a holy nation, a nation of people united in their common calling as God's prophets. This is why Nigerian unity means for the late Gumi, leader of Izala, the conversion of Christians and non-Muslims to Islam (*Quality* October 1987: 37).

Militant Muslims favour a military approach, a jihad, to recapture the national space from the secular evil world and establishing a holy Nigerian nation with tenure from Allah. Mallam Yahaya, the leader of militant Islam in Katsina, claims that 'a battle will be fought and Allah has promised to help his people' (*Tell* 6 May 1991: 19). Mallam Zakzaky, the leader of the Islamic movement, observed that: 'Eventually the movement will swallow up all of the Muslim population. And when finally the Islamic system triumphs, the Christians will find that it is much better than the present set up' (*The Guardian* 7 May 1991: 11). By such apocalyptic visions of Nigeria, Muslim activists are not only asserting Islam's rejection of the separation of politics and religion, but also promoting their idea of the nation based on a Muslim space.

The Christian vision of Nigeria is also based on only one space, a Christian space. This will be brought about, not by a holy war, but by divine intervention, the Holy Spirit. This approach has been referred to as the 'Christian Liberation Movement, the Nation's Liberation in the Spirit realm through Christ Jesus' (Johnson 1990: iii). The major weapon for the liberation of the national space from the devilish forces of Islam and traditionism is prayer. For instance, the CSSMN stated that:

> 1983 is the year of destiny for Nigeria ... It will be the turning point spiritually for Nigeria. The political, economic and social situations will be the result of what goes on in the spiritual realm. Therefore EVERYONE has to be a WATCHMAN for NIGERIA. Learn to DAILY pray and intercede for at least a prayer item concerning Nigeria. (CSSMN 1983d: 1)

Therefore in the imaginaries of both religious groups, Nigeria is established as a nation-state. What is not yet established is which God rules the state.

Each of the two groups believes that Nigeria is God's promised land for its members. For instance, the CSSMN urged the faithful to 'speak healing' to the Nigerian economy because: 'if Nigeria were to go down we cannot carry out God's assignment for us as has been revealed by prophecy: we cannot run to Chad, Cameroon, Niger, Benin or the Atlantic Ocean. We must therefore have a good economy' (CSSMN 1983a: 5).[7] Muslim fundamentalists, on the other hand, behave as if an Islamic state is a *fait accompli*. As they see it, Muslims are the majority and Islam is a total way of life. Mallam Zakzaky claimed that Christians had nothing to fear from the triumph of Islam in Nigeria as their religion expressed no views on the political and socio-economic aspects of daily life (*The Guardian* 7 May 1991: 11). The late Gumi made similar claims, observing that Muslim rule in Nigeria is imperative for Nigerian unity. 'We have to divide the country' if Christians do not accept Muslim leadership (*Quality* October 1987: 35). What is therefore seen to be at stake by both groups is which religious system provides the sacred, the holy, normative substance to their identity as Nigerians. It is this substance that ultimately enables individuals and communities to accept as permanent and meaningful the suffering which is integral to a national identity. For most people, identity is simply a necessary stigmatic emblem one must learn to carry without disguise (De Vos and Romanucci-Ross 1975: 389). Holy nationalism is the ideology that enables the stigmatic emblem of the nation to be carried with pride, and national loyalty to have a special appeal as a 'secular transformation of fatality into continuity, contingency into meaning' (Anderson 1983: 19).

The dilemma for Nigeria, however, remains. Although the politicisation of religion and religionisation of identities may seek to resolve the crisis of identity facing Nigerians, it also raises the delicate question of where their ultimate loyalties lie: religion, ethnic group or state? As religion increasingly reinforces the sense of identity, the old dialectic between ethnicity and nationalism continues in a new form and setting to divide Nigeria and confuse visions of its future destiny as a nation. However Nigeria has the potential for reconciling religion with modernity via public policy. Such a policy should, among other things, synthesise nation-building and the Nigerian peoples' religious heritage, elevating traditional religion to the national status now being accorded Islam and Christianity in Nigeria.

Official policy towards traditional religion is ambivalent. A National Advisory Council on Religious Affairs (NACRA) was inaugurated by the government on 29 June 1987 with equal numbers of Christians and Muslims. Traditional religionists were not invited to the council, a measure that might have mediated the extreme positions of the two camps and enhanced cultural nationalism. Through the promotion of 'traditional culture', indigeneous religious beliefs were accorded rights in law, administrative policy, medicine, psychiatry and pharmacology, and so on (Kalu 1989: 23). Marriages and contractual obligations sealed customarily were legitimated. The government has in recent years set up two different panels to study traditional healing that is tied to traditional religion. Practitioners of indigeneous religion have now been recognised. Whereas it was previously referred to as paganism and animism, it is now referred to as Traditional Religion with a capital T and R. The minister of internal affairs, Col. Shagaya, pointedly told the journalist who referred to TR as paganism that 'there is nothing like paganism, rather they are called Traditional Religion because they also recognise the existence of God and therefore have a religion.'[8] In official forms, TR now respectably appears where it was once not an acceptable alternative to Christianity and Islam. For example, in the 1973 census all Nigerians were required to identify themselves as *either* Muslim or Christian and thus, the government was already inadvertently promoting a cleavage between Christianity and Islam (Gilliland 1986: 171). Traditional African religion is now taught in schools as part of religious knowledge (Kunu 1987: 276). Despite all this, it has not been accorded any significant role in nation-building. At the inauguration of the council, the chief of general staff and second-in-command to President Babangida, Vice-Admiral Aikhomu, warned the members not to forget that there are other religions in Nigeria besides Islam and Christianity. The warning was futile as members can only represent their respective religions. The government ought to have made formal provision in the council for those other religions if it felt so strongly about their interests (Onaiyekan 1987: 8). By providing only for Christians and Muslims in the council the government is effectively indicating that traditional religion, unlike Islam and Christianity, has no place in nation-building, as well as inadvertently reinforcing the existing cleavage between the two organised religious blocs.

NOTES

This chapter has here been abridged and reproduced, with the kind permission of Blackwell publishers. The full version of this article was first published in *Nations and Nationalism*, vol. 1, part 3, November 1995, pp. 327–55, published by Blackwell.

1 Although there are different versions as to how and when Islam came to Hausaland, the majority of scholars agree that it reached Hausaland through Mali. See for instance Doi (1984: 19–22).

2 For details of the Christian missions in Nigeria, see Ayandele (1996: *passim*).

3 Revelations about the growth of cults in Nigerian universities was of great public concern in 1991 as it involved ritual killings and injuries to many students. See *The African Guardian* (Lagos), 9 April 1991.

4 See *African Concord*, 23 April 1987, 7–15.
5 Issues of the *Bulletin* are filed at the CSSMN office, 2 Akanbi Street, Satellite Town, Lagos.
6 For Biblical echoes, see Colossians 1: 3, Romans 8: 38, 2 Corinthians 3–4.
7 Healing is here used in the sense of order.
8 Interview, 'All religions are encouraged in Abuja', *Thisweek*, 14 March 1988, 26.

REFERENCES

Agi, S. P. I. (1987), 'The influence of religion on politics in Nigeria: Yesterday, today and ...?', in S. O. Olugbemi (ed.), *Alternative Political Futures for Nigeria*, Lagos: Nigerian Political Science Association.

Anderson, Benedict (1983), *Imagined Communities*, London: Verso.

Ayandele, E. A. (1966), *The Missionary Impact on Modern Nigeria 1842–1914*, London: Longman.

Berger, Peter L. (1969), *The Social Reality of Religion*, London: Faber and Faber.

Breuilly, John (1985), *Nationalism and the State*, Manchester: Manchester University Press.

Christian Students' Social Movement of Nigeria (1983a), *Prayer Bulletin* 14, 16 June.

Christian Students' Social Movement of Nigeria (1983b), *Prayer Bulletin* 12, 24 May.

Christian Students' Social Movement of Nigeria (1983c), *Prayer Bulletin* 8 February.

Christian Students' Social Movement of Nigeria (1983d), *Post-prayer Conference Letter*, January.

Clarke, Peter B. and Ian Linden (1984), *Islam in Modern Nigeria: A Study of a Muslim Community in a Post-Independence State 1960–1983*, Munich: Kaiser Grunewald.

De Vos, George and Lola Romanucci-Ross (1975), *Ethnic Identity: Cultural Communities and Change*, Chicago: University of Chicago Press.

Doi, Abdurrahman I. (1984), *Islam in Nigeria*, Zaria: Gaskiya Corporation Limited.

Ekoko, A. E. and L. O. Amadi (1989), 'Religion and stability in Nigeria', in J. A. Atanda et al. *Nigeria Since Independence: The First 25 Years, Volume IX, Religion*, Ibadan, Nigeria: Heinemann Educational.

Ellah, F. J. (1983), *Nigeria and States Creation*, Port Harcourt: Chief J. W. Ellah, Sons and Co.

Gellner, Ernest (1983), *Nations and Nationalism*, Oxford: Blackwell.

Gilliland, Dean S. (1986), *African Religion Meets Islam: Religious Change in Northern Nigeria*, Lanham, MD: University Press of America.

Hackett, Rosalind (ed.) (1987), *New Religious Movements in Nigeria*, Lewiston, NY: Edwin Mellen Press.

Ibrahim, Jibrin (1989), 'The politics of religion in Nigeria: The parameters of the 1987 crisis in Kaduna State', *Review of African Political Economy*, 45–6: 65–82.

Igwara, Obi (1993), *Ethnicity, Nationalism and Nation-building in Nigeria, 1970–1992*, Ph.D. thesis, London School of Economics.

Ikara, Bashir (1989), *The Greater Future of Nigeria: A Cultural Perspective*, Lagos: Books.

Johnson, Segun (ed.) (1990), *Readings in Selected Nigerian Problems*, Lagos: Okanlawon Publishers.

Juergensmeyer, Mark (1993), *The New Cold War? Religious Nationalism Confronts the Secular State*, Berkeley: University of California Press.

Kalu, Ogbu (1989), 'Religions in Nigeria: An overview', in Atanda et al., *Nigeria Since Independence: The first 25 Years,* Ibadan: Heinemann.

Kukah, Matthew Hassan (1990), *Religion and Politics in Northern Nigeria since 1960*, Ph.D. thesis, University of London, SOAS.

Kukah, Matthew Hassan (1991), 'Religion and the politics of deprivation: A case study of the religious riots in Kaduna State', paper presented at the International Conference on Religion and Protest in Africa, Cornell University, Ithaca, NY, 25–7 April.

Kunu, Atome (1987), 'The nationalist movement in Nigeria', in J. U. Obot (ed.), *Nigeria: The People and their Heritage*, Calabar: Wusen Press.

Laitin, David (1986), *Hegemony and Culture: Politics and Religious Change among the Yoruba*, Chicago: University of Chicago Press.

Lubeck, Paul (1985), 'Islamic protest under semi-industrial capitalism: Yan Tatsine explained', *Africa: Journal of International African Institute* 55, 4: 369–89.

O'Brien, Conor Cruise (1988), *Godland: Reflections on Religion and Nationalism*, Cambridge, MA: Harvard University Press.

Olupona, Jacob K. (1988), 'Muslim–Christian relations in Nigeria: Then and now', paper presented to the Oxford African Society Seminar, Oxford University, 27 January.

Onaiyekan, John, Bishop of Horin (1987), 'Secularism and the Nigerian state', paper presented at Ahmadu Bello University, Zaria, 11 July.

Ozay, Mehmet (1990), *Islamic Identity and Development: Studies of the Islamic Periphery*, London: Routledge.

Parrinder, O. (1953), *Religion in an African City*, Oxford: Oxford University Press.

Peel, J. D. Y. (1989), 'The cultural work of Yoruba ethnogenesis', in E. Tonkin et al. (eds), *History and Ethnicity*, London: Routledge.

Smith, Anthony D. (1983), *Theories of Nationalism*, London: Duckworth, 2nd edn.

Usman, Bala (1987), *The Manipulation of Religion in Nigeria (1977–1987)*, London: Vanguard Publishers.

Magazines and newspapers

African Concord, Lagos.
The African Guardian, Lagos.
The Guardian, London.
New Nigerian, Kaduna.
Newswatch, Lagos.
Quality, Lagos.
Tell, Lagos.
Thisweek, Lagos.
West Africa, London.

Chapter 18

ETHNIC DEMOBILISATION:
THE CASE OF THE AFRIKANERS

David Welsh and J. E. Spence

Afrikaner nationalism's roots lay in the last third of the nineteenth century as a response to British imperialism. In its subsequent development it invoked many symbols of what it assumed to be a Golden Age in which Boer Trekkers had moved beyond the clutches of imperial rule and established independent republics: the trek, ox wagon, rifle, *kruithoring* (power-horn) and the laager into which wagons were formed when trekker groups were under attack. These were powerful symbols of cultural cohesion and continuity, as well as group identity. The Trekkers were also powerfully influenced by religion, and subsequent interpreters claimed that they were a 'chosen people'. The Old Testament, moreover, supposedly offered many analogies to the situation of the Afrikaner people, including theological justifications of segregation and apartheid. Anthony D. Smith's brief writings on South Africa acutely analyse the powerful effects of this symbolic apparatus and the accompanying civil religion as it was yoked to the rising nationalism of the late nineteenth and twentieth centuries (Smith 2003).

The focus of this chapter, however, is on the decline of this traditional invocation of ethnosymbolism. As Afrikaners urbanised, became better educated and more secular – in short, the process of *embourgeoisiement* – the nationalist movement began to disintegrate. Finally, demobilisation occurred. Few young, modern-minded Afrikaners nowadays pay much attention to the traditional symbols. Many regard them as little more than historical curiosities, as well as embarrassing reminders of Afrikaner nationalism's association with racial conflict and domination.

Since South Africa's transition in 1994 to a democratic and inclusive polity, Afrikaner nationalism, the dominant force in the country since 1948, has fallen into disarray. Its institutional embodiments have either disappeared, like the National Party (NP), or are groping to adapt themselves to the radically changed circumstances in which racial exclusivity is prohibited. The transition, accordingly, offers a rare case study of the demobilisation of a once-powerful ethnic nationalism. This chapter provides a brief overview of the rise of Afrikaner nationalism, followed by an analysis of how its solidarity began to fray and crack in the decades after the 1960s when its cohesiveness was at its zenith. The circumstances of the transition in the early 1990s are examined, followed by an exploration of current issues and the options that a now powerless minority sees itself as having.

Afrikaner nationalism's roots lay in the late nineteenth century, principally as a reaction to British imperialism's quest for control of southern Africa. The events leading up to the Anglo-Boer War (1899–1902), which devastated the defeated Boer republics, gave the nascent movement a huge stimulus. Efforts by Louis Botha and Jan Smuts, both former Boer generals, to establish a unified white bloc at the time of unification in 1909 foundered on the rocks of Afrikaner sentiment. J. B. M. Hertzog, also a former Boer general, who was dropped from the cabinet in 1912 for his demands that Dutch be accorded its (constitutionally) rightful place, formed the National Party in 1914, thereby beginning the process of separate Afrikaner organisation. Hertzog propounded the 'two-stream' policy 'whereby the Afrikaner and Englishman's cultural streams would continue to flow alongside each other, but would not become a mishmash that did no honour to either' (van den Heever 1943: 313, translation).

The building of Afrikaner nationalist solidarity was a lengthy and complex process that suffered many vicissitudes, despite the NP's electoral victory in 1923 (in a pact with the predominantly English-speaking Labour Party), and Hertzog's tenure as prime minister until 1939. Hertzog was no radical: his conciliatory attitude to English-speakers and his soft-pedalling of the republican issue alienated more radical nationalists. A critical split occurred in 1933–4 when, faced with an economic crisis, Hertzog formed a coalition government with his old enemy Smuts, and thereafter led the NP into fusion with Smuts's South Africa Party, forming the United Party (UP).

To the radicals, led by D. F. Malan, this was a betrayal. It also comprehensively split Afrikaner nationalism. The Malanites, now constituted as the 'Purified' NP, propounded a radical version of Afrikaner nationalism. It was a classic manifestation of 'ethnic outbidding'. By 1945, the NP had emerged triumphant and, despite defeat in the 1943 election, the seeds of their victory in 1948 were being sown: the tide of a resurgent nationalism was flowing strongly beneath stormy surface waters.

The narrow victory won by Malan's NP and the tiny Afrikaner Party (consisting mostly of residual supporters of Hertzog) in the general election of May 1948 came as a surprise to all, not least to Malan himself. In a famous utterance, he declared: 'We feel at home again in our own country'. It was a sentiment that suggested the Nationalists' attitude to other groups, and the symbolic importance of the land to Afrikaners. Earlier, in 1941, Malan had told a party congress that '[w]e are no party political organisation in the ordinary sense of the word. We are much more than that' (Malan 1964: 38, translation).

The 1948 election was fought less on the issue of apartheid than on the appeal to Afrikaner unity. Exploiting the colour issue, a familiar tactic in South African electoral history, was a means to an end, namely fanning the fears of Afrikaners that the traditional policy of segregation was breaking down under UP rule. The election strategy centred on an effort to win back Afrikaner support from those who had declined to follow Malan and his 'Purified' Nationalists. Between 70 and 80 per cent of Afrikaners heeded the call for Afrikaner unity, a per centage that would increase in future elections.

It was a long-standing manifestation of Afrikaner nationalist paranoia that the perfidious English would seek to compensate for their numerical inferiority in relation to Afrikaners by using African votes (until they were abolished) and Coloured votes to tip the electoral scales against the NP. If (white) politics was to continue to be based upon the approximately 60:40 Afrikaner to English population ratio, Afrikaner nationalist political hegemony was secure. It was the NP's assumption that Coloured voters would vote largely against it that made it determined to go to extreme lengths to abolish common roll voting rights. After a series of shabby manoeuvres this was finally achieved in 1956.

The NP was part of a wider nationalist movement that spanned all spheres of Afrikaner community life. Hertzog's original two-stream approach was confined to politics and the protection of Afrikaners' language rights. The approach, however, was carried further, and, as far as possible, an effort was made to separate Afrikaner spheres of interest or community activities from their English counterparts. Afrikaner society was 'bureaucratised' (Slabbert 1975: 115). The spheres were demarcated along functional lines (political, economic, labour, religious, educational, press and cultural), each being regarded as relatively autonomous.

The task of coordinating the spheres, thereby resolving friction between them in the name of Afrikaner unity, fell to the Afrikaner Broederbond (AB), the secret society founded in 1918 to further Afrikaner interests. Membership of the AB was confined to male, Protestant Afrikaners, generally 30 years of age or more, and occupying positions of actual or potential influence in their communities. Moreover, membership was by invitation and prospective members were vetted to ensure that they were of blameless character. By 1978 the AB had some 12,000 members among whom were clergy, university administrators and professors, schoolteachers, editors, senior civil servants, businessmen, and judges. Politicians were also strongly represented: from D. F. Malan to F. W. de Klerk all prime ministers or state presidents, as well as most cabinet ministers, were members. The AB was the elite of Afrikanerdom.

Exactly how influential the AB was has been a matter of ongoing debate. There is no evidence, however, to suggest that it dictated to government after 1948. Nevertheless, the AB manoeuvred to ensure that 'right-minded' people were nominated for, and appointed to, important positions in the community. Rectors of the Afrikaans universities, for example, were invariably AB members, as were the senior office-bearers in the biggest Afrikaan church, the Nederduitse Gereformeerde Kerk (NGK), often caustically referred to as 'the NP at prayer'.

The penalties for dissent within the AB and NP were severe: they included effective ex-communication, social ostracism, having the details of a messy divorce widely publicised, denial of promotion or even loss of a job. In Dr H. F. Verwoerd's time (prime minister from 1958 to 1966), it was prudent to acquiesce, and only a few hardy souls declined to do so. That Verwoerd's term of office represented the zenith of Afrikaner nationalism's cohesion was no coincidence: he, after all, had delivered to Afrikaners the greatest symbolic prize of all, the coming of the Republic in 1961 – and, as a bonus, withdrawal from the Commonwealth. His seeming omniscience and ruthless onslaughts on black resistance caused him to be deified by a large segment of the Afrikaner population. No previous leader had ever exerted such total control of Afrikanerdom.

Inadvertently, however, Verwoerd created two indirect openings for future dissent in the ranks of Afrikaners, one for the far-right wing (which had grumbled, *sotto voce*, about 'too much' being done for the blacks) and one for more moderate Afrikaners. These two categories were subsequently to be labeled the *verkramptes* and *verligtes*, respectively.

In the first instance, Verwoerd, scenting an opportunity to woo English-speaking voters to the NP, broke with tradition and appointed two (undistinguished) English-speakers to his cabinet in 1961. Further wooing reaped electoral gains, since at least 25 per cent of English-speaking voters supported the NP in the 1966 election. In all subsequent elections a substantial minority of English-speakers voted for the NP.

Although anti-English sentiment had declined among most Afrikaners, the two white communities still lived largely separate lives. For the hardliners, however, Verwoerd's and his successors' détente with the old enemy was a betrayal. When the *verkramptes*, led by an eccentric former minister, Albert Hertzog, were flushed out of the NP by Vorster in 1969, they formed the Herstigte Nasionale Party (HNP) (the Reconstituted National Party). Their policy proposed the relegation of English to a secondary status. Their other grievances arose from Vorster's ultra-cautious moves to permit sporting tours of South Africa by racially mixed teams; and permitting the exchange of diplomats with the few African states with whom South Africa had relations. For the HNP apartheid in its full Verwoerdian rigour had to be maintained.

If the NP reaped benefits from co-opting some English-speakers into its camp, there was also a downside: the Party could no longer thump an Afrikaner nationalist drum and simultaneously hope to win English-speaking support. This, and the supposed deviations from past orthodoxy, created space for ethnic outbidding, with the HNP portraying itself as the true custodian of Afrikaner interests. Although only four NP MPs joined the HNP, the split caused hysteria in the NP The question was whether the split heralded the beginning of the break-up of Afrikaner nationalism.

Vorster reacted by calling an election in April 1970, over a year ahead of schedule, with the aim of destroying the HNP before it could organise itself. The tactic succeeded: the HNP contested 76 seats and was defeated in all of them, winning 53,504 votes (or 3.5 per cent of the total number of votes cast). After the election Vorster caused HNP supporters to be flushed out of the AB, notwithstanding its supposed stance above party politics. The defeat of the HNP was not the end of the *verkrampte* revolt. Many NP MPs who sympathised with the HNP kept their heads down and remained within the fold. These included the man who became the spiritual leader of the *verkrampte* cause, Dr A. P. Treurnicht.

The second opening indirectly created by Verwoerd was more subtle. In launching his vision of independent African homelands, Verwoerd had emphasised that racial domination was no longer an option: subject peoples had to be given the right of self-determination. 'Separate development' was South Africa's form of decolonisation:

[We are] not fighting for anybody's permanent subordination. It is true that there is a transition period during which there are certain forms of separation and even certain forms of discrimination against the Black man within the White area and against the White man within the Black area. But these are transition periods.(Pelzer 1966: 527)

Could the new vision of apartheid offer an acceptable form of freedom to its supposed beneficiaries? Or would the Bantustans merely be a façade that tried to hide the reality of continuing white domination? And what if a majority of Bantustans declined to accept the kind of freedom that Verwoerd was offering? Equally pertinent was the question of accommodating the Coloured and Indian minorities, neither of whom possessed homelands. Verwoerd's comment about a 'transition period' sounded suspiciously as though freedom might be deferred indefinitely.

It is unnecessary to describe why apartheid failed. It is relevant to note that Afrikaner nationalism had hitched its wagon to the apartheid star, and it rose or fell with that star. Apartheid was the scaffolding that held it together. The morality of apartheid had always been a core issue for supporters and opponents alike. Verwoerd's statement sharpened the focus of the moral question for supporters, and many raised moral qualms in the post-Verwoerd era as the gap between his vision and the reality of policy as it was implemented widened.

By the 1970s it was clear to all who wished to see that apartheid was failing. Although the large majority of Afrikaners continued to vote for the NP, it was apparent that a more critical and questioning attitude to authority was developing. The change was most clearly to be seen among writers and some intellectuals. A younger generation of novelists, Die Sestigers (literally, 'The Sixty-ers'), addressed new themes, challenged cultural taboos and in some cases mocked the moralistic pretensions of the old guard. Their writings, as well as the poetry of the avant-garde poet Breyten Breytenbach, were avidly read, especially by younger people.

Comparable evidence of stirrings could be seen in other spheres: in the churches, for example, the number of clergy who were disquieted by the churches' apparently unquestioning support for apartheid grew, if only slowly. More outspoken criticism came from one of the smaller Afrikaans churches, the Gereformeerde Kerk. Their credo was a straightforward one: what was morally wrong could not be politically right and, as their journal *Woord en Daad* regularly pointed out, much in the implementation of apartheid lacked moral foundation.

In the economic sphere, public criticisms of apartheid were rare. Nonetheless, a number of enterprises were bursting out of their nationalist seams. The earlier efforts by Afrikaners to break into commerce and industry, then dominated by English-speakers, had relied on Afrikaner sentiment to build their businesses, commonly invoking the slogan 'Buy Afrikaans!' The man who became the doyen of Afrikaner entrepreneurs, Anton Rupert, discovered early in his career that sentiment was insufficient: 'the focus on an exclusively Afrikaans clientele narrowed their market considerably' (Dommisse 2005: 54). Other Afrikaner businesses reached the same conclusion.

It was apparent from the changes mentioned above, as well as others, that many modern Afrikaners had lost the fervour which was associated with the radical nationalism of an earlier generation. Folk memories of the Anglo-Boer War, the depression of the 1930s and poor-whiteism were fast disappearing. The enthusiasm for *volksfeeste* (*volk* festivals) commemorating historical events and for cultural organisations had also declined. Afrikaners had benefited from a (racially) protected environment which ensured that whites with skills could easily obtain jobs. Approximately 30 per cent of Afrikaners acquired higher educational qualifications after leaving school, thanks in part to the state's generous provision of Afrikaans-medium institutions, but also to the Afrikaners' own determination to ensure that their children received a good education.

Much of the old inferiority complex, itself a product of conquest and subsequent colonisation, had disappeared. Entrepreneurs like Rupert had been determined to break down the perception among Afrikaners that they could not compete in the English-dominated world of business. He and many others succeeded in doing so.

During the twentieth century Afrikaners became a preponderantly urban population – the old self-appellation of *Boerenasie* ('nation of farmers') was an anachronism: by 1970, 81.6 per cent of Afrikaners were urban, and by 1975 commercial agriculture, always a precarious occupation in South Africa, contributed only 7.2 per cent to Gross Domestic Product. Afrikaners' share of the private sector (excluding agriculture) had risen from 9.6 per cent in 1948–9 to 20.8 per cent in 1975. Moreover, by 1970 over 50 per cent of Afrikaners held white-collar jobs, compared with 29 per cent in 1946. Correspondingly, the percentage of Afrikaners classified as working class declined to 31.5 per cent of the Afrikaner population by 1980. In short, a slow but steady process of *embourgeoisement* was occurring.

In a shrewd analysis of Afrikaners after twenty-five years of NP rule, Schalk Pienaar, a leading Afrikaner journalist, noted the emotional effect: 'There was an explosion of energy in all fields', and the Afrikaner 'having become conscious of his own power, especially after the coming of the Republic [in 1961], had become a much calmer [*rustiger*] person in his relations with those of other languages'. The greater sense of security that victory in 1948 had brought, 'gradually made him a much more liberal person towards other population groups.' The various changes had caused the Afrikaner to loosen ties with his establishment (Pienaar 1975: 70–2, translation).

None of the shifts identified by Pienaar halted the continuing gains of the NP, which increased its majority in the 1974 and 1977 elections. Moreover, tough security action against black protestors continued, as was demonstrated in the Soweto Uprising of 1976–7. The uprising, the most serious challenge to the state since Sharpeville in 1960, arose out of a foolish attempt by the authorities to require the teaching in Afrikaans of certain subjects in certain grades in African schools in the white-controlled areas (that is, outside the Bantustans). The move was opposed by even the most conservative African educationists. Warnings of impending major protests went unheeded by the authorities, with the tragic consequence that in Soweto on 16 June 1976 a small detachment of unprepared police, finding themselves surrounded by what they took to be a menacing crowd of 10,000 or more youthful protesters, opened fire. The resulting disturbances spread to other parts of the country, and it was not until early in 1977 that resistance petered out.

Undergirding the protests was a relatively new phenomenon that had influenced young Africans since the late 1960s. This was Black Consciousness, and its principal advocate was a medical student named Steve Biko. For some Afrikaners, Black Consciousness, with its core demand that blacks (including Coloureds and Indians) had to shake off the 'colonisation of the mind' caused by racial domination, reminded them of Afrikaner nationalists' earlier quest for *eiewaardigheid* (a sense of one's own dignity) and *selfstandigheid* (independence, implying the ridding of a dependency complex). There were parallels between the two phenomena, both being reactions to the pathologies caused by conquest and subordination. An even more striking parallel was the attempts by the British High Commissioner, Lord Alfred Milner, forcibly to anglicise Afrikaner school-children in the aftermath of the Anglo-Boer War. This, too, was not lost on many Afrikaners.

South Africa would never be the same again after the Soweto Uprising: as a young Afrikaner, Tienie Swanepoel, put it, 1976 marked the splitting of two generations among both black and white. For him, traditional explanations by their parents of what was happening no longer sufficed: 'some of us listened even less to our parents' forceful answers. Because they no longer made sense' (Swane-poel 1997: 8, translation). Many Afrikaners were deeply shocked by the callous words used by Jimmy Kruger, the Minister of Justice, at an NP Congress in 1977 when he said of the murder of Steve Biko while in police detention that 'it leaves me cold'. What exacerbated matters was that many in the audience applauded this barbaric comment.

Throughout the 1970s and into the 1980s conflict between the *verligtes* and *verkramptes* continued unabated. Vorster's twelve years in office had produced little reform but his looser grip on Afrikanerdom permitted freer debate than before. The *verligtes* were trying to reform the NP from within; while *verkramptes*, led by Treurnicht, hoped to capture control of the NP and the bureaucracy of Afrikaner nationalism. The reformist intentions of the *verligtes* were derided by a number of fellow-Afrikaner critics as being little more than a cosmetic make-over of the underlying reality of apartheid. The criticism of the *verligtes* was often true: few had made the paradigm shift away from a somewhat modified apart-heid system to one in which the whites had lost exclusive control. Afrikaners have continued to debate the role of the *verligtes*. The *verligte* phenomenon reflected the ferment inside the Afrikaner block; and they were harbingers of a more funda-mental change than they had originally contemplated.

Polarisation among Afrikaners continued after P. W. Botha became prime minister in 1978. For the next three years, Treurnicht (now a full cabinet minister, albeit occupying minor portfolios) and the group of conservatives around him played a cat-and-mouse game with Botha, who had announced reformist inten-tions from the outset of his premiership. Treurnicht and his acolytes favoured the retention of hardline Verwoerdian apartheid, their belief being that any conces-sion would be the thin end of the wedge that would lead to loss of power. (In a perverse way this turned out to be true.) He opposed the relaxation of 'petty' apartheid (the myriad laws enforcing social apartheid), racially mixed sport of any kind, and moves to incorporate Coloureds and Indians into a joint power-sharing arrangement with whites.

The latter issue triggered the eventual split. Botha's proposals for the tricameral parliament involved a single parliament consisting of white, Coloured and Indian chambers; legislation affecting a particular group's interests could be enacted by the relevant chamber, but legislation affecting all three groups had to be passed by all three chambers. Treurnicht considered the proposal to be a violation of 'white sovereignty'. At a stormy caucus meeting of the NP on 24 February 1982, twenty-two MPs voted against a motion of confidence in Botha proposed by a lieutenant. The dissident members were expelled and thereafter they established the Conservative Party (CP) with Treurnicht as leader.

The dreaded *skeuring* (split) had occurred. The Conservatives were better packaged than the crude, street-fighting style of the HNP. Treurnicht himself was dignified, and an orator of distinction, who spoke in the florid manner of the NGK clergyman that he formerly had been. The Conservatives' expulsion, however, was to have consequences for every component of Afrikaner nationalism's bureaucracy, including the churches, the AB, agricultural organisations, cultural societies and the like. The new party, moreover, could exploit the fears of whites as the turbulent 1980s unfolded, the noose of economic sanctions tightened, and white working-class living standards declined.

For the NP, the odium incurred by having caused *skeuring* was more than compensated for by the shedding of the group that had become a millstone around its neck. For many Nationalists the racism of the Conservatives' view held up a mirror to what they themselves had accepted not that long before. There was now an impetus to widen the space between the NP and the CP. Henceforth, the NP would be more dependent on English-speakers' votes to ensure that it retained a majority.

The first trial of strength between the NP and the CP took place in November 1983 when a referendum on the tricameral constitution was held. Despite a vigorous campaign and a high turnout of its supporters, the CP was badly beaten. The 'yes' vote, supporting the introduction of the constitution, won 66 per cent of the total, while the 'no' votes amounted to 33.5 per cent, mostly coming from CP and HNP supporters.

In subsequent elections the CP gained a bigger foothold in parliament, winning 23 seats in the 1987 election, slightly more than half the number of votes won by the NP; in 1989, it won 39 seats, with 31 per cent of the votes, the NP's share of the overall vote dipping below 50 per cent for the first time since 1958. By 1989 estimates suggested that up to 40 per cent of Afrikaner voters now supported the CP. The split was irrevocable. Treurnicht spurned appeals for the restoration of Afrikaner unity, declaring that this could not be achieved unless the NP returned to the apartheid policy of old.

The turbulent 1980s and a widespread sense of impending fundamental change had spurred the establishment of a large number of ultra-right-wing organisations, some ostensibly committed to defending 'white' South Africa by force if necessary. The most significant was the paramilitary Afrikaner Weerstandsbeweging (AWB), literally, the Afrikaner Resistance Movement, founded in 1973 and claiming by the mid-1980s a membership of some 15,000, although 'active sympathisers' numbered 150,000 (Kemp 1990: 150). Its leader, Eugene Terre'Blanche, a former policeman, was a demagogue whose powerful oratory could whip up frenzy among the crowds he attracted. Despite this ability, Terre'Blanche, whose weakness for women and alcohol was widely known, was more bark than bite.

Many of the ultra-right-wing organisations, including the AWB, hammered on themes familiar to old-style Afrikaner nationalism, regularly invoking the threat to the *Boerenasie* and their determination to defend it to the death. Collectively, the ultra-right-wing was responsible for a fair amount of violence in the late 1980s and early 1990s, but none of it seriously threatened the transition that began with F. W. de Klerk's speech on 2 February 1990 in which he unbanned the African National Congress and other organisations, announced the impending release of Nelson Mandela and other political prisoners, and committed his government to negotiating an inclusive, democratic constitution. The far-reaching, unanticipated scale of de Klerk's proposals caused outrage among the ultra-right-wingers. The most serious incident that came close to precipitating a crisis was the assassination in April 1993 of the popular ANC/South African Communist Party leader, Chris Hani, by Clive Derby-Lewis, an English-speaking CP member, and Janus Walusz, an anti-communist Polish immigrant and AWB member. The country trembled on the brink of violence that was averted only by Nelson Mandela's appeal for calm – and his pointing out that it had been a young Afrikaner woman who had witnessed the killing and then reported the assassins' car registration number to the police.

The most impressive figure to emerge from the ranks of the ultra-right was Constand Viljoen, a former chief of the South African Defence Force, who enjoyed huge esteem among troops, past and present. Despite his military background Viljoen was essentially a man of peace, who avoided the bellicose language used by many right-wingers and exhorted his followers not to resort to violence. More than any other individual, Viljoen could take the lion's share of the credit for defusing any attempt at an ultra-right-wing 'counter-revolution'. Viljoen's efforts were directed largely at trying to achieve some unity of purpose among the fragmented ultra-right (van Rooyen 1994: 114).

The confusion caused by de Klerk's reforms was aggravated by his decision, after the NP had lost a series of by-elections to the CP, to hold a referendum among whites in March 1992, in which whites would be asked to pronounce on whether the process of constitutional reform should continue. It was a high-risk decision.

Some commentators believed that de Klerk might lose. This was unlikely, though a narrow victory might well have been a Pyrrhic one, with serious consequences for the transition. Although the CP, AWB and HNP campaigned vigorously for a 'no' vote, de Klerk won easily, securing 69 per cent of the vote.

The massive defeat caused more confusion among the ultra-right, whose claims to represent a majority of Afrikaners had been decisively beaten. Demands to restore Verwoerdian-style apartheid were now scaled down, being replaced by calls for the creation of a *volkstaat*, a white Afrikaner-controlled enclave vested with the right of self-determination. It was a chimerical quest: apart from the NP's and the ANC's strong opposition to the idea, few proponents of a *volkstaat* could agree where its borders might be. Moreover, few Afrikaners, whatever their doubts about future ANC rule, contemplated uprooting themselves and migrating to a *volkstaat*. A fatal defect was the demographic fact was that there was no substantial block of territory, potentially viable as a *volkstaat*, in which whites, let alone Afrikaners, were a majority. Threats of a unilateral declaration of independence – forcibly seizing a block of territory as a *volkstaat* – came to nothing.

None of the ultra-right-wing organisations formally participated in the constitutional negotiations of the early 1990s. It was a period of complex and messy internecine relations. Eventually, Viljoen, frustrated by the debates, acknowledged that extra-parliamentary action would achieve nothing, and proceeded to form the Freedom Front, with a view to negotiating a *volkstaat*. In bilateral dealings with the ANC, Viljoen extracted an agreement to allow the possibilities of a *volkstaat* to be investigated by the Volkstaat Council, a body to be set up after the elections in April 1994. He also took the Freedom Front into the election, in an attempt to prove Afrikaner support for a *volkstaat*. It would require, he said, the votes of between one-third and one-half of the 1.8 million Afrikaner voters to demonstrate adequate support. His party received 2.17 per cent of the national vote, which, according to Johann van Rooyen's calculations, amounted to approximately 27 per cent of the Afrikaner vote. In the provincial elections, however, the Freedom Front did significantly better, winning an estimated 41 per cent of the Afrikaner vote (van Rooyen 1994: 104). The votes made little impression on the ANC, whose large majority (over 62 per cent support) assured it of the dominant position in the political system. It is likely that agreement to the *Volkstaat* Council was nothing more than a sop to induce Viljoen to participate in the election – and thereby reduce the threat of ultra-right-wing violence. The Council deliberated for several years, achieving nothing. All that came of the *volkstaat* idea was the tiny settlement of Orania, in a remote part of the sparsely populated Northern Province, where 600 Afrikaners live, apparently contentedly, in relative isolation.

During the constitutional negotiations the NP's proposals for an elaborate system of power-sharing, in which no group could dominate others, came to virtually nothing. By mid-1992 the ANC had gained the upper hand in the country, being able, in effect, to hold it to ransom and call the shots in the negotiations. It was not amenable to any significant restraints on its power that the quasi-consociational proposals of the NP sought. It equated 'democracy' with 'majority rule' and turned a deaf ear to any notion of minority rights or the potential tyranny of the majority. The 'sunset' clause whereby parties winning ten per cent or more of the vote would have cabinet representation in a 'government of national unity', as well as a deputy-presidency for a party that won 20 per cent of the vote, lowered the stakes in the 1994 election, but it was not genuine power-sharing. It fell apart in 1996 when de Klerk pulled the NP out of the arrangement three years before it was due to expire, and announced his retirement from politics in 1997.

De Klerk's achievement had been a considerable one, and he entitled his autobiography *The Last Trek*, bringing the curtain down on one of the historic symbols of Afrikaner nationalism. He had known well before 1990 that the ANC would easily win an election based upon universal franchise, and consequently looked for allies across the colour line in the hope that the NP's winning about 35 per cent of the vote would at least constrain the ANC's use of its power. In 1994, the now non-racial NP won little more than 20 per cent of the vote, but the interesting fact about its support was that white voters accounted for fewer than 50 per cent of its votes. Obviously, its historic role as the vehicle of Afrikaner nationalism was now dead and buried.

The final Constitution of 1996 recognised no fewer than eleven official languages – English and Afrikaans, together with nine African languages. This was obviously an unworkable provision. The Constitution (section 30) provides that everyone has the right to use the language and to participate in the cultural life of their choice; and in section 29(2) everyone is given the right to receive education in the official language(s) of their choice in public educational institutions 'where that education is reasonably practicable.' The state must consider 'all reasonable educational alternatives, including single medium institutions', taking into account (a) equity; (b) practicability; and (c) the need to redress the results of past racially discriminatory laws and practices. As Afrikaans language activists soon discovered, this was not a watertight safeguard for single-medium Afrikaans educational institutions, one of the foremost demands of traditional Afrikaner nationalism.

The national anthem and flag, major symbolic issues, were defused: the national anthem, determined by the President (the conciliatory Nelson Mandela), consists in separate, though conjoined by a linking phrase, renditions of *Die Stem* (The Voice), the sole national anthem prior to 1994, and *Nkosi Sikelel'iAfrika* (God Bless Africa); and the flag was of an entirely new design.

After de Klerk's retirement, the NP went into decline. Under its new leader, Marthinus van Schalkwyk, it sought to dissociate itself from apartheid by renaming itself as the New National Party (NNP). The change achieved nothing: indeed, its share of the vote in the 1999 election slipped to a derisory 6.87 per cent, and coming second to the ANC in the only province it had controlled, the Western Cape. In 2000 the NNP formed an alliance with the Democratic Party which broke down in 2001, leaving the NNP to contest the 2004 election on its own. It won only 1.7 per cent of the national vote, which meant that its days were numbered. Van Schalkwyk, after dropping broad hints to the ANC, announced that the NNP would disband and be absorbed into the ANC, which occurred in 2005. It was an ignominious end.

The fragmentation of Afrikaner nationalism, and the decline, after 1994, of its main political instrument, the NP, was paralleled by the growth of more militant black resistance. Indeed, the two processes interacted dialectically, creating the circumstances that enabled the transition to occur. In an inclusive, (supposedly) non-racial democracy, there was little or no scope – or pay-off – for an ethnic remobilisation that included the culturally and genetically linked Coloured people, some 80 per cent of whom are Afrikaans-speaking. Unlike the Francophone Quebeckers, who form a large majority in Quebec, Afrikaners were dispersed far and wide over South Africa. Apart from frustrating any possibility of a *volkstaat*, the absence of a solid majority of Afrikaners in any region also frustrated the possibility of genuinely federal arrangements that might have benefited Afrikaners – which, in any case, the ANC would have opposed.

Considerations of space preclude an analysis of the impact that the steady fragmentation of the NP and its loss of *élan* had on the spheres that constituted the bureaucratic organisation of Afrikanerdom – or the reciprocal impact of developments in the spheres on the NP. Especially during the 1980s, the obvious failure of apartheid and the need for a viable alternative that safeguarded Afrikaner interests, was widely debated. For example, the NGK steadily, though not without considerable resistance from within, abandoned its attempted theological justifications of apartheid, many being refuted by its own theologians, and condemned the implementation of apartheid as inconsistent with Christian principles.

The AB, long demonised by its critics as a citadel of reactionary Afrikaner nationalism, emerged in the 1980s as a reformist organisation. In 1986 a policy document entitled *Basiese staatkundige voorwaardes vir die voortbestaan van die Afrikaner* (Basic constitutional preconditions for the survival of the Afrikaner) was approved by the Executive Council. The policy proposals included findings of significance: 'Abolishing statutory discriminatory measures is a condition for survival'; 'All citizens must be afforded effective participation in the legislative and political processes'; 'An entrenched white government is no longer acceptable'.

The document committed the AB unambiguously to a negotiated settlement, even though it pointed out that the ANC regarded negotiation 'as an instrument in its liberation struggle'. There could be no guarantees: 'We have to think in terms of probabilities, calculated risks. The biggest risk we could take was to avoid risks altogether' (Afrikanerbond: 1997).

In 1993 the AB made significant changes: its secrecy was ended, it changed its name to the *Afrikanerbond*, and opened its membership to women and members of other races. It remains committed to further the interests of Afrikaners and all South Africans.

More than ten years after the coming of democracy Afrikaner reactions to their loss of power vary. According to estimates, emigration has been substantial, as it has been among English-speakers: there are probably some 50,000 Afrikaners in Britain alone, and many others in Australasia and North America. While this is a serious haemorrhaging of the community, since it is invariably 'the best and the brightest' who leave, the large majority will stay.

Analyses of the condition of the Afrikaners abound in the Afrikaans press, which flourishes, and the topic is a staple at conferences of Afrikaner organisations. Several books, moreover, address the question. For example, Willem de Klerk (brother of F. W. de Klerk and a former theologian and newspaper editor) writes:

> Loss of power. Loss of influence. Loss of esteem. Loss of security. Loss of privilege. Loss of credibility. Loss of language. Even loss of profession. And many more debits. We are in a state of shock. Shock causes hysteria, or paralysed silence, or panicked anxiety, or a victim complex, or an emotion of being lost [*verlorenheidsemosie*]. This is true of many Afrikaners today. At the moment we suffer from a poverty of political, clerical and cultural leadership. (de Klerk 2000: 52, translation)

There is a belief among Afrikaners that, notwithstanding the liberal terms of the constitution, Afrikaners and Afrikaans are being systematically marginalised. The ANC denies this, but Afrikaner leaders point to the pressure on Afrikaans-medium schools and universities to admit non-Afrikaans-speakers, which, they believe, will lead to the elimination of Afrikaans. English, moreover, is the language of the public service, armed services, police, courts and, with limited exceptions, Parliament. A related grievance is the systematic drive to Africanise place-names, the most notable case being the renaming of Pretoria (except for a few central blocks) as Tshwane.

There is also an awareness of the association between apartheid and 'the language of the oppressor', namely Afrikaans. The link will not easily be snapped. In turn, there is a huge process of introspection among many, even a sense of guilt at the recognition of predominantly Afrikaner government's responsibility for an odious system.

Few, if any, Afrikaners believe that Afrikaners could ever be reunited under a single political banner. There is hope, though, that whatever political differences there may be, Afrikaners and their fellow Afrikaans-speakers in the Coloured community could at least come together to resist the further marginalisation of Afrikaans. Some have proposed dropping the word Afrikaner because of its racial and political connotations, and replacing it with the term '*Afrikaanses*' to denote all those whose mother-tongue is Afrikaans. Thus far it has not caught on.

Loss of power and fragmentation do not necessarily entail a loss of ethnic sentiment. A majority of Afrikaners remain attached to their language, although acquiescence in its marginalisation is widespread. Some, recognising the dominance of English, choose to send their children to English-medium schools in the hope that greater fluency in English will facilitate their entry into the labour market, especially in times when affirmative action is vigorously enforced in favour of 'previously disadvantaged' categories of people.

Language activists, nevertheless, remain vigorous, and several civil society organisations as well as newspapers keep a watchful eye on attempts further to marginalise Afrikaans. During 2005 Stellenbosch University, the cradle of Afrikaner nationalism, was convulsed by a decision of the university authorities to introduce dual-medium (50/50 Afrikaans and Engilsh tuition in the same class) in the Faculty of Arts and Philosophy. Opponents mobilised a substantial number of students, graduates and faculty members, together with several distinguished writers, to force the rescinding of the decision. They argued that introducing a dual-medium system was the start of the slippery slope towards anglicisation. The poet Breyten Breytenbach, a radical opponent of apartheid and a dedicated foe of Afrikaner nationalism, memorably described the dual-medium option as, 'It is, by way of saying, the sheep moving over in bed, in the name of equal rights, to make space for the elephant' (quoted in *Rapport*, 30 October 2005).

NOTE

Translations from Afrikaans into English are by David Welsh.

REFERENCES

Afrikanerbond (1997), *Bearer of an Ideal: 1948–1996*, Johannesburg: Afirkanerbond.

de Klerk, Willem (2000), *Afrikaners: Kroes, kras, kordaat*, Cape Town: Human and Rousseau.

Dommisse, Ebbe, in cooperation with Willie Esterbuyse (2005), *Anton Rupert: A Biography*, Cape Town: Tafelberg.

Kemp, Arthur (1990), *Victory or Violence: The Story of the AWB*, Pretoria: Forma Publishers.

Malan, D. F. (1964), *Glo in u Volk*, Cape Town: Tafelberg.

Pelzer, A. N. (ed.) (1966), *Verwoerd Speaks: Speeches 1948–1966*, Johannesburg: APB Publishers.

Pienaar, Schalk (1975), *10 Jaar politieke kommentaar*, ed. Ton Vosloo, Cape Town: Tafelberg.

Slabbert, F. van Zyl (1975), 'Afrikaner nationalism, white politics, and political change in South Africa', in Leonard Thompson and Jeffrey Butlery (eds), *Change in South Africa*, Berkeley: University of California.

Smith, Anthony D. (2003), *Chosen Peoples: Sacred Sources of National Identity*, Oxford: Oxford University Press.

Swanepoel, Tienie (1997), *My Hart wil Afrika*, Cape Town: Queillerie-Uitgewers.

van den Heever, C. M. (1943), *Generaal J. B. M. Hertzog*, Johannesburg: AP Boekhandel.

van Rooyen, Johann (1994), 'The White Right', in Andrew Reynolds (ed.), *Election '94 South Africa: The Campaign, Results and Future Prospects*, Cape Town: David Philip.

Part VIII

ETHNOSYMBOLISM IN THE AMERICAS

Chapter 19

WOMEN, WAR AND THE CONFEDERATE ETHNOSCAPE

Bruce Cauthen

—————◁▷—————

It is not surprising that as an agrarian people whose culture was based upon the cultivation of crops, antebellum Southerners demonstrated a profound affinity for the soil which they tilled; and, this was hardly an exclusively masculine orientation.[1] Catherine Clinton correctly observes that 'many southern women felt a powerful identification with the land' (Clinton 1982: 164). Although Keziah Brevard maintained a handsome townhouse in Columbia she spent little time there, instead preferring to reside on her plantation in rural Richland County. There she was spiritually inspired by the bright, sunny mornings – sufficient, she thought, to 'invite man to purity ...' – and where her daily routine hummed with the myriad tasks of managing her extensive acreage (Brevard 1993: see 14; *passim*; 43). Arriving as a refugee in New Orleans, Sarah Morgan was immediately rattled by the urban blight of the Confederacy's largest city. She complained in her journal:

> This dreary city! I never knew how much I loved the country until this, my first summer in New Orleans. How I long for the green woods and open fields! This melancholy sight which I never expected to see – that of grass growing in the streets of this once populous city – makes me pine for the greener, fresher grass of my home – Baton Rouge. If it could be once more what it has been – if we could again be there – if Sophie and I could stand hand in hand on our beautiful terraces, watching the glorious sunsets over the mighty Mississippi. (Morgan 1991: 513)

In her memoirs, Parthenia Antoinette Hague of Alabama recalled a carriage ride in Harris County, Georgia, her birthplace and girlhood home, which was:

> ennobling to the soul, as nature's great book unrolled its series of beautiful scenes. Far in the azure blue the great white banks of clouds seemed to lie at anchor, so slow of sail were they; the gloom of the dense forest, gently waving

its boughs to the morning breeze would greet the eye; the dulcet murmur of gurgling streams would break on the ear never so gently; quiet cottages, surrounded with flowers and fruits, seemed the abode of peace and content. Grass-green marshes all flecked with flowers of varied tints, with here and there a tall pine or somber cypress standing as sentinels of the blooming mead; song-birds caroling their sweet lays as they flitted from bough to bough, or lightly soaring in space; fields of deadened trees, all draped with the long gray Spanish moss, reminded me of the ancient Romans mantled with the toga, as they were silhouetted against the sky; groups of great oaks, with clusters of the mistletoe pendent, calling to mind the ancient Britons with their strange and terrible religion of the Druids, when they met together in sacred groves for the celebration of mystical rites. (Hague 1888: 11–12)

Yet, such sentiment represented much more than simply a nostalgic preference for a bucolic idyll and the country life. The majority of women in the Old South were psycho-socially bound to the rural panorama: its fertile cotton-fields, its banks of red clay, its meandering rivers, and desolate swamps shaped the very conception of their lives. Yet, far more than a merely scenic landscape, their natural environment possessed a vibrant persona uniquely its own which moulded the identity of its inhabitants. It was a verdant and fecund habitat which had given birth to, and paternally sustained, a proud and distinctive people who lived in ecological harmony with the biosphere. The sons, and particularly the daughters, who sprang from Southern soil extolled the beauty of *their* land which inspired intense patriotic loyalty in a time of political turmoil. In 1861, Ada Bacot, a South Carolina planter, rejoiced in her journal:

Oh! The beautiful Sunny South The home of my birth my childhood and of my womanhood, could I leave thee, could I clame another home[.] Ah! No, thou art dearer to me than all else earthly. As long as I live let it be on Southern Soil and when I die let my remains be covered by her warm and genial Sod. Truly I am a child of the South, I love her as a fond Mother. (Bacot 1994: 51)

A woman in northeast Louisiana declared, 'The Southerners are a noble race, let them be reviled as they may, and I thank God that He has given my birthplace in this fair land among these gallant people and in a time when I can show my devotion to my Country' (Stone 1955: 110).

Clearly the words of these women exemplify Anthony D. Smith's concept of ethnoscape – 'the idea of a historic and poetic landscape, one imbued with the culture and history of a group, and vice versa, a group part of whose character is felt by themselves and outsiders to derive from the particular landscape they inhabit ...' (Smith 1997: 11). Through a collective and profound identification with the landscape, the ethnic group appropriates topographical features such as rivers and mountains as essential and distinctive components of the community itself. And, as this is the same ground tread upon by heroic ancestors, and the terrain on which they accomplished great deeds, as well as the eternal earth which cradles their remains – the land assumes an even more emotive dimension. It is the corporate contemplation of the ethnoscape which incorporates the natural environment into the genealogical continuum and thereby unites community and homeland in the trans-historical bonds of organic interaction (Smith 1997: *passim*; 2003: 130–7). Certainly some Southern women considered the soil and all things rooted in it an inseparable part of the Confederate nation. For them, the land possessed a peculiarly Southern, indeed Confederate, character.

The collective female inclination to see the environment as an active participant in Southern secession is evident by the extent to which Southern women discerned the interaction between political events and meteorological phenomena. A South Carolina widow – already depressed by the bleak and rainy weather – became infinitely more so when she learned the news of Lincoln's election in a letter from a friend. She recorded in her journal: 'This is a cloudy, drizly day – well Abolitionists you desire our blood ... This day corresponds with the note, it is so gloomy looking ... Nature seems to be weeping o'er our cause' (Brevard 1993: 50). Although she was an ardent proponent of Southern Independence, Eliza Rhea Anderson Fain nevertheless regretted the dissolution of the American Republic – which, as she saw it, was largely the result of Northern corruption, apostasy, and intransigence. She berated the North for not allowing the South to secede peace- fully and was apprehensive of the prospect of extensive socio-political upheaval. On 16 April 1861 – a cold, dark and rainy day – Fain penned the following entry in her diary: 'Our natural world is presenting the same gloomy phase as our political. Days are dark in the extreme in the history of our country' (Fain 2004: 6). Kate Cumming also emphasised that which she saw as the natural connec- tion between sacrifices on the battlefield and the consequent inclement weather. After the battle of Shiloh, she wrote, 'It is raining torrents. Nature seems to have donned her most somber garb, and to be weeping in anguish over the loss of so many of her noblest sons' (Cumming 1959: 10–11).

Yet, just as the elements could commiserate and console, in the imagination of some Confederate women, the climate might also signal chastisement or portend tragedy. This was the ominous interpretation which Betty Ross was compelled to contemplate during the summer of 1864. In a letter to her son – a surgeon who had been ordered from Richmond to the front – the Virginian wondered how he would be able to make it there as many of the streams had been flooded by recent torrential rains and fretted, 'This very unusual weather seems a dark judgment on us. It must be for our sins' (Ross in Bartlett 1952: 158). On 28 December of that same year, as Sherman had completed his March to the Sea and turned toward North Carolina, Ellie M. Andrews noted in her diary, 'A cloudy gloomy day, which suits our state and present condition as a nation' (Andrews 1984: 124). It is, however, interesting to note that following the ultimate Confederate collapse in 1865, Eliza Frances Andrews (no relation to Ellie Andrews) did not mind the overcast firmament above her Georgia home that summer. Considering that Confederate uniform, of which she was so fond, had been banned and she now only witnessed the ubiquitous blue of the conqueror, Andrews confessed in her journal: 'I can better endure the gloomy weather because it gives us gray skies instead of blue' (Andrews 1908: 311).

The emotional attachment of women to the land – and hence their commitment to the nationalist struggle – was reinforced by the war as many a Confederate belle was disturbed that the Sunny South was being darkened by the shadow of the Yankee foe and its soil contaminated by their stride. On the evening of 29 December 1861, Lucy Rebecca Buck was disturbed by the roar of cannons and pondered the threat to her homeland:

> The evening was lovely and I turned to look on the landscape spread before me. In the foreground the smooth lawn-like meadows and the little Happy Creek like a silver thread meandering through them. Then the quiet village with the crimson sunset on its windows, and its bright wreaths of curling smoke, and beyond the undulating hills – and in the distance like a fitting frame to this sweet picture stretched the blue mountains all with a cloudless heaven over-head, painted with the sunset pencils forming altogether a scene of surpassing loveliness. So tranquil did everything seem that I could scarce persuade myself of the fact that just beyond those mountains barriers lay the camp of an invading foe cruel and relentless, who had come with the avowed purpose of deluging this beautiful land with the blood of the noblest and best of its sons. They were our enemies who would fain see the dun-cloud of the battle-field or the sombre smoke from our pillaged burning homes ascending to the blackened heavens instead of the sweet Sabbath atmosphere which pervaded the scene now. Those who would ensanguine that little stream with human gore, those who would mar and devastate the face of the earth that they might blot out from remembrance everything of beauty from our now beautiful Virginia. (Buck 1997: 8–9)

Indeed this ineffable glimpse of paradise is subverted by an apocalyptic vision of wanton ruination.

As war came to coastal North Carolina in 1862, a local woman remarked,

'What a blessing that the future is veiled from our eyes! How life would have been poisoned if we had known that those hills, those peaceful valleys, smiling with their luxuriance, would so soon have echoed to the horrid tramp of War!' And, nine months later, she added this disturbing postscript: 'This note of horrid War which comes blooming over the peaceful fields and through the still quiet swamps and woods, awakening echoes which until now have slept to all save peaceful sounds' (Edmonston 1979: 246; 336–7). Kate Stone despaired, 'fair Louisiana with her fertile fields of cane and cotton, her many bayous and dark old forests, lies powerless at the feet of the enemy'. A subsequent entry in her diary reported that Union gunboats 'are polluting the grand old Mississippi' (Stone 1955: 110, 122). Kentuckian Catherine Reynolds, who even though spent most of the war in a luxurious exile in Europe, empathised profoundly with her country-women trapped back home behind enemy lines. When she learned that a dear friend in Virginia was now confined in a zone of military occupation adminis-tered by the draconian Union General Benjamin F. Butler, Reynolds lamented in a letter, 'How sorry I feel for her, for any Southern lady who is compelled to breathe the same air as the animal (I can't call him a man) Butler does. Oh! That such a creature should be allowed to live in civilised times – to tyranise over refined people' (Reynolds in Bartlett 1952: 139). After the fall of New Orleans, a sixteen-year-old girl reiterated the same sentiment as she strolled down the street: 'With what a different feeling had I last trod that path. Then I breathed the air of a free city, now I breathed the air tainted by the breath of three thousand Federals and trod a soil polluted by their touch' (Solomon 1995: 354). In 1863, Catherine Charlotte Rebecca Burckmyer professed her fear for the city she loved: 'Dear old Charleston may she never be polluted by the presence of the enemy' (Burckmyer and Burckmyer 1926: 25).

Rose O'Neal Greenhow would not even tolerate Yankee corpses on Southern soil. She complained that the enemy was slow to bury their fatalities after Manassas 'when the hetacombs of their dead lay manuring the sacred soil' (Greenhow 1863: 44). And at least one Southern woman was so disturbed by the threat of ecolog-ical contamination that it compelled her to alter her diet. Indeed, the elderly dowager in Virginia issued the seemingly eccentric solicitation to her neighbors for salted fish – preferably that which was a year old. She absolutely refused to consume the fresh catch from the river as she heard that the corpses of Federal soldiers had been thrown into its depths (Frobel 1986: 46). Yet, the collective female obsession that somehow the Union Army would actually defile the soil may not have been completely misplaced. When an aged woman in Arkansas defiantly confronted, with a club, a Federal soldier after he had just slaughtered one of her hogs, he turned, exposed his backside to her, and defecated in her yard (Ash 1995: 202).

Numerous scholars of nationalism have argued that the family is the most basic unit of the nation (Connor 1994: ch. 8; Horowitz 2000: ch. 2; Grosby 1994). This being the case, it should then be logical to infer that it is the rural homestead situated among the picturesque bounties of a lush natural habitat which constitutes the very nucleus of the ethnoscape. This was certainly the view of Confederate women and it was this intimate retreat and familiar refuge which was now most vulnerable to the manifold hazards of war and its proximity. The exquisite gardens which graced her family's home on the Potomac, Wilton Hill, had been a source of infinite pride and enjoyment to Anne Frobel. The cultivated landscaping reminded her of her parents and was a welcoming sight to her brothers serving in the Confederate Army; and, Frobel despaired that the priorities of war necessitated the neglect of the once meticulously manicured and florid grounds:

> But O it grieves us sorely that to see our dear beautiful flowers running to waste, flowers and shrubs collected and planted under our dear parents [*sic*] supervision, and such a source of pleasure to them, and the dear boys too, both loved flowers dearly, I cannot bear to think of their coming back and finding the old home looking so bare and desolate after fighting for us to so many years – O for magical power to make them bloom like an Eden when they come. (Frobel 1986: 137)

Another Virginia woman was confronted with a dreadful dilemma when her homeplace came under Federal occupation. Although she was utterly repulsed by the prospect of having to submit to taking the Oath of Allegiance to the United States, she realised that failure to comply would likely result in the confiscation of her property and her forcible eviction. Yet, she was perplexed by the calculation of sentimental rather than financial loss as she sought counsel from a friend:

> Pray that grace may be given me to do my duty; it will be hard to give up all here, not as property, – for I do not believe that we care more for that than we should, – but there are associations with one's home that cannot be severed without distress. I was born in this house, and here my father and blessed Mother breathed their last, – every tree and plant has a memory connected with it. (Tazewell in Bartlett 1952: 128)

In 1862, a North Carolina matron was interested to learn that Confederate General Armistead had been stationed near his boyhood residence; she reflected: 'Well may he strike, for it is in defence of his home, his sisters, his parents [*sic*] graves!' (Edmonston 1979: 246). A lady in occupied Tennessee also worried about the security of the tombs of her forebears and seemed almost relieved that death had already rescued several of her family members from seeing their beloved hearth afflicted by the calamity of invasion:

> The sound of cannon, the tramp of horse, the tread of the soldier, the firing of arms disturbs not the sweet repose of the grave. I fear that precious spot has been sadly desecrated. There sleeps my uncle, my mother and my loved sisters with many, many other dear friends. O my loved sister what anguish would have passed that heart couldst thou have known that in six months thy house where thy precious treasures were was to pass through such a trial. (Fain 2004: 91)

After Union troops torched her home in the Shenandoah Valley, Henrietta Bedinger Lee sent a blistering indictment to the commanding officer: 'Hyena like you ... have torn my heart to pieces! for all hallowed memories cluster around that homestead ...' [2] However, many Confederate women would no doubt have subscribed to the pronouncement of South Carolinian Grace Brown Elmore who wrote in her journal: 'Homes and firesides is but a term for love of country, we could never love those homes and firesides were they elsewhere as we do when placed upon our native soil' (Elmore 1997: 51).

For some Southern ladies, the soil itself possessed qualities which were essential and restorative. In a letter to a Confederate officer on assignment in Europe, Ella Tazewell wrote: 'I wish I could fill this with our spring violets from your old friend, tho' you may have an abundance of far more brilliant flowers, they cannot be sweeter, and if I was as far from home as you are, I believe I would enjoy even a *grain of Virginia soil*' (Tazewell in Bartlett 1952: 151). Tallulah Hansell sympathised with, and consoled, a bereaved mother over the loss of her son at Manassas with the following words: 'Our tears flow, but we know that *he* would have sought no *nobler* fate than to die for his land and home!' (Hansell in Joslyn 1997: 57). And, as the blood of their kinsmen spilled on the ethnoscape's fertile fields which they once carefully tilled and the remains of the heroic dead were interred in the eternal earth, the soil began to acquire an even more emotive dimension in the minds of Confederate women and one which reinforced the imperative of an unrelenting prosecution of the war effort. In April 1861, Dolly Lunt Burge of Covington Georgia was so impressed with a sermon she heard concerning 'the present state of our country at War and the soil stained with the blood of our brethren' that she made this note of it in her journal (Burge 1997: 117). A woman in Tennessee mourned the catastrophic loss of Stonewall Jackson in her diary: 'His ashes will mingle with his native soil but his blood crieth for vengeance on his oppressor' (Fain 2004: 72).

Eleanor Hull of Suwanee County, Florida, was moved when she learned that during her sister's visit to their aunt in Savannah the two women visited Laurel

Grove Cemetery where the body of her cousin, killed in the war, lay buried. Hull conveyed her immense satisfaction in a letter to her aunt in which she described the cemetery as 'that dear beautiful spot' (Hull in Joslyn 1997: 165). Bessie King wrote to her husband at the front that she had visited the grave of his brother who had given his life in the Battle of Chickamauga: 'it is so still and sad and sweet there, two pine trees have fallen across the enclosure, and the precious earth will now be protected from the desecration of the enemy – don't tell it but the Yankees rode all round and round it, and made their horses *paw it*!' (King in Galloway 2003: 100).

The graveyard became a venerable shrine of regular pilgrimage for the grieving daughters of Dixie and many a tomb was reverently tended by fastidious feminine hands. Yet, not every Southern family was afforded the psychological closure of burying their slain soldier in the ancestral plot or hometown cemetery. In an increasingly debilitating war of attrition which inflicted staggering casualties on both sides, military expediency necessitated that many Confederate fatalities be hastily interred in unadorned mass graves where they fell (Loughridge and Campbell 1985: 21). Although these rapidly multiplying makeshift cemeteries were hardly welcome landmarks to the Southern countryside, they nevertheless further sanctified the hallow soil and therefore more assiduously wedded Confederate women to the ethnoscape and convinced them that only complete victory could justify the mass self-sacrifice. The journal entry of 28 April 1865 of a Louisiana woman powerfully articulated this reality:

> I cannot bear to hear them talk of defeat. It seems a reproach to our gallant dead. If nothing else can force us to battle for our freedom, the thousands of grass-grown mounds heaped on mountainside and in every valley of our country should teach us to emulate the heroes who lie beneath and make us clasp closer to our hearts the determination to be free or die. (Stone 1955: 334)

Women were particularly concerned that the South be cleansed of its alien intruders. Judith McGuire wondered incredulously in her diary as to how the men could allow the ethnoscape to be alienated to the Yankees: 'Can they see the spot of earth which they have perhaps inherited from their fathers covered with the tents of the enemy; ... ancestral trees laid low, to make room for fortifications, thrown across their grounds, from which cannon will point to the very heart of their loved South?' (McGuire 1867: 67). And, in an evocative statement, Sallie Bird declared, 'I believe if I were a man I would never lay down my arms in this glorious struggle, till the fiendish invader was driven back step by step from our soil' (Bird and Bird 1988: 76).

As Southern territory was dismembered by Federal incursion, the Confederate ethnoscape which resonated in the feminine imagination was molested by warfare and its peculiar character was corrupted by the occupation of the enemy. Some Confederate women could not bear the fact that their beloved homeland was now in Yankee hands; and, as one historian recalls, 'Thousands of women voluntarily left occupied areas rather than to submit to the enemy's will ...' (Massey 1966: 235). As Union troops marched across the South, the land was robbed of its national essence. Southerners who lived in areas which had fallen to Federal forces found themselves outside the political boundaries of their ethno-cultural community. Consider the complaint of Ellen Renshaw House as she spent the hot and dusty summer of 1863 in Federally-occupied Knoxville: 'Every breth you draw about a peck of dust goes into your throat and you can feel it down to the end of your toes. If it was Confederate dust I would not care half as much, but Yankee dust and I don't agree at all' (House 1996: 10). As Fanny Cohen Taylor spent the unhappy Holidays of 1864 in occupied Savannah she lamented in her journal, 'This is the saddest Christmas that I have ever spent and my only pleasure during the day has been in looking forward to spending my next Christmas in the Confederacy' (Taylor in Jones 1964: 94–5). A woman who was exiled from Winchester, Virginia, which had been captured by Union forces in 1864, remarked how 'wonderfully, fresh, pure and free' the air seemed behind Confederate lines (McGuire 1867: 285–6).

The proud Charlestonian Emma Holmes would have profoundly empathised with the Virginian refugee as for her the charter of Southern freedom was rooted in the physical environment. Holmes declared, 'Liberty "sprang full-statued in an hour" from the wave rock "City by the Sea" and then its triumphant [?] was reechoed by every hill and dale of the far inland. Thank God, Charleston is my home' (Holmes 1994: 485).

Catherine Edmonston recognised the earth itself as an ally – indeed an active combatant – in the battle against Northern domination. She saw a unique justice in the fact that a Southern turncoat met his demise on his native sod. An indignant entry in her journal of 5 August 1864 reads: 'Amongst the Yankee dead within our lines was found that renegade and traitor Gen. Thomas, a base son of Va. Meet was it that her soil should drink his blood when he turned against her and led to the conquest of his native land a band of negro assassins which he had organised' (Edmonston 1979: 601). A Virginia woman concurred; she revelled in her diary that '*ancestral* marshes are yielding their malaria and mosquitoes with an unstinting hand, and aiding unsparingly the sword of the South in relieving it of invaders' (McGuire 1867: 130). Nation and land were united in the struggle to preserve Southern liberty.

Yet not even the most resolute coalition of people and earth could prevail against a numerically superior and industrialised adversary. During those desperate days of 1865 when much of their homeland was reduced to ruin, Southern women continued to contemplate the Confederate ethnoscape. Emma LeConte could hardly bring herself to witness the smouldering rubble of South Carolina's capital – a city which had once been celebrated for its stately trees and broad expanses of florid lawns. She despaired, 'Poor Columbia! Sometimes I try to picture it as it now is, but I cannot, I always see the leafy streets and lovely gardens – the familiar houses' (LeConte 1957: 56). Just a few blocks away, however, another young woman was comforted by the view of her yard which had not been trampled by the invading army:

> The garden is lovely all the trees out and the roses in bloom, not withstanding all our trouble I do enjoy it's [*sic*] beauty, and even forget the wickedness of man in gazing upon the glories of nature. As Mother says, there are things that even the Yankee cannot destroy, the works of God, the trees and the flowers, the sunlight and the blue sky, that have already thrown their mantle around the hideous ruins of Columbia. (Elmore 1997: 115)

However, Cornelia Phillips Spencer was not nearly so confident that ethnoscape had escaped the Federal onslaught. Her account of the capture of Raleigh reveals that Confederate political authority was not the only Southern dominion yielded to the Yankees – the very trees, like the people to whom their branches provided shade, sank beneath the chains of conquest:

> The very air seemed shriveled. In the brief interval that elapsed from the retreat of her protectors to the arrival of her foes, the beautiful city of Raleigh stood under the outstretched arms of her noble oaks, embowered in the luxuriant shrubbery of a thousand gardens, just touched with vernal bloom and radiance – stood with folded hands and drooping head in all the mortal anguish of suspense in a silence that spoke awaiting her fate. (Phillips in Jones 1964: 298)

The wartime writings of Southern women powerfully demonstrate their profound affinity for landscape, providing a vivid illustration of Anthony D. Smith's concept of the ethnoscape. Indeed, many Confederate women regarded the landscape as the natural extension of their embattled nation which, like them, increasingly confronted the disruptions of a rapidly escalating war. It was the fertile and formative cultivator which maternally nurtured a proud and distinctive people whose destiny was patriotically rooted in the soil. It was a moral barometer which decisively demonstrated its tender empathy with the nationalist project through the dramatic display of meteorological signals. It was an arcadian and bosky habitat in which ancestral lodgings were intrinsically situated and which implanted and preserved memories of noble forebears in the natural environment. It was the virtuous incubator of liberty itself; a strategic catalyst in the military campaign; and the sacred repository of martyred heroes whose blood further glorified the ground on which they fell. It was, for them, a pristine and purified domain vulnerable to the profane trespass of a base enemy and one which had to be liberated from alien occupation in order to retain its essential and ineffable character. And so it was this constant preoccupation of Southern women toward the ethnoscape which powerfully reinforced their commitment to Confederate nationalism.

NOTES

1 A preliminary version of this chapter was presented as a paper at the eighth Annual ASEN Conference Roundtable, London, March 1998.
2 Lee's remarks are cited in Rable (1991: 170). Rable provides an interesting discussion of the reaction of Confederate women as Federal troops invaded their homes; see chapter 9.

REFERENCES

Andrews, Eliza Frances (1908), *The War Time Journal of a Georgia Girl*, New York: D. Appleton and Company.

Andrews, Ellie M. (1984), *Ellie's Book: The Journal Kept by Ellie M. Andrews from January 1862 through May 1865*, ed. Ann Campbell MacBryde, Davidson, NC: Briarpatch Press.

Ash, Stephen V. (1995), *When the Yankees Came: Conflict and Chaos in the Occupied South, 1861–1865*, Chapel Hill and London: University of North Carolina Press.

Bacot, Ada W. (1994), *A Confederate Nurse, The Diary of Ada W. Bacot, 1860–1863*, ed. Jean W. Berlin, Columbia, SC: University of South Carolina Press.

Bartlett, Catherine Thom (ed.) (1952), *'My Dear Brother': A Confederate Chronicle*, Richmond, VA: Dietz Press.

Bird, Edgeworth and Bird, Sallie (1988), *The Granite Farm Letters: The Civil War Correspondence of Edgeworth and Sallie Bird*, ed. John Rozier, Athens, GA and London: University of Georgia Press.

Brevard, Keziah Goodwyn Hopkins (1993), *A Plantation Mistress on the Eve of the Civil War: The Diary of Keziah Goodwyn Hopkins Brevard, 1860–1861*, ed. John Hammond Moore, Columbia, SC: University of South Carolina Press.

Buck, Lucy Rebecca (1997), *Shadows on My Heart: The Civil War Diary of Lucy Rebecca Buck of Virginia*, ed. Elizabeth R. Baer, Athens, GA and London: University of Georgia Press.

Burckmyer, C. L. and Burckmyer, C. R. (1926), *The Burckmyer Letters, 1863–June 1865*, Columbia, SC: The State Company.

Burge, Dolly Lunt (1997), *The Diary of Dolly Lunt Burge, 1848–1879*, ed. Christine Jacobson Carter, Athens, GA and London: University of Georgia Press.

Clinton, Catherine (1982), *The Plantation Mistress: Woman's World in the Old South*, New York: Pantheon.

Connor, Walker (1994), *Ethnonationalism: The Quest for Understanding*, Princeton: Princeton University Press.

Cumming, Kate (1959), *Kate: The Journal of a Confederate Nurse*, ed. Richard Barksdale Harwell, Baton Rouge: Louisiana State University Press.

Edmonston, Catherine Ann Devereux (1979), *'Journal of a Secesh Lady': The Diary of Catherine Ann Devereux Edmonston, 1860–1866*, ed. Beth G. Crabtree and James W. Patton, Raleigh, NC: Division of Archives and History.

Elmore, Grace Brown (1997), *A Heritage of Woe: The Civil War Diary of Grace Brown Elmore, 1861–1868*, ed. Marli F. Weiner, Athens, GA and London: University of Georgia Press.

Fain, Eliza Rhea Anderson (2004), *Sanctified Trial: The Diary of Eliza Rhea Anderson Fain, a Confederate Woman in East Tennessee*, ed. John N. Fain, Knoxville: University of Tennessee Press.

Frobel, Anne S. (1986), *The Civil War Diary of Anne S. Frobel of Wilton Hill in Virginia*, ed. Mary H. Lancaster and Dallas M. Lancaster, Birmingham, AL: Birmingham Printing and Publishing Company.

Galloway, T. H. (ed.) (2003), *Dear Old Roswell: Civil War Letters of the King Family of Roswell, Georgia*, Macon, GA: Mercer University Press.

Greenhow, Rose O'Neal (1863), *My Imprisonment And The First Year of Abolitionist Rule At Washington*, London: Richard Bentley (facsimile reprint, Ann Arbor and London: University Microfilms International, 1981).

Grosby, Steven (1994), 'The verdict of history: The inexpungeable ties of primordiality – A Response to Eller and Coughlan', *Ethnic and Racial Studies*, 17:2, 164–71.

Hague, Parthenia Antoinette (1888), *A Blockaded Family: Life in Southern Alabama During the Civil War*, Boston, MA: Houghton, Mifflin and Company (facsimile reprint, Lincoln and London: University of Nebraska Press, 1991).

Holmes, Emma (1994), *The Diary of Miss Emma Holmes 1861–1866*, ed. John F. Marszalek, Baton Rouge and London: Louisiana State University Press.

Horowitz, Donald (2000), *Ethnic Groups in Conflict*, Berkeley, Los Angeles and London: University of California Press.

House, Ellen Renshaw (1996), *A Very Violent Rebel: The Civil War Journal of Ellen Renshaw House*, ed. Daniel E. Sutherland, Knoxville: University of Tennessee Press.

Jones, Katharine M. (ed.) (1964), *When Sherman Came: Southern Women and the 'Great March'*, Indianapolis: Bobbs-Merrill Company.

Joslyn, Mauriel Phillips (ed.) (1997), *Charlotte's Boys: Civil War Letters of the Branch Family of Savannah*, Berryville, VA: Rockbridge Publishing Company.

LeConte, Emma (1957), *When the World Ended: The Diary of Emma LeConte*, ed. Earl Schenk Miers, New York: Oxford University Press (reprint, Lincoln and London: University of Nebraska Press, 1987).

Loughridge and Campbell, Edward D. C., Jr (1985), 'Life after death: Mourning in the Old South and the confederacy', in *Women in Mourning* (Catalog of the Museum of the Confederacy's corollary exhibition held November 14 1984 through January 6 1986, Richmond, Virginia), Richmond, VA: Museum of the Confederacy.

Massey, Mary Elizabeth (1966), *Bonnet Brigades,* New York: Alfred A. Knopf.

McGuire, Judith W. (1867), *Diary of a Southern Refugee During the War by a Lady of Virginia*, New York: E. J. Hale and Son (facsimile reprint, Lincoln and London: University of Nebraska Press, 1995).

Morgan, Sarah (1991), *The Civil War Diary of Sarah Morgan*, ed. Charles East, Athens, GA and London: University of Georgia Press.

Rable, George C. (1991), *Civil Wars: Women and the Crisis of Southern Nationalism*, Urbana and Chicago: University of Illinois Press.

Smith, Anthony D. (1997), 'Nation and ethnoscapes', *Oxford International Review*, 8: 2, 11– 18.

Smith, Anthony D. (2003), *Chosen Peoples: Sacred Sources of National Identity*, Oxford and New York: Oxford University Press.

Solomon, Clara (1995), *The Civil War Diary of Clara Solomon: Growing Up in New Orleans, 1861–1862*, ed. Elliot Askenazi, Baton Rouge and London: Louisiana State University Press.

Stone, Kate (1955), *Brokenburn: The Journal of Kate Stone, 1861–1868*, ed. John Q. Anderson, Baton Rouge: Louisiana State University Press.

Chapter 20

ETHNIC ORIGINS AND INDIGENOUS PEOPLES: AN APPROACH FROM LATIN AMERICA

Natividad Gutiérrez Chong

Indigenous peoples or Amerindians, the original inhabitants of the American continent, are dynamic carriers of historical ethnicity. The ethnic past and origin have been persistent and recurrent concepts in our modern understanding of nationalism and nation-building. In Latin America, cultural origin and ethnic past are embodied in Indigenousness but as such they are perceived in a very different way within each nation-state. In its turn, every nation has developed a particular way to deal with and manage historical and present-day ethnicity. Fear towards Indian peoples persists throughout Latin America, because historically they have been regarded as agents of insurrection and political instability, while discrimination and exclusion are frequent variables in the handling of ethnicity.

This chapter addresses three main issues related to the social construction of Indian identity, which may be opposite or complementary to national identity. Firstly, it is important to determine if ethnicity, the cultural system of Amerindian peoples, establishes a close association to ethnic origins in the revival of indigenous claims seeking to alter and transform the traditional structure of the nation-state, that is, Mexico and Ecuador in the twenty-first century. Secondly, I will bring into this discussion the span of Anthony D. Smith's theoretical work, which has contributed to the understanding of ethnic mobilisation and its dynamics through one of his most classic arguments: the power of the ethnic self and the myth of the ethnic origin. Thirdly, and linked to the second issue, it is necessary to point out some difficulties expressed by Indigenous intellectuals and writers in their attempt to find out the vitality of the combination of myths, memories and symbols in the social construction and reproduction of their ethnicity as it is perceived within the ethnic group. These issues will be discussed in relation to the cases of Mexico and Ecuador. The overall aim of this chapter is to illustrate how ethnicity expresses itself among indigenous groups who have played a major role in the democratic process of Latin America.

THE USES OF THE ETHNIC PAST

For Indian peoples, the past is a key concept in the definition and negotiation of their identity, but it also often represents a problem for nationalists. The use of the ethnic past as posited by the builders of the Latin American liberal state (eighteenth century), and by the present policies of national integration from assimilation to multiculturalism, follows four main routes: (1) an explicit reference to the past; (2) a rejection of the past; (3) a denial of such a past despite its evidence; and (4) a rejection of the past because it involved the memory of conquest by neighbouring people. As said above, these routes have interacted throughout the foundation of the liberal state in the nineteenth century and up to the present as vital components of nation-building and national identity.

1. An explicit reference to the past can be found in the glorification and exaltation of Prehispanic times[1] mainly through its monumental architecture and exceptional art. This explicit claim of early Mexican nationalists (friar Servando Teresa de Mier, Carlos María de Bustamante), who sought political independence from the Spanish crown (in the first decades of the nineteenth century), was rooted in the complex idea of achieving authenticity and originality for the former colony of New Spain (Mexico). Such grandiosity – mainly Aztec – was the native and ancestral evidence of a prestigious culture developed without the concourse of European culture, mind and religion. Mexico is the classic example of this and wide-ranging and prolific research has been carried out using historical sources (Phelan Leddy 1960; Brading 1991; Lòpez and Lòpez 2001).

2. Within the same span of time of the political Independentist movements (early nineteenth century), Peruvian intellectuals and nationalists (Josè Manuel Dàvalos, Hipòlito Unanue and Josè Eusebio de Llano Zapata) were inclined to exclude the Prehispanic past, notwithstanding the splendid vestiges of the Inca empire, and saw themselves as agents in the creation of a new national culture. Frequent rebellions between 1708 and 1783, as well as the great revolt of Tupac Amaru in 1780, were reasons for avoiding Indigenous cultural revivals. Instead, these intellectuals and nationalists took the route of eulogising the nation from another angle and searched for evidence of originality and authenticity in the admiration of its impressive Andean nature, mountainous landscape and weather (Lewin 1957; Lynch 1986; Valcarcel 1965; Durand 1973).

3. For the founders of further Southern states the explicit denial of the past was a recurrent concept and a project integrating different modalities. In the early nineteenth century, for example, nationalists of the Southern cone (today's Argentina, Chile and Uruguay) deplored the lack of civilisation expressed in archeological remains and the barbaric ways of their native inhabitants, while emphasising the superiority of European peoples and cultures. From this perspec-

tive, Amerindians and their cultures could not add value to a nation in formation, but were rather impeding progress and prestige (Quijada, Bernand and Schneider 2000).

4. Other cases, and from a different perspective, involving native internal conflicts, are to be found in Ecuador (and Bolivia). In the formation of these nations, local Creole elites have also been selective, including the glorification of the Prehispanic past in the composition of their nation and identity. To redeem the past was to accept defeat and domination from their neighbours (Peru and later Chile). The glorification of the past in Ecuador was to recognise the superiority of the Peruvian Inca Empire –Tahuantinsuyo– and their recurrent wars of conquest and territorial expansion (Almeida 1999; Larson 2004; Flindell Klaren 2000).[2]

The Mesoamerican and Andean worlds are inevitably linked to their ethnic past, but this past has been appropriated and reformulated by non-indigenous, European elites for purposes of national-identity-making. For these nationalist elites the past became a problematic issue since its foundation was not clearly European. While Amerindians had to face other problems such as the search for and interpretation of their original roots. In what follows, my concern is to discuss the importance of the past and of ethnic origins in the making and continuity of Indigenous identities.

ETHNICITY

Ethnicity, as said earlier, is here understood as the cultural system of Amerindians. By that I mean certain features historically shared by these groups, mainly a non-European origin, deep attachment to land and territory, and complex symbolism expressing their profound relationship with nature. Other features, such as colonialism and rejection or manipulation by nationalisms, have also imprinted modern Indianness. Of course, not all Indian groups in the continent, about 33,219,814 individuals, according to the Interamerican Indigenous Institute (1993), could be subsumed in one category. Other important categories emerging from colonial societies throughout Latin America are the Mestizo (half breed) and Creoles (White people born in the New Continent). However, the Amerindian cultural system, canalised through different types of identity, is persistent and it proves its unpredictable malleability and capacity of response and organisation through significant political mobilisations, thereby illustrating an instrumentalist approach of ethnicity construction (Koonings and Silva 1999; Baud 1996). Ethnicity is also marginal, persecuted, unrecognised and, thus, it survives in the realm of discrimination and exclusion (Loayza 2004). Exclusion and discrimination have imprinted in the ethnic actors capacity for mobilisation and innovative leadership in the democratisation process of Latin America (as in the case of Mexico and Ecuador).

Ethnicity must have a solid ground to be able to express itself in political terms. What kinds of sources are modern Indigenous peoples using in order to have original means to express themselves politically? Here is where, in my opinion, lies one of the most interesting methodological challenges to the work of Anthony D. Smith in relation to Latin America.

THE MYTH-SYMBOL COMPLEX

In the Mixe, Nahua or Maya groups of Mexico, or in the Quechua-Aymara peoples of Ecuador and Bolivia, ethnicity is vividly expressed through symbolic codes of dress and adornment, social relations, domestic behavior, gender roles, religious rituals, festivities and cults of nature. It is also found in subjective, intellectual and artistic activities, such as literary production, language and music. Landscape is also deeply rooted in the Andean memory. Modern Quechua culture is widely making use of modern and electronic ways of informing and enjoying their identity: videos, electronic pages and so on. But the important connection of present ethnicity with the past is established through a wealth of symbolism expressed in myth and ritual, cosmovision or a vision of the world. When referring to a past, we basically mean Prehispanic times, the span of time previous to the European arrival in the new continent (sixteenth century). There is no one single way in which such past is homogenously expressed. The following situations illustrate how the past is revived and perceived among different Amerindian societies of Latin America.

The celebration of *Fiesta* provides a collective space to socialise. The Mixe people of Oaxaca, Mexico, organise a festivity called *Fiesta de Santa Cruz*, in which the symbol of a cross is the main motif. It is a giant offering, a ritual of purification and a petition for a prosperous season. This ceremony is devoted to the reproduction of the spiritual life of the people and the assurance that they will keep having their main food: maize. Ancient rituals are repetitive acts; they take the form of cultural messages whose purpose is to establish patterns, cycles, celebrations and remembrances in a routinely and organised fashion. Santa Cruz Festivity is an example of how continuity with the past can be expressed; it is the reinterpretation of a historical discourse used by ancient Prehispanic cults with regards to the rainy season (Torres 2003).

Local festivities are one of the most advantageous settings for the realisation of ethnic projects. For example, the Quechua people of Ecuador, in the town of Otavalo, have carried out an important activism in order to recover their traditions and ancient ways of life. But this activism has also played an important role in fabricating/inventing new traditions (Hobsbawm and Ranger 1983), such as the Yamor Festival (September). The festivity was apparently invented by Otavaleños, then appropriated by Mestizos and Whites, and after an intense struggle, the Otavaleños are fighting for controlling the festivity again. Interestingly enough, the Yamor festival is not linked to any Prehispanic calendar, equinoctials or cycle of agriculture (which are crucial in determining the organisation of time and space in the Andean world as we shall see below). One of the most noticeable activities of this festival is a beauty contest, which promotes archetypes of female Indian beauty largely discredited by the non-indigenous society. The festivity began in 1957 through the initiative of young intellectuals who aimed at fabricating a new cult based on the synthesis of two female characters: the birth of the Virgin Mary and the symbol of Koya Raymi (a woman belonging to the Inca aristocracy) thus arriving at a new symbol of fertility (Posern-Zielinski 1999). Unlike the ancient spirituality involved in the Santa Cruz Festivity, the Yamor festival may be characterised as a recent 'invented tradition' which seeks to refashion and recombine Prehispanic female symbols for purposes of social cohesion and commercial benefit.

The Aymara and Quechua though continue to have tremendous vitality in Andean societies. There are two main concepts that illustrate how the Andean world is organised and how people are inserted within it: *Pachakutik* and *Pachamama*, both deeply rooted in rural areas and urban towns. *Pacha* has many meanings: it may be sun's time or land (*tierra*). Both conjure up the central idea involved in the well-being of an Aymara or Quecha with respect to time and space: totality and abundance (Bouysse-Cassagne et al. 1987; Urbano n/d; Sarkisyanz 1992; Waskar Chukiwanka 2004).

Pachakutik is an ancient name that today frames the political role played by Quechuas in the democratisation of the nation-state. It is interpreted as the 'time of war' or as the specific moment when a process changes direction, when there is a radical change of the world. *Pachakutik* has thus acquired modern significance for an Aymara or Quechua person.[3] *Pachakutik* is also the name of an organisation, organically linked to the Confederation of Indigenous Nationalities in Ecuador (CONAIE), which has played a leading role in the political movement that has shaken Ecuador since the Indigenous uprising of 1990. In 1992 and 1994 indigenous mobilisations claimed the construction of the plurinational state and rejected the Agrarian Law of 1994. After overthrowing President Abdala Bucaran in 1997, there emerged a proposal for a new Constituent Assembly which resulted in the New Constitution issued in 1998. Furthermore, CONAIE has been the leading force behind the overthrowing of presidents Jamil Mahuad in 2000 and Lucio Gutièrrez in 2003 (Ibarra 1992; McDonald Jr 2002; Montes de Oca Barrera 2004).

Pachamama is the name of an Andean divinity. Pacha as mentioned above is interpreted as totality or abundance and mama in Aymara language does not necessarily mean mother but lady. In any case, the phrase is associated with the concept of abundance being reutilised in the political discourse of Aymara women organised along the defence of their lands and territories facing privatisation of the oil industry in Bolivia. An interviewee expressed the potency of the concept: '*pachamama* is our land, our mother, we cannot sell our mother, as simple as that' (AS, Federación de Mujeres Bartolina Sisa, La Paz, Bolivia, 25 July 2005). In Mexico, it is possible to say, however, that key concepts of indigenous thought have not managed to influence any political or social organisation, nor are they included in ideological discourses serving as guiding principles for collective action.

These two sets of examples, on the one hand, the official use of the ethnic past as forming part of a national identity, while on the other, the continuous vitality of myth, ritual or symbolic thought used and reproduced by the indigenous societies for their own social cohesion or political action, show the following patterns: (1) When the state takes over ethnic origins and past to legitimise a broad national identity, a myth or a ritual may persist in the indigenous realm, a community in a rural area. However, the formulation and transmission of a coherent tradition of an ethnic past is weaker among Indian peoples themselves (Mexico); (2) When the state rejects the past because of its Indigenous origins, which are considered inappropriate for a broad national identity, the Indigenous thought has its own dynamism and has a potential for inventiveness and continuity (Otavalo). Moreover, it serves as an innovative ground for democratic transformation on a large scale and nationalisation of natural resources (Ecuador and Bolivia).

Oral tradition is the vehicle for reproducing Indigenous thought and culture mainly. Modern institutions such as media and the standard school are available but not widespread within indigenous societies. Amerindian mythology is a body of information and it is communicated by several means and made of verbal and non-verbal symbols. The Indian world communicates itself through artistic expressions, paintings, embroideries, language, to mention just a few, and they depend largely on symbolism, signs and signals (Urbano n/d).

INDIGENOUS INTELLECTUALS IN SEARCH OF THE MYTH-SYMBOL COMPLEX

There is one more aspect requiring further discussion. The reinterpretation or revisitation of myths is a current conceptual obstacle for the political and ideological thinking of most Indigenous peoples. As I have already indicated, there is abundant and rich archeological evidence of the past, as well as mythological information about the origin of any group. The basic question expressed in the myth-symbol complex (Smith 1984, 1986) 'where do we come from?' is the central idea of numberless narratives. For example, ethnocentric ideas expressed in myths of origin and descent refer to the initial formation of the group: many present-day indigenous peoples owe their prestige to antiquity, presenting themselves as the first inhabitants, the first who spoke a language, the first men, the first nations. Such primordial ideas of origin attached to Indian peoples reveal an extraordinary symbolical weight. However, these ideas have a limited influence because, as stated above, they are known to the group by means of oral tradition. Furthermore, narratives telling the ethnic origin of Amerindians have been largely replaced or diminished in importance by a more recent and powerful myth of descent: the Mestizo myth of descent from the idealised couple formed by a Spanish male and an Indigenous female of the colonial caste structure, whose ideological – not biological – influence has guided nation-building policies throughout the twentieth century, especially in Mexico (Gutièrrez 1999, 2005).

The methodological challenge referred to above is the claim that most of this important knowledge, that is to say, narratives of origin, or foundation, is not easily accessible, and is not in the possession of Indigenous peoples. According to this claim, the study of Amerindian societies and their past is, largely, a specialised knowledge produced by experts and academics engaged in disciplines such as Epigraphy, Paleontology, Archeology and so on. Indian peoples have little access to such information; the school system does not encourage this type of knowledge and to have access to it involves professional training in these disciplines, a fact that is neither common nor widespread. While there are a growing number of poets and literary men and women writing in Indigenous languages, ethnic experts on Indian antiquities are very few. One can think of the historian Luis Reyes of Nahua ethnic origin, or the internationally known readers of ancient texts (codices) such as Ubaldo Lòpez or Juan Julian Caballero from the Mixtec group (Mexico). In Bolivia, the multifaceted role of ethnic intellectuals like Inka Waskar Chukiwanka[4] and Luis Macas[5] from Ecuador shows how the study and revival of ancient culture can nurture ideology construction.

In this scenario, present indigenous identity (mainly for Mexico) locates its 'myth-symbol complex' (myths, memories and symbols) in the highly diverse and creative symbolic arena, such as rites and rituals of petition (for example, rain), that use and combine Catholic with indigenous imagery. To this I should add that the past in Mexico has an officially constructed solid stand which displays its prestige and antiquity through monumental architecture and splendid museography. Grandiosity and prestige imbued in concepts, narratives and romanticised ways of life are far away from the imagination of the current Indigenous peasant or the immigrant in search of a better life.

For the Andean societies where the past has not been taken over by official institutions and where memories of such past refer to acts of conquest by neighbouring peoples, the recovery of ancient traditions takes place through direct interchange with nature. These may not require science and discipline as in the case of the study of antiquities; they are part of nature itself. They are associated with the land and territory which they possess and enjoy or aim at recovering. This explains to a certain extent the fierce defence of these resources by the Aymara and Quechua people above everything else; language and culture for them may come later. These peoples are somehow united by common referents, the *Pachamama,* the *Pachakutik,* which guide their action for the future and have a firm stand in the ancient ways of managing and understanding nature (Bouysse-Cassagne et al. 1987).

Contemporary official definitions of Indian peoples make the assumption that there is an inevitable attachment to an ethnic past. Let us bring as examples the Political Constitutions of Mexico and Ecuador: in article 2 of the Mexican Constitution of 2001, we read: 'The Mexican nation has a pluricultural composition originally endorsed by their indigenous peoples who descend from populations inhabiting the present territory before the beginning of colonisation ...' Similarly, article 83 of the Constitution of Ecuador of 1998 claims that 'Indigenous peoples self-identified as nationalities of ancestral roots ... form part of the unique and indivisible Ecuadorian state' (Montes de Oca Barrera 2004).

It is somehow assumed that the link connecting the past with contemporary Indigenous peoples is possible through the incessant fluidity of oral traditions. But memory, recovered and communicated through oral tradition, is dispersed and leads to fragmentation. Therefore, dependence on oral traditions only interferes with the continuity or uniformity of a myth or narrative which, in the ideal paradigm, may foster supra-ethnic social cohesion, that is, a cohesion that goes beyond the village. Because memories are fragmented and different versions may exist with respect to a myth, it is not possible to claim unity of thought among Indigenous peoples. Furthermore, there are generational gaps regarding how this ethnic information is transmitted from one generation to the next. From a romanticised view, it is believed that the elderly must carry ethnic information and wisdom, but, very often, they do not hold memories about the origin or foundation of the group simply because, as already mentioned, this is part of specialised knowledge.

If ethnicity is expressing vitality, but does not necessarily emerge from a homogeneous collective awareness of belonging such as a belief in common ethnic origins and a common past, where does this leave us in relation to Smith's theory and the methodological challenge set to us by the Latin American data? In Smith's approach, myths, symbols and legends are fundamental ideas which encourage the reproduction and continuity of a group, especially in times of invasion or, more generally, when the group is in some kind of peril. I am, thus, inclined to suggest that Smith has largely focused on the ethnicity of dominant groups or groups who have historically gone through stages of cohesion either by state or religious institutions. Ethnicity transmitted by institutional means, and not merely by oral tradition, has more opportunities to reproduce itself and develop accordingly. Ethnicity of marginal peoples is not expressed in glorious ideas of the past. Marginal peoples largely survive due to their capacity to fabricate, invent and recombine a variety of elements which are embedded in their daily life, such as the respect of nature, and harness them to various forms of political discourse summoning defence and resistance (Otavalo in Ecuador).

CONCLUSION

This chapter has addressed the importance of the past for nationalists and Indigenous peoples in Latin America. I called nationalists the European founders of the nineteenth-century Latin American States, distinguishing them from the Indigenous Amerindian peoples. In Latin America, the State has been instrumental in building up a type of homogeneous, horizontal and liberal national community emulating the Western concept of nation and in doing so four main routes are to be found: (1) acceptance and glorification of the past; (2) rejection of the past despite its evident existence; (3) denial of the past on the ground that it did not exist or it is not worth it; and (4) rejection of the past because it involved experiences of conquest and invasion by neighbouring populations.

As a result, the use or neglect of the past by official bodies had important consequences for the present identity of Amerindians. In Mexico, the Prehispanic past is an issue of national pride and prestige, and one that has also received worldwide recognition and respect. Therefore, it is preserved by official institutions. In contrast, the Indigenous peoples themselves lack substantial information regarding their roots and have no impact on political thinking or the construction of a wider, ethnic consciousness. Ancient rituals of, say, rain petition, are widely practised in rural towns. However, they manage to influence only small fragments of the ethnic group, in this case, the inhabitants of the village.

On the other hand, in Ecuador, Quechua people from the Otavalo town are politically visible and economically prosperous; there is even a Quechua upper class with close links to financial markets. But their present identity is not based on ideas of a *continuum* emerging either from a prestigious ethnic past or origin. Quechua intellectuals, activists and even merchants have influenced Mestizo political parties and founded indigenous ones. They have played an important ideological role and activism in the democratisation of the Ecuadorian state and they have used the ancient and powerful myth of *Pachakutik* to organise mobilisation on a solid symbolic platform. Similarly, the Aymara and Quechua in Bolivia have found in ancient mythology linked to the protection of nature powerful arguments against dispossession of land and resources by foreign companies.

Modern Indigenous peoples are in a creative process of reinventing themselves but generally lack the means to conceptualise and adapt their past to their purposes. Mexico is less developed in this respect when compared to Bolivia and Ecuador who have given new meaning to their mythologies for their collective defence. Like the rest of Amerindian societies, they have lacked institutional means and effective political power to put them into motion. Nevertheless, there is one exception to this: the Mexican Mestizo myth. Although this myth of ethnic origin lacks cultural, historical or biological evidence to support it, nevertheless, it has been widely disseminated by state schools for over fifty years.

Otavalo people at present are searching and readapting everything in their desire to affirm their identity. They are recovering ancient names to rename objects, rituals, even first names, which have been eroded as a consequence of hostility and discrimination by the dominant Mestizo and White society. They are also interested in emphasising their distinctive cultural characteristics which nurture their identity: music and instruments, vestment, adornment (which includes a male symbology of wearing long hair), and symbols to decorate the streets of the emblematic Otavalo town, to mention but a few.

If there is an active process of invention, revival and fabrication, this by no means implies that Indigenous peoples have fake cultures. They have to follow another route, different from that of the dominant group whose culture is embodied in the official, national narrative. Their own route is to create a complex culture and ethos which also integrates information about their origins and history.

The Prehispanic age is of capital importance for the revitalisation of Indigenous peoples because it constitutes unmistakable evidence of their ancestry, uniqueness and authenticity. Consequently, and as a second point, new amendments to constitutional charts brought about by mobilisations in Mexico (Liberation Zapatist Movement, EZLN, 1994 and Pachakutik, 2000) have put the Indian question at the heart of debates about the nature of the Mexican nation. Interestingly enough, the Southern Mexican EZLN has made noticeable its lack of ethnic symbolism in its ideological claims against the state. In these new constitutions, there is the explicit criterion of ancestry as a condition for the recognition of Indianness. Such recognition activates rights for autonomy and self-determination and, in some cases, enables collective access to natural resources. This unprecedented legal framework is beginning to characterise the transition of homogeneous nation states into pluricultural or multiethnic ones. But the past, as reinterpreted by Indigenous peoples themselves, is a thing in the making; it needs to be taken away from the hands of the dominant nation.

The Mesoamerican and Andean ethos is giving place to a more dynamic process of ethnicity construction embodying, using and recovering symbols associated with nature, concepts of Amerindian thought based on abundance and totality, inventing new festivals and performing both old and new rituals. Indeed, ethnicity among Indigenous peoples in Latin America is largely symbolic as Smith has argued, while the use of the past as a key component of identity is variable. The myth-symbol complex is most evident in identity-construction of dominant ethnicities because it relies on and is disseminated by institutional means which present it as the national identity. However, the same symbolical complex is not so clear in the case of Indigenous societies, which lack their own institutions and thus, have been exposed to denial, extermination, discrimination and manipulation.

Finally, and considering Smith's contribution from another angle, I am inclined to add to my conclusion that the idea of ancestry, as a distinct concept that helps to figure out the past, keeps playing a leading role in the present era which demands recognition, especially for minority and unprivileged peoples. If Indian societies manage to reinvent themselves and become firmly incorporated in a reconfiguration of the multicultural state, the Amerindian past will have a long and creative future.

ACKNOWLEDGEMENT

The author acknowledges PAPIIT–UNAM funding (2005–6).

NOTES

1 Periodisation of Prehispanic times is divided in three stages: Preclassic, 2500 BC–200 AD; Classic, 200 AD–900 AD; and Postclassic, 900 AD– 1521 AD.

2 The Inca State also known, in Quechua language, as Tawantinsuyo, emerged and developed between the twelfth and sixteenth centuries. It was extended from the South of present Colombia to the Northeast of Argentina and a central portion of Chile. It, of course, included Ecuador, Peru and part of Bolivia. The territorial expansion from Inca rulers from Peru meant the *quechuizacion* of the different ethnic groups of these territorial areas as well as the introduction of the quechua culture and language. This expansion was not always pacific and meant violent and cruel wars of conquest and subjugation against non-quechua groups, for example, the Kayanbis, Karankis y Pastos inhabiting Ecuador. The present quechua people is estimated in 8 million and they are disseminated in Peru, Bolivia, Ecuador and frontier zones of Argentina, Chile and Colombia (Almeida 1990: 290).

3 The active participation of social movements led by Movimiento de Unidad Plurinacional Pachakutik – Nuevo País, in a scenario of permanent crisis, created poles of alternative politics which managed to capitalise social unrest as a result of privatisation policies (Barrera 2004: 16).

4 A leading ideological figure in the foundation of cultural and political institutions concerned with the cultural revival of the Aymara people. He was a national deputy from the Pachakuti Indigenous Movement.

5 Well-known anthropologist, lawyer and political leader. He is president of CONAIE and regarded as a leading moral guide of the indigenous movement.

REFERENCES

Almeida, Ileana (1999), *Historia del pueblo kechua*, Quito: Abrapalabra Editores.

Almeida, José, Carrasco Hernán (1993), *Sismo étnico en el Ecuador*, Quito: Abya-Yala.

Barrera, Augusto (ed.) (2004), *Entre la utopia y el desencanto*, Quito: Planeta.

Baud, Michiel (1996), *Etnicidad como estrategia en Amèrica Latina y el Caribe*, Quito: Abya-Yala.

Bouysse-Cassagne Theresse, Olivia Harris, Tristan Platt, Verónica Cereceda (1987), *Tres reflexiones sobre el pensamiento andino*, La Paz: Hisbol.

Brading, David (1991), *The First America: The Spanish Monarchy, Creole Patriots and the Liberal State 1492–1866*, Cambridge: Cambridge University Press.

Durand Flores, Luis (1973), *Independencia e integración en el plan político de Tupac Amaru*, Lima: PLU Editor.

Flindell Klaren, Peter (2000), *Peru. Society and Nationhood in the Andes*, Oxford: Oxford University Press.

Gutiérrez, Natividad (1999), *Nationalist Myths and Ethnic Identities: Indigenous Intellectuals and The Mexican State*, Lincoln: Nebraska University Press.

Gutiérrez, Natividad (2005), 'Myth and Sexuality in the Making of the Mexican National Identity', unpublished manuscript.

Hobsbawm, Eric J. and Terence Ranger (eds) (1983), *The Invention of Tradition*, Cambridge: Cambridge University Press.

Ibarra, Alicia (1992), *Los indígenas y el estado en el Ecuador*, Quito: Abya-Yala.

Instituto Indigenista Interamericano, *Amèrica Indígena*, vol. LIII (4), October–December 1993.

Koonings, Kees and Silva Patricio (eds) (1999), *Construcciones étnicas y dinámica sociocultural en América Latina*, Quito: Abya-Yala.

Larson, Brooke (2004), *Trials of Nation Making. Liberalism, Race and Ethnicity in the Andes, 1810–1910*, Cambridge: Cambridge University Press.

Lewin, Boleslao (1957), *La rebelión de Tupac Amaru y los orígenes de la emancipación americana*, Buenos Aires: Hachette.

Loayza Bueno, Rafael (2004), *Halajtayata. Etnicidad y racismo en Bolivia*, La Paz: Fundemos.

Lòpez, Austin Alfredo and Lujan Leonardo Lòpez (2001), *El pasado indígena*, 2nd edn, México: Fondo de Cultura Económica.

Lynch, John (1986), *The Spanish American Revolutions, 1808–1826*, 2nd edn, New York: W. W. Norton.

Macdonald, Theodore, Jr (2002), 'Ecuador's Indian Movement: Pawn in a Short Game or Agent in State Reconfiguration?', in David Maybury-Lewis (ed.), *The Politics of Ethnicity. Indigenous Peoples in Latin American States*, Cambridge, MA: Harvard University Press.

324											*Nationalism and Ethnosymbolism*

Montes de Oca Barrera, Laura Beatriz (2004), "Ladinoamerica' reconfigurada: Reformas constitucionales en materia indígena. Estudio comparativo entre México y Ecuador', Tesis de maestría, Instituto de Investigaciones Dr José María Luis Mora.

Phelan Leddy, John (1960), 'Neo-Aztecism in the nineteenth century and the genesis of Mexican nationalism', in Stanley Diamond (ed.), *Culture in History: Essays in Honour of Paul Radin*, New York: Columbia University Press.

Posern-Zielinski, Alexander (1999), 'La fiesta del yamor: etnicidad, tradición y conflictos étnicos en Otavalo, Ecuador', in Kee Koonings and Patricio Silva (eds), *Construcciones étnicas y dinámica sociocultural en América Latina*, Quito: Ediciones Abya-Yala.

Quijada, Mónica, Carmen Bernand and Arnd Schneider (2000), *Homogeneidad y nación. Con un estudio de caso: Argentina, siglos XIX y XX*, Madrid: Consejo Superior de Investigaciones Científicas.

Sarkisyanz, Manuel (1992), *Temblor en los Andes. Profetas del resurgimiento indio en el Perú*, Cayambe: Abya-Yala.

Smith, Anthony D. (1984), 'National identity and myths of ethnic descent', *Research in Social Movements, Conflict and Change*, 7: 93–130.

Smith, Anthony D. (1986), *The Ethnic Origin of Nations*, Oxford: Blackwell.

Torres, Gustavo (2003), *Mej xeew. La gran fiesta del señor de Alotepec*, México: Comisión Nacional para el Desarrollo de los Pueblos Indígenas.

Urbano, Henrique (n/d), *Mito y simbolismo en los Andes. La figura y la palabra*, Cusco: Centro de Estudios Regionales Andinos.

Valcarcel, Daniel (1965), *La rebelión de Tupac Amaru*, 2nd edn, México City: Fondo de Cultura Económica.

Waskar Chukiwanka, Inka (2004), *Wiphala Guerrera. Contra símbolos coloniales 1492–1892*, La Paz: Fondo Editorial de los Diputados.

Interviews

AS, Federación de Mujeres Bartolina Sisa, La Paz, Bolivia, 25 July 2005.

Epilogue

THE POWER OF ETHNIC TRADITIONS
IN THE MODERN WORLD
Anthony D. Smith

Rome and Jerusalem: two kinds of city, two different images, two opposed ideals. On the one hand, a great metropolitan city, centre of the known world in antiquity; on the other hand, a small provincial city, centre of a local cult and a singular people. Rome presented the image of a world city, imperial, polyglot and multicultural, though at first foreign cults were expelled; Jerusalem that of an ethnic city, forging its people through an ancient lawcode and focused on its Temple cult, though Greek influence was strong. Hence, the two ideals: the open, polyethnic and inclusive society of 'cosmopolis'; and the exclusive, monoethnic and authentic world of 'ethnopolis'.

'COSMOPOLIS' AND 'ETHNOPOLIS'

It is a contrast that has considerable resonance in the modern world, and it presents two antithetical images of global society. The cosmopolitan vision embraces a series of civic nations, based on the voluntary association of individual citizens, who agree to live according to common values and laws which are essentially utilitarian and instrumental, and whose relationship to the state is direct and unmediated. Uniformity of laws, equality before the law, and universal reciprocity of rights and duties, are the guiding principles of a 'civic' conception of nationhood. The nation itself is seen as an autonomous legal-political community, defined by common territory, shared civic history and common laws, its members united by a common public culture and political symbols such as flags, anthems, assemblies and public days of commemoration (Viroli 1995).

But the horizon of cosmopolis extends beyond the borders of the nation, taking in regional-continental associations of national states. The civic ideal of nationhood is profoundly political: it is predicated on the union of nation and state, and on a political type of nationalism, and this allows cognate national states, related either by history or geography or both, to pool some of their resources and hand over some of their functions to a higher authority in an overarching union with its own institutions and political symbolism, such as the European Union (Gowan and Anderson 1997).

Of course, such unions are only stepping-stones to the ideal of the world as 'one place', a truly universal city. Indeed, globalising trends of economic interdependence and mass communications have lent credence to the cosmopolitan ideal. Hence its thrust is towards a world that, for all its inclusiveness, is politically highly centralised, with a global, scientific discourse and technology serving as cultural cement for a universal society directed by a unified polity and political elite.

At the other pole, the reverse holds for the vision of ethnopolis. Globally, it sees a world composed of a multitude of ethnic communities and nations, disparate power centres, each of them unique in terms of size, extent, resources and values. For such an ideal of decentralised communities, ethnicity becomes the necessary source of value and power, and the basis of the many different peoples and cultures that seek political self-expression, and which a global society must represent.

Similarly, the continental-regional level of cosmopolis finds its counterpart in various pan-nationalisms and cultural unions of cognate nations and ethnic communities. Historically, this ideal was exemplified in centripetal movements like PanSlavism and PanTurkism, and in contemporary terms by PanLatinAmericanism, PanAfricanism and PanArabism. Of course, great power interests have been involved in several of these; nevertheless, they sought to build on the cultural dimensions of proximate ethnic nations.

To the civic nation of cosmopolis, the ethnic vision opposes the intimacy of ethnically defined national communities, that is, named communities of presumed common ancestry and shared descent, sharing common origin and foundations myths and historical memories. In this conception, nations are seen as unique, incommensurable and autochthonous communities of historic culture and shared destiny, embedded in ancestral homelands and recognised by distinctive public cultures and common laws and customs rooted in ethno-national history. Unlike the civic nation, the ethnic nation prides itself on its 'authenticity', its rootedness in 'nature' and in popular consciousness (Connor 1994: ch. 8; Smith 1999: Introduction).

VARIETIES OF ETHNOCULTURAL COMMUNITY

Normatively, there is much to be said for spelling out the nature and consequences of these two visions of community. But, as many have pointed out, the contrast does not hold up in practice, for most empirical cases of national community are composed of elements of both models, albeit in varying manner and degree. 'Civic' and 'ethnic' conceptions of the nation may serve as heuristic devices and normative ideals, but they hardly do justice to the variety and complexity of individual nations. In what follows I shall attempt to trace the ways in which ethnic elements are not only interwoven with civic dimensions, but infuse the latter with ethnic intimacy, energy and uniqueness, albeit in attenuated form in certain domains (Miller 1995; Yack 1999).

Although the concept of 'ethnicity' is a mere half century old, the adjectival form 'ethnic' was much used in Greek antiquity. Signifying a sense of kinship and similarity among the members of a group, *ethnos* came to stand for a group of persons related by imputed ties of kinship (a *myth* of descent), sharing common cultural elements and hailing from a particular area. In the ancient world, such cultural elements included worship of specific gods, their statues, temples and cults, as well as shared speech. For the Christian Fathers, *ta ethne* signified the Gentiles, recalling the biblical *goyim*. This suggests that, from the first, the adjective 'ethnic' has denoted more than genealogical attributes; it has always included cultural, and even territorial elements. Hence, in what follows, I shall be concerned with the influence of this broader concept, and will treat 'ethnic' interchangeably with 'ethno-cultural' (Tonkin et al. 1989: Introduction; Hall 1997: ch. 3).

Ethnic groups vary, of course, not only in size and power, but also in their complexity. Here I shall be concerned with *ethnic communities* (or *ethnies*, to use the French term) where the members possess myths of origin, shared memories and a sense of communal solidarity, defining the *ethnie* as 'a named and self-defined group possessing a myth of common origins, shared memories and elements of common culture, linked to a particular territory, and infused with a sense of solidarity'. Such communities, though their members may appeal to primordial ties, are created over the long term, and the contents of their myths, memories, values and symbols often change over the generations. Nevertheless, some of these communities have persisted through many generations, and a few of them for many centuries, even when the memory of their presumed common ancestry grows faint (Smith 1986: ch. 2).

Now, as is often pointed out, 'ethnicity' is only one of several collective identities that human beings share; and were that to represent the sum total of its presence in human affairs, we should regard ethnic identity as interesting, at times perhaps important, but for all that limited in influence. This is not the case. Ethnic relations in the broader sense remain so potent and pervasive because they so easily mesh with other cultural and political dimensions and, as a result, form a series of related communal types, both historically and in the contemporary world. The domains most frequently cited in the historical record include territory, language and literature, political history, and religion and ritual, giving rise to such well-known types as ethno-territorial, ethno-linguistic, ethno-political and ethno-religious communities, which I illustrate briefly below.

Ethno-territorial communities

'Ethnicity' is so often opposed to 'territory' as representing two alternative principles of social organisation, that we forget how often they have been aligned in history as well as in the modern world. The idea that the ethnic community is 'earth-born' and emerges from the soil is not just a figment of the Romantic imagination. In fifth-century Athens, the belief that Athenian citizens were native-born descendants of Erechtheus and that all who could not trace their descent from common Athenian ancestors were foreigners took root, and in 451 BC was enacted into law. Bounded and sanctified land, of course, played a crucial role in ancient Israel, as it did in ancient Egypt, where *kemet*, the black land of a bountiful Nile valley, was seen as the only place for an Egyptian to be, and, as the Tale of Sinuhe informs us, the only place for an Egyptian to die and be buried (Cohen 2000: ch. 4; Grosby 2002: 32).

In the modern world, too, territory, elevated through the Romantic return to Nature, increasingly defined the community of presumed kinship and ancestry. We see this in the attempts by the Jacobins and their republican successors to forge a clearly bounded 'France' on the basis of the old (enlarged) hexagon, but now endowed with 'natural frontiers'. Much the same can be said of the 'nation-building' efforts of the Young Turks who, spurred by the French example, aimed to consolidate the Anatolian lands as an ethnic Turkish heartland, at the cost of its cultural others (Gildea 1994; Kushner 1976).

Ethno-linguistic communities

Here the community of presumed descent is aligned with that of common vernacular speech and writing. This, too, is not simply a Romantic conceit. It is not true, as is so often averred, that language was of no political importance before the French Revolution. Certainly by the sixteenth century, with its series of translations of the Vulgate Bible into so many vernaculars, native languages were recognised as possessing social, and hence political, importance. But we also find examples of language as the prime expression of the ethnic community in medieval Europe – among the French and English, Irish and Welsh, and Catalans and Basques – not to mention older examples such as the Armenians and Georgians, Arabs and Persians. On the other hand, nationalism undoubtedly strengthened the equation of language and ethnicity, the obvious case being the otherwise decentralised Germans, divided into several states, but 'rediscovering their essence' through philology and poetry, in accordance with the philosophy of Johann Gottfried Herder. Language here becomes not just a badge and expression of *Deutschtum* but a treasury of the intimate bonds that unify all Germans and reveal their 'inner being'. In their wake, many of the smaller East European *ethnies* from the Finns to the Slovaks and Slovenes rediscovered their common filiation in the lineaments of their vernaculars, which then became the *raison d'être* of their political separatism (James 2000: ch. 2; Hroch 1985).

Ethno-political communities

Ethnies have also been aligned through common mores and institutions which focus on shared memories, legends and myths of military adventure, great heroes and 'golden ages' of glorious statehood. Ancient Egypt again provides the proto-type, with a complex set of political institutions and public mores that expressed the unity and exclusive destiny of an Egyptian *ethnie*. Despite frequent interac-tion with foreigners both inside and outside Egypt, the Egyptian elite generally despised the cultures of their Asiatic and Nubian neighbours, and sought to build an Egyptian 'nation' through political culture and ideology (T. Smith 2003).

In the modern world, the French example of the glorious age of the French Revo-lution again springs to mind, but we find similar ethno-political communities in Tsarist Russia, Japan and modern Ethiopia. In each, the idea of a common heroic ethno-history – a tale retold by members of the community to each other and to the next generations – has been central to the self-definition of the community, as it has been to the state built on these epic foundations, though this more inclusive ethno-political community based on shared memories and a former state and/or heroic age may conflict with religious or linguistic bases of communal self-definition and 'golden ages' (Smith 1997).

Ethno-religious communities

This has been perhaps the most influential and intense kind of communal self-definition in the past. Here the community of presumed common ancestry is equated with the community of the faithful, as the pre-modern examples of the Druse, Sinhalese, Jews and Irish confirm. In these cases, religion and ethnicity cross-fertilised each other; hence the appearance of specific ethnic liturgies, tradi-tions and customs in a world religion, as among the Orthodox Greeks, the Mono-physite Copts and the Roman Catholic Poles; and the ethnicisation of religion among the Armenians, Jews and Maronites (see Atiyah 1968).

In the modern world, too, a revitalisation of ethno-religious communities is taking place. Examples include the Shi'ite Persians, the Sikhs and the Hindu Tamils. In the case of Saudi Arabia, Iran, Pakistan, Sri Lanka and Israel, religion continues to play a large part in the self-definition of dominant-*ethnie* states. In others, it continues to define the vast majority of the state's population, who constitute the dominant *ethnie*, as in Catholic Ireland, Poland, and the Philippines, Orthodox Greece and Muslim Turkey (despite the official secularism) (Kepel 1995).

ETHNIC TRADITIONS IN MODERN NATIONS

What this brief survey confirms is that ethnic traditions – myths, symbols and values, memories – are present in or 'flow' into all kinds of communities, and can be used by nationalists for what John Hutchinson has termed a 'mythic overlaying' (Hutchinson 2005). Ethno-cultural identities and ethnic relations are not simply another type of community alongside existing communities, nor do they consti-tute ingredients added to, and complicating, existing communities and relations. Rather, they infuse, rejuvenate and remould all kinds of communities and identi-ties, not least modern nations and national states. Indeed, it is from these ethnic sources that the members of nations derive much of their power and distinctive character. We need to remember that most 'civic' nations rely on an ethnic core, a dominant *ethnie* around which the state was formed, and whose members still, for the most part, compose the state elites and dominate its political institutions. Of course, these ethnic traditions themselves are not static; they are frequently supplemented, reinterpreted, selected and recombined in response to external challenges, and can therefore be seen as novel or even 'invented' traditions, partic-ularly in nations whose elites are bent on presenting a 'civic' image of the nation and who therefore relegate earlier kinship ties to the background. Intellectuals of all kinds play a large part in these processes of selection and reinterpretation, but they are constrained by numerous factors, including the geopolitical situation of the community, its cultural heritage and resources, and its economic and social composition (Hutchinson 2005).

Above all, to be successful, ethnic innovations need to accord with the culture and outlook of the majority of the population whom it is desired to form into a distinct nation. Peasant cultures may be remoulded, and much may be forgotten by urban intelligentsia, but it is hazardous to jettison them entirely and start again *de novo*. For the *raison d'être* of any nation must, in the first place, reside in its people and their (alleged) distinctive character: their vernacular language and literature, their land, their history and collective memories, their religion and public rituals. These constitute the 'sites' of national distinctiveness, and it is here that ethnic tradi-tions are revived and often reconstituted, as I aim to show below.

Landscape

We saw briefly how ethnic territory has been crucial to national self-definition in the modern world. But the effect of nationalist ideologies since Rousseau has been to turn 'territory' into 'landscape', ethnoscapes into 'homeland'. This is equally true of 'civic' nations: it was in France that the earlier English preoccupa-tion with depicting native landscapes took hold, notably in the Barbizon school of painters around Fontainebleau and later among the Impressionists; and land-scapes became increasingly invested with national expression, as embodying the virtues and destiny of the community (Hooson 1994).

A striking example is the sudden emergence of the characteristic landscapes of Russia into national consciousness. This was, in the first place, an achievement of Russian intellectuals, starting with the Slavophiles in the 1830s, but it soon spread to others, particularly after the Wanderers (*Peredvenniki*), artists who had seceded from the Academy in the 1870s, popularised the vast Russian forest, steppe and tundra landscapes. Through their realism and attention to detail of field, hill, tree, river and weather, they hoped to evoke the Russian 'soul' of a countryside that was viewed no longer just as local and given, but as a specifically Russian and national possession, an intrinsic element of Russian national identity (Ely 2002).

Similar preoccupations can be found among artists in the United States. Thomas Cole had initiated the portrayal of the equally colossal spaces of North America, albeit in allegorical vein. His successors, men like Edwin Church and Robert Bierstadt, went out into the American 'wilderness' to meditate on the dilemma of nature and progress, the painful destruction of nature's desolate magnificence by the settlers' ever expanding pursuit of an American manifest destiny. In fact, this reveals the conflict between two moral visions: on the one hand, the providentialist messianism of the colonial settler on the American frontier, on the other hand, the divinely infused imagery of a solitary American grandeur, so memorably evoked by Church in his painting entitled *Wilderness* (Wilton and Barringer 2002).

In England, we can distinguish several kinds of national landscape depiction. The earliest was the seascape, with its images of island peace and tranquillity, on the one hand, and of seafaring and naval warfare, on the other hand; here England and Britain were often conflated. A second vision, specifically of England, became current in the early nineteenth century, that of the idyll of meadow and copse in the southern counties, which the paintings of Constable helped to establish as the true face of England among the middle classes. There was also a landscape of the indus-trial North, anticipated in the work of Joseph Wright of Derby, with its stress on coal, machines and smoking factories, icons of Britain's industrial primacy. Finally, there emerged a new cult of the 'wild' Scottish Highlands in Victorian Britain; initiated by the novels of Walter Scott and popularised by various Scots painters, it won the seal of royal approval when Queen Victoria took up residence in Balmoral (Howkins 1986; Edensor 2002: ch. 2).

Language and literature

If national landscapes expressed the national 'spirit' of the people, language mirrored its inner being and, according to Romantic 'organic' nationalists, distilled its very 'essence'. Even today, in a post-Romantic age, language is often treated as the true bond of ethnic intimacy among native language-speakers, and the touch-stone of the 'authentic' nation.

Though several nations do not possess a unique language, a vernacular language and literature provide significant fields for the rejuvenation of many nations through authentic ethnic traditions. This has been particularly true of nations that possessed their own distinctive scripts like the Armenians and Geor-gians, or a language unrelated to others like the Basques. But even in cases where the language belongs to a wider family like the Slav or Finno-Ugric languages, the intimacy and sense of authenticity created by the linguistic bond is precisely matched by its capacity for erecting a symbolic barrier against outsiders. Ethnic intimacy and national differentiation appear here as two sides of the same coin. Through lexicography, philology, language renewal and language spread, the potential for ethnic regeneration is created on a national scale. Though there have been few cases of successful language restoration such as Hebrew, the selection of specific dialects or forms to create a national language, as occurred in Croatia and Greece, has given a powerful impetus to ethno-national renewal (Edwards 1985: ch. 2).

This process is greatly enhanced by the creation, or rediscovery, of a national literature, based preferably on ancient chronicles, epics and the like. Its main value resides not so much in 'fixing' the linguistic limits of a national reading public, as in its revelation of 'authentic' collective experience. For Herder and his followers, a nation's literature formed the main repository of its individuality and origi-nality, but even before the Romantics, the literary canon of the nation had sprung up alongside vernacular translations of the Bible. In the modern period, the reau-thentication of the nation, through the recovery of its ancient literature, has been a vital part of its ethnic overlay. A striking example is the recovery of Karelian ballads and their collection in the Finnish *Kalevala*, which Elias Lönnrot edited in 1835, with a longer version in 1849. This was a work of considerable creative writing, but the atmosphere and legends that it purveyed became a living part of the ethno-national Finnish revival under Russian domination. The same was true of much of German literature, notably the recovery of the *Nibelungenlied*, the work of the Minnesanger, and the collection of fairy tales by the Grimm brothers. Today, national languages continue to be nurtured by national education systems and media – sometimes as part of a conscious programme like that pursued by the Académie Française in defence of the purity of the French language faced by the intrusion of global English – and to give rise to varied national literatures expres-sive of the ethno-cultural heritage and character of even self-proclaimed 'civic' nations (Branch 1985: Introduction; Kohn 1965: chs .3–4).

Ethno-history

This kind of 'history', consisting essentially in shared memories of great events, heroes and ages, has been particularly salient for ethnopolitical communities and dominant-*ethnie* nations. The lack of clear alternative cultural bases of nationhood brings shared memories, particularly of great deeds and self-sacrifice, to the fore, stories which, after all, the descendants of outsiders can come to adopt as their own, as we see in immigrant nations like the United States and Australia. Of course, their national integration is not accomplished without conflict; the various strands of shared memories provide plenty of room for rival ethno-histories. This is equally apparent in long-settled countries like England and France. The role of ethnic conflict between 'Anglo-Saxon' and 'Norman' histories, and between Franks and Gauls, in the shaping of modern English (and British) and French political mores and institutions, is well known. So is the rivalry of Hellenism and Byzantinism in modern Greece: on the one hand, a vision of ancient Greece, especially Athens, articulated by the Greek diaspora intelligentsia and merchants, as the basis for a regenerated and modernised Greece, on the other hand, a restoration of Byzantium and its imperial seat in Constantinople, as the one true and glorious manifestation of the Greek spirit (Koliopoulos and Veremis 2004: Part V).

Similar ethno-historical dualities can be observed in neighbouring states. Against an inclusive 'civic' Ottomanism, the political elites from 1908 opted for a narrower Turkism, based increasingly on the ideal of ethnic Turkish nation-building in Anatolia, which entailed massive displacement and extermination of non-Turkish peoples in the Turkish 'heartland'. Subsequently, Ataturk opted for a secular state and westernised society on the French model, while adopting an ethnicist stance by advancing a Sun Language theory of Turkish origins in Central Asia, and rediscovering a Turkish nation based on the language and history of the Turkish tribes who had migrated to Anatolia, but shorn of their Islamic identity. By contrast, in Egypt, such a radical reform met with little success. The movement of Pharaonicism in the early twentieth century, which envisaged a secular, westernised Egypt returning to its sources of native greatness in the environment and ancient civilisation of the Nile valley, remained largely a preserve of intellectuals. It failed to dislodge the dominant Arab-Islamic ethnic identity of the masses and the heritage of medieval Egypt, which was reaffirmed by modernisers and is now accorded a central place (Poulton 1997: ch. 4; Gershoni and Jankowski 1987: chs 6–8).

Religion and public rites

Whereas religion is often the preserve of the most exclusive ethnicism in ethno-religious communities, when it is translated into a form of national regeneration, it tends to become a 'civic religion' based on the cult of self-sacrifice. Both of these phenomena can be seen side by side in Israel. On the one hand, there is the strong Orthodox presence with its insistence on creating a Jewish state, one that is ruled according to the precepts of the Torah and its rabbinic guardians. On the other hand, the Israeli state sponsors a set of public rituals on the Day of the Holocaust, the Day of Memorial for the fallen soldiers, and Independence Day, over and above the ancient Jewish festivals that have also acquired a national meaning. There is a similar dualism of monuments: ancient tombs of rabbis and the Western Wall of the Temple alongside modern, secular tombs of Zionist leaders like Herzl and Rabin, and the shrine of the Holocaust, *Yad VaShem*. Here, too, ethnic traditions flow into and infuse with Jewish meanings modern festivals and monuments; are they not all situated in the ancestral and holy land of Israel (Handelman 2004: chs 6–8)?

This is perhaps an extreme case, but much the same can be said of long-established national states like France and Britain. In France, the eighteenth-century cult of French heroes was extended through the secular martyrs of the Revolution – Marat, Bara and le Peletier – and thence in the Panthéon to the cult of *les grands hommes, la patrie reconnaissante*. But there was also a Catholic ethnic tradition which revived the cults of the Virgin Mary, with whom Marianne was closely identified, and Joan of Arc (canonised in 1920), with festivals and statuary. Nevertheless, in France, the civic religion has predominated: its culmination is Bastille Day with its ceremony at the Tomb of the Unknown Warrior under the Arc de Triomphe, symbolising the mass self-sacrifice of the nation in the Great War, followed by the military parade to the Place de la Concorde (Prost 2002: chs 1, 7; Bell 2001: ch. 4).

In Britain, too, there has been a parallel celebration of heroes. For example, in the eighteenth and nineteenth centuries, Wolfe, Nelson, Wellington were publicly celebrated and the Victorian cult of great men ranged from Alfred and Arthur to Shakespeare and Milton. It found similar expression in monumental statuary, mainly located near the tombs of the kings in Westminster Abbey, but also in St Paul's and Trafalgar Square. However, unlike France, the rituals of Britain's 'civic religion' are linked to the monarchy: Coronations, State Opening of Parliament, Trooping of the Colour, Royal Weddings and Funerals. For historically, the monarchy has been the fulcrum of English ethnic traditions as well as of broader British national aspirations, and this is most strikingly exemplified in its pivotal role in the great ceremony of the annual Remembrance Day commemorations for the 'Glorious Dead' who fell for 'King and Country' in the two World Wars. This wreath-laying ceremony is held at the Cenotaph in Whitehall in the presence of royalty, politicians, ecclesiastics and military, and is followed by a popular march-past of participant regiments in these and other wars, signifying the resolve of a nation to renew itself through the example of the mass sacrifice of its youth (Smith 2003: ch. 9).

CONCLUSION

The domains of landscape, language, ethno-history, and public religion and ritual reveal how ethnic traditions and symbols infuse and give meaning to wider national identities, even in national states that are in their own eyes most determinedly 'civic' in orientation. We might hypothesise that, though ethno-cultural elements flow into each of these domains, they tend to be more intense and salient in the more intimate setting of family life, the personal attachment to the native landscape and the interpersonal experience of linguistic and religious affinity; whereas they are more diffuse at the political level, especially where the national state organises their expression and strives for more civic representations of national identity and unity. Nevertheless, even here, we note the capacity for ethno-cultural symbols, memories, myths and traditions to shape the destiny of the nation and the role of the state.

REFERENCES

Atiyah, A. S. (1968), *A History of Eastern Christianity*, London: Methuen.
Bell, David (2001), *The Cult of the Nation in France: Inventing Nationalism, 1680–1800*, Cambridge, MA: Harvard University Press.
Branch, M. (ed.) (1985), *Kalevala, the Land of Heroes*, tr. W. F. Kirby, London: Athlone Press.
Cohen, E. (2000), *The Athenian Nation*, Princeton: Princeton University Press.
Connor, W. (1994), *Ethno-nationalism, The Quest for Understanding*, Princeton: Princeton University Press.
Edensor, T. (2002), *National Identity, Popular Culture and Everyday Life*, Oxford and New York: Berg.
Edwards, J. (1985), *Language, Society and Identity*, Oxford: Blackwell.
Ely, C. (2002), *This Meager Nature: Landscape and National Identity in Imperial Russia*, Dekalb, IL: Northern Illinois University Press.
Gershoni, I. and J. P. Jankowski (1987), *Egypt, Islam and the Arabs: The Search for Egyptian Nationhood, 1900–1930*, Oxford: Oxford University Press.
Gildea, R. (1994), *The Past in French History*, New Haven: Yale University Press.
Gowan, P. and P. Anderson (eds) (1997), *The Question of Europe*, London and New York: Verso.
Grosby, S. (2002), *Biblical Ideas of Nationality, Ancient and Modern*, Winona Lane, IN: Eisenbrauns.

Hall, J. (1997), *Ethnic Identity in Greek Antiquity*, Cambridge: Cambridge University Press.

Handelman, D. (2004), *Nationalism and the Israeli State*, Oxford and New York: Berg.

Hooson, D. (ed.) (1994), *Geography and National Identity*, Oxford: Blackwell.

Howkins, A. (1986), 'The discovery of rural England', in R. Colls and P. Dodd (eds), *Englishness: Politics and Culture, 1880–1920*, London, Sydney and Dover, NH: Croom Helm, 62–88.

Hroch, M. (1985), *Social Preconditions of National Revival in Europe*, Cambridge: Cambridge University Press.

Hutchinson, J. (2005), *Nations as Zones of Conflict*, London: Sage.

James, H. (2000), *A German Identity, 1770 to the Present Day*, London: Phoenix Press.

Kepel, G. (1995), *The Revenge of God*, Cambridge: Polity Press.

Kohn, H. (1965), *The Mind of Germany*, London: Macmillan.

Koliopoulos, J. and T. Veremis (2004), *Greece: The Modern Sequel, From 1821 to the Present*, London: Hurst.

Kushner, D. (1976), *The Rise of Turkish Nationalism*, London: Frank Cass.

Miller, D. (1995), *On Nationality*, Oxford: Oxford University Press.

Poulton, Hugh (1997), *Top Hat, Grey Wolf and Crescent: Turkish Nationalism and the Turkish Republic*, London: Hurst.

Prost, A. (2002), *Republican Identities in War and Peace: Representations of France in the Nineteenth and Twentieth Centuries*, Oxford and New York: Berg.

Smith, Anthony D. (1986), *The Ethnic Origins of Nations*, Oxford: Blackwell.

Smith, Anthony D. (1997), 'The "Golden Age" and national renewal', in G. Hosking and G. Schopflin (eds), *Myth and Nationhood*, London: Routledge, 36–59.

Smith, Anthony D. (1999), *Myths and Memories of the Nation*, Oxford: Oxford University Press.

Smith, Anthony D. (2003), *Chosen Peoples: Sacred Sources of National Identity*, Oxford: Oxford University Press.

Smith, S. Tyson (2003), *Wretched Kush: Ethnic Identities and Boundaries in Egypt's Nubian Empire*, London and New York: Routledge.

Tonkin, E., M. McDonald and M. Chapman (eds) (1989), *History and Ethnicity*, London: Routledge.

Viroli, M. (1995), *For Love of Country: An Essay on Nationalism and Patriotism*, Oxford: Clarendon Press.

Wilton, A. and Barringer, T. (2002), *American Sublime: Painting in the United States, 1820–1880*, London: Tate Publishing.

Yack, B. (1999), 'The myth of the civic nation', in R. Beiner (ed.), *Theorising Nationalism*, Albany: State University of New York, 103–18.

INDEX

⟫◁▷⟪